THE REVELS PLAYS

Former general editors
Clifford Leech
F. David Hoeniger
E. A. J. Honigmann
J. R. Mulryne
Eugene M. Waith

General editors
David Bevington, Richard Dutton, Alison Findlay,
Helen Ostovich and Martin White

OLD FORTUNATUS

Manchester University Press

THE REVELS PLAYS

ANON *Thomas of Woodstock or King Richard the Second, Part One*

BEAUMONT *The Knight of the Burning Pestle*

BEAUMONT AND FLETCHER *A King and No King The Maid's Tragedy Philaster, or Love Lies a-Bleeding*

CHAPMAN *All Fools*

CHAPMAN *Bussy d'Ambois An Humorous Day's Mirth*

CHAPMAN, JONSON, MARSTON *Eastward Ho*

DEKKER *The Shoemaker's Holiday*

FORD *Love's Sacrifice The Lady's Trial*

HEYWOOD *The First and Second Parts of King Edward IV*

JONSON *The Alchemist The Devil Is an Ass Epicene, or The Silent Woman Every Man In His Humour Every Man Out of His Humour The Magnetic Lady The New Inn Poetaster Sejanus: His Fall The Staple of News Volpone*

LYLY *Campaspe* and *Sappho and Phao Endymion Galatea* and *Midas Love's Metamorphosis Mother Bombie The Woman in the Moon*

MARLOWE *Doctor Faustus Edward the Second The Jew of Malta Tamburlaine the Great*

MARSTON *Antonio and Mellida Antonio's Revenge The Malcontent*

MASSINGER *The Roman Actor*

MIDDLETON *A Game at Chess Michaelmas Term*

MIDDLETON *A Trick to Catch the Old One*

MIDDLETON AND DEKKER *The Roaring Girl*

MUNDAY AND OTHERS *Sir Thomas More*

PEELE *The Troublesome Reign of John, King of England David and Bathsheba*

WEBSTER *The Duchess of Malfi*

THE REVELS PLAYS

OLD FORTUNATUS

THOMAS DEKKER

edited by David McInnis

MANCHESTER
UNIVERSITY PRESS

Introduction, critical apparatus, etc.
© David McInnis 2020

The right of David McInnis to be identified as the editor of this work has been asserted by them in accordance with the Copyright, Designs and Patents Act 1988.

Published by Manchester University Press
Oxford Road, Manchester M13 9PL
www.manchesteruniversitypress.co.uk

British Library Cataloguing-in-Publication Data
A catalogue record for this book is available from the British Library

ISBN 978 0 7190 8943 5 hardback
ISBN 978 1 5261 5605 1 paperback

First published 2020

The publisher has no responsibility for the persistence or accuracy of URLs for any external or third-party internet websites referred to in this book, and does not guarantee that any content on such websites is, or will remain, accurate or appropriate.

Typeset
by Toppan Best-set Premedia Limited

For Emma, Imogen, and Kit

Contents

LIST OF ILLUSTRATIONS	*page* viii
GENERAL EDITORS' PREFACE	ix
ACKNOWLEDGEMENTS	xii
ABBREVIATIONS	xiv
INTRODUCTION	1
Authorship and the lost play(s)	1
The text	6
The German play	11
Sources	18
Performance history	29
Critical reception	45
Act and scene divisions	59
Press-variants	63
OLD FORTUNATUS	79
INDEX	247

Illustrations

1 Title-page of Thomas Dekker, *The Pleasant Comedie of Old Fortunatus* (London: Printed by S. S. for William Aspley, 1600), leaf A1r (Folger STC 6517). Used by permission of the Folger Shakespeare Library. page xviii

2 'Actus Primus' from *Comoedia von Fortunato und seinem Seckel und Wünschhütlein in Engelische Comedien und Tragedien* (1620), leaf L2v (Folger PR1246.G5 E59 Cage). Used by permission of the Folger Shakespeare Library. 12

3 Fortunatus tricks the Sultan of Babylon and obtains his wishing-hat; woodcut from the German *Volksbuch*, *Fortunatus Eyne Hystorye* (Augsburg, 1509), Bayerische Staatsbibliothek München, Rar. 480, fol. 68r. 22

4 'Court scene from the Old Fortunatus production, 1906', Digital Collections and Archives, Tufts University (http://hdl.handle.net/10427/003511). 42

5 'Fortune, Virtue, Vice and attendants in the Old Fortunatus production, 1906', Digital Collections and Archives, Tufts University (http://hdl.handle.net/10427/003510). 43

General Editors' Preface

Clifford Leech conceived of the Revels Plays as a series in the mid-1950s, modelling the project on the New Arden Shakespeare. The aim, as he wrote in 1958, was 'to apply to Shakespeare's predecessors, contemporaries, and successors the methods that are now used in Shakespeare's editing'. The plays chosen were to include well-known works from the early Tudor period to about 1700, as well as others less familiar but of literary and theatrical merit. 'The plays included', Leech wrote, 'should be such as to deserve and indeed demand performance'. We owe it to Clifford Leech that the idea became reality. He set the high standards of the series, ensuring that editors of individual volumes produced work of lasting merit, equally useful for teachers and students, theatre directors and actors. Clifford Leech remained General Editor until 1971, and was succeeded by F. David Hoeniger, who retired in 1985.

Ever since then, the Revels Plays have been under the direction of four or five general editors: initially David Bevington, E. A. J. Honigmann, J. R. Mulryne, and E. M. Waith. E. A. J. Honigmann retired in 2000 and was succeeded by Richard Dutton. E. M. Waith retired in 2003 and was succeeded by Alison Findlay and Helen Ostovich. J. R. Mulryne retired in 2010. Published originally by Methuen, the series is now published by the Manchester University Press, embodying essentially the same format, scholarly character, and high editorial standards of the series as first conceived. The series now concentrates on plays from the period 1558–1642. Some slight changes have been made: for example, starting in 1996 each index lists proper names and topics in the introduction and commentary, whereas earlier indexes focused only on words and phrases for which the commentary provided a gloss. Notes to the introduction are now placed together at the end, not at the foot of, the page. Collation and commentary notes continue, however, to appear on the relevant pages.

The introduction to each Revels play undertakes to offer, among other matters, a critical appraisal of the play's significant themes and images, its poetic and verbal fascinations, its historical context, its characteristics as a piece for the theatre, and its uses of the stage for which it was designed. Stage history is an important part of the story. In addition, the introduction presents as lucidly as possible the criteria for choice of copy-text and the editorial methods employed in presenting the play to a modern reader. The introduction also considers the play's date and, where relevant, its sources, together with its place in the work of the author and in the theatre of its time. If the play is by an author not previously represented in the series, a brief biography is provided.

The text of each Revels play, in accordance with established practice in the series, is edited afresh from the original text of best authority (in a few instances, texts), in modern spelling and punctuation and with speech headings that are consistent throughout. Elisions in the original are also silently regularised, except where metre would be affected by the change. Emendations, as distinguished from modernized spellings and punctuation, are introduced only in instances where error is patent or at least very probable, and where the corrected reading is persuasive. Act divisions are given only if they appear in the original, or if the structure of the play clearly points to them. Those act and scene divisions not in the original are provided in small type. Square brackets are also used for any other additions to, or changes in, the stage directions of the original.

Rather than provide a comprehensive and historical variorum collation, Revels Plays editions focus on those variants which require the critical attention of serious textual students. All departures of substance from the copy-text are listed, including any significant relineation and those changes in punctuation which involve to any degree a decision between alternative interpretations. The collation notes do not include such accidentals as turned letters or changes in the font. Additions to stage directions are not noted in the collations, since those additions are already made clear by the use of brackets. On the other hand, press corrections in the copy-text are duly collated, as based on a careful consultation of as many copies of the original edition or editions as are needed to ensure that the printing history of those originals is accurately reported. Of later emendations of the text by subsequent editors, only those are reported which still deserve attention as alternative readings.

One of the hallmarks of the Revels Plays is the thoroughness of their annotations. Besides explaining the meanings of difficult words and passages, the annotations provide commentary on customs or usage, on the text, on stage business – indeed, on anything that can be pertinent and helpful. On occasion, when long notes are required and are too lengthy to fit comfortably at the foot of the page below the text, they are printed at the end of the complete text.

Appendices are used to present any commendatory poems on the dramatist and play in question, documents about the play's reception and contemporary history, classical sources, casting analyses, music, and any other relevant material.

Each volume contains an index to the commentary, in which particular attention is drawn to meanings for words not listed in the *OED*, and (starting in 1996, as indicated above) an indexing of proper names and topics in the introduction and commentary.

Our hope is that plays edited in this fashion will promote further scholarly and theatrical investigation of one of the richest periods in theatrical history.

DAVID BEVINGTON
RICHARD DUTTON
ALISON FINDLAY
HELEN OSTOVICH

Acknowledgements

Editing Dekker's wonderful play has been an immense source of pleasure for me and has created opportunities to benefit from the insights and kindness of many people over the years. The genesis of the project was a chance meeting with Helen Ostovich in Prague; her encouragement then and since (including at the inaugural conference of the Asian Shakespeare Association in Taiwan, where we presented together) has been greatly appreciated.

One of the great joys of preparing a critical edition is the opportunity to visit some of the finest libraries in the world. For their generous assistance and advice when I was collating the surviving quartos of Dekker's play, I would like to thank Yvonne Lewis (National Trust) and Andrew Loukes (House and Collections Manager, Petworth House); Lyndsi Barnes, Isaac Gewirtz, Jessica Pigza, and Ted Teodoro at the New York Public Library; Margaret Tenney at the Harry Ransom Center; Clive Hurst at the Bodleian; Rowan Watson at the Victoria & Albert Museum; Michael Woods at the British Library; Rachel Bond and Lucy Gwynn at Eton College; Jaeda Snow at the Huntington; and, as usual, the staff at the Folger (in particular, LuEllen DeHaven, Alan Katz, Rosalind Larry, Camille Seerattan, Heather Wolfe, and the now late Betsy Walsh). A Faculty of Arts research grant at the University of Melbourne helped defray the cost of travel to research libraries and of digitization of quartos from the libraries I could not visit in person. For assistance with research into the production history of the play, I'm grateful to Molly Bruce (Tufts University); Shalimar Abigail Fojas White and Alyson Williams (Dumbarton Oaks Research Library and Collection, Washington, DC); Christopher Scobie (Music Reference Service, British Library), for advice on the Henry Bishop manuscript score for the Covent Garden production; Lucie Desjardins (University of Ottawa Archives), for providing a copy of the 1953 production's programme; Toby Malone and the members of the Canadian Drama listserv; and the staff at the library of Shakespeare's Globe.

Elena Benthaus provided extensive assistance working with the German texts of the 1620 play and the seventeenth-century puppet play, and Kathryn Vomero Santos kindly offered her knowledge of Spanish for the Insultado passages; Ian Donaldson and Roslyn L. Knutson read pieces of my work in progress and offered advice; Maria Kirk, Lisa Hopkins, and June Schlueter provided helpful advice and pre-publication access to their work; Brett Greatley-Hirsch, Alan Farmer, Karolina Fit, Matthew Lorenzon, Ruth Lunney, Kirk Melnikoff, Lucy Munro, and Jolynna Sinanan helped with fiddly questions; and Penelope Woods, Tim Fitzpatrick, and Andrew Lynch's contributions to performance-as-research experimentation with the 'echo scene' on the New Fortune stage at the University of Western Australia provided useful insights that would not otherwise have occurred to me. I presented work towards this edition at several venues, including Tiffany Stern's Folger Institute Symposium and Martin Wiggins's 'Dekkerthon' reading at the Shakespeare Institute (both in 2016) and conferences convened by the Australian and New Zealand Shakespeare Association, the Marlowe Society of America, the Society for Renaissance Studies, the Asian Shakespeare Association, and the Shakespeare Association of America; I'm grateful to all who provided feedback on those occasions.

Sadly, David Bevington – who examined my PhD dissertation on mind-travelling (in which I first began thinking about *Old Fortunatus* and the pleasures of travel) and who greeted news of this current edition being contracted by Manchester as 'part of a heartwarming surge of activity with the Revels series' – passed away in early August 2019, before he could see the fruits of that surge of activity. His kindness will be missed.

From sharing pre-publication access to his *Catalogue* entries to discussing editing choices, using my draft text for the Shakespeare Institute reading in 2016 and providing detailed feedback on that text, Martin Wiggins has been exceptionally generous with his expertise and time: thank you, Martin. Thanks, too, to John Banks for his keen editorial eye, which saved me from errors and improved the edition in many ways. Finally, every editor owes a significant debt both to previous editors of the play and to their General Editor: in my case, Richard Dutton has been a constant source of support and advice, and I have been most fortunate in having his discerning eyes look over my work.

Abbreviations

EDITIONS AND TEXTUAL REFERENCES

Q   Quarto of 1600. *The Pleasant Comedie of Old Fortunatus. As it was plaied before the Queenes Maiestie this Christmas, by the Right Honourable the Earle of Nottingham, Lord high Admirall of England his Seruants.* London: Printed by S. S. for William Aspley, 1600.

Bowers   *Old Fortunatus* in vol. 1 of *The Dramatic Works of Thomas Dekker*, ed. Fredson Bowers, 4 vols. Cambridge University Press, 1953.

Capell   Edward Capell. *The School of Shakespeare: or, authentic Extracts from divers English Books, that were in Print in that Author's Time; evidently shewing from whence his several Fables were taken, and some Parcel of his Dialogue: Also, further Extracts, from the same or like Books, which or contribute to a due Understanding of his Writings, give Light to the History of his Life, or to the dramatic History of his Time*, 3 vols. London: Printed by Henry Hughs, for the Author, 1779–80.

Daniel   P. A. Daniel. MS notes towards a critical edition in his copy of Shepherd (Folger PR 2480 1873 v.1).

Deighton   Kenneth Deighton, *The Old Dramatists: Conjectural Readings on the Texts of Marston: Beaumont and Fletcher: Peele: Marlowe: Chapman: Heywood: Greene: Middleton: Dekker: Webster*. Westminster: Archibald Constable and Co., 1896.

Dilke   *Old Fortunatus* in vol. 3 of *Old English Plays; Being a Selection from the Early Dramatic Writers*, ed. Charles Wentworth Dilke, 6 vols. London, 1814–15.

Hoy   Cyrus Hoy, *Introductions, Notes, and Commentaries to Texts in 'The Dramatic Works of Thomas Dekker', Edited by Fredson Bowers*, 4 vols. Cambridge University Press, 1980.

Rhys   *Old Fortunatus* in *The Best Plays of the Old Dramatists: Thomas Dekker*, ed. Ernest Rhys. London: Vizetelly, 1887. The Mermaid Series.

ABBREVIATIONS xv

Schelling *Typical Elizabethan Plays*, ed. F. E. Schelling. New York: Harper and Brothers, 1926.
Scherer *The Pleasant Comedie of Old Fortunatus by Thomas Dekker*. Münchener Beiträger zur Romanischen und Englischen Philologie, vol. 21, ed. Hans Scherer. Erlangen & Leipzig: A Deichert'sche Verlagsbuchh, Nachf. (Georg Böhme), 1901.
Shepherd *Old Fortunatus* in vol. 1 of *The dramatic works of Thomas Dekker: now first collected with illustrative notes and a memoir of the author, in four volumes*, ed. R. H. Shepherd. London: John Pearson, 1873.
Smeaton *Old Fortunatus: A Play*, ed. Oliphant Smeaton. London: J. M. Dent, 1904. The Temple Dramatists
Tufts *The Pleasant Comedy of Old Fortunatus by Thomas Dekker. As Presented at the Court of Queen Elizabeth*. Boston: The Tufts College Press, 1906.

OTHER REFERENCES

Allot Robert Allot, *Englands Parnassus: or the choysest flowers of our moderne poets, with their poeticall comparisons*. London, 1600.
Conover James H. Conover, *Thomas Dekker: An Analysis of Dramatic Structure*. The Hague: Mouton, 1969.
CWBJ *The Cambridge Edition of the Works of Ben Jonson*, Gen. Ed. David Bevington, Martin Butler and Ian Donaldson. Cambridge University Press, 2012.
Dent R. W. Dent, *Proverbial Language in English Drama Exclusive of Shakespeare, 1495–1616: An Index*. Berkeley: University of California Press, 1984.
Duffin Ross W. Duffin, *Some Other Note: The Lost Songs of English Renaissance Comedy*. Oxford University Press, 2018.
Ellis Anthony Ellis, *Old Age, Masculinity, and Early Modern Drama: Comic Elders on the Italian and Shakespearean Stage*. Farnham: Ashgate, 2009.
Fischer Sandra K. Fischer, *Econolingua: A Glossary of Coins and Economic Language in Renaissance Drama*. Newark: University of Delaware Press, 1985.
Foakes *Henslowe's Diary*, ed. R. A. Foakes, 2nd edition. Cambridge University Press, 2002.

Ketterer	Elizabeth Ketterer, '"Govern'd by stops, aw'd by dividing notes": The Functions of Music in the Extant Repertory of the Admiral's Men, 1594–1621', unpublished PhD dissertation, University of Birmingham, 2009.
McInnis	David McInnis, *Mind-Travelling and Voyage Drama in Early Modern England*. Basingstoke: Palgrave Macmillan, 2013.
McKerrow	Ronald B. McKerrow, *Printers' and Publishers' Devices in England and Scotland, 1485–1640*. London: Chiswick Press, 1913.
OCD	*Oxford Classical Dictionary*, ed. M. Cary et al. Oxford: Clarendon Press, rpt 1961.
OED	*Oxford English Dictionary. OED Online*. Oxford University Press.
Ovid, *Met.*	Ovid, *Metamorphoses*, trans. Mary M. Innes. London: Penguin, 1955.
Schlueter	June Schlueter, 'New Light on Dekker's *Fortunati*', *Medieval and Renaissance Drama in England* 67 (2013), 120–35.
Spenser	Edmund Spenser, *The Faerie Queene*, ed. Thomas P. Roche, Jr with C. Patrick O'Donnell, Jr. London: Penguin, 1978.
SR	*A Transcript of the Registers of the Company of Stationers of London, 1554–1640 A. D.*, ed. Edward Arber, 5 vols. London, 1875–94.
Wiggins	Martin Wiggins, in association with Catherine Richardson, *British Drama, 1533–1642: A Catalogue*. Oxford University Press, 2012.

OTHER TEXTS BY DEKKER

Dekker	*The Dramatic Works of Thomas Dekker*, ed. Fredson Bowers, 4 vols. Cambridge University Press, 1953.
Shoemaker's Holiday	*The Shoemaker's Holiday*, ed. R. L. Smallwood and Stanley Wells Manchester University Press, 1979. Revels Plays series.

TEXTS BY SHAKESPEARE

Quotations from Shakespeare are from Gary Taylor, John Jowett, Terri Bourus and Gabriel Egan, Gen. Eds, *The New Oxford Shakespeare: The Complete Works (Modern Critical Edition)*. Oxford University Press, 2016.

THE
Pleasant Comedie of
Old Fortunatus.

As it was plaied before the Queenes
Maieſtie this Chriſtmas, by the Right
Honourable the Earle of Nottingham, Lord high Admirall of England his Seruants.

LONDON

Printed by S. S. for William Aspley, dwelling in
Paules Church-yard at the ſigne of the
Tygers head. 1600.

1 Title-page of Thomas Dekker, *The Pleasant Comedie of Old Fortunatus* (London: Printed by S. S. for William Aspley, 1600), leaf A1r (Folger STC 6517).

Introduction

AUTHORSHIP AND THE LOST PLAY(S)

In the spring season of 1596, Philip Henslowe, manager of the Rose playhouse, recorded the following references to a Fortunatus play in the repertory of the Admiral's company:[1]

3 of febreary 1595	Rd at the j p of fortewnatus . . . iij li
10 of febreary 1595	Rd at fortunatus. . . . . xxxx^s
20 of febreary 1595	Rd at ffortunatus . . . . xxij^s
14 of ap^{r}ell 1596	Rd at fortunatus. . . . . xviij s
11 of maye 159[5]6	Rd at fortunatus. . . . . xviij s
24 of maye 1596	Rd at ffortunatus . . . . xiiij s

Later, in 1599, Henslowe recorded a series of transactions with Thomas Dekker, as follows:[2]

the ixth of november
Receued of phillipp Hinchlow to pay
Thomas Deckker in earnest of abooke } xxxx^s
cald the hole hystory of ffortunatus
xxxx^s by me Thomas downton . .

Lent vnto Thomas dickers the 24 of. . . .
novmb[er] 1599 in earneste of his Boocke called } iij^{li}
the wholle history of fortewnatus the some of
wittnes   John: Shaa.

[Receaued of Mr Henshlowe this xxxth of
novemb^r 1599 to pay M^r deckers in full } xx^s
payment of his booke of fortunatu[s]
          By me Robt Shaa

Henslowe proceeded to pay an additional 20s the very next day ('the 31 of novmb[er] 1599') for alterations. He subsequently authorised the spending of £10 on properties for the play and paid another 40s to Dekker on 12 December 1599 'for the eande of fortewnatus for the corte'.[3] The anticipated court performance took place that Christmas, and Dekker's play was ultimately entered in the Stationers' Register as 'A commedie called old FORTUNATUS in

1

his newe lyuerie' on 20 February 1600, before appearing in print in quarto form later that year.[4]

This string of payments raises a number of questions about texts, chronology, authorship and the interpretation of historical records in general. E. K. Chambers noted that £4 was the minimum payment but £6 was the normal payment for a new play.[5] The £6 paid by Henslowe for 'abooke cald the hole hystory of ffortunatus' is thus on par with the usual payment for a completely new play, and would be excessive for mere revisions. Roslyn L. Knutson similarly notes that 'the phrasing of the diary entries is the same Henslowe used to show the payment by installments for new plays: "in earneste," "in full payment of his booke"' and that '[p]laywrights often wrote their own versions of popular subjects'.[6] What, then, is the relationship (if any) between the Dekker play bought by Henslowe in 1599, and the earlier Fortunatus play performed in 1596?

The 1596 entries tell us that the earlier play was moderately successful, averaging just over 28s per performance, and receiving at least six stagings where other plays (e.g. 'The Merchant of Emden', 1594; 'Paradox', 1596) appear to have been performed only once. Unfortunately, these entries also raise a number of questions that, for the moment, remain insoluble. Henslowe often inscribed an enigmatic 'ne' next to titles, possibly to designate a play as new to a company's repertory or newly revived; or perhaps, as R. A. Foakes suggests, because the play incorporated such substantial revisions that it required a new licence for performance by the Master of the Revels.[7] Why was there no 'ne' next to this, the first record of a Fortunatus play in Henslowe's diary? Was it a continuing play, rather than a new or revised play?

If '1 Fortunatus' (as I shall call it) was indeed a continuing play, how much earlier was it actually written? Presumably it would have to antedate 3 June 1594, when the series of Rose playhouse entries that include the Fortunatus records began. Frederick Gard Fleay confidently declared that '[t]he date of writing the first part [i.e. '1 Fortunatus'] is fixed at 1590 by Sc. 1', based on an assumption that Fortunatus's line about an 'almond for a parrot' and 'crack me this nut' (1.57) is a specific reference to the anti-Martinist tracts *An Almond for a Parrat* (c.1590), and *Pap with a Hatchet, alias A Fig for my Godson, or Crack Me This Nut* (1589).[8] But aside from that line being merely proverbial (Dent A220 and N359), the passage is intelligible without resorting to textual allusions. Fortunatus uses a series of puns on nuts to describe his hunger and weariness from wandering endlessly through the wood; each metaphor suggests the next. His teeth grind like *nutcrackers*, his body is about to break out into glandular swellings (waxing *kernels*), he craves food like a parrot wants *almonds*, and he seeks a way out of the wooden maze as one might seek the solution to a paradox ('crack me this *nut*'). Fortunatus's line cannot be used to date anything with confidence.

Who wrote '1 Fortunatus'? Henslowe did not begin recording dramatists' names until 1597, so there is nothing unusual about the anonymity of the records. Nor is there any cause to exclude from authorship considerations any of the playwrights subsequently named in the diary: they may well have been working with Henslowe in 1596 without their names being recorded. It seems unlikely to me that Dekker would have been paid the handsome fee of £6 to write a Fortunatus play in 1599 if he had also been paid to write a Fortunatus play previously for the same company, but in the absence of greater evidence about payments to playwrights for duplicate titles, my opinion remains precisely that: an opinion. Robert Greene has emerged as the proposed candidate for authorial ascription by a variety of scholars, for different reasons, none of which are especially convincing. Chambers, for example, wrote: 'I should not wonder if Greene, who called his son Fortunatus, were the original author',[9] as if tenuous biographical connections were sufficient grounds for authorship attribution. Martin Wiggins, who is very open about his assumptions (declaring his guess 'unprovable speculation'), also notes the name of Greene's bastard son, and adds that Greene 'built much of his early play-writing career on shadowing Marlowe's innovations', which in this context he specifies as the supernatural bargain, the two-part play, and the appeal of riches. He adds the 'impressionistic judgement' that a couplet in Dekker's play (10.266–7) resembles the final lines of Greene's *James IV*, and assigns a date of c.1590 to the lost play on the basis that '[i]t and its sequel might fill a gap in Greene's datable activity from September 1589 to March 1590'.[10] Enticing though this position might sound, reducing both Greene and '1 Fortunatus' to mere Marlowe imitators involves a considerable value judgement that Wiggins himself advances with reservations, and that critics might shy away from in light of revised understandings of Marlowe's influence on the repertory theatre. Undermining critical assumptions about the centrality of Marlowe's work to the Admiral's repertory, Holger Schott Syme has used quantitative analysis of the data in Henslowe's diary to show that 'while Marlowe was played a lot, those performances were less lucrative than the company's non-Marlovian offerings', and that Henslowe's diary 'does not tell us that a single play or author dominated the company's stock'.[11] Might it accordingly be problematic to assume that Greene's work habits were governed by a desire to emulate Marlowe, or that the '1 Fortunatus' play's chief virtue was its resemblance to Marlovian drama?

Henslowe's entries raise further questions. What is meant by the reference to 'the j p' in the entry for 3 February? This is the only occasion on which Henslowe designates the play as being a first part, and there is no identifiable record of a second part anywhere in Henslowe's diary.[12] Wiggins breaks his usual rule 'that a known first part need not imply an otherwise unknown second part' on this occasion, arguing that, because '1 Fortunatus' was not marked 'ne', it must have been old by 1596 – and, if it was old by 1596, 'the suggestion of a second play is retrospective rather than prospective'.[13] In other words, Henslowe must have deliberately written 'the j p' because he knew that the second part existed. This proposition sounds logical enough, and accords with Knutson's observation that, whilst Henslowe habitually marks the second part of a play as the second part, he does not designate the first part as such until the second part is already in performance — but Henslowe's designations are not always consistent.[14] When he enters 'Tamar Cham' as 'ne' on 6 May 1596, unlike '1 Fortunatus' he does *not* describe it as 'the 1 p' — even though he knew full well that a second part existed: he had already introduced '2 Tamar Cham' as 'ne' on 28 April 1592. Henslowe might also simply have been mistaken in his belief that the '1 Fortunatus' play was a first part; it is unlikely that he would have corrected his mistake, since the 1591–97 series of entries in the diary do not generally exhibit the 'correction' feature that becomes common in the later, 1597–1603 series of entries.

Yet critical belief in a conjectured '2 Fortunatus' has persisted despite the absence of evidence, and debate has revolved around the question of what use Dekker made of these two lost precursors. Fleay thought that the first six scenes of Dekker's play corresponded to '1 Fortunatus'.[15] W. W. Greg, concurring with Fleay on the c.1590 date, exercised greater caution in noting only that 'a second part had been planned', and that '[t]his, however, was for some reason delayed and in the confusion following on the inhibition of July 1597 the project was for the time abandoned'.[16] Greg in fact believed that the '1 Fortunatus' of 1596 was part of a revision of an older (c.1590) Fortunatus play, and that Dekker was responsible for the 1596 text. Without justifying this conjecture, he proceeded to assume that Dekker 'was entrusted with the recasting of the whole' again in 1599.[17] Bowers assumes that the 'payments [by Henslowe] were made for combining two old plays on Fortunatus into one'.[18] Critics naturally tend to assume that '1 Fortunatus' dramatized the life of Fortunatus himself, and '2 Fortunatus' dramatized (or would have dramatized) the adventures of his sons, Ampedo and Andelocia.[19] (This seems to be the model used by Bernard Fonteyn for his Dutch Fortunatus plays published in 1643, for example.)[20] This conjecture may well be correct, but the evidence offered by Fleay and Greg – that Andelocia's line, 'See, here's a story of all his travels; this book shall come out with a new addition: I'll tread after my father's steps' (5.396–7) is a metatheatrical allusion to the second part – does not offer sufficient interpretative warrant for such conclusions. Such an allusion is not implausible, but the sentence is equally (if not more) intelligible as a simple pronouncement by the sons that they will continue travelling as their father had done, recording their adventures along the way.

Chambers advances alternative evidence for the theory that Dekker's *Old Fortunatus* is merely a revision of an older play or plays. In a rare lapse of judgement, he uses the Stationers' Register as evidence for textual issues, suggesting that the wording of 'A commedie called old FORTUNATUS *in his newe lyuerie*' suggests a new version of the play.[21] Bowers concurred, noting that '[t]he "new livery" referred to was provided by Dekker during November, 1599'.[22] If this were the meaning of the Stationers' Register entry, it would be the only example of 'lyuerie' being used in such a context, and the *OED* does not support the use of 'new livery' in this sense.[23] A more logical inference to draw from the Stationers' Register entry is simply that the rise in stature experienced by Dekker's Fortunatus was a memorable feature of that play: Fortunatus enters '*meanly attired*' (1.0 SD) but, after the visitation by Lady Fortune, appears finely dressed or '*gallant*' (2.140 SD). This sartorial transformation was ostentatious enough to warrant explicit stage directions and much commentary within the scene; it probably also accounts for the Stationers' Register entry, '*in his newe lyuerie*'.

There is much at stake in the unsubstantiated 'lumping' together of similar titles that sees '1 Fortunatus' and *Old Fortunatus* described as a single play, or versions of a single play.[24] Bundling together lost plays with other lost or extant titles on a similar theme potentially distorts our view of early modern theatre history: it can mean the difference between recognizing a trend in subject matter that transcends company and authorial lines, or confining the influence of a topic by reductively assuming that it was dealt with by only one play or playwright. In the case of *Old Fortunatus*, there is no compelling evidence to support the hypothesis that Dekker merely revised, extended or otherwise rewrote an earlier Fortunatus play or plays. On the contrary, there *is* documented evidence that Dekker was paid the usual new play sum for his *Old Fortunatus* in 1599. The identity of the anonymous author of the lost '1 Fortunatus' play remains pure conjecture.[25] For these reasons, this edition resists the long-standing critical tendency to conflate the stage histories of '1 Fortunatus' and Dekker's play. The more logical inference is simply that the Fortunatus legend was popular with early modern playgoers: so much so that an early 1590s play appears to have been revived successfully in the spring of 1596, the respectably high takings on that first recorded performance (£3) suggesting high demand for a title that had not been performed since at least June 1594 (when Henslowe's records for this run of performances begins). Henslowe's confidence in the enduring interest of the Fortunatus legend is reflected in his acquisition of a new play on the topic (Dekker's), introduced in late 1599. This new play was deemed worthy of a performance at court, and appears to have enjoyed a steady afterlife on the Continent (see 'Performance History', below).

THE TEXT

No manuscript of Dekker's play exists. The copy-text for *Old Fortunatus* is the quarto (*Q*) of the play printed by Simon Stafford in 1600 (STC 6517) (see Fig. 1):[26]

> [Ornament] | THE | Pleasant Comedie of | Old Fortunatus. | As it was plaied before the Queenes | *Maiestie this Christmas, by the Right* | Honourable the Earle of Notting-|ham, Lord high Admirall of Eng-|land his Seruants. | [printer's device, McKerrow 281] | *LONDON* | Printed by S. S. for William Aspley, dwelling in | Paules Church-yard at the signe of the | Tygers head. 1600.

In his Temple Dramatists edition of 1904, Oliphant Smeaton made the bizarre and unsubstantiated claim that '[f]urther editions appear to have been issued in 1603, 1622, and 1624, the last-mentioned in Edinburgh, but of these no copy exists save one in the library of the Duke of Buccleuch at Dalkeith Palace'.[27] There is no evidence to corroborate any of Smeaton's claims, and no trace of the 'Edinburgh' edition in the current Duke of Buccleuch's libraries.[28] The quarto printed in 1600 seems to be the only early edition of the text in English.

Bowers is surely correct that Dekker's own papers, with some markings for performance, were used at the court presentation, and subsequently became the copy-text for the printer.[29] The extensively detailed directions for Virtue's and Vice's clothing (3.0 SD) are most likely Dekker's own, and the printing of 'Tho. Dekker' at the foot of the text (after the Epilogue, on sig. L3v) may indicate that the playwright's signature was included at the end of the manuscript used by the printer. Further indications that the author's papers lie behind the printed text include the faulty stage direction (which would have been caught by a prompter) on sig. I4v, '*Puts Gallowayes hornes off*' (corrected in this edition, following Dilke, to '*Pulls Montrose and Longueville's horns off*', 9.131 SD), and the puzzling reference to a gardener and a smith in *Q* (sig. A3v) even though Fortune subsequently introduces her captives as a 'carter' (1.206–7), and a 'botcher' (i.e. tailor) (1.211). Aside from the inclusion of the 'Prologue at Court' and 'Epilogue at Court', there are stage directions printed in *Q* that point to a manuscript that had been adapted for performance. The first scene contains the imperative, 'Kneel down' (1.290 SD), prompting an act of supplication by the actor playing Fortunatus. Later in the play, Andelocia and Agrippine's entry is marked twice, at Cho.2.32 SD ('*Enter* ANDELOCIA *and* AGRIPPINE') and then again three lines later at 7.0 SD ('*Enter* ANDELOCIA *with the wishing-hat on,* AGRIPPINE *in his hand*'). The Chorus here may have been a late inclusion as part of Dekker's revisions for performance at court; it summarizes a scene which was apparently excised to make room for alternative material. Its brief direction for Andelocia's and Agrippine's entrance is probably a playhouse annotation, whereas the detailed (but redundant) second direction is probably authorial, and a remnant from the pre-court draft of the play. That Dekker's manuscript, rather than a formal prompt-book, was used at court is suggested by two passages in the printing of *Q*. First, there was evidently some confusion over the printing of Echo's speech prefixes in Scene 1, where they appear as if part of a long monologue by Fortunatus. Presumably, as Bowers suggests, the copy-text did not have 'the conventional rules drawn between the end of one speech and the beginning of the next'.[30] Second, the stage direction at 9.171 ('CORNWALL *and some other*[*s*] *run out and enter presently*') was printed as part of Athelstan's speech in *Q* (sig. K), presumably because its status as a direction was not sufficiently clear in the manuscript.

As Bowers noted in his Introduction, summarizing earlier findings, an 'interesting post-publication incident attaches itself to the 1600 quarto'.[31] Bowers observed that 'four of the eleven preserved copies of the play are imperfect in sheet E', and that leaf E2 in particular appears to have given cause for offence, leading him to conjecture that this leaf 'was torn out of unsold copies at some date following publication, and was not replaced by a cancellans'.[32] This is an exceptionally unusual occurrence, and I am unaware of any comparable case. The four defective copies identified by Bowers are the Eton, Folger, and Harvard A and B copies — over one-third of the extant copies, in his estimation.[33] It is now possible to supplement and extend Bowers's hypothesis with further information. In the course of collating the *Old Fortunatus* quartos for this present Revels edition, I have consulted two additional extant copies: one at Petworth House in West Sussex, and a second NYPL copy, both of which appear to contain original E2 leaves (see 'Press-variants' below). This brings the number of preserved copies up to thirteen. Moreover, some details of the copies known to Professor Bowers were either missed or misreported to him, hence it is worth revisiting this curious situation.

First, Bowers noted that 'leaves D_1, F_{1-4}, and L_{2-3}' from the Harvard B copy 'have been subtracted at some early date to complete the present Pforzheimer copy', and that 'the Pforzheimer quarto appears to have its original $E_{2.3}$'.[34] This is incorrect; Bowers may have relied on the Pforzheimer collection catalogue assembled in 1940 by Frederick Warde and Bruce Rogers, which confirms that 'the outer margins of Sig D, F1-4, and L2-3 are extended', and which adds that although the Pforzheimer copy bears the bookplate of Frederick Locker-Lampson (1821–95), '[t]here were two Locker copies; the other, from which the extended leaves in the present were taken, is now at Harvard'.[35] The Pforzheimer copy, now at the Harry Ransom Center, does indeed exhibit extended outer margins on the leaves noted by Bowers and by Warde and Rogers; but leaves E2-3 also show signs of extended margins – E2 on the inner margin, E3 on the outer margin. In other words, the Pforzheimer quarto once lacked its E2 leaf also, and has been completed at a later stage, probably with leaves from the Harvard B copy.[36]

Second, Bowers believed that the Bodleian and the Victoria & Albert copies were in original (i.e. uncancelled) condition. This is

INTRODUCTION 9

also incorrect. Although an original E2 leaf is present in both copies, it was a late addition to the binding of both. The Bodleian copy belonged to Edmond Malone, who not only excised Dekker's autograph from Henslowe's papers and affixed it to the endpaper of his *Old Fortunatus* quarto, but also appears to have acquired a genuine E2 leaf to insert into the binding of his copy to make it perfect. The torn stub of the cancelled E2 leaf is clearly visible before E3, and Malone appears to have inserted an E2 from another quarto to replace it. The inserted copy's inner margin is extremely close to the binding and the stub of this inserted copy is still visible jutting out between E3v and [E4]r. This pattern of 'inserted E2 – E3 – protruding stub of inserted E2' also occurs in the Victoria & Albert copy, which was owned by another collector and editor of early modern drama, the Rev. Alexander Dyce. Accordingly, both the Bodleian and Victoria & Albert copies should be considered examples which lack their original E2 leaves.

Bowers knew of eleven copies, four of which (i.e. over a third) he deemed to lack sig. E2. Of the thirteen known copies collated for this Revels edition, only six have their original E2 leaves. *Seven* lack sig. E2: four have facsimiles (Eton, Folger, Harvard A, Harvard B); three have genuine leaves inserted from other copies (Pforzheimer, Bodleian, Victoria & Albert). The majority of extant quartos are thus defective.

The explanation offered by Bowers is that the offending lines must have been the following:

Fortunatus. In some courts shall you see Ambition
Sit piecing Daedalus' old waxen wings,
But being clapped on and they about to fly,
Even when their hopes are busied in the clouds,
They melt against the sun of majesty
And down they tumble to destruction.
For since the heavens' strong arms teach kings to stand,
Angels are placed about their glorious throne
To guard it from the strokes of trait'rous hands.

(5.217–25)

Bowers concludes that 'no other event between 1600 and 1603 parallels Dekker's lines so closely as the fall of Essex', although he hastens to add that the case is entirely conjectural.[37] (Presumably Bowers had in mind the rhetoric of Francis Bacon's letter to Essex, dated 20 July 1600, in which he lamented: 'I was ever sorry that your Lordship should fly with waxen wings, doubting Icarus' fortune').[38] It seems unusual that a play written in 1599 and printed in 1600 could be misconstrued by its early readers as specifically anticipating the rebellion of 1601, but Essex's downfall had begun much earlier. The sensational events of September 1599, when Essex disobeyed the Queen's orders and returned from Ireland prematurely, bursting in on her private apartments, unannounced, had only just occurred when Dekker was writing the play. Even if the Master of the Revels, Edmund Tilney, allowed the lines above from E2 to be presented at court that Christmas (which he may have done, if he thought their overall message was essentially loyalist), the same lines would have seemed increasingly dangerous once printed and made public, as it became obvious to all that there was to be no quick reprieve for Essex. Certainly, given the significant incidence of cancellations (which exceeds sheer coincidence), some explanation is required, and the probably unintentional parallel with Essex is the likeliest one.[39]

The passage may no longer appear exceptional, but it was notable in its own time: Robert Allot selected the first six of these lines ('In some courts ... destruction') for inclusion under the heading 'Ambition' in his *Englands Parnassus* (1600), published the same year as Dekker's play.[40] He also found the following three lines ('For since ... trait'rous hands') worthy of mention under the rubric 'Kings'.[41] It might be significant that Allot altered the plural form of 'thrones' and 'trait'rous hands' to the singular 'throne' and 'hand', as if a single ambitious individual were the subject of the passage. Bowers's argument 'for some post-publication event which would cause the stationer, doubtless on advice, to rip the leaf – suddenly given a specific and dangerous application – from his unsold copies to avoid trouble with the authorities' represents a unique case in the printing of English drama; I am unaware of any other incident that comes near the circumstances of this alleged cancellation.[42] There is, however, evidence of at least one other playwright self-censoring out of fear that his work might be read as an oblique reference (though not intentionally so) to Essex. In his *Dedication to Sir Philip Sidney*, Fulke Greville describes the reasoning behind the immolation of his now lost play, 'Antony and Cleopatra' (c.1600–1):

> Lastly, concerning the tragedies themselves, they were in their first creation three, whereof *Antony and Cleopatra*, according to their irregular passions in foresaking [sic] empire to follow sensuality, were sacrificed in the fire; the executioner, the author himself, not that he conceived it to be a contemptible younger brother to the rest, but lest, while he

seemed to look over-much upward, he might stumble into the astronomer's pit: many members in that creature (by the opinion of those eyes which saw it) having some childish wantonness in them apt enough to be construed or strained to a personating of vices in the present governors and government.

From which cautious prospect I ... seeing the like instance not poetically, but really, fashioned in the Earl of Essex then falling (and ever till then worthily beloved both of Queen and people) – this sudden descent of such a greatness, together with the quality of the actors in every scene, stirred up the author's second thoughts to be careful.[43]

Perhaps booksellers shared Greville's 'second thoughts' about the prospect of being found in possession of a text that suddenly (if inadvertently) resonated with contemporary politics.

In or around 1609, Sir John Harington had a copy of Q, bound with twelve other plays: *The Three Ladies of London* and *The Three Lords of London*, both parts of *Tamburlaine*, *Faustus*, *Captain Thomas Stukeley*, *Arden of Faversham*, both parts of *Edward IV*, *A Warning for Fair Women*, *A Looking Glass for London*, and *The Fair Maid of Bristow*.[44] John Horne, Vicar of Headlington, Oxfordshire, had a copy some time in the 1630s or 1640s (catalogued by Anthony Wood in the 1670s), as did Henry Oxinden of Kent in c.1663–65.[45] It was still being advertised for sale as late as 1656, when it appears in bookseller lists appended to *The Careless Shepherdess* and *The Old Law*. A copy has been in the Petworth House collection since at least 1690, when it was catalogued, but was probably there as early as the 1630s when the tenth Earl of Northumberland, Algernon Percy, was collecting playbooks.[46] It is bound with nine other plays: *The Phoenix* (1607), *King Lear* (1608, i.e. 1619), *When You See Me You Know Me* (1621), *The Bond Man* (1624), *Henry IV* (1632), *The Insatiate Countess* (1631), *The English Traveller* (1633), *Love's Sacrifice* (1633) and *The Late Lancashire Witches* (1634).

THE GERMAN PLAY

Although no other early printing of Dekker's play survives in English, a German play which is clearly related to Dekker's appeared in print in *Engelische Comedien und Tragedien*, an octavo volume of German plays deriving from English originals, published in 1620, probably in Leipzig. The collection was compiled by Frederick Menius (1593–1659) and contains versions of *Titus Andronicus*, *Nobody and Somebody*, and six other plays related to the London stage,

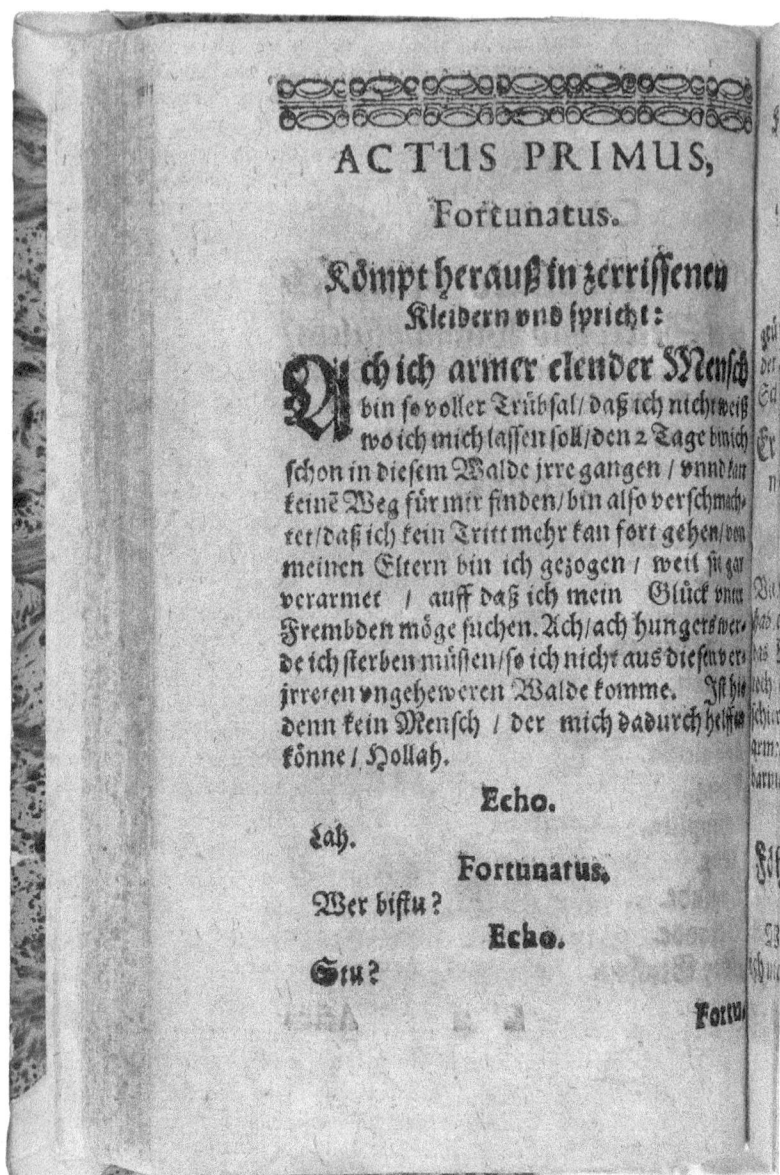

2 'Actus Primus' from *Comoedia von Fortunato und seinem Seckel und Wünschhütlein* in *Engelische Comedien und Tragedien* (1620), leaf L2v (Folger PR1246.G5 E59 Cage).

including a play called *Comoedia von Fortunato und seinem Seckel und Wünschhütlein, darinnen erstlich drei verstorbenen Seelen als Geister, darnach die Tugend und Schande eingeführet warden* (or *Comedy of Fortunatus and his Purse and Wishing-Hat, in which first three dead Souls as Spirits, and afterwards Virtue and Shame are introduced*).

The *Von Fortunato* play opens with an echo scene and a young Fortunatus lost in the woods after having attempted to escape the poverty of his parents (see Fig. 2). Fortune, blindfolded, offers him the choice of virtues, but, whilst he deliberates, three ghosts enter the stage, each warning Fortunatus to avoid Fortune's gifts and the misfortune they bring. Fortunatus nevertheless chooses riches and receives the magic purse, offering Fortune his services in gratitude. Fortune demands that Fortunatus perform three tasks for her annually, regardless of where he is: first, to celebrate the day he received the purse and not work that day; second, to find a husband for a poor man's daughter, clothe her and her parents, and give them 400 gold coins; and finally, to delight a virgin every year (*als du heute von mir bist erfrewet worden / so erfrewe du auch alle Jahr eine Jungfrawe*). Fortunatus agrees, is shown the way out of the woods, and tests his purse at a local tavern. A Pickelherring (German clown) interlude marks the end of the act. The second act takes place sixty years later, at the Turkish court, where Fortunatus, well-dressed (*hat schöne Kleider an*), obtains the wishing-hat from the Sultan by deception. In the next scene, Fortune reprimands him for abusing her gift, and punishes him with almost immediate death by poking his breast (*stosset sie ihn auff die Brust*) with a little stick (*ein Stöcklein*). Andelocia and Ampedo appear for the first time; Fortunatus bequeaths the purse and hat to his sons (on condition that the treasures are not to be separated), and implores his sons to use them wisely. The sons drag their father's body off the stage at the end of the act, and Pickelherring enters once again.

Act 3 commences a year after Fortunatus's death, with the brothers dividing the two gifts, taking six-year turns to enjoy each. Andelocia anticipates travelling the world like his father, whilst Ampedo is content to lead a frugal life at home. Andelocia declares his intention to travel to London to see the princess Agrippine and woo her by holding tournaments in her honour ('*demnach wil ich ihrenthalben alle Tage ein Turnier halten*'). After another Pickelherring interlude, the scene shifts to London a few years later. The king and Agrippine attempt to discover the secret of the low-born Andelocia's fabulous wealth. Andelocia tries to prepare a banquet to impress

Agrippine but finds he's been blocked from buying firewood; he sends his servant (*Jung*, a 'young man') to the Venetian grocer (*den Venediger Krämern*) to buy spices as an alternative fuel for the kitchen fire. Agrippine flatters Andelocia, who reveals to her the secret of his wealth: the purse. She invites him to her chamber to sleep with her at midnight, then tells the king what she has learnt. The king concocts a plan whereby Agrippine will use her charms to get close to Andelocia, drug him, and substitute a counterfeit purse for the magic purse. In the next scene, music accompanies an elaborate dumbshow in which Andelocia drinks the drugged wine, kisses Agrippine and passes out in her arms, and has his purse replaced with a counterfeit. Andelocia wakes up, tries to give his servant money but discovers his loss instead, and attempts to dismiss the servant whom he can no longer afford to employ. The loyal servant, however, offers to sell his own horse, give Andelocia the money, and remain in his service (*'mein Pferd und Harnisch wil ich verkauffen / und euch das Geldt geben / und zu Fuß nachlauffen / wohin ihr kommet'*). Agrippine refuses to give her father the purse, keeping it for herself and filling her treasure chamber with its contents instead.

Ten years later, in a scene without analogue in Dekker's play, Andelocia admits to his brother that he lost the purse. Ampedo startles violently, wrings his hands, and rips his jerkin open (*Ampedo erschricket heftig / wircket die Hände / reisset das Wambs auff*). He recovers from his shock and suggests writing to the Sultan and offering to sell him his wishing-hat back in order to secure financial security for the rest of their lives. However, Andelocia rejects the suggestion and instead tricks his brother so he can use the hat to go to Venice and acquire treasure, then return to England to retrieve the purse from Agrippine. Act 4 begins with Virtue (wearing a fool's cap; *ein Narrenhuetlein auf*) and Vice with their apple trees, in a forest in Ireland (*Hibernia*). This is followed by another scene not found in Dekker's version: Andelocia, disguised as a jeweller, tricks Agrippine into revealing the location of the purse, then abducts her. They arrive in the woods and spy Vice's apple tree. Whilst Andelocia scales it to pick an apple for Agrippine, she escapes with his hat. Andelocia eats the apple and sprouts horns on his head. Fortune appears, denies Andelocia his wish to die, and instead shows him the way out of the woods – but not before pointing him in the direction of Virtue's tree and the apples he needs as an antidote. He picks a few apples from each tree to take back to London.

INTRODUCTION 15

In the final act, Andelocia and his servant sell Vice's apples to two dukes and Agrippine in London. The king orders the dukes to find a doctor who can cure them all of their horns, paving the way for the disguised Andelocia to arrive and introduce himself as a foreign doctor, fresh from the court of Spain ('*ich ein* DOCTOR DER MEDICIN *bin / komme jetzt auß Barbarien / habe den König in Spanien 6. Jahr mit meiner Kunst gedienet*'). He succeeds in abducting Agrippine again, and confronts her in a remote wilderness where she begs for mercy and to be sent to a convent. In the following scene he takes her to one, paying 600 gold coins towards the convent's expenses. Andelocia returns to Famagusta and offers his brother the hat and purse. Ampedo declines, opting to live peacefully without either. Andelocia has a change of heart and leaves to free Agrippine from her horns and return her to her father, stopping in the woods along the way to acquire more apples. Back in the convent, Agrippine tells Andelocia that she longs to go home to her father and (cf. Dekker) her mother ('*so begehrte ich nichts liebers denn zu Lunden bey meinem hertzlieben Herrn Vater / und lieben Fraw Mutter der Königin zu seyn*'). He removes her horns and takes her back to London, then departs again for Cyprus, where the horned dukes seek revenge. They stab the servant, tie up Andelocia, and take him off-stage to torture him for information about the source of his riches. Ampedo burns the hat and dies of grief. The dukes re-enter and test the purse, then strangle Andelocia with a rope. Upon his death, the purse loses its magic, but each of the dukes think that the other has deceived him somehow when the purse doesn't yield gold. A sword fight ensues. The king, Agrippine, and a servant enter and restore the peace, demanding to know the cause of the altercation. The king authenticates the now defunct purse and Agrippine seeks justice for Andelocia's murder; the king sentences the dukes to death. Fortune enters and reclaims the purse, and the king and Agrippine kneel before her, thanking her for her generosity toward them and asking her to be generous to their kingdom thereafter. She grants them their wish. (Virtue and Vice do not reappear.)

The relationship of the German *Comoedia von Fortunato* to Dekker's *Old Fortunatus* has long interested critics. Charles H. Herford was generally dismissive of the 'barbarous pieces' presented in Germany by the English players, and regarded the German Fortunatus play as 'a meagre epitome of its original—which was undoubtedly Decker's play'. He accounted for the differences between the German and English plays by assuming the German text has been 'eked out ... by direct quotation from the German *Volksbuch*'.[47] Julius Tittman similarly concluded that the German play was a loose adaptation of Dekker's, interspersed with material from the Fortunatus *Volksbuch* of 1509.[48] Paul Harms thought rather that the deficiencies of the 1620 play were attributable to the faults of memorial reconstruction, and Emile Herz argued that the mistakes and carelessness of the German redactor indicated a superficiality and lack of dramatic technique.[49] Orlene Murad later agreed with these negative evaluations of the German play (which she referred to as a 'garbled, degraded, and barbarized' version of *Old Fortunatus*), but was more generous than Herford in describing it as a 'very loose adaptation' of Dekker's play. Murad observed important differences between the two (the German play's inclusion of a 'Pickelherring' clown character; its dramatization of Fortunatus as a young man; and Fortunatus's wish to transport himself to the West Indies), noting the omission of characters and abbreviation of scenes in the 1620 text but pointing to such distinctive devices as the opening 'Echo' scene (shared by *Old Fortunatus* and *Von Fortunato* but not found in the *Volksbuch* or other possible sources) as evidence that Dekker's play must have been 'a principal model' for the German play.[50] Cyrus Hoy sided with Harms in treating the German play as a reported text. In the introduction he provided for Fredson Bowers's edition of Dekker's play, Hoy asserted that '[t]he first two-and-a-half acts of the German *Comoedia* are clearly a redaction of Dekker's play', but claimed that the redactor's attempt at memorial reconstruction subsequently failed him, prompting a return to the *Volksbuch* for missing details.[51]

But there is another, more satisfying possibility which has been explored in great detail by June Schlueter, who proposes an alternative genealogy for the German play.[52] Schlueter posits that the 1620 text derives not from the quarto of Dekker's play published in 1600 (which incorporates the revisions for performance at court) but rather from Dekker's pre-court manuscript of the play, which somehow made its way to the Continent in the early 1600s. Following Henslowe's terminology in November 1599, she calls this earlier version *The Whole History of Fortunatus*. If Schlueter's hypothesis is correct, Dekker's 'altrenge of the boocke of the wholl history of fortewnatus' included not merely the prologue and epilogue for court but the introduction of the Chorus, Insultado's cameo appearance, and a more prominent and extensive supernatural plot.[53] Shadow's absence from the German text isn't necessarily indicative of his absence from the pre-court production though: he may have been part of Dekker's original conception but subsequently cut in favour of pleasing the German audience with a Pickelherring clown part.[54] Likewise, some of the discrepancies between Dekker's play and the German text must have resulted from performance and printing considerations; it was presumably the English players (not a playwright or a translator) who translated Dekker's text for their German audiences, and Schlueter notes that the German compiler, Frederick Menius, 'provided stage directions, compulsively', even when they were clearly redundant.[55] Although 'Dekker's revisionary efforts were heavily invested in the supernatural subplot', the presence of supernatural characters in *Von Fortunato* suggests their role may have been amplified only as part of the revisions for court, rather than being completely new and superficial additions.[56] The complicated ending of Dekker's play may thus reflect the late and hasty addition of an amplified Virtue/Vice narrative, whereas 'the final scene of the 1620 text brings closure to a leaner Virtue/Vice subplot [i.e. featuring Fortune but not the other supernatural figures] – the plot, in short, that Dekker created before he was commissioned to alter the play'.[57]

Further support for Schlueter's hunch that the German text derives from the pre-court version of Dekker's play can be found in the 'jeweller' scene of Act 4 in *Von Fortunato* (described briefly above), a scene not present in the printed text of *Old Fortunatus*.[58] At this point in the play, Andelocia still has the wishing-hat but Agrippine has taken his purse. Having stolen three pieces of valuable jewellery in Venice, Andelocia arrives back in London with the intention of selling them to Agrippine. He disguises himself by tying a mask to his face and altering his voice, in order to deceive and abduct Agrippine, and waits for her along the route she takes to church. Introducing himself to her as a jeweller from foreign lands ('*ich bin ein Jubilirer und gekommen auß fernen Landen*'), he claims to have followed her for several hundred miles in the hope of selling her his precious jewels. Agrippine inspects the merchandise and they haggle extensively over the price, eventually settling on the extravagant sum of no less than 4,000 gold coins (*vier tausend Kronen und kein heller ringer*). The bargaining is in fact a ploy by Andelocia to create a situation in which Agrippine must use the stolen purse and thereby disclose its whereabouts. The disguise as a jeweller is thus integral to the ruse. No sooner does she retrieve the purse than he grabs her by the arms (*Sie holet den Glückseckel auß dem Sack / ANDOLOSIA machet sich alsobald zu ihr / fasset sie umb die Armen gar feste*). With the help of the wishing-hat, he abducts her and transports them both to a wilderness (*Nun wünsche ich mich in einen wilden Wald da keine Leute innen sind*).

In Dekker's play, by contrast, these events are merely summarized by the Chorus:

> If your swift thoughts clap on their wonted wings,
> In Genoa may you take this fugitive,
> Where having cozened many jewellers,
> To England back he comes. Step but to court
> And there (disguised) you find him bargaining
> For jewels with the beauteous Agrippine,
> Who wearing at her side the virtuous purse,
> He clasps her in his arms and as a raven
> Gripping the tender-hearted nightingale,
> So flies he with her, wishing in the air
> To be transported to some wilderness.
>
> (Cho.2, 21–31)

Dekker's decision to describe this episode in the second Chorus is confusing unless doing so was the result of cutting and altering the play for performance at court. The choric summary provides many specific details (Genoa, cozening jewellers, returning to England, disguise and bargaining) yet fails to convey the central point: that the specificity of this subterfuge is what enables Andelocia to recover the purse. It would seem, then, that the Chorus is awkwardly summarizing events that could no longer be accommodated within the play after the alterations. The alternative explanation – that the scene was *added* to the German play – is less compelling, since *Von Fortunato* is uniformly a much abbreviated text. The presence of the 'jeweller' scene in *Von Fortunato* can best be explained if it were part of the copy-text used in Germany, and the most likely cause for this would be if the copy-text derived from the pre-court version of Dekker's play.

Wherever details of the German play shed light on Dekker's play or form a significant contrast, they have been recorded in the commentary notes of this edition.

SOURCES

Folklore sources

The Fortunatus story was translated and printed so prolifically throughout the early modern period that tracing its ancestry to a single point of origin is a complicated affair. Folklore lies behind it: specifically, the tale classified as 'AT 566: The Three Magic Objects and the Wonderful Fruits' in the Aarne-Thompson typology.[59] Versions of the story appeared in such languages as German, Polish, Danish, Hungarian, French, English, Dutch, Icelandic, Swedish and Italian in around forty editions between the sixteenth and eighteenth centuries.[60] It exists in at least an embryonic form as early as the fourteenth-century: Francis Douce suggests that the Fortunatus story, 'unless itself of oriental origin', may ultimately derive from the medieval *Gesta Romanorum* (chapter 120 of the Latin, 54 of the English).[61] Herford succinctly summarises the key episodes in the *Gesta*:

> There the dying Darius bequeaths three gifts to his three sons. To the eldest he leaves what he had himself inherited; to the second what he had conquered; to the third three *iocalia*, – a ring, a necklace, and a rich cloth, of which the first gave him the favour of all, the second fulfilled all his wishes, and the third transported him wherever he wished to go. These three gifts, which obviously did not all belong to the original story, he successively loses through the seductions of a mistress. Her triumph seems complete when after Jonathas [the youngest son] has carried her off by the aid of the cloth into a desert place, – 'in tantam distantiam, ubi nullus hominum venit,' – she contrives, like Agrippina, to get the cloth into her own possession, wishes herself at home and leaves him there. The remedy is as in Fortunatus. The frustrated lover discovers as he wanders, water which blisters the flesh, and fruit which produces leprosy. Shortly afterwards he finds other water and other fruit which cure the inflictions of the first. He takes samples of both sorts, and sets out homeward. On the way he finds occasion to heal a leprous king with his second sample, and the renown thus acquired gives him the opportunity of punishing his faithless mistress with the first, and recovering his stolen treasures.[62]

The *Gesta* and this story in particular were known to Thomas Hoccleve (c.1367–1426), who translated it as 'The Tale of Jonathas' in his *Series*, written towards the end of his life. Hoccleve's redaction was subsequently included in William Browne's *The shepheards pipe* (1614), with the claim that it was 'never til now imprinted'.[63]

Both Hoccleve and the *Gesta* decline to discuss the elder brothers, focusing solely on Jonathas's exploits with the ring, brooch and cloth (the purse, notably, is not amongst the magical items yet in these accounts). Jonathas is drip-fed the inherited items by his mother rather than possessing them simultaneously: he first loses the ring to Fellicula (the mistress), who sleeps with him in order to learn the secret of his wealth, then persuades him that the ring will be safer with her than with him. She subsequently claims to lose the ring, and Jonathas returns home to his mother in shame; she chides him for associating with dishonest women, but gives him the brooch (which he also loses to Fellicula in identical circumstances), and finally the cloth, which Jonathas uses to wish himself and Fellicula away to the end of the world. There, he falls asleep with his head on her lap, and she extricates herself and the cloth, then wishes herself back home, abandoning Jonathas in the wilderness. Jonathas discovers fruit and water that each induce leprosy, and others that cure it; he chances upon a king who suffers from leprosy, thus providing an opportunity to use the newfound remedies. He begins practising as a doctor with the aid of his fruit and water samples. When he subsequently encounters Fellicula once again, she is serendipitously in need of a physician, and Jonathas uses the opportunity to solicit a confession from her (honesty being billed as the only remedy) regarding the lost ring and brooch. Instead of offering her the cure, though, he exacts his revenge by giving her the water and fruit that produce illness: as Browne describes it, 'Her wombe opened, & out fell each intraile / That in her was'.[64]

These elements provide the basis of the German *Volksbuch* of Fortunatus, *Von Fortunato und seynem Seckel auch Wünschhütlein* (Augsburg, 1509), which is the ultimate source in print for the Fortunatus legend. It adds 'a religious and moral colouring' to the outline found in the *Gesta* and Hoccleve, including the dual focus on the father and the next generation (thereby enabling a pattern of temptation to emerge); the introduction of Fortune and her choice of gifts (especially wisdom), as well as her requirement that Fortunatus use his newfound wealth for good (i.e. provide four hundred pieces of gold to a poor man's daughter who would otherwise be without a dowry); the provision of the Ampedo character to contrast with the Andelocia–Jonathas type; and the use of the magical fruit not just to punish the Fellicula–Agrippine character but subsequently to cure her too.[65] To this is added a prehistory for the main protagonist, in which the exploits of his youth are recounted in ten chapters constituting a 'romance adventure' (as Herford calls it): how his father Theodorus's lavish spending led their family to poverty; how Fortunatus subsequently left home to became a servant to the Earl of Flanders; how the threat of castration forces him to flee to London; his service there to a Florentine merchant, how he was framed for murder and his narrow escape from execution; and the subsequent fleeing which ultimately sees him lost in a wood in Brittany where he kills a wild bear for sustenance, and where he then encounters Fortune.[66] Dekker chooses to open his play with the episode in which Fortune bestows her gift on the already old Fortunatus, leading James H. Conover to observe that '[a]pparently Dekker's interest in the story centers on the effects of the magic gifts rather than on the life stories of the heroes'.[67]

The *Volksbuch* Fortunatus proceeds to find himself in trouble when the mismatch between his dishevelled appearance and his fabulous wealth leads a tavern owner to suspect him of theft. He is arrested but released, and makes his way to Nantes where the nobleman Lüpoldus becomes his travelling companion. They venture to Hibernia (Ireland) to visit St Patrick's Purgatory and have many other adventures. In Constantinople, Fortunatus tries to follow Fortune's injunction to provide a poor woman with a dowry; his inquiries rouse the suspicions of his host, who twice tries to steal the magic purse (he is caught red-handed, killed, and the body thrown in a well). Upon returning to Cyprus, Fortunatus learns of his parents' death. The King of Cyprus arranges a marriage between Fortunatus (whose wealth elevates his social status) and Cassandra, the daughter of a count. They marry, and, shortly thereafter, Lüpoldus dies. Cassandra gives birth to the two boys, Ampedo and Andelocia, and after twelve years Fortunatus sets off again on his travels. In Alexandria he acquires the Sultan's wishing-hat (see Fig. 3), which enables him to conveniently travel to distant lands without having to be away from his family for long stretches at a time. At the end of his life, he bequeaths the purse and hat to his sons and instructs them not to separate the treasures.

Andelocia takes the purse and travels to France, offers a gentleman's wife an indecent proposal but is himself the victim of a bed-trick that sees him sleep with the wife's neighbour. He travels to England, fights against the Scots on the unnamed English king's behalf, and falls in love with the English princess Agrippina. When the King prevents Andelocia from purchasing firewood, Andelocia uses his fabulous wealth to purchase expensive spices to burn instead, and prepares a banquet. The king and queen task Agrippina with discovering the source of Andelocia's riches; she sedates him and steals the purse. Impoverished, he returns to Cyprus, takes his brother's wishing-hat, and uses it to transport Agrippine to a remote wilderness. Unfortunately, whilst climbing an apple tree to pick fruit for her, he lets her wear the hat, and she wishes herself back to

3 Fortunatus tricks the Sultan of Babylon and obtains his wishing-hat; woodcut from the German *Volksbuch*, *Fortunatus Eyne Hystorye* (Augsburg, 1509).

safety. Andelocia eats the apples, and horns sprout from his head. A hermit advises him that there are other apples that will remove the horns. Andelocia returns to England in disguise, sells the bad apples to Agrippine, then disguises himself as a doctor with the ability to cure her of the horns. He gets close enough to the princess to recover the purse and hat, then transports her to a convent near St Patrick's Purgatory, where he abandons her. Hearing that the King of Cyprus wants to marry Agrippine, Andelocia retrieves her from the convent and cures her. In Cyprus, Andelocia leads a lavish lifestyle, and his prowess at jousting provokes the jealousy of two earls (Theodorus and Limosy), who imprison him and extract, by torture, the secret of his wealth. Ampedo burns the hat, Theodorus strangles Andelocia, and, when the earls discover that the purse no longer works after the death of both sons, they fight each other. The king has them both executed.

After the Augsburg edition of the *Volksbuch*, a variant appeared in Frankfurt in 1550. Herford describes it as being less detailed, less indebted to the romance form, with different woodcuts, and in general inferior to the Augsburg version.[68] Herford's account can be supplemented with the textual differences between the Augsburg and Frankfurt editions presented by Alexis F. Lange, who notes that the Augsburg edition 'is subjective and didactically interpretative' but the Frankfurt edition 'aims at an objective recital of incidents'.[69] The general narrative remains the same in all versions of the Fortunatus legend, though, and Dekker's use of the *Volksbuch* material is characterised by Herford as a 'cutting away':

> He chooses the three most piquant adventures of Fortunatus, – the presentation of the purse, the stealing of the hat, and his death. The whole of his early history is omitted; the play beginning when he is already 'olde,' and his two sons of an age to take up the tale at his death. ... The adventures of Andelosia are less curtailed, and at certain points even amplified. The punishment of the faithless Agrippina by the horn-producing apples was a trait too congenial to Elizabethan taste to be neglected; Decker has accordingly made the two courtiers Longaville and Montrosse share the fate of the princess; obtaining at the same time a better ground for the vengeance which here as in the *Volksbuch* they wreak upon the sons of Fortunatus.[70]

Dekker's handling of the Andelocia character has been viewed in sharply contrasting ways by key critics. Herford thought that whereas in the *Volksbuch* 'he is a hero to the last; his death is told with undisguised sympathy, and savagely avenged', in Dekker's play, Andelocia 'is a prodigal who has spent his gifts in riot, *luxuriose vivendo;* and his ruin becomes a retribution, of which Fortune is again the instrument'.[71] David Blamires argues precisely the opposite: 'Andelocia is no hero at all: he is a negative exemplary figure and a strong contrast to his father. The fact that he is immediately ready to contravene his father's instructions to keep the two magic gifts together demonstrates his arrogance and imprudence and prepares us for his final undoing and pitiful murder at the hands of Earl Theodorus'.[72] Blamires further observes that Dekker's Fortunatus is a 'static figure' where the *Volksbuch* equivalent is depicted 'as a hero who, after various false starts, learns to use the gift of endless wealth with prudence and wins a place of honour for himself in the world'.[73]

One of the more substantial changes that Dekker made to the story is the supernatural plot featuring not just Fortune but Virtue,

Vice, and their respective entourages; their planting of the apple trees that cause horns to sprout or to be removed; and the concluding compliment to Queen Elizabeth. Critics have typically assumed this allegorical framework was devised as part of the alterations for court in late 1599. Herford calls them an 'after-thought'.[74] But if Schlueter's hypothesis about the relationship of the German and English plays is correct (see 'The German Play' above), the supernatural elements were present in Dekker's play prior to the revisions for court; they were amplified but not invented for the court performance, and they are actually of a piece with the moralizing tone found throughout Dekker's play.

But how would an English dramatist like Dekker have had access to either version of the German *Volksbuch*? Dekker's surname implies Dutch ancestry, and his familiarity with Dutch is evident from *The Shoemaker's Holiday*: possibly he read German too.[75] Alternatively, Dekker may have consulted an intermediary text. Although Hans Sachs dramatized the Fortunatus story in 1553, no critic has detected any influence of Sachs in Dekker's work. The earliest extant English translation was previously thought to be an undated quarto called *The History of Fortunatus*, which had been assigned a conjectural date of 1650 by its custodians, the British Library (shelfmark 12410. bb.8).[76] The reasons for this nominal dating are unknown, since the BL quarto begins at sig. B and lacks the prefatory pages that contained its full title and publication date. *Early English Books Online* (*EEBO*) facilitates comparison with other extant Fortunatus narratives not held by the British Library; it reveals that the BL *History of Fortunatus* is in fact an imperfect copy of a much later text: the anonymous *The history of the birth, travels, strange adventures, and death of Fortunatus* ... (London: Printed for T. Haly, 1682), and is thus no longer a contender for the title of earliest extant English translation.[77]

In fact, the earliest surviving English translation, published in 1640, appears to have passed unnoticed by Dekker scholars (with the exception of Blamires), perhaps on account of a cataloguing error whereby the ESTC misattributes authorship to the sixth-century Christian poet Venantius Honorius Clementianus Fortunatus:

The right pleasant and variable tragicall historie of Fortunatus: whereby a yong man may learne how to behaue himself in all worldly affaires, and casuall chances / first penned in the Dutch tongue; therehence abstracted, and now first of all published in English, by T.G. London: Printed by George Miller, dwelling in the Blacke-Friers, 1640.

The unique extant copy of this 92-leaf octavo is held by Yale's Beinecke Rare Book and Manuscript Library (shelfmark Ih F779 640; STC (2nd ed.) 11197.5). It was reprinted with minor variations in 1676, with attribution of the translation to 'T.C.' rather than 'T.G.'. Because the 1676 edition was well known to scholars and the 1640 edition surfaced only during the 1990s, the translator has typically been thought to be Thomas Churchyard (an identification first made by John Payne Collier, without evidence); Thomas Gainsford has been tentatively proposed by the Yale cataloguer, but neither attribution is by any means certain.[78]

Yale's 1640 text does not appear to have been the earliest English translation, however; it is merely the earliest extant. Gainsford died in 1624, Churchyard in 1604; if either of these men was the English translator, he must have drafted his edition considerably earlier than 1640, and may even have published it. The earliest record of an English version of the Fortunatus legend (no longer extant) in the Stationers' Register, '*The Historye of* FORTUNATUS', was registered on 22 June 1615.[79] This is too late for Dekker's purposes, but Cyrus Hoy may have been too quick to categorically state that '[n]o English version of the story seems to have been available in the sixteenth century'.[80] Schlueter represents the prevalent thinking on the subject when she observes that '[w]ithout extant sixteenth-century English or Dutch editions, we can only assume, without evidence, that Dekker read the *Volksbuch* in the original German'.[81] In short, there has been a general consensus that Dekker either consulted the *Volksbuch* directly or revised the earlier Fortunatus play(s), which were in turn supposedly based on the *Volksbuch*. This edition contests both of these claims. I have already presented my arguments against the hypothesis that Dekker merely revised older drama; I wish now to suggest that Dekker, and any other dramatist adapting the Fortunatus legend for the stage, may actually have had ready access to an English source text.

In *The lives and characters of the English dramatick poets* ... (London, 1699), an expansion of the bibliographic work of Gerard Langbaine, Charles Gildon states of *Old Fortunatus* that 'the story is taken from the stitch'd Book of *Fortunatus*', without elaborating on this clue.[82] Although quires of an elaborate folio might be sold stitched, larger books would typically have at least a cheap binding, and it is unlikely that something so large would be referred to as a 'stitch'd' book. Gildon was more likely referring to cheap print, probably pamphlets (which were always sold stitched). A roughly contemporaneous advertisement appended to John Owen's *A guide to church-fellowship* ... (1692) gives a sense of the size of a stitched publication, advising that 'There is Newly Printed a Stitch'd Book, containing six Sheets', and Silius Titus's pamphlet *Killing No Murder* (1657) was described disparagingly by Richard Atkyns in his *The original and growth of printing* ... (1664) as having 'but eight Leaves in all, stitcht up without binding'.[83] Thus the stitched book of Fortunatus would likely have been a slim, stab-stitched pamphlet.[84]

In *Vertue's Commonwealth* (1603), Henry Crosse appears to confirm Gildon's observation, referring to what may have been Dekker's source text when he complained of the 'pye-bald Pamphlets' like 'the Pallace of Pleasure, *Guy of Warwicke*, *Libbius* and *Arthur*, *Beuis* of *Hampton*, the wise men of *Goatam*, *Scoggins* Ieasts, *Fortunatus*, and those new delights that haue succeeded these, and are now extant'.[85] No extant copy of this pamphlet has yet been identified, but in the dedicatory epistle prefacing his translation of Eusebius (1577), Meredith Hanmer likewise makes mention of an extant Fortunatus narrative available in England:

> Many nowe adayes had rather reade the stories of Kinge *Arthur*: The monstrous fables of *Garagantua*: the Pallace of pleasure: the Dial of Princes, where there is much good matter: ... Reinard the Fox: *Beuis* of Hampton: the hundred mery tales: *skoggan*: *Fortunatus*: with many other infortunate treatises and amorous toies wrytten in Englishe, Latine, Frenche, Italian, Spanishe ...[86]

Interestingly, whether a cheap print version of the Fortunatus legend was available in England for dramatists to consult would affect the debate about whether Dekker revised Henslowe's 'the j p of fortewnatus' (and its possible sequel) or whether, as seems more likely to me, he composed his drama independently. Wiggins assumes that Dekker revised earlier drama, and supports the hypothesis that there was a lost second part. He consequently argues that '[i]t is more economical to assume only one writer using the German text, at the time the play was originally written', and that Dekker combined two lost plays rather than having access to the German *Volksbuch* and using it himself to continue the story begun in 'the j p'.[87] Blamires, who also believes that Dekker revised earlier drama, nevertheless argues that '[t]he most economical explanation ... would be the hypothesis that there was a single [English Fortunatus] text current from about 1577 or slightly earlier' and that '[t]his text (rather than the German *Volksbuch* directly) would also be the most plausible source for *The First Part of Fortunatus* (1596)'.[88] The stitched English pamphlet referred to by Crosse, by Hanmer, and by Langbaine's successor (Gildon), would circumvent the problem of either Dekker or the '1 Fortunatus' playwright needing to read German, and would do away with any linguistic necessity of Dekker relying on a lost English play and its possible sequel.

Legendary analogues
Although Dekker is named by Henslowe for the first time only in January 1598, Francis Meres's testimony in *Palladis Tamia* that Dekker was 'amongst our best for Tragedie' implies that he had been working as a playwright earlier, and presumably he would have been aware of the lost '1 Fortunatus' play which had been in the Admiral's Men's own repertory in 1596.[89] As he drafted his own version of the story for the company who had performed the lost play, comparisons would have been inevitable. However, the possible dramatic sources potentially extend beyond the lost '1 Fortunatus' play, as the vestigial traces of the Fortunatus story may also have lain behind another, older lost play. Henry Peacham recalled seeing a play in the mid-1580s featuring Richard Tarlton and a death-bed scene.[90] The dying father, a very rich man, bequeathed his land to his eldest son and an allowance in perpetuity to his second son (a scholar) to purchase books. Both responded with tears and an ardent desire that their father live long enough to enjoy these gifts himself. Tarlton played the comical part of the dying man's third son, an ill-dressed 'rogue' and 'ungracious villaine' with a history of being fetched out of Newgate and Bridewell by his long-suffering father. To this son the father could bequeath only 'the gallowes and a rope', to which news Tarlton's character duly wept and responded, like his brothers, by announcing a desire that the old man should live to enjoy these gifts himself too. On its own, this point might not bear comparison with Fortunatus's death and asset division in Scene 5 of Dekker's play, but the Tarlton play has some analogy with an anonymous Scottish poem of 1698 which *is* a liberal redaction of the Fortunatus legend.[91] It is possible that a source common to both was in circulation in the 1580s. In the Scottish *A Delectable Little History in Meter: Of a Lord and His Three Sons*, the dying lord's eldest son receives his father's land, the middle son receives a 'purse both good and fine' which has a 'vertue' ('As oft thou puts thy hand in it, / A Ducat of Gold thou shalt find there'), and the youngest

son, who is a scholar, and had actually requested books as his inheritance, receives the equivalent of the wishing cap: a 'mantle' whose 'virtue none does understand' ('Wherever thou wishes for to be, / Thou shalt be there right speedilie: / Were it a thousand miles and mair, / Into a clap thou shalt be there').[92]

The responsible land-owning elder brother is immediately forgotten and the narrative focuses on the remaining two brothers. As in Dekker's play, the ability to travel does not attract censure, but '[t]he midmost brother played the fool' with the purse, growing proud and 'wanton of gold and treasure'. (The revelation that he '[d]efiled women above all measure' may shed further light on Agrippine's fear that Andelocia will rape her, 7.35.)[93] In this poem, the Andelocia-character visits a Portuguese king and his only daughter, and his lavish spending rouses the king's curiosity.[94] The princess assumes the brother has come to woo her with his riches; she invites him to drink wine with her and inquires after the source of his fantastic wealth: 'For as long here as ye have spended, / I marvel, that your gold's not ended'.[95] He discloses the source of his riches in exchange for the princess's hand in marriage, but after they spend the night together the man wakes up to discover his purse is missing. When he sends message to the princess to return the purse, she orders him on pain of his life to flee the country; impoverished, he turns to farming swine.

Meanwhile the youngest brother, the scholar who inherited the mantle, has been crowned Pope. He chances upon his needy brother and supports him, but within a month the middle brother's thoughts turn once again to the princess, and he resolves to use the wishing-mantle to help him reclaim the stolen purse. He wishes himself into the princess's bedchamber where he kisses her in her sleep; she wakes, terrified, and demands to know how he gained access to her room. In the process of explaining the wishing-mantle, the brother inadvertently wishes them both '[u]nto a green place' (cf. Dekker's 'wilderness', Cho.2, 31), where he promptly falls asleep with his head on the princess's knees.[96] She extricates herself, takes the mantle, and wishes herself back to her chamber, leaving him stranded ('Both Purse and Mantle wants he now').[97] He is rescued by passing ships and, after disembarking, ends up wandering around a wood, 'almost dead' from hunger until he spies a tree with the fairest and sweetest apples he'd ever seen.[98] Unfortunately, consuming the apples gives him leprosy ('He was as lipper as *Lazarus* / ... / His head ov'rspread with byles black'); fortunately, he spies a magical

INTRODUCTION 29

pear tree, the fruit from which cure leprosy.[99] (There is no mention of the *Gesta* and Hoccleve's waters that also provoke and cure leprosy; the poem, like Dekker's play, restricts itself to the magical fruit.) Taking threescore apples and twice as many pears with him, he travels in search of the princess and waits for her outside a church, selling the apples for ten ducats each.[100] The princess purchases apples and 'ate of them three, and thought them right dulce, / Till she was as lipper as *Lazarus*'.[101] The brother disguises himself as a doctor of medicine capable of curing leprosy, and is brought to the court to aid the princess. There, he guarantees relief on the condition that she confess her sins and keep a promise she once made (i.e. to marry him). She eventually confesses and surrenders the purse and mantle to the disguised brother, who wishes himself back to Rome. His brother the Pope urges him to return to cure the princess and marry into royalty.

PERFORMANCE HISTORY

The Admiral's Men and early repertorial contexts
The title-page of the quarto announces that *Old Fortunatus* was played 'before the Queenes Maiestie this Christmas, by the Right Honourable the Earle of Nottingham, Lord high Admirall of England his Seruants'. The Admiral's Men played at court twice that season, and, since Q1 of *The Shoemaker's Holiday* advertises on its title-page that it was performed on New Year's Day (1 January 1600), *Fortunatus* must have been played on 27 December 1599. The venue for the Christmas and Shrove courts in 1599–1600 was Richmond.[102] The significant sum of £10 received by Thomas Downton 'ffor to by thinges for ffortunatus' (recorded by Henslowe sometime between 6 and 12 December 1599) suggests, as Richard Dutton observes, that '[n]o expense was to be spared in making an impression with this play' at court.[103]

No records document performances of the play in public theatres, either before or after the Christmas presentation at Richmond. The reference in the regular Prologue to a 'small circumference' must be an allusion to the Rose, and may thus be a hangover from the pre-court playtext: it would not make sense as a reference to the Fortune, which was square. Despite an absence of evidence, the Admiral's Men were more likely to have given the play a public run than not. Although critics would once have assumed that the play's registration at Stationers' Hall on 20 February 1600 (and its appearance in print that same year) might suggest only a limited stage run in England, there is no evidence to substantiate such claims, which rest on a network of false assumptions on the relationship of playhouse operations and the book trade. Holger Syme has questioned the traditional narrative concerning the relationship between the commercial viability of plays on stage and their registration and printing, arguing that, by the mid-1590s, the challenge for stationers 'was not how to give theatrically faded plays a new life as books but how to choose those plays whose stage popularity could be translated into print popularity'.[104]

The repertorial context of the earlier, lost play called '1 Fortunatus' may offer some insight into the types of plays and pairings that would presumably also work well for performances of Dekker's play at the turn of the century. For example, Henslowe's earliest records of the lost play occur alongside performances of Marlowe's *Jew of Malta* (featuring a fascination with infinite riches, exotic locations, and eastern Others); Chapman's *Blind Beggar of Alexandria* (a romance/disguise play also set in the exotic east); the lost 'Wise Man of West Chester' play (probably a pseudo-history; possibly involving magic, which would complement the wishing-hat and magic purse of Fortunatus); and Marlowe's *Tamburlaine* (again featuring eastern travel; it was performed the day after '1 Fortunatus' on two occasions). The Admiral's Men's repertory at that point also included such journeying plays as *Doctor Faustus* (which features diabolically enabled global travel) and the lost 'New World's Tragedy', as well as a number of histories or pseudo-histories ('Longshanks'; 'Harry the 5'; 'Chinon of England') that would pair well with the Athelstan material if it were present in the earlier Fortunatus play.[105]

When Dekker was writing *Old Fortunatus* at the end of 1599, the Admiral's Men were contemplating their move to the Fortune playhouse and appear to have considered the size and age of their repertory in anticipation of the move. (The name of the new playhouse may even have provided the impetus for Dekker to write *Fortunatus* when he did: his play's title would call attention to that of the new venue.) As Knutson suggests, part of the Admiral's Men's repertorial planning at this date may have been in response to the arrival of the Chamberlain's Men just across Maid Lane, at the Globe, but the expansion of plays in the Admiral's Men's repertory may also simply be the product of the very real expectation of a need to 'fill out the schedule' at their new playhouse, 'thus saving themselves the expense of new productions (when their other costs were up)'.[106]

INTRODUCTION   31

An allusion to Dekker's play in Marston's *Antonio's Revenge* (Paul's, c.1600) increases the likelihood that *Old Fortunatus* was being performed publicly in conjunction with its court performance: 'I tell thee, Duke, / I have old Fortunatus' wishing-cap, / And can be where I list, even in a trice'.[107] W. Reavley Gair observes that Marston 'assumes that his audience is familiar with contemporary theatre', imitating language and stagecraft from Shakespeare's *Richard III* and *Romeo and Juliet* in addition to Pandulpho's allusion to Dekker.[108] If *Fortunatus* were playing in the spring of 1600, as Marston's allusion suggests, its title would by then have had the serendipitous effect of advertising the company's new venue, the contract for which had been signed on January 8 that year.[109]

Old Fortunatus would have been a potentially valuable inclusion in the Admiral's Men's repertory for a number of reasons. The pseudo-Anglo Saxon setting of Athelstan's court complements the company's investment in legendary (i.e. Trojan and Arthurian) British history at a time when the Chamberlain's Men continued to invest in Tudor history by playing *Henry V* and probably *2 Henry IV*. Also, the choric-narrated geographical oscillations of *Old Fortunatus* and *Henry V* offer a strong parallel between the companies at the Rose and Globe. On the London stage, the competition between Orleans, the Prince of Cyprus, and Andelocia for the affection of Agrippine would have been a familiar enough motif, a version of which had been seen by the Swiss tourist Thomas Platter some time between 6 September and 14 October 1599 at either the Curtain or Boar's Head. His diary records that he 'beheld a play in which they presented diverse nations and an Englishman struggling together for a maiden'.[110] Indeed, comedies account for about half of the plays at the Rose in the 1590s, and a play such as *Fortunatus* – which contains love intrigue and romance elements, disguise motifs and fantasy – would have been perfectly at home in the repertory of many of the London commercial companies.[111]

As a form of romance, Dekker's play would complement the Admiral's Men's own two-part 'Fair Constance of Rome', 'Seven Wise Masters', and the Chinon spin-off (if that's what it was), 'Tristram of Lyons'.[112] It may also have paired especially well with Richard Hathaway and Anthony Munday's 'Valentine and Orson' (1598), a romance play which may have featured magical travel: in his *Defence of Poesy*, Philip Sidney meditated on 'the difference betwixt reporting and representing', noting that it was one thing to describe Peru and Calicut, 'but in action, I cannot represent it without *Pacolets* horse', a reference to the Valentine and Orson story, in which (as Cyrus Mulready explains) 'a dwarfish enchanter named Pacolet fashions a magical wooden horse that allows him to travel throughout the world'.[113] The fantasy of instantaneous transportation also apparently featured in an anonymous play about the King of England's son and the King of Scotland's daughter (c.1598).[114] This play, which survives in German but not in its original English, features a necromancer named Runcifax (subsequently also known as Barrabas; the text appears corrupt) who boasts that he can command twelve spirits to venture forth to Italy, Germany, Spain, and India on a whim (much as Faustus procured winter fruit for the pregnant Duchess of Vanholt).

Alternatively, Dekker's play might be viewed alongside such moral plays as *A Looking Glass for London and England* and Nashe's *Summer's Last Will and Testament* (which had been reprinted in 1598 and 1600 respectively), amongst others. On account of its 'insistent morality' and the supernatural subplot featuring Virtue and Vice as characters, *Old Fortunatus* has been treated as 'a later but intentional morality' by some critics.[115] David Kathman's reattribution of the plot of 'The Second Part of the Seven Deadly Sins' from the Lord Strange's Men to the Chamberlain's, and his redating of the plot from the early 1590s to 1597–98, provide an important revision to the repertorial context for *Old Fortunatus*. It draws attention to the fact that 'even as Shakespeare was honing his skills and presenting the Chamberlain's Men with more sophisticated fare (by our standards) in the late 1590s, the public still had an appetite for old-fashioned, morality-style play[s] such as *The Seven Deadly Sins*'.[116] It should not be surprising that shortly after '2 Seven Deadly Sins' was being prepared for performance in one of the Chamberlain's Men's Shoreditch playhouses, the Admiral's Men at the Rose were investing in a heavily moralizing play of their own.

Other plays in the Chamberlain's Men's repertory in 1600–1 potentially contain points of analogy with *Fortunatus*. The situation of the banished Duke Senior in the forest of Arden (*As You Like It*, 1600) loosely resembles the pastoral setting of Fortunatus's exile in the Cypriot wood, and Duke Orsino's lovesick musings in *Twelfth Night* (c.1601) appear to directly recall Orleans's music-accompanied melancholy in scene 6 of Dekker's play. In May 1601, the Admiral's Men revived *The Jew of Malta*, which had paired with the earlier, lost Fortunatus play, and whose revenge motif would go well both with Andelocia's quest to punish Agrippine for stealing his purse and with Longueville and Montrose's desire for vengeance against Andelocia and Shadow for being duped in the Irish costermonger episode.

Seventeenth-century German performances
The precise details of the play's stage run in London might remain ambiguous, but as June Schlueter has noted, Old Fortunatus 'appears to have been a staple of the English actors' repertory' on the Continent.[117] A play about Fortunatus and his Purse and Wishing-Cap (*'Fortunatus peitl und Wünschheitel'*) was performed in 1608 at the court of Styria in Graz, Austria, by a visiting English troupe led by the Englishman John Green. According to a letter sent by Archduchess Maria Magdalena to her brother, the Archduke Ferdinand, the visitors performed ten plays. Dated 20–2 February 1608, this 'theatre letter' – as its translator, Orlene Murad, calls it – provides a detailed report of 'what plays the Englishmen put on':

> First of all, as they had arrived here on Wednesday after Candlemas, they rested on Thursday. On the following day, Friday, they gave the play about the prodigal son, as at Passau, but on Saturday about a pious lady of Antwerp, certainly an excellent and chaste play. On Sunday they had Doctor Faustus, on Monday about a Duke of Florence who fell in love with a nobleman's daughter. On Tuesday they had a play about nobody and somebody, which was mighty clever. On Wednesday they played Fortunatus's purse and wishing-hat, also very nice.

The remaining entertainments included 'the play about the Jew', 'another play about the 2 brothers, King Ludwig and King Friderich [*sic*] of Hungary', a play 'about a King of Cyprus and a Duke of Venice', and a play 'about the rich man and Lazarus'.[118]

Murad suggests that the German Fortunatus play performed in Graz in 1608 corresponds to the text printed in *Engelische Comedien und Tragedien* (see 'The German play' above).[119] The subsequent availability of this play in print also makes it the prime candidate for use in the performance of a German Fortunatus play (*von Fortunato Wünschhütlein*) by English players in Dresden, at the court of Saxony, in July 1626. In addition to the detailed discussion of the German play above, it may be worth noting that the text contains a possible clue to staging choices: every time the wishing-hat is used to transport the bearer to a new location, the stage directions say '*fahret davon*' (or one of the different conjugations of '*fahret*'), which literally translated means 'drive' or 'travel' away; by contrast, every time a character walks off the stage, the German verb *'gehen'* (to walk) is used.[120] It is just possible that these choices of verb indicate that there might be either a mechanism for lifting characters out of the scene (flying) or a trapdoor into which they vanish and from which they return. But there is nothing further in the text, beyond the use of the different verbs, which would indicate different means of transportation. Albert Dessoff has suggested that a German play referred to as *'Von der Agrippina'*, performed in Dresden in 1630, may also have been this German Fortunatus play; the alternative title being plausible on account of the significant role played by Agrippine in Dekker's play.[121] If the suggestion is correct, presumably the 1620 German text would again be the most likely candidate for use in performance.

There is also another extant German Fortunatus play, which exists in a unique manuscript in Germany's Landesbibliothek und Murhardsche Bibliothek der Stadt Kassel (8o Ms. theatr. 4).[122] It is one of two plays in the manuscript, the first (in the same hand) being *Ariodante und Ginevra*. Schlueter has suggested an English connection by noting that Richard Mulcaster's Merchant Taylors' School boys performed an 'Ariodante and Genevra' play at court on 12 February 1583, and that the Landgrave Moritz, who presided over the Kassel court, kept English actors (including a Robert Browne) at Kassel from c.1594 to 1613.[123] Despite these tantalising English connections, Paul Harms concludes his study of the Fortunatus texts with the suggestion that the Kassel MS derives from Hans Sachs's German drama of 1553, rather than Dekker's; a position which Schlueter continues to find problematic:

> Given the ready availability of Hans Sachs's play, though, it is curious that such a manuscript, with line-by-line parallels with the earlier play but not identical to it, would exist at all. More importantly, given the sustained association of the Kassel court with the *englische Komödianten*, it would be surprising if this manuscript were not related in some way to the English players.[124]

The absence of Dekker's distinctive opening 'Echo' scene and the presence of characters named 'Rosina', 'Theodorus' and 'Limosi', however, weaken the possibility that it was a version of Dekker's play that was performed in Kassel.

Later in the seventeenth century, especially during the Thirty Years War (1618–48), *Puppenspiel* (puppet plays) were a significant form of public entertainment in Germany. Schlueter suggests that the Englishman Robert Browne may have been restaging English plays as German puppet plays in the 1620s and early 1630s, when he was in his seventies.[125] A German Fortunatus puppet play called *Glückssäckel und Wünschhut* shows indebtedness to the 1620 German redaction of Dekker's play, including opening with Dekker's distinctive Echo scene, Fortunatus's encounter with Fortune, the appearance of the three ghosts, and Fortunatus's choice of riches.[126] The Pickelherring character who replaced Shadow in the 1620 play, however, is now replaced by 'Hans Wurst', a popular coarse-comedic figure in seventeenth- and early eighteenth-century German impromptu comedy (*Stegreifkomoedie*). The fifth scene of the puppet play, for example, is performed extempore by this character, who enters the stage and recounts how he travelled through twenty kingdoms and the experiences he has had. He performs a comic improvisation (*lazzi*) about Fortunatus's torn clothes (*zerrissene Kleider*) and is interrupted by Fortunatus, who recounts how he tore them on thorny bushes and explains that he is actually a rich count who is travelling the world to accumulate knowledge (*um kenntnisse zu sammeln*). Hans Wurst doesn't believe him until Fortunatus shows him the purse. Fortunatus is delighted by Hans Wurst's gaiety and asks Hans Wurst to join him as a servant. An enthusiastic negotiation scene (*Sie halten Scene à la gusto*) follows and they reach an agreement before exiting.

In the second act, Fortunatus steals the magic hat from the Sultan but incurs the wrath of Fortune for doing so: she makes his heart weak and sick (*schwach und krank*) as a punishment, accelerating his demise. The third act does not differ significantly from the German play: Andolosia sets out to travel, prepares a banquet for the king, and loses the purse to the princess. The fourth act retains the scene in which Andelocia is disguised as a jeweller in order to abduct Agrippine. In the fifth act, Andelocia and Hans Wurst sell their apples to Duke Theodor and Duke Limoso (as in the Kassell MS, but not in Dekker) as well as to Agrippine. Andelocia subsequently appears with a long beard (*einen langen bart*) and Hans Wurst carries a large syringe (later used to administer an antidote to the horns); both appear disguised as doctors (Act 5, scene 7). This is followed by an interlude featuring Hans Wurst (in the guise of 'Famulus') and Limoso in conversation about the horns, which ends in a '*scene ad libitum*'. (This scene is not in the 1620 play, and serves to integrate Hans Wurst more deeply into the puppet play.) The final act of the puppet play contains the most drastic departures from earlier dramatizations. In the penultimate scene, Hans Wurst is given another *lazzi* in which he improvises an account of an astounding air travel sequence (*diese furiose Luftfahrt*) in which he and his master, Andelocia, flew through the air from London to Famagusta. He sits beneath a tree, starts a fire, and announces his plan to fry an amazing sausage he bought from London (*eine schöne Wurst aus London*). In the final scene, Andelocia returns to Famagusta (having returned Agrippine to her family in London) and Ampedo reveals that he has filled their treasure chests with enough gold from the purse to provide for them and their descendants. The brothers survey their property and wealth, and voluntarily sacrifice the magic purse and wishing-hat to the fire, recognising that whoever owns them has to live in constant fear for their life (as their father's travel diary – *Gedächtnisses Reisebuch* – attests). Ampedo explicitly states that burning the items will help the brothers live happily ever after (*auf daß wir ruhig und zufrieden leben immerdar*), and Fortune, having witnessed their temperate decision, intervenes to offer her congratulations and blessings: 'Live happily, wisely, and justly!' (*Lebt glücklich, weise und gerecht!*).

The nineteenth century
Amongst the collection of plays submitted to the Lord Chamberlain for licensing between 1737 and 1824 is a manuscript copy of *Fortunatus, and His Sons; Or, The Magic Purse, and Wishing-Cap*, a melodramatic romance in two acts.[127] Its title-page advertises that the play was 'founded' on Dekker's play, and a note by John Larpent, Examiner of Plays, indicates that on 1 April 1819 he licensed it for performance at the Theatre Royal, Covent Garden, where Henry Harris was the theatre manager. The play was performed at that venue as an 'Easter afterpiece' on 12 April 1819 and reprised for a total of eleven further productions.[128]

The Covent Garden adaptation is a much shorter play than Dekker's. The celebrated choruses and prologues are omitted, and there is much cutting to the dialogue to expedite the action. Fortune's entourage of debased kings is omitted altogether, as is the episode with the planting of apple trees by Virtue and Vice. For reasons that are not entirely clear, there is a Caliph instead of a Sultan, and a character named Egbert replaces Cornwall at Athelstan's court (but the Prince of Cyprus and the Lords Longueville, Montrose, and Chester become merely numbered 'lords'). At the same time, there are additional minor characters including a tailor, mercer, hatter, and shoemaker who attire Fortunatus 'superbly' (p. 21), and a sea captain who, being bound for Alexandria, becomes Fortunatus's initial means of travelling to Egypt (Scene 3). There are also additional songs. Ampedo has an aria ('Oh! Place me in some lowly shed') espousing the value of 'mild content' (rather than extravagance) after his father, brother and servant rush off to spend their money at the end of the second scene (p. 20); the Alexandrian citizens sing a glee (punctuated by 'loud Huzzas') heralding Fortunatus's arrival by boat (p. 24); and, when Fortunatus has received the purse and is about to leave the woods, a chorus provides 'Aerial Music':

> Fortunatus, why delay?
> No longer in the Greenwood stay!
> Haste! On all, thy gold to shower,
> Purchase pleasure, honor, power!
> To Famagosta haste away,
>   No longer stay!
> Fortunatus, haste away!
>
> (p. 10)

There is also much rewriting of the dialogue in the subplot with the brothers and the servant Shadow, mostly to replace obscure references with more intelligible banter.

Besides these relatively minor changes are some major discrepancies. The Egyptian Caliph loses the wishing-cap through greed rather than naivety; whereas Dekker's Sultan trusts Fortunatus to weigh the cap and see for himself how light it is, the Covent Garden Caliph 'holds out the cap, & Fortunatus keeps dropping golden coin in it, from his purse', until the Caliph 'scarce can hold it' (pp. 29–30). Fortunatus 'keeps on pouring out gold rapidly', forcing the Caliph to rest the cap on a table, whereupon Fortunatus 'upsets the gold in it, puts the cap on' and wishes himself back to Cyprus (p. 30). In these moments of instantaneous transportation, the elaborate stage directions provide glimpses of the stagecraft at Covent Garden:

> *The Curtains at the back of the Pavilion fly open the moment he utters this – the seat, on which he is, rises with him into the air, thro' which he is carried with the utmost swiftness over the distant sea, which is discovered.* (p. 30)

Fortunatus is '*seen flying over the sea, in the distance, as the Curtain drops*' (p. 31) and the first act ends.

Fortunatus does not die in the Covent Garden adaptation. The spendthrift role played by Andelocia in Dekker's play is instead reassigned to Fortunatus. It is not until the second half that we see Fortunatus return triumphantly with the Caliph's wishing cap, interrupting the lavish banquet Andelocia has been hosting (with funds left to him by his father). Fortunatus stays only briefly, then transports himself to Athelstan's court where he (not Andelocia) falls for the Princess Agrippine. Like Dekker's Andelocia, Fortunatus succumbs to a sleeping potion and the soporific effect of lullabies, and wakes to find that Agrippine has robbed him of his purse. He catches up with her and transports her to a wilderness. The episode in which Agrippine escapes the desert setting – by accidentally activating the wishing-cap lent to her for shade – is retained, with elaborate details: '*The Princess Disappears – Fortunatus falls from the Tree – The trees open, & from them comes forward Fortune, Vice, & Virtue. Fortunatus as he falls, appears with a pair of horns on his head. They surround him and laugh*' (p. 51). Fortunatus eats one of the apples from the trees (whose true import here is obscure, since Dekker's earlier scene with Virtue and Vice planting the trees has been cut), and *he* is punished with the horns reserved for Agrippine and the lords and in Dekker's play. Fortunatus begs Fortune to remove the horns, but she refuses, telling him: 'thou must live to see / Worse torments for they follies light on thee' (p. 52). However, Virtue and Vice offer their apples, and Fortunatus wisely chooses Virtue's; the horns fall off and the deities grant him the opportunity to recover his purse and cap.

Oddly, despite the absence of the Irish costermonger scene in which Agrippine acquires Vice's apples and is subsequently transformed, the Covent Garden production still includes the moment when Agrippine seeks medical assistance with removing her horns, only here 'a learned Armenian' rather than French doctor arrives to save the day ('*Enter Fortunatus, disguised as an Armenian, with long beard &c.*', p. 55). He offers her Virtue's fruit as an antidote: '*She eats – the mask drops off – she runs to a mirror, & then comes forward*' (p. 58). When she offers to reward the 'Armenian', he kneels in feigned supplication then snatches back his purse from her and transports them both to Cyprus: '*He forces her on a Couch – the whole apartment changes – and they are seen in a chamber at his house in Famagosta. A Tripod of fire rises*' (p. 60). Shadow mistakes Fortunatus for a ghost and pleads for his life; Andelocia and Ampedo are relieved to see their father return, but he proudly presents Agrippine, 'this peerless gem, / From Britain's court' (p. 62), as his latest

INTRODUCTION 39

acquisition. Horrified, Ampedo demands to know 'what / Evil power tempted you to force this / Virtuous maid from her native land?' (p. 62). Fortunatus reminds him of his filial duty to respect his father, but Ampedo retorts, 'My duty, father, is to protect the virtuous / Whensoever she calls upon me', adding 'while I've life, none / Shall oppress the helpless form / Of beauteous women!' (pp. 62–3). Andelocia challenges his brother to a duel, precipitating the entrance of Vice, then Fortune, and finally Virtue, who enters on a bright cloud when Ampedo thrusts the hat and purse into the fire (p. 65). In a final scene back at Athelstan's court, Virtue restores Agrippine to her father, urges him to bestow her 'on this virtuous youth' (Ampedo) (p. 65), and delivers what were Fortune's lines in Dekker: 'England shall ne'er be poor, if England strive, / Rather by virtue, than by wealth to thrive'. The play ends with a new Chorus celebrating the beginning of Virtue's reign (p. 66).

From the information supplied by John Genest in his *Some account of the English stage* (1832), the following cast list can be reconstructed:

Fortunatus:	Farley
Ampedo:	Duruset
Andelocia:	Abbott
Shadow:	Blanchard
Athelstan:	Chapman
Agrippina:	Miss Foote
Fortune:	Miss Beaumont
Virtue:	Mrs Faucit
Vice:	Miss Logan.[129]

Charles Farley's libretto and a musical score by Henry R. Bishop containing the 'Overture, Song, Glee, Chorusses, and Melo-Dramatic Music' for voice and piano were published in 1819.[130] Ampedo's aria, 'Oh! place me in some lowly shed' is accompanied by the advertisement, 'The Poetry by D. Terry Esq.'', referring to the actor and playwright Daniel Terry.[131] In addition to the piano reduction, Bishop's full score is extant in autograph manuscript with some spoken cues (British Library Add. 27711, ff. 1–69v), and as a neater copy which generally omits these cues (BL Add. 33570, ff. 1–73).[132]

The piano score uses standard Classical period (1750–1820) 'Eastern'-sounding compositional devices, including 'topics' like the exotic military march of the opening overture 'alla turca', which sets the scene. The Ottoman empire was generally depicted by a military march with some dissonant notes decorating the melodic line, and the Bishop piece exemplifies this with dissonant melodic decoration on the very first note (the grace note, a G sharp, is at the interval of an augmented fourth, the most dissonant interval in the chromatic scale).[133] Bishop's score provides a 'Characteristic March, of the trains of Fortune and Vice, with Chorus', accompanied by the parenthetical notes, 'Fortunatus lies down to sleep' and 'The Wood sinks and discovers the Temples of Fortune & Vice'.[134] This is followed by the first verse of lyrics from Dekker's song, 'Fortune smiles, cry holiday' (1.72–5), which was supplemented in the Covent Garden production by alternative subsequent verses as follows (repetitions omitted):

> Vice o'er mortals holds her sway,
> With tempting treasure stor'd,
> Her will, with pleasure we obey,
> For Vice and Fortune are ador'd.
>
> See Virtue all alone descend,
> In vain she courts Mankind:
> No vot'ries at her shrine attend
> No convert can she find![135]

There are also explicit stage directions ('Fortunatus starts on perceiving Fortune &c') and information about the logistics of staging ('The wood closes'; 'Wind Instruments, behind Scenes').[136]

Just a few years after the Covent Garden production, a letter from Charles Lamb to Samuel Taylor Coleridge (dated 22 March 1826) implies that Coleridge had planned to adapt a Dekker play into a pantomime for the actress Fanny Kelly:

> Your query shall be submitted to Miss Kelly, though it is obvious that the pantomime, when done, will be more easy to decide upon than in proposal. I say, do it by all means. I have Decker's play by me, if you can filch anything out of it.[137]

Coleridge's early biographer James Dykes Campbell suggested that the pantomime was 'possibly to be founded on Decker's *Old Fortunatus*'.[138] Coleridge was certainly familiar with the Fortunatus legend: he referred to transportation 'by a swifter vehicle than Fortunatus's Wishing Cap' in the appendix to *Church and State* (1829), and referred to his publisher's faith in him 'possessing a Fortunatus's wishing-cap or Jack's seven-league Boots' (in order to

INTRODUCTION   41

have his essay appear in Saturday's paper in London) in a letter to John Brown, c.9 April 1809.¹³⁹ The success of the spectacular Covent Garden production suggests that a Fortunatus pantomime project had merit, but nothing seems to have come of Coleridge's plans, despite Lamb's enthusiastic encouragement to 'do it by all means'. The Coleridge archives of Victoria University, Toronto includes a holograph manuscript outline for another Dekker play, however: 1 *Honest Whore*.¹⁴⁰ Whether the projected entertainment mentioned by Lamb was this, or whether it was another Dekker adaptation—possibly of *Old Fortunatus*—remains ambiguous.

University productions and play readings
There do not appear to be any major productions of the play since the Covent Garden run, although university and amateur groups have occasionally staged it, as for example when the Department of English in the then Tufts College performed *Old Fortunatus* outdoors in June 1906, with a cast of approximately 75 students. Photographic stills of this production, rediscovered in 2007, reveal the extent of the lavish costuming and sets (see Figs 4 and 5).¹⁴¹ The open-air production was staged on one of the terraces of the south campus, where by all accounts the woodland scenes were staged very effectively. A special amphitheatre was erected with a seating capacity of just over five hundred. The production was directed by Prof. Thomas Whittemore, and was noted for being more elaborate than his production of Milton's *Comus* some seven years earlier. Whittemore's prompt-book includes cuts, alterations, cues for music, entrances, and very occasionally specific directions such as 'A[grippine] sits in chair' and 'Bow. Lower eyes' for the scene where Galloway and Orleans observe Agrippine talking with Cyprus (Scene 6), or 'Andel. should be looking for his hat' for the scene where Andelocia disguises himself as a French doctor in order to retrieve the wishing-cap (Scene 9).¹⁴² Interestingly, the dramaturgical problem posed by the rapid changes of location in Dekker's play seems to have been solved through the use of sceneboards (like those discussed by Tiffany Stern in the context of early modern stage practices): Whittemore included frequent instructions to 'Hang sign' or 'Change sign' (in order to convey location) at the start of new scenes.¹⁴³

The 'Final Announcement' advertising the performances explains that rather than using the Covent Garden musical score ('Sir Henry Bishop's Fortunatus music (1819) interested only his

4 'Court scene from the Old Fortunatus production, 1906', Tufts production.

contemporaries'), Prof. Leo R. Lewis sourced an assortment of music from the Elizabethan period.[144] The production was reportedly well attended. On Tuesday 5 June 1906, the *Boston Evening Transcript* related that, owing to the popularity of Tufts' production, it would be staged for an unscheduled fourth time that coming Saturday (p. 14). A contemporaneous reference in a 1907 book on New England notes that '*Old Fortunatus* was marvellously well presented in the rich garb of the day on the grounds of Tufts College, by the undergraduates, in June 1906'.[145] That 'rich garb' was (according to the programme notes) created with 'all available accuracy', the costumes made 'from special designs based upon portraits in the National Gallery'.[146] The production was intended to emulate the historical conditions of the first performance at court, with actors impersonating Queen Elizabeth, her nobles and servants, who appear to have remained present for the duration

5 'Fortune, Virtue, Vice and attendants in the Old Fortunatus production, 1906', Tufts production.

of the Tufts performance. The programme draws attention to the fact that the dances, like the costuming, were drawn from historical inspiration: 'The most helpful authority has been Thoinot Arbeau's "Orchésographie." Three dances will be used: the Pavan danced by Insultado, the Double Branle by the English courtiers, and the Nymph Dance'.[147] A new edition of the play, based on Rhys but prepared specifically for performance, was published by Tufts College Press. Its corrections and omissions 'for convenience in acting', where significant, have been collated in the notes of this Revels edition.[148]

The University of Ottawa Drama Guild also produced the play, directed by Jack McCreath, on 4 and 5 December 1953. Both the production's programme notes (by Prof. L. E. Stock) and *The Ottawa Citizen* newspaper advertised the performance (incorrectly, given the Tufts production) as the first production to appear in North America.[149] Stock acknowledges that *Old Fortunatus* was regarded as an obscure choice for performance at the time, but that through a 'remarkable coincidence' Mr Ian Fellows had independently prepared his own edition of the play (based on Dilke's text) recently, which formed the basis of the Ottawa production. The performance was in three acts, with ten-minute intervals between them, and a writer for *The Ottawa Journal* reported that Fellows's edition provided 'a workable text of slightly more than two hours'.[150] Fellows also assisted with 'textual correction, production, coaching, and costume selection'.[151]

Stock's programme notes praise Dekker as being 'one of the most attractive of Shakespeare's contemporaries, with a kindliness and charm even in his satire, which is a pleasant contrast to the arrogance of Jonson or the bitterness of Marston'. Critics seem to have agreed. In a review of the opening night's performance, *The Ottawa Journal* reporter noted numerous 'faults of acting' but praised 'the achievement in bringing this play to the stage'.[152] The staging itself was 'simply done': 'A platform stage for space and movement and spare settings against velvet and gilt drapes are set off by the color of the costumes'. Whatever faults the reviewer found with the acting, he or she was consistent in their praise of the play itself: 'Here is a witty piece of theatre, shot through with telling phrases and moments of lyric beauty, which does credit to any age'; 'While the plot of Old Fortunatus may seem somewhat thin and naive and full of cupboard superstitions, its wit shines clearly and the grace of its verse is pleasant to the ear'.

The Ottawa Citizen relates that producer Steve Dupré and wardrobe mistress Paulette LeBlanc were to stage the play 'in costumes of the 10th century, the period of the original Hans Sachs story on which Dekker based his play'.[153] A student newspaper advertisement similarly emphasized the authenticity of the scene and costuming which contributed to the beauty and the spectacle of the production.[154] Jean-Paul Riopel played Fortunatus and Cyprus, Jack Richardson and Ed O'Reilly played Fortunatus's sons, and Veronica Faeghan, R. B. Omanique, and Fran Dumais played Fortune, Vice, and Virtue respectively. The production was at Academic Hall and featured an offstage choir and musical accompaniment; the music was a combination of settings taken from the Elizabethan composer John Dowland (1563–1636) (including his 'Mrs. Nichol's Almand', 'Captain Piper's Galliard', and 'Pavan Lachrimae') and new settings for Dekker's songs, written by commission by William France (an Ottawa musician and composer).

INTRODUCTION   45

More recently, *Old Fortunatus* was included in the Globe Theatre's 'Read Not Dead' programme on Sunday 5 November 2006, coordinated by Lucy Jameson. The Rhys edition was used as the performance text, with a cast of seventeen covering the roles. The accompanying programme notes by Maggie Williams promoted the play as 'a generically eclectic piece which relies heavily on music, dance and spectacle' and 'a play in which visual effects are as important as dialogue and where episodes are included largely for their entertainment value'. As is the usual practice for the Read Not Dead series, the musical accompaniment (mostly strings) seems to have been largely improvised, rather than drawing on Bishop's score from the Covent Garden production. *Old Fortunatus* was also selected for the *Shakespeare Bulletin*–sponsored play reading at the Shakespeare Association of America's 43rd Annual Meeting (Vancouver, 2015) and was included in the chronological reading of Dekker's plays (the 'Dekkerthon') led by Martin Wiggins at the Shakespeare Institute, Stratford-upon-Avon, 13 June – 1 July 2016 (a draft of the present Revels text was used).

CRITICAL RECEPTION

Aesthetics, ambivalence, and unrealized potential
A common theme unites the nineteenth- and early twentieth-century responses to *Old Fortunatus*: that, aesthetically, it is a beautiful play which, at its best, surpasses most of the dramatic output of Dekker's period, but that it suffers from inconsistency in its execution and consequently from critical neglect. The play's first editor, Charles Wentworth Dilke, was certain that *Old Fortunatus* was languishing through neglect: 'the "Honest Whore" has long been admired, and "Old Fortunatus," I trust, requires only to be equally known'.[155] Those who did know Dekker's play consistently found charm in its poetry and conceptualization. Charles Lamb famously declared that 'Decker, who wrote Old Fortunatus, had poetry enough for anything' and Felix E. Schelling believed that '[c]ould Dekker have written always as he wrote in the best scenes of this beautiful play, he could challenge a place beside the great poets of his age'.[156] Mary Lelund Hunt was similarly impressed by the 'abundance of poetry' in *Old Fortunatus*, 'the pure magic of which Dekker never surpassed', and found 'a fresh childlike joy in the marvellous' in this play.[157]

Anthony Trollope's previously unpublished thoughts on *Old Fortunatus*, recorded in his personal copy of the Shepherd edition of Dekker's works and dated 23 November 1873, contain a similar mixture of ambivalence and praise:

> The story of the various wishes and the folly of the wish for wealth has come to us in many shapes – but in none more tedious than this. Yet there is such a richness of language in the play that it is worth reading. The childishness, of all the persons, and the simple superlativeness of Vice and Virtue did not strike an audience temp: Eliz: as it does us.[158]

If Trollope's response was ambivalent at best, disparaging or dismissive at worst, his approximate contemporary the British poet Algernon Charles Swinburne evidently had a more positive experience of Dekker's play. Comparing *Old Fortunatus* with Shakespeare's *A Midsummer Night's Dream*, Swinburne effused that 'Dekker had as much of the peculiar sweetness, the gentle fancy, the simple melody of Shakespeare in his woodland dress' and that 'Shakespeare has nothing more exquisite in expression of passionate fancy, more earnest in emotion, more spontaneous in simplicity, more perfect in romantic inspiration'.[159] Yet Swinburne's praise of Dekker, like Trollope's, was tempered by his perception of the playwright's apparent limitations: 'his finest and rarest gifts of imagination and emotion, feeling and fancy, colour and melody, are as apparent as his ingrained faults of levity and laziness'.[160] Swinburne was an avid reader of Elizabethan and Jacobean drama, and appears to have enjoyed *Old Fortunatus* sufficiently to be inspired to write his own 'prologue':

> Prologue to Old Fortunatus
>
> The golden bells of fairyland, that ring
> Perpetual chime for childhood's flower-sweet spring,
> Sang soft memorial music in his ear
> Whose answering music shines about us here.
> Soft laughter as of light that stirs the sea
> With darkling sense of dawn ere dawn may be,
> Kind sorrow, pity touched with gentler scorn,
> Keen wit whose shafts were sunshafts of the morn,
> Love winged with fancy, fancy thrilled with love,
> An eagle's aim & ardour in a dove,
> A man's delight & passion in a child,
> Inform it as when first they wept & smiled.
> Life, soiled & rent & ringed about with pain
> Whose touch lent action less of spur than chain,
> Left half the happiness his birth designed,

And half the power, unquenched in heart & mind.
Comrade & comforter, sublime in shame,
A poor man bound in prison whence he came
Poor, & took up the burden of his life
Smiling, & strong to strive with sorrow & strife,
He spake in England's ear the poor man's word,
Manful & mournful, deathless & unheard.
His kind great heart was fire, & love's own fire,
Compassion, strong as flesh may feel desire,
To enkindle pity & mercy toward a soul
Sunk down in shame too deep for shame's control.
His kind keen eye was light to lighten hope
Where no man else might see life's darkness ope
And pity's touch bring forth from evil good,
Sweet as forgiveness, strong as fatherhood.
Names higher than his outshine it and outsoar,
But none save one should memory cherish more:
Praise & thanksgiving crown the names above,
But him we give the gift he gave us, love.[161]

It is not certain which edition of the play Swinburne read: in the Sotheby, Wilkinson & Hodge sale of Swinburne's library (19 June 1916), only the four-volume Shepherd edition of Dekker's *Works* (1873) is listed (lot 184), but it is explicitly described as '*uncut*'.[162] However, the sale catalogue does not accurately describe Swinburne's entire literary collection: his friend Theodore Watts-Dunton allowed the bibliophile T. J. Wise to raid the library prior to auction, and many first editions from Swinburne's Elizabethan collection appear to have disappeared at this point, before public access was granted.[163]

The influence of Marlowe on Dekker

From at least 1886 (when Charles Herford included *Fortunatus* as part of what he called a 'Faustus Cycle') until well into the early twentieth century, the supernatural bargain, the morality play inheritance, and the magical transportation in Dekker's play encouraged critics to draw comparisons between *Fortunatus* and Marlowe's *Doctor Faustus*.[164] Common to such accounts is Dekker's apparent inability to emerge from Marlowe's shadow, yet the affinity between *Doctor Faustus* and *Old Fortunatus* needn't imply a chain of influence so much as confirm Dekker's business acumen as a commercial playwright.

Comparisons between *Faustus* and *Fortunatus* are inevitable. The protagonists' names encourage us to link them as prosperous or 'fortunate' men.¹⁶⁵ Both plays involve supernatural travel, moral choices, and choric devices. Both playwrights drew on German folklore as their immediate sources: Marlowe relied on the *Faustbuch*, Dekker on some version of the German *Volksbuch*. None of this proves influence, but these superficial similarities appear to have made the Faustus and Fortunatus stories appropriate repertorial partners. The lost Fortunatus play was performed by the Admiral's Men at the Rose in the same repertory as Marlowe's *Faustus*. After Dekker's play was performed at court in 1599, a version of it appeared on the Continent (see 'Performance History' above). A troupe led by John Green visited Graz in February 1608 and performed ten plays there: on Sunday 10 February they played *Faustus*, on Wednesday 13 February *Fortunatus*.¹⁶⁶ On 11 July 1626, the Fortunatus play was again performed, this time in Dresden, again with *Faustus* in repertory.¹⁶⁷ Like *Faustus*, a puppet version of Dekker's *Fortunatus* was performed during the Thirty Years War in Germany when the theatres were closed. The plays shared enough similar interests to make them work well together; but this is not the same as positing *Faustus* as a direct source.

Nevertheless, several critics have made disparaging comparisons between Dekker and Marlowe. Mary L. Hunt, for example, assumed Dekker merely combined and revised older Fortunatus plays, retaining 'the most striking features' whilst he 'relegated the rest to a chorus that seems modelled on that of "Doctor Faustus"'.¹⁶⁸ C. F. Tucker Brooke thought 'it seems clear that *Faustus* inspired important elements in the plot of *Old Fortunatus*'.¹⁶⁹ A. W. Ward connected the two on account of German ancestry, and criticised Dekker for his flattery of Elizabeth and overly allegorical scenes 'full of historical allusions which it is hardly worth while to verify', dismissing Dekker's play as 'even ruder than Marlowe's'.¹⁷⁰ Perhaps the most far-fetched claim to a relationship between the two playwrights comes from John Payne Collier, who forged evidence in the form of an entry in Henslowe's diary to suggest that Dekker was paid for additions to *Faustus*.¹⁷¹

Cyrus Hoy spoke rather more cautiously than most about '[t]he story of Fortunatus' having 'certain Faustian overtones', suggesting that 'the model afforded by Marlowe's tragedy was not lost on Dekker when he addressed himself to the adaptation of the story to the stage'.¹⁷² Hoy pointed to the 'insistent morality' of Dekker's play and argued that in *Faustus* and *Fortunatus*, 'the protagonist's character is promptly revealed by an act of choice that has a decisive effect on all that follows. Riches are to Fortunatus what knowledge is to Faustus.[173] There are reasons to believe, however, that this 'insistent morality' in Dekker's play was significantly expanded for the court performance (see 'The German play', above), driven more by a perception of the Queen's preferences than by any desire to imitate Marlowe, which makes it difficult to endorse Hoy's suggestion that such moral interest is a significant connection between *Faustus* and *Fortunatus*.

Certainly this moral dimension has interest in and of itself; Herford drew attention to Dekker's 'unprecedented' depiction of Fortune as severe, noting that 'Fortune is not the benevolent fairy casting favours on her favourite child, but a stern goddess who confers them with contempt and calls him inexorably to account for their abuse'.[174] Although Herford raises this observation to establish a parallel between Fortune and Mephistopheles, Frederick Kiefer has shown in his study of Fortune and Elizabethan tragedy that 'Dekker had, in the native dramatic tradition, the precedent of Fortune's close relationship to the Vice and ... he appears to follow this in several scenes of the play'.[175]

Sidney R. Homan, Jr made the boldest claims for the derivative and inferior nature of Dekker's play relative to Marlowe's. He cast Fortunatus as a 'lower level' hero with simpler aspirations, dominated by his passions where Faustus is governed by reason, and explicitly claimed that Dekker copies the Chorus from Marlowe. His argument turns on a series of parallels, many of which had been devised earlier by Herford. According to Homan:

> Old Fortunatus, like Faustus, sells his soul, though to Fortune instead of the Devil, and for riches, not wisdom. For a time he enjoys the wages of his sin, among other things tricking the Soldan as Faustus tricks the Pope. There is for each man a fixed time for his death, and at the bitter hour Fortunatus repents his choice as does Faustus, though instead of being carried off by devils, he is taken from the stage by satyrs.[176]

It may be worth considering each of these ostensible parallels in turn. First, it isn't quite true that Fortunatus sells his soul for riches: when he is woken in the woods by Fortune, the only thing he asks for is forgiveness ('Oh, pardon me, for to this place I came / Led by my fate, not folly', 1.156–7). Fortune introduces herself and explains that only she can guide him out of the woods, at which point she advises him, 'Thou shalt be one of Fortune's minions' (1.176). There is no offering of a soul, no hint of a pact, and no initiative on Fortunatus's part. Fortune offers a choice of gifts, warning only that there's 'no recanting a first choice' (1.224); hardly a Mephistophelian contract. When Fortunatus chooses riches, the only warning is Fortune's caveat, 'The virtue ends when thou and thy sons end' (1.311), which doesn't really justify Herford's 'At the fixed hour Fortune appears, like Mephistophilis, to claim her victim' or Homan's declaration that 'There is for each man a fixed time for his death'.[177] When Fortune later advises Fortunatus that his death is imminent, he is taken completely by surprise: 'O sacred deity, what sin is done, / That Death's iron fist should wrestle with thy son?' (5.244–5). It is only now that Fortune reveals that Fortunatus is to die when he's most fortunate, because she takes greatest pleasure in casting him down when he's at his happiest.

Homan is particularly interested in Fortunatus choosing riches over wisdom. Noting that Fortune offers wisdom first and riches last, Homan considers these polar opposites, and detects a contrast between Faustus and Fortunatus accordingly: 'Dekker purposely casts his hero on a lower level, and his aspirations are therefore simpler'.[178] In fact, we find lengthy deliberations over Fortune's offerings in Dekker's play, and, if Dekker were writing another *Faustus*, it seems particularly odd that Fortune is unaware of how Faustus's aspirations for knowledge worked out for *him*: without a hint of irony she criticises Fortunatus for choosing 'dross' over 'Wisdom's divine embrace' (1.314–15). Homan also finds Marlovian imitation in the protagonists' enjoyment of their blessings: 'For a time he enjoys the wages of his sin, among other things tricking the Soldan as Faustus tricks the Pope'. Fortunatus's tricking of the Sultan and theft of the Sultan's wishing cap is an integral part of the legend as found in the German *Volksbuch* and its later reincarnations; it seems unlikely that Dekker *introduced* a deliberate parallel to the boxing of the Pope's ears.

Finally, Homan observes that 'at the bitter hour Fortunatus repents his choice as does Faustus, though instead of being carried off by devils, he is taken from the stage by satyrs'.[179] This appears to be his strongest parallel, though again, closer inspection shows the inaccuracy of the comparison. In the German sources there is no mention of satyrs dragging Fortunatus away. This alteration for *Old Fortunatus*, then, does indeed sound like a visual echo of Marlowe's *Faustus*, where infernal retribution is exacted as the devil claims what is contractually his to claim. But there may be important differences in *Fortunatus*. For one thing, the role of the satyrs appears to be occasional, belonging to alterations produced for the performance at court. In the German play printed in 1620, Fortunatus simply dies and the sons carry off the body — there are no satyrs. If the satyrs are unique to the court performance of Dekker's play, what is the likelihood that they are imagined under the influence of Marlowe? There may be a much simpler explanation for the satyrs' presence — one that is more pragmatic than Marlovian imitation. Unlike Faustus being dragged off-stage by devils, Fortunatus is already dead when the satyrs enter and remove his body. Their purpose is rather more simply to clear the stage than to exact retribution. Having satyrs perform this task is more spectacular and interesting than having the sons do it, and would give the Admiral's Men at court an extra chance to use the prosthetic horns that they already had on hand for the supernatural episodes later in the play — also thought to be a court addition — where Andelocia eats Vice's magic apples and sprouts horns (and subsequently fools Agrippine, Montrose, Longueville, and others to do likewise). This would accord with Frederick Kiefer's judgement that *Fortunatus* is written 'as much for the amusement of a courtly audience as for moral edification'.[180]

Although a strong case can be made for the potential for *Faustus* and *Fortunatus* to appeal to playgoers with similar tastes, and the logic of making these plays repertorial partners (as they were in Germany) is evident, it also seems that the specifically Marlovian influence has been somewhat overstated by critics too eager to find Marlowe's fingerprints everywhere they look.

Revaluing Dekker's play
George R. Price moved beyond the comparison of Dekker's play to either Marlowe or the German *Volksbuch* to reinstate the belief of nineteenth-century critics that 'the play has much more depth than has usually been found in it'.[181] He thrice takes issue with Herford's account of Dekker's handling of the *Volksbuch* material. First, he disagrees with Herford's analysis of Fortune, claiming that 'it is not essentially the choice of riches that she condemns; it is his abuse of riches'. Second, Herford notes that whereas Andelocia is 'the lucky hero' of the *Volksbuch*, he becomes a prodigal son-type in *Old Fortunatus*; but, as Price points out, 'the theme of evil prodigality is a favourite with Dekker throughout his life; he dwells on it in both plays and tracts. The contrast between Andelocia and Ampedo, therefore, is a parable'. Finally, he agrees with Herford that the

Fortune–Vice–Virtue material is presented somewhat incoherently, but, where Herford assumes the cause to lie in Dekker's alterations for court (amongst which he includes the personification of Virtue and the demonstration of her 'supremacy over Fortune'), Price attributes the incoherence to the modern audience's lack of familiarity with the 'abundant literature and iconography' associated with Fortune.[182]

In his study of Dekker's dramatic structure, James H. Conover takes a more lenient view of the seeming incoherence of plot elements in *Fortunatus*. The common perception of the play's disjointedness, split as it is between the adventures of Fortunatus and those of his sons, is all but dismissed by Conover, who notes that Fortunatus himself appears only in four scenes and that '[t]he focus of the story is not divided; it is clearly on Andelocia'.[183] The Fortunatus scenes provide the exposition (which would otherwise have to be narrated rather than depicted) required by the playwright in order to focus on the incidents that follow 'after the sons have acquired the magic gifts'.[184] The play thus takes on a tripartite form consisting of the expository material involving Fortunatus and the acquisition of the gifts, Andelocia's 'first failure', and 'his second chance with the gifts and his ultimate death'.[185] The execution is deemed imperfect, however, with the lack of an appropriate relationship between the action of the supernatural plot and the play's denouement (in which the final judgement is left to the adjudication of Elizabeth herself), and the lack of 'dramatic' purpose to be found in the Orleans plot (which according to Conover serves only the 'theatrical' function of enabling changes of costume and so forth).[186] Despite these apparent shortcomings, Conover ultimately praises Dekker's skill, suggesting that the inability of critics to classify the play according to standard genres (it has been labelled a 'fairy tale' and even a 'domestic tragedy' in addition to the more common classifications)[187] is evidence 'that the playwright has written a unique and highly imaginative work'.[188] The perceived structural failures of the interwoven plots are tempered for Conover by Dekker's unifying 'devices of repetition' which lend the work an overall appearance of 'an artistic whole'.[189] These include 'repetitions of situations, music, and images' that 'tend to relate and unite elements that otherwise might be considered isolated and irrelevant'.[190] One such cluster of images and situations involves variations of 'food, hunger, thirst, gluttony, and greed', whilst another pertains to 'appearances, deformity, and transformation'.[191] These clusters, operating across the various plots and applying to multiple characters, provides 'a consistency of texture' and 'poetic unity' that overcomes the episodic plotting of the play.[192]

More recent criticism has historicized the play in relation to the emergence of capitalism and the effect of travel and the English nation-state on the identity of the individual. William H. Sherman has pointed to the novelty of gold functioning as a universal medium of exchange as the late-Elizabethan society experienced 'the birth-pangs of a modern market economy'.[193] Gold, he argues, 'had not yet become a straightforward commodity and an abstracted standard for exchange' but, in this 'transitional market mechanism, gold was playing a new and complex role, bringing drastic changes to forces of production, exchange transactions, and social relations'.[194] The concerns about currency's essential transferability, its universality and therefore lack of integral identity, is emblematic of an attendant concern about the fragility of personal identity in an age of trade and exchange. Such a reading is eminently sensible, given that the Fortunatus legend is proverbially associated with the perils of gold. The moral of infinite riches was invoked by Karl Marx, for example, in his description of England during the period of 1846–66: 'No period of modern society is so favourable for the study of capitalist accumulation as the period of the last 20 years. It is as if this period had found Fortunatus' purse'.[195] It was, however, also integral to the German *Volksbuch* a century before Dekker's play, for, as David Blamires observes, '[t]he Crusades had expanded the horizons of Western Europe in all kinds of ways. With the growth in agricultural productivity, the increase in general population, and the specialization of labour in the towns there had been a gradual change from a barter to a money economy.'[196]

Anthony Ellis joins Sherman in analysing the corrupting influence of gold within the world of *Fortunatus*, but attends specifically to the context of old age and its effect on the social critique on offer: for him, the play 'commingles the themes of old age, mortality, and the place of gold in English society to achieve its own scathing portrayal of rampant materialism'.[197] He argues that by making an old man his 'pivotal' character, Dekker associates 'social corruption' with the embodiment of 'physical decline', thereby offering the audience 'a physical correlative for a more pervasive deterioration'.[198] This attention to the figure of the *senex* (or old man) leads Ellis to conclude that the seemingly unjust death of Ampedo alongside the more reasonable punishment of Andelocia is explicable in terms of a moral lesson:

> the sins of the father shall be visited on the sons. The failure of the patriarch to observe an old man's gravity produces a dysfunctional younger generation: one son adopts his father's dissolute behavior, while the other overcompensates and cannot enjoy life at all.[199]

Dekker in fact shows Fortunatus in two different 'old man' guises: first as 'the penniless itinerant' in the opening scenes and subsequently as 'the appetite-driven, affluent *senex*' who enjoys his magical treasures. This 'dual representation of the comic old man' enables Dekker to 'represent a set of English social problems arising out of the unequal distribution of wealth'.[200] Daniel Vitkus also reads the play in relation to economic developments, suggesting that the 'divergent modes of representing the journey on stage (as painful ordeal and as fantastic fun) indicate the ideological tensions and contradictions produced under an emergent capitalism in the early modern context'.[201] Accordingly, he finds in the purse and wishing-hat only superficial or short-lived pleasure: 'What at first seems a miraculous boon, like the magical returns or fortunes accrued by successful merchant-travelers, produces an ever more restless activity driven by desire, rather than quiescent satisfaction'.[202]

The relationship between gold and travel can also be read more symbolically, through the rich literary tradition (biblical and mythological) associating forbidden fruit – in this case, golden – with desire and knowledge. They can, for example, be read alongside the 'ball of gold that set all Troy on fire' (4.44) – the golden apple whose inscription, 'To the fairest', forced Paris to judge between Hera, Athena and Aphrodite, thus ultimately precipitating the downfall of Troy. It is in this vein that Lowell Duckert reads *Mandeville's Travels* and *Fortunatus* 'pomologically' – attending to the role of golden apples in the context of 'liquid gold' and its connotations of mobility and motion. In Dekker's play, gold is thirsted after (10.87), sufficiently mutable to be withdrawn from Fortune's purse in any currency (1.305–7), and poured as 'golden showers' into laps by the newly enriched Fortunatus (2.155): it is mobile as well as enabling mobility, it circulates as well as making circulation possible. The malleability of gold comes to stand for a dangerous kind of transformation in the play: as Duckert asks, 'Where is "home" or the "self" in this play which amplifies, perhaps even valorizes, the liquidity of gold and its corollaries of relentless (re)turning, dissembling, and transformation?'[203]

INTRODUCTION 55

But however desirable, the aspirations of social-climbing produced by gold, and the lengths to which characters go to acquire gold, makes the pursuit of gold an ambivalent venture at best:

> Just as the faith in gold of the Golden Age is challenged by Dekker's ambivalence towards gold in the play – Sherman's contention – the aspiration to travel is rendered ambivalent as well. Gold, apples, and travel can transform, for better or for worse – just make sure to choose the unostentatious apple of Virtue.[204]

At a time when the English national identity was barely nascent and identity was conceived of as fluid and malleable, subject to a host of external pressures including the environment and corruption by foreign cultures, travel was often regarded as an unprofitable pursuit.[205] Travellers (e.g. Jonson's Sir Politic Would-Be in *Volpone*) were frequently criticized for their cultural amorphousness; for exhibiting a pastiche of borrowed fashions and cultural markers, for diluting or overwriting their Englishness.[206]

Dekker was familiar with such opposition to the perceived effects of travel; in *The Seven Deadly Sins of London* (1606), he devotes a lengthy section to the vice of 'apishnesse', which is predicated on the fear that English character will be corrupted:

> *Apishnesse* rides in a Chariot made of nothing but cages, in which are all the strangest out-landish Birds that can be gotten: the Cages are stucke full of Parats feathers: the Coach-man is an *Italian Mounti-banck* who drives a Fawne and a Lambe.[207]

Andelocia anticipates precisely such a degenerate transformation upon his father's return:

> Come, come, when the old traveller my father comes home like a young ape full of fantastic tricks, or a painted parrot stuck full of outlandish feathers, he'll lead the world in a string. (5.26–9)

Despite this display of a typically English anxiety over the detrimental effects of travel, Fortunatus's tales of foreign lands prove too tantalizing for Andelocia, who is in turn inspired to travel. It has been suggested that Andelocia appears to lose hold of his own identity in the process, that he 'epitomizes shape-shifting and getting "lost" in the play', given that '[w]hile in England he disguises himself as a Genoese jewel-seller, Irish apple-monger, and French physician'.[208] However, these shape-shifting activities pertain specifically to his failed romance and subsequent quest for revenge. As I have argued elsewhere, a notable aspect of Dekker's play is that none of the travelling characters are punished for their extravagant voyaging, only for their riotous waste of riches.[209] When Fortune claims Fortunatus's life it is his waste of riches that she laments: 'endless follies follow endless wealth' (5.256). When she denounces his sons, she explains that 'their riots made them poor' (10.218). In other words, it is the spendthrift nature of their lavish expenses that attracts condemnation from Fortune (and, we assume, the audience), not their fanciful transportation. *Old Fortunatus* was written after a period of financial difficulty for Dekker: he was imprisoned for debt in 1598 and again in 1599.[210] It is interesting that this personal financial hardship coincides with a play about the (mis)use of fabulous, inexhaustible riches.

Dekker's play, then, censures the spendthrift or the prodigal, but seems to celebrate the traveller, hence Vitkus's characterization of the play as offering 'what is perhaps the most extended fantasy of instantaneous and labor-free travel' on the early modern stage.[211] Like Faustus's dragon-driven chariot (or Aladdin's magic carpet and Jonathas's cloth, for that matter), Fortunatus's wishing-hat serves primarily to satisfy curiosity and provoke wonder.[212] The early modern theatre encouraged such imaginary travel, providing a vicarious experience of exotic climes for mind-travelling playwrights and playgoers in London.[213] Such fantasies of whimsical voyaging are underappreciated by critics of early modern drama, but are shown (in Dekker's play) to be a deliberate and informed desire that knowingly runs counter to the prescriptions for profitable travel advocated by the *ars apodemica* treatises of the period. The Sultan declares that he uses the hat temperately for statecraft, exploiting its powers for espionage in order to avoid conflict with his enemies:

> By this I steal to every prince's court
> And hear their private counsels and prevent
> All dangers which to Babylon are meant.
>
> (4.90–2)

In the hands of Fortunatus – the character with whom playgoers are presumably more likely to identify – the benefits of instantaneous transportation are purely pleasurable:

> I'll travel to the Turkish emperor,
> And then I'll revel it with Prester John
> Or banquet with great Cham of Tartary,
> And try what frolic court the Sultan keeps.
>
> (2.210–13)[214]

Even the magical purse – supplied by Fortune, not by the Sultan who owned the wishing-hat – is unusually well placed to facilitate travel fantasies; it provides 'bright gold' that is specifically '[c]urrent in any realm' (1.306–7), thereby suggesting that an expectation of travel is inextricably bound up in the fantasy of wealth. There is also a third item linked importantly to travel in the play: Fortunatus's travel diary, which he bequeaths to his sons along with the purse and hat. Having announced that he will 'sit and read what story my father has written here', Andelocia describes the contents of Fortunatus's book as 'a story of all his travels' (5.348–9, 396), which inspires him to 'tread after' his father's footsteps and 'measure the world' (5.397–8). (In the German play, the book is said to contain notes of all his travels from throughout his lifetime, and how in his youth he traversed half the world including all Christian kingdoms and heathendom; Andelocia is there certain that, if his brother reads the book also, he too will be infected with its charm.)[215] Fortunatus's travel book offers a stimulus to travel, whetting his son's appetite for adventure; the majority of playgoers attending a performance of Dekker's play would not have been able to embark on such exotic travels themselves if Fortunatus's example kindled their own wanderlust, but the theatre offered at least a vicarious travel experience to partially satisfy the mind-travelling playgoer. Characters who travel (and whose travels are celebrated) can serve as a proxy for playgoer desires, carrying them many miles 'on the wings / Of active thought' (Cho.1, 8–9).

The imaginative connection between playgoer and player has been constructed along alternative lines by Hillary M. Nunn in her study of how the presence of food on-stage fosters playgoer empathy with characters' 'physical hunger' and 'moral struggles with temptation' whilst simultaneously 'encouraging refreshment sales within the playhouse'.[216] Nunn claims that '*Old Fortunatus* offers the most vivid instance of apples' mutually dependent commercial and thematic roles onstage, integrating the fruits into the plot as emblems of both temptation and virtuous eating'.[217] Fortunatus's hunger in the opening scene is used 'to establish a connection with the audience', and partially explains why he chooses riches: 'his physical hunger deprives him of wisdom, leading him to choose the more immediate, and desperate, reward of bodily relief' which gold can afford.[218] Fasting, being lean, serving lean banquets to the eye (1.299) and other references to hunger permeate the play and plague its impoverished characters; conversely, Fortunatus aspires to 'banquet with great Cham of Tartary' (2.212) and Andelocia aspires to entertain Athelstan's court royally with a lavish banquet (Scene 6). But as the play progresses it becomes clear that food, as much as riches, becomes a source of moral temptation, as epitomized by various characters' consumption of Vice's apples. It may be significant that the on-stage embodiments of temptation – the apples – were probably also available for playgoers to purchase from vendors circulating within the playhouse, thus collapsing the distance between diegetic and extradiegetic worlds and eliminating 'the comfortable distance that might separate playhouse viewers from the moral dilemmas represented through food onstage'.[219] According to Nunn, '[t]he similarities between the foods appearing on- and offstage allowed the plays and audience members to consider, together, profound questions about the nature of hunger, temptation, and human desire'.[220]

A number of the foregoing issues – the question of form, the perceived quality of Dekker's play, and the topicality of travel for early modern playgoers – coalesce in Cyrus Mulready's reading of the play, in which *Fortunatus* is a response both to developments in the English knowledge (and acquisition) of foreign lands and to the 'geographically expanded imaginations of playgoers'.[221] Citing the experimental form of Dekker's play (a hybrid of stage romance, morality play, masque, tragedy and fable) and the playwright's disregard for the Classical unities of time and place, he argues that 'England's expanded horizons were exercising pressure on the matter of the theater in particular plays, but also on dramatic practice and the very categories of dramatic representation itself'.[222] Mulready situates *Fortunatus* amidst the vogue for stage romances (which began, in London, in the late sixteenth century) and the 'mounting demand for plays that gave audiences representations of an expanded world'.[223] In his *Defense of Poesy*, Sir Philip Sidney famously denounced plays that attempt to represent rather than report sweeping geographical shifts, quipping facetiously about the need for the instantaneous transportation afforded by Pacolet's magical wooden horse (a device with obvious analogy to Fortunatus's wishing-hat).[224] But rather than reading *Fortunatus* through this Sidneian lens and criticizing its 'explicit resistance to neoclassical unity', Mulready positively revalues the generic innovations of Dekker's play, arguing instead that it 'shows us the appeal that this genre had for its audiences'.[225]

ACT AND SCENE DIVISIONS

In editing Dekker's other sole-authored play of 1599, *The Shoemaker's Holiday*, Fredson Bowers followed the lead of earlier editors by imposing act divisions, but placed them at new positions. Smallwood and Wells object to the arbitrariness of this editorial intervention:

> The ease with which Bowers can propose a radical rearrangement of the traditional division of *The Shoemaker's Holiday* suggests that this is a superficial division, corresponding to no structural principle in the mind of the author as he disposed his material.[226]

They argue that, in direct contrast to the nominal definition of the act divisions, the scenic unit held 'indisputable' significance for Dekker and fellow playwrights vis-à-vis 'narrative function'.[227] Accordingly, the Revels editors of *The Shoemaker's Holiday* omitted the editorially imposed act divisions and reverted to continuous scene numbering.

Just as Smallwood and Wells found nothing in the design of *The Shoemaker's Holiday* to suggest that Dekker had a five-act structure in mind when composing that play, so too there is no evidence for imposing a five-act structure on *Old Fortunatus*. The quarto printed in London in 1600 is not divided into acts, and Dekker's practice elsewhere suggests that the scenic unit was of primary importance to him; his 1 *Honest Whore* (1604, STC 6501), for example, includes partial through scene numbering (headings for scenes 1, 7, 8, 9, 10, 11, and 13), but not act divisions beyond the initial 'ACTVS PRIMVS. SCÆNA PRIMA'. As Wilfred T. Jewkes has observed, although act division was a 'theatrical necessity' as well as 'a literary habit' in the indoors playhouses, act intervals do not appear to have been observed in the amphitheatres, and nor did the playwrights of the 1590s practise the same literary habits as the Terence-inspired 'university wits' of the 1580s either.[228] (Jonson, as ever, was the exception.) Following Jewkes, Henry L. Snuggs noted that the handful of surviving prompt-books from the Elizabethan to Caroline periods 'indicate the optional character of act-division in the later sixteenth-century ... and the growth of division as a regular practice as the seventeenth century progresses'.[229] The general consensus of Jewkes and Snuggs is that in the 1590s and early 1600s (at least until the King's Men began performing at the indoors Blackfriars playhouse as well as their open-air Globe),[230] the five-act structure was not observed for amphitheatre plays. Imposing a five-act structure on to Dekker's *Old Fortunatus* not only supplies a structure that was not intended but obscures the playwright's original intentions. The matter is complicated, however, by the fact that at the court performance of 27 December 1599, the practical consideration of candles needing to be trimmed periodically to prevent hot wax spilling on to those below would have necessitated breaks at some point in the play, which couldn't therefore have been a continuous performance as it may have been at the Rose or Fortune. Playgoers might in fact have been expected to recognize a tripartite movement in Dekker's play (and perhaps the court performance entailed just two breaks, accordingly). Snuggs notes that '[p]lays are sometimes divided or punctuated by other means than the numbering of acts, especially by the chorus'.[231] Although the *Fortunatus* quarto is undivided, it contains a heading for an induction called 'The Prologue at Court' as well as for the regular 'Prologue' (who begs to 'serve as Chorus' to the 'scenes'). Scenic units are evident, marked by a combination of line breaks, directions for clearing the stage, or musical or choric markers of a new scene's commencement. The appearance of the Chorus on sigs E4v and H1r, however, implies a theatrical division that would have been observable to audiences even if it wasn't explicitly presented by headings in the quarto. (Interestingly, the Ottawa production of 1953 was presented in three acts with ten-minute intervals between each.) Accordingly, the scene division of Prol., sc. 1–3, Cho.1, sc. 4–6, Cho.2, sc. 7–10 might be conceived in a three-part form as follows (with the Prologue at Court and Epilogue at Court added):

1: Prol., sc. 1–3
2: Cho.1, sc. 4–6
3: Cho.2, sc. 7–10.

A three-part structure to Dekker's play corresponds neatly with his use of source material. As mentioned above, a distinctive aspect of Dekker's treatment of the legend is the fact that his play opens with Fortunatus already old. The German *Volksbuch* of 1509 and the later chapbooks (see 'Sources', above) begin with the adventures of Fortunatus as a young man. Herford summarizes the four-part outline of the *Volksbuch* version:

> The first (chapters i. – xx.) comprises the early history of Fortunatus preceding the encounter with Fortune which first entitled him to his name. The second (c. xi. – xxiii.) is the history of *Fortunatus and the purse*. After receiving the purse from Fortune, he enters on a career of successful

INTRODUCTION   61

adventure in Venice and elsewhere, and finally marries with great splendour in his native Cyprus. The third (c. xxv. – xxx.) contains the story of *Fortunatus and the hat*. After twelve years of domestic happiness the instinct for enterprise stirs once more in the old adventurer; disguised as a merchant, he visits the Sultan, robs him by a simple stratagem of the wishing hat, returns home and dies, leaving the purse and hat to his two sons Andolosia and Ampedo. The fourth (c. xxxi. to the end) contains the *Adventures of Andolosia*, his intrigue with the English princess Agrippina, the loss, recovery, and final loss of purse and hat, and lastly, the violent death of both sons.[232]

Dekker can thus be seen to have omitted entirely the first part of the *Volksbuch* material and turned each of the remaining three parts into what would, in performance, appear as three distinct movements. The first is the story of the purse: it includes Fortunatus's first encounter with Fortune and his choice of riches (Scene 1); Ampedo, Andelocia, and Shadow meeting a gallant Fortunatus, receiving money from him before he embarks on his travels (Scene 2); and Virtue and Vice planting their trees and competing for patronage (Scene 3). The second is the story of the hat: Fortunatus acquires the wishing-hat from the Sultan (Scene 4); he returns to Famagusta where he presents his sons with his new treasure (the hat), is admonished by Fortune, and dies, leaving his sons follow in their father's footsteps (Scene 5); and Andelocia loses the wishing-hat via the machinations of Agrippine and Athelstan (Scene 6). Dekker's third movement covers Andelocia's story, including the loss of the hat and the death of the brothers. Andelocia abducts Agrippine, but she escapes with the hat. In a parallel with the opening scene of the play, Fortune visits Fortunatus's son in the remote wilderness where *he's* now trapped (Scene 7). To retrieve the hat and purse, Andelocia and Shadow first disguise themselves as Irish costermongers selling Vice's apples (which cause their eater to sprout horns) (Scene 8), then Andelocia returns disguised as a French doctor peddling an antidote (Scene 9). Ampedo argues with his brother, takes the hat and burns it. Ampedo expires, Andelocia is strangled, and, as the lords fight for possession of the purse, the whole court arrives, as do Fortune, Vice, and finally Virtue, who ultimately triumphs (Scene 10).

I refer to these as 'movements' rather than proposing a three-'act' structure because the occasional nature of the copy-text (corresponding to performance at court in 1599) obscures the playwright's original conception of the action in such complicated ways.[233] The excision and addition of material – including, significantly the 'jeweller' episode summarised by the second Chorus (which may in turn have necessitated the inclusion of that Chorus at that juncture) – makes it difficult to ascertain what Dekker initially envisaged for the structure of his play; or what, indeed, the play looked like if it were subsequently performed in a public playhouse. The Choruses may simply have been expedient inclusions for performance at Richmond, and the distribution of *Volksbuch* material less obvious in their absence. Although the German *Von Fortunato* play printed in 1620 has act divisions, and the seventeenth-century German puppet play (*Glückssäckel und Wünschhut*) has both act and scene divisions, in England the five-act practice was being established from around 1607–8 and had become sufficiently common by 1616 that act divisions were being retrospectively imposed on printed playtexts.[234]

Previous editors have distributed the scenes differently. For Fredson Bowers, the play's most recent editor, sc. 1–3 = 1.1–3; sc. 4-5 = 2.1–2; sc. 6 = 3.1; sc. 7–8 = 4.1–2; sc. 9-10 = 5.1–2. Such division into five acts did not begin until the late nineteenth century. Ernest Rhys, in his edition of 1887, was the first to attempt an act- or scene-division (288). (Charles Dilke's critical edition of 1814 noted that *Q* is not divided into acts, but did not attempt to impose a five-act structure or to number the scenes.) Rhys's distribution of scenes influenced subsequent editors; he differs from Bowers in that he includes a scene division immediately prior to the dumbshow in which Agrippine steals the purse from the sleeping Andelocia; but Andelocia remains sleeping on stage, '*Music sounding still*', and, to make his scene division work, Rhys has to ignore *Q*'s explicit direction 'Manet Athelstane' and add a stage direction for Athelstan to exit – only to then add a further direction for him to re-enter immediately after Agrippine secures the purse. (Bowers doesn't divide the scene, and neither do I.) Hans Scherer made no attempt at act- or scene-divisions in his 1901 edition. Oliphant Smeaton subsequently attempted a fresh division of acts and scenes in 1904, though by his own admission it corresponds 'in some respects' to the division imposed by Rhys.[235] Smeaton's structure differs from Rhys's in three points: he starts a new scene (designated 2.3) where the company of satyrs enter to steal away Fortunatus's body whilst Ampedo and Andelocia sleep; he starts a new scene where Athelstan, Agrippine, and the lords enter (designated 3.2; he then proceeds to observe Rhys's scene division at the start of the dumbshow, and designating

INTRODUCTION   63

it 3.3); and he creates a new scene (4.2) when the supernatural figures discover Andelocia asleep under a tree, having recently lost the wishing-hat to Agrippine. Bowers, finally, follows the usual division of Act 1 into three scenes; does not adopt Smeaton's insertion of scene division with the satyrs' entrance in Act 2; does not divide Act 3 at all; has 4.1 end when the action moves to Athelstan's court; and divides his Act 5 into two scenes as usual.

Smeaton's creation of a new scene simply to mark the entrance of the king and his entourage (at what he calls 3.2) seems particularly unnecessary; likewise, where Rhys and Smeaton introduce divisions, Dekker has placed a character asleep on-stage (Ampedo and Andelocia at Smeaton's 2.3; Andelocia alone at Smeaton's 3.3 and 4.2). Neither editor, though, sees fit to mark a scene division when Fortunatus falls asleep in Scene 1, despite there being an analogy of circumstances. In all these instances, music is introduced or sustained (explicitly so, as in 'Music sounding still' at 6.373 SD of this edition) and the sleeping character, although silent, is the focal point, ensuring continuity of action. I therefore follow Bowers in avoiding formal scene divisions if a character remains on-stage (even if they are asleep), but differ from him by omitting act divisions altogether, for the reasons described above. This strikes me as the most consistent and defensible division of scenic units, and produces fifteen discrete scenes as follows: Prologue at Court, Prologue, Scenes 1–3, Cho. 1, Scenes 4–6, Cho. 2, Scenes 7–10, Epilogue at Court.

PRESS-VARIANTS

There are currently thirteen known copies of *Q* extant. In the UK: British Library C.34.c.26 (Garrick's copy) and C.12.f.3.(1.) (King George III's copy); Victoria & Albert Dyce 2857 (Dyce's copy, from the Heber collection); Eton S.178 Plays 45 (1-6); Bodleian Mal.235 (1) (Malone's copy, into which he has pasted Dekker's autograph); and Petworth House NT 3007480, vol. 14 (the Earl of Egremont's, from the ninth or tenth Earl of Northumberland). In the US: Huntington C 6517 X60132 (the Bridgewater copy); Harvard STC 6517 (A) (W. A. White's copy) and (B) (also White's, from Frederick Locker / the Rowfant library); Folger STC 6517 (the Rev. John Mitford's copy, later W. Carew Hazlitt's); Pforzheimer / Harry Ransom Pforz 277 (previously also from the Locker/Rowfant collection); and NYPL Berg (the Kemble–Devonshire copy) and Arents

S113 (Corser/Huth/Murton/Jones/Clark). All thirteen copies have been inspected (in person or via digital photography) during the preparation of this Revels edition, the Petworth copy and one of the NYPL copies not having been collated previously. See 'The text' (above) for collation details and information about missing leaves supplied in facsimile or from other original copies of *Q*.

Q is printed in black-letter with roman (and occasionally italics) for speech prefixes, stage directions, etc.; this edition presents the text in roman with italics (respectively). Only two minor press-variants occur in the surviving copies:

Sheet A (*inner forme*)
Corrected: Bodleian, British Library C.34.c.26, Eton, Harry Ransom, Harvard STC 6517 (A), V&A.
Uncorrected: British Library C.12.f.3.(1.), Folger, Harvard STC6517 (B), Huntington, NYPL Arents, NYPL Berg, Petworth.

Sig. A4 / scene 1.81 *Radiance*] Radianee

Sheet B (*outer forme*)
Corrected: Bodleian, British Library C.34.c.26, Eton, Harry Ransom, Harvard STC 6517 (A).
Uncorrected: British Library C.12.f.3.(1.), Folger, Harvard STC 6517 (B), Huntington, NYPL Arents, NYPL Berg, Petworth, V&A.

Sig. B1 / scene 1.149 *court*] Court

Accidentals in *Q* have been collated and emended throughout the text; my practice has been to check Bowers's notes against the quartos he collated (the only discrepancy being at 9.25, where Bowers stated that the comma was clearly inked only in the Harvard (B) copy, but it is clear in the Bodleian copy also); and to supplement his observations with information from the two quartos he did not collate: the Petworth and NYPL Berg copies (the only addition being at 10.337 the colon is inked in the Berg copy but not the Petworth).

In general I have preserved the spelling of early modern texts, but have silently emended i/j, u/v, vv/w and expanded contractions using the tilde to the full form throughout.

NOTES

1 Foakes, 34–7. Henslowe routinely applied the Old Style calendar, according to which the year ended on 25 March; hence the February 1595 performances belong to 1596 in the New Style calendar.
2 Foakes, 126–7.
3 Foakes, 127–8.
4 *SR* 3.156.
5 E. K. Chambers, *The Elizabethan Stage* (Oxford: Clarendon Press, 1923), 1.373.
6 Roslyn L. Knutson, 'Influence of the Repertory System on the Revival and Revision of *The Spanish Tragedy* and *Dr. Faustus*', *English Literary Renaissance* 18 (1988), 258n.
7 Foakes, xxxiv–xxxv.
8 Frederick Gard Fleay, *A Biographical Chronicle of the English Drama, 1559–1642* (London: Reeves & Turner, 1891), 1.126.
9 Chambers, *Elizabethan Stage*, 3.291.
10 Wiggins, #843.
11 Holger Schott Syme, 'The Meaning of Success: Stories of 1594 and Its Aftermath', *SQ* 61.4 (2010), 500, 505.
12 'Long Meg of Westminster', for which no known sequel ever existed, was marked with a marginal 'j' on its initial entry in the diary, on 14 February 1594. It is unclear what Henslowe meant by this 'j', but it may be analogous to his use of 'the j p' or similar. (See Knutson, 'Influence', 267n.)
13 Wiggins, #851; see also #843. Wiggins also appeals to a second reason for positing the existence of a '2 Fortunatus' play: he argues that 'there are indications that Thomas Dekker later combined the two parts into a single play'. I will return to this point below.
14 Roslyn L. Knutson, 'Henslowe's Naming of Parts: Entries in the *Diary* for *Tamar Cham*, 1592–3, and *Godfrey of Bulloigne*, 1594–5', *N&Q* n.s. 30.2 (1983), 157–60.
15 Fleay, *Biographical Chronicle*, 1.125.
16 Walter W. Greg, ed. *Henslowe's Diary, Part II. Commentary* (London: A. H. Bullen, 1908), 179. Greg's initial caution hardened into conviction by 1927, when he declared: 'It is clear that the extant text of Dekker's *Old Fortunatus* is refashioned from the two-part play performed by the Admiral's men, and it is probably this fact that was in mind when the piece was entered as 'A commedie called old Fortunatus in his newe lyuerie' on 20 February 1599/1600' ('Some Notes on the Stationers' Registers', *The Library* s4-VII (1927), 382).
17 Greg, *Henslowe's Diary, Part II*, 179.
18 Bowers, 1.107.
19 See Wiggins, #843 and #851; Fleay, *Biographical Chronicle*, 1.125; Greg, *Henslowe's Diary, Part II*, 179; C. H. Herford, *Studies in the Literary Relations of England and Germany in the Sixteenth Century* (Cambridge University Press, 1886), 210–11; and Albert Feuillerat, *The Composition of Shakespeare's Plays: Authorship, Chronology* (New Haven: Yale University Press, 1953), 18.
20 Bernard Fonteyn, *Fortunatus Beurs en wensch-Hoedt. Bly-droef-eyndend spel. Gespeelt op de Amsterdamsche Schouw-burgh. T'Amsterdam, gedruckt

by Nicolaes van Ravesteyn. *Voor Dirck Cornelisz Hout-Haeck, Boeckverkooper op de Nieuwe-zijds Kolck, Anno 1643*; Bernard Fonteyn, *Fortunatus Soonen, Op en Onder-gangh. Tweede deel. T'Amsterdam, gedruckt by Nicolaes van Ravesteyn. Voor Dirck Cornelisz Hout-Haeck, Boeckverkooper op de Niewe-zijds Kolck, Anno 1643*. Digitizations of both are available via *Early European Books*.

21 Chambers, *Elizabethan Stage*, 3.291.
22 Bowers, 1.107.
23 Martin Wiggins has suggested in personal correspondence that an analogous case might be 'The Whore New Vamped' (1639, lost), in which case it is unclear whether the titular character has a new costume or a new text; *The Knave in Grain New Vamped* is a clearer example of textual alteration being signalled by the title. But again, the *OED* offers no support for such an interpretation in the textual domain, its earliest use of 'new-vamped' in this context being 1649.
24 The term 'clumping', misremembered from Darwin, was used by John H. Astington to describe this reductive practice for effacing the often scant historical records for a play's existence. See Astington, 'Playing the Man: Acting at the Red Bull and Fortune', *Early Theatre* 9.2 (2006), 136. Astington revised the terminology to the more accurate 'lumping' in his chapter, 'Lumpers and Splitters', in *Lost Plays in Shakespeare's England*, ed. David McInnis and Matthew Steggle (Basingstoke: Palgrave Macmillan, 2014), 84–102.
25 If there is anything of '1 Fortunatus' in Dekker's extant text, stylometric analysis (in the form of a Jensen-Shannon Divergence test, a Zeta test, and an Iota test) does not support the hypothesis of Greene's involvement, but instead supports the conclusion that *Old Fortunatus* is stylistically of a piece with Dekker's other plays. The tests were performed by Brett Greatley-Hirsch with Hugh Craig.

The Jensen-Shannon Divergence test measures the similarity between two probability distributions; it establishes what a 'typical' Greene text is stylistically, so that Dekker texts (or segments of text) can be tested for their divergence from this mean. Plotting 2000-word segments of Greene's *James IV, Alphonsus, Friar Bacon*, and *Orlando* against Dekker's *2 Honest Whore, If It Be Not Good, Old Fortunatus, Shoemaker's Holiday*, and *Whore of Babylon* shows that *Old Fortunatus* behaves like a typical Dekker play in this sample. None of the 2000-word blocks of *Old Fortunatus* shows any unusual affinity with any 2000-word blocks of Greene's works.

A Zeta test is a technique commonly used for authorship attribution. It relies on identifying words that appear frequently within one author's known corpus of writing (set 1) and plotting these against words appearing frequently in another author's known corpus (set 2). The disputed text is then graphed against these sets to see where its most frequently used words fall. Dekker's plays and Greene's plays differentiate quite obviously in this test, with *Old Fortunatus* behaving stylistically like Dekker's other plays.

The Iota test identifies words that occur not just more frequently, but *exclusively* in one author's works: i.e. words that occur at least once in each 2000-word segment of a given play, and not at all in the work of the other author being examined. This test reveals that *Old Fortunatus* consistently uses a higher proportion of words which are more frequently used by Dekker and not used by Greene. The results show a clear separation between the two authors' works, with no overlaps and no outliers.

26 The printer's device representing Opportunity (signified by having long hair at the front but being bald at the back; and thus easily seized when approaching but not once past) standing on a wheel which floats in the sea accompanied by the Latin motto *aut nunc aut nunquam* was apparently passed from John Danter (who used it, for example, on the *Romeo and Juliet* quarto of 1597) to Simon Stafford in 1599 (McKerrow, device 281); the initials 'S. S.' on the title-page also point to Stafford.
27 Smeaton, xi.
28 I am grateful to the Duke's secretary, Sandra Howat, for searching book records in the libraries of all the Buccleuch houses. The only Dekker text currently in the Buccleuch Collection is *The Whole Magnificent Entertainment* (1604), which is held at Bowhill House. The Dukes of Buccleuch called Dalkeith home until 1913, only nine years after Smeaton's edition was published. It is technically possible that, if the Edinburgh edition did exist, it may have moved from Dalkeith at this date, its present whereabouts remaining unknown.
29 Bowers, 1.108–9.
30 Bowers, 1.108.
31 Bowers, 1.109.
32 Bowers, 1.109.
33 Fredson Bowers, 'Essex's Rebellion and Dekker's *Old Fortunatus*', *RES* 3.12 (1952), 365.
34 Bowers, 'Essex's Rebellion', 365n.
35 Frederick Warde and Bruce Rogers, *The Carl H. Pforzheimer Library: English Literature, 1475–1700*, vol. 1 (New York: Privately Printed, 1940), 270 (entry #277). Both Harvard copies come from the collection of William Augustus White, whose library was catalogued in 1926. The catalogue confirms that the B copy belonged to the Rowfant estate (i.e. Frederick Locker-Lampson) (Henrietta C. Bartlett, *Catalogue of Early English Books; Chiefly of the Elizabethan Period* (New York, Priv. Print. for Mr. W. A. White by the Pynson Printers, 1926), 33).
36 At that stage, the B copy (i.e. the second Locker copy) lacked only 'D1, F1–F4, L2, L3' (Bartlett, *Catalogue*, 33). The whereabouts of the Pforzheimer quarto (i.e. the bookplated Locker copy) are unaccounted for between 1905 (when the Locker-Rowfant library was dispersed) and 1940 (when Carl H. Pforzheimer acquired it). Presumably at some stage between 1926 and 1940, leaves E2–3 were transferred from the now severely imperfect Locker copy (Harv.B) to complete the virtually restored Locker copy (Pforzheimer).
37 Bowers, 'Essex's Rebellion', 366.
38 Francis Bacon, 'To the Earl of Essex' in *The Letters and the Life of Francis Bacon*, vol. 2, ed. James Spedding (London: Longman, Green, Longman and Roberts, 1862), 191.
39 Curiously, as long ago as 1874, Richard Simpson, in his survey of turn-of-the-century plays engaging with the Essex controversy, noted that

Fortunatus 'seems quite innocent of all political allusion', yet asked: 'But in those days could Fortunatus and his fate be played without a hidden reference to Essex and his catastrophe?' ('The Political Use of the Stage in Shakspere's Time', *The New Shakspere Society's Transactions* 2 (1874), 394).

40 Robert Allot, *Englands Parnassus: or the choysest flowers of our moderne poets, with their poeticall comparisons* (London, 1600), 5.

41 Allot, *Englands Parnassus*, 156. A total of 17 passages are attributed to Dekker in *Englands Parnassus*; of these, one is actually from Peele's *Battle of Alcazar* (p. 255), one is from *Lucrece* (pp. 280–1), two are untraced (pp. 259 and 416), and two subsequently occur in Heywood's *Love's Mistress* (1636), and may be remnants of the lost 'Cupid and Psyche' play by Chettle, Day and Dekker (Admiral's, 1600) (pp. 372–3 and 478).

42 Bowers, 'Essex's Rebellion', 366.

43 John Gouws, ed., *The Prose Works of Fulke Greville, Lord Brooke* (Oxford: Clarendon Press, 1986), 93.

44 British Library Add. MS. 27632, fol. 43.

45 Bodleian Wood MS D. 18; see Albert C. Baugh, 'A Seventeenth Century Play-List', *The Modern Language Review* 13.4 (1918), 401–11; *Miscellany of Henry Oxinden [manuscript]*, ca. 1642–1670, Folger Shakespeare Library MS V.b.110, http://luna.folger.edu/luna/servlet/s/82ikiu (see Giles E. Dawson, 'An Early List of Elizabethan Plays', *The Library* s4-XV (4) (1935), 445–56).

46 Maria Kirk, 'Books and Their Lives: The Petworth House Plays', in *Writing the Lives of People and Things, AD 500–1700: A Multi-Disciplinary Future for Biography*, ed. Robert F. W. Smith and Gemma L. Watson (Farnham: Ashgate, 2016), 203–24.

47 Herford, *Studies in the Literary Relations*, 218.

48 Julius Tittman, ed., *Die Schauspiele der Englische Komödianten in Deutschland* (Leipzig: Brockhaus, 1880), XXXVIff.

49 Paul Harms, *Die deutschen Fortunatus-Dramen und ein Kasseler Dichter des 17. Jahrhunderts* (Hamburg and Leipzig, 1892), 17; Emil Herz, *Englische Schauspieler und englisches Schauspiel zur Zeit Shakespeares in Deutschland. Theatergeschichtliche Forschungen, 18* (Hamburg and Leipzig: Verlag von Leopold Voss, 1903); 97.

50 Orlene Murad, *The English Comedians at the Habsburg Court in Graz, 1607–1608*, Salzburg Studies in English Literature 81 (Salzburg: Institut für Englische Sprache und Literatur, Universität Salzburg, 1978), 58–9.

51 Hoy, 1.90.

52 June Schlueter, 'New Light on Dekker's *Fortunati*', *Medieval and Renaissance Drama in England* 67 (2013), 120–35.

53 Foakes, 127.

54 Schlueter, 'New Light', 128.

55 Schlueter, 'New Light', 129–30.

56 Schlueter, 'New Light', 124.

57 Schlueter, 'New Light', 123.

58 See *Comœdia von Fortunato* in Manfred Brauneck, ed., *Spieltexte der Wanderbühne*, vol. 1 (Berlin: Walter de Gruyter, 1970), p. 168, line 10 – p. 170, line 4.

INTRODUCTION 69

59 The tale is classified as 'AT 566: The Three Magic Objects and the Wonderful Fruits' in Hans-Jörg Uther, *The Types of International Folktales: A Classification and Bibliography. Based on the System of Antti Aarne and Stith Thompson* (Helsinki: Suomalainen Tiedeakatemia, 2004).
60 See Luisa Rubini, 'Fortunatus in Italy: A History between Translations, Chapbooks and Fairy Tales', *Fabula* 44 (2003), 25; Hans-Gert Roloff, ed., *Fortunatus. Studienausgabe nach der Editio Princeps von 1509* (Stuttgart: Bibliographie Jörg Jungmayr, 1996), 336–48; Debra Prager, '*Fortunatus*: "Auß dem Künigreich Cipern"': Mapping the World and the Self', *Daphnis* 33 (2004), 123–4; Michael Haldane, 'The Translation of the Unseen Self: Fortunatus, Mercury and the Wishing-Hat', *Folklore* 117 (2006), 171; and David Blamires, *Fortunatus in His Many English Guises* (Lewiston: Edwin Mellon Press, 1996), 9–21.
61 Francis Douce, 'Dissertation on the *Gesta Romanorum*', in *Illustrations of Shakspeare, and of Ancient Manners* (London, 1807), 2.362, 390–1.
62 Herford, *Studies in the Literary Relations*, 207. For a full translation of the *Gesta* tale, see appendix 1 to Blamires, *Fortunatus in His Many English Guises*, 101–7.
63 William Browne, *The shepheards pipe* (London, 1614), sig. C7r; the redaction of the Jonathas tale is found on sigs B3v–C6r.
64 Browne, *The shepheards pipe*, sig. C5v.
65 Herford, *Studies in the Literary Relations*, 208–9.
66 Herford, *Studies in the Literary Relations*, 209. For an excellent summary of the *Volksbuch* material and its history, see Blamires's chapter on 'The German *Fortunatus*: Background and Sources', in his *Fortunatus in His Many English Guises*, 9–21. My overview of the *Volksbuch* material follows Blamires.
67 James H. Conover, *Thomas Dekker: An Analysis of Dramatic Structure* (The Hague: Mouton, 1969), 56.
68 Herford, *Studies in the Literary Relations*, 205n.
69 Lange, 'On the Relation of *Old Fortunatus* to the *Volksbuch*', *Modern Language Notes* 18.5 (May 1903), 141–4, 143.
70 Herford, *Studies in the Literary Relations*, 212–13.
71 Herford, *Studies in the Literary Relations*, 215.
72 Blamires, *Fortunatus in His Many English Guises*, 18.
73 Blamires, *Fortunatus in His Many English Guises*, 47–8.
74 Herford, *Studies in the Literary Relations*, 212.
75 On Dekker's possible ancestry and his familiarity with Dutch in particular, see Christopher Joby, *The Dutch Language in Britain (1550–1702): A Social History of the Use of Dutch in Early Modern Britain* (Leiden: Brill, 2015), 316–22.
76 Hoy, for example, describes this BL copy as 'apparently the earliest extant English translation' (1.74).
77 Anon., *The history of the birth, travels, strange adventures, and death of Fortunatus wherein is contained such variety both of comical and tragical discourse, that the like is not afforded in any histories of this nature: there being added likewise several new additions which was not in the original copy from whence it was translated ...: with the illustration of several new pictures.*, London: Printed by and for T. Haly ..., 1682. Wing / H2145, Henry E. Huntington Library and Art Gallery. Accessed through *EEBO*.

78 J. Payne Collier, 'Thomas Churchyard and the Romance of "Fortunatus"', *N&Q* s4-I (1) (1868), 2–3; Michael Haldane, 'The Date of Thomas Combe's Fortunatus and its Relation to Thomas Dekker's *Old Fortunatus*', *MLR* 101 (2006), 313–24. Michael Haldane has nominated Thomas Combe as the 'T.C.' recorded in the Stationers' Register entry for 1615.

79 *SR* 3.568.

80 Hoy, 1.74.

81 Schlueter, 'New Light', 122.

82 Gerard Langbaine, *The lives and characters of the English dramatick poets also an exact account of all the plays that were ever yet printed in the English tongue, their double titles, the places where acted, the dates when printed, and the persons to whom dedicated, with remarks and observations on most of the said plays / first begun by Mr. Langbain; improv'd and continued down to this time, by a careful hand* (London, 1699), 36.

83 John Owen, *A guide to church-fellowship and order according to the gospel-institution* ... (1692), [81]; Richard Atkyns, *The original and growth of printing collected out of history, and the records of this kingdome* ... (1664), 17.

84 In his *Pamphlets and Pamphleteering in Early Modern Britain*, Joad Raymond has noted '[b]y the later seventeenth century, in some contexts, "stitched book" was used synonymously with "pamphlet"', and cites a 1586 agreement by the Stationers' Company and London Aldermen which specifies the maximum size of stitched books to be 40 sheets for folio, 12 sheets for octavo, and 5–6 sheets for decimosexto (quartos would presumably be between 12 and 40 sheets). These figures may have been optimistic, and the Stamp Act of 1712 appears to have revised the maximum lengths pragmatically in terms of what could actually be stitched: it leads Raymond to conclude that 'according to the customs of the book trade in Britain, a stitched quarto book or pamphlet was not more than twelve sheets in length, or 96 pages in total' (Joad Raymond, *Pamphlets and Pamphleteering in Early Modern Britain* (Cambridge University Press, 2003), 81, 82).

85 Henry Crosse, *Vertues common-wealth: or The high-way to honour Wherin is discouered* ... (London, 1603), sig. Ov.

86 'To the righte honourable, the Godly, wise and vertvovs Ladie Elizabeth, Countesse of Lyncolne ...', *The auncient ecclesiasticall histories of the first six hundred yeares after Christ, wrytten in the Greeke tongue by three learned historiographers, Eusebius, Socrates, and Euagrius* ... (1577). STC (2nd ed.) / 10572. (no sig.). Blamires independently identified the Crosse and Hanmer references in *Fortunatus in His Many English Guises*, 27–8.

87 Wiggins, #851.

88 Blamires, *Fortunatus in His Many English Guises*, 31.

89 Francis Meres, *Palladis Tamia* (London: Cuthbert Burby, 1598, STC 17834), sig. Oo3.

90 Henry Peacham, *The Truth of our Times: Revealed out of one Mans Experience, by way of Essay* (London, 1638), 102–5; see also McInnis, 'Evidence of a Lost Tarlton Play, c. 1585, Probably for The Queen's Men' *N&Q* 59.1 (2012), 43–5, and Wiggins, #780 ('Play with a death-bed scene').

INTRODUCTION   71

91 W. Carew Hazlitt, who first noticed Peacham's account of the lost
    Tarlton play, also edited the Scottish poem and drew the connection
    between them; see his MS note in Folger Shakespeare Library, W.a.501,
    Hazlitt's own copy of his *A manual for the collector and amateur of old
    English plays* (London, 1892), 137n.; a digitization is available in the
    entry for the 'Lord and his Three Sons' play in the *Lost Plays Database*
    (https://lostplays.folger.edu). See also Hazlitt's revision of David Laing's
    Early popular poetry of Scotland and the northern border (London, 1895),
    2.211.
92 *A Delectable little history in metre of a lord and his three sons, containing his
    latter will and legacy to them upon his death-bed, and what befell them after
    his death, especially the midmost and the youngest* (Edinburgh: [s.n.],
    1698), Wing / D900, 4–5.
93 *A Delectable little history*, 5.
94 *A Delectable little history*, 7.
95 *A Delectable little history*, 8.
96 *A Delectable little history*, 14.
97 *A Delectable little history*, 15.
98 *A Delectable little history*, 16.
99 *A Delectable little history*, 16.
100 *A Delectable little history*, 17.
101 *A Delectable little history*, 18.
102 John H. Astington, 'Appendix: Performances at Court 1558–1642', in
    English Court Theatre, 1558–1642 (Cambridge University Press, 1999),
    236; W. R. Streitberger, *The Masters of the Revels and Elizabeth I's Court
    Theatre* (Oxford University Press, 2016), 285–6. There is no evidence
    to support Paul Frazer's assertion that the court performance of *Old
    Fortunatus* took place at Whitehall Palace (Frazer, 'Performing Places
    in Thomas Dekker's *Old Fortunatus*', *Philological Quarterly* 89.4 (2010),
    460).
103 Foakes, 128; Richard Dutton, 'The Court, the Master of the Revels,
    and the Players', in *The Oxford Handbook of Early Modern Theatre*, ed.
    Dutton (Oxford University Press, 2009), 369.
104 Holger Schott Syme, 'Thomas Creede, William Barley, and the Venture
    of Printing Plays', *Shakespeare's Stationers: Studies in Cultural Bibliography*
    (Philadelphia: University of Pennsylvania Press, 2013), 31.
105 Foakes, 34–7. It is harder to say what the content or relevance might
    be of Classical period plays including 'Julian the Apostate' or 'Phocas',
    or such proverbially titled plays as 'A Toy to Please Chaste Ladies' and
    'Crack Me This Nut'.
106 Roslyn L. Knutson, *The Repertory of Shakespeare's Company, 1594–1613*
    (Fayetteville: University of Arkansas Press, 1991), 80.
107 Pandulpho, 2.2.78–80 in John Marston, *Antonio's Revenge. Revels
    Plays*, ed. W. Reavley Gair (Manchester University Press, 1978, rpt
    1999).
108 W. Reavley Gair, ed., 'Introduction', *Antonio's Revenge*, 32. That this
    allusion to '*old* Fortunatus' (my emphasis) is to Dekker's play, rather
    than being merely legendary, is supported by the fact that in Dekker
    (unlike any of the extant sources), the protagonist is already old when
    the play commences.

109 Knutson suggests that '[m]uch of the repertory acquired in 1599–1600 probably made the move' with the Admiral's Men to the Fortune, 'particularly plays advertising their new venue such as *Old Fortunatus*'. See Roslyn L. Knutson, 'Toe to Toe Across Maid Lane: Repertorial Competition at the Rose and Globe, 1599–1600', in *Acts of Criticism: Performance Matters in Shakespeare and His Contemporaries*, ed. June Schlueter and Paul Nelsen (Madison and Teaneck: Fairleigh Dickinson University Press, 2005), 31.

110 Clare Williams, *Thomas Platter's Travels in England, 1599* (London: J. Cape, 1937), 166. See Wiggins, #1200, 'Play of a Maiden's Suitors'.

111 On comedies in the 1590s, see Knutson, *The Repertory*, 40–4.

112 Knutson, 'Toe to Toe', 28–9.

113 Sidney, *The Defence of Poesy* (London, 1595), sig. K1v; Cyrus Mulready, *Romance on the Early Modern Stage: English Expansion Before and After Shakespeare* (Basingstoke: Palgrave Macmillan, 2013), 52. The Queen's Men also apparently had a Valentine and Orson play in their repertory; it was registered for possible publication by Thomas Gosson and Raffe Hancock on 23 May 1595 (*SR* 2.298), and passed to William White, who re-registered it on 31 March 1600 (*SR* 3.159) – a little over a month after Aspley registered *Old Fortunatus* (20 February 1600).

114 *Eine schöne lustige triumphirende Comoedia von eines Königes Sohn auß Engellandt vnd des Königes Tochter auß Schottlandt* was published in the Leipzig volume of 1620 (*Engelische Comedien und Tragedien*) alongside the German Fortunatus play. See the *Lost Plays Database* entry for this play, and Wiggins, #1112.

115 Hoy, 1.85; Sidney R. Homan, Jr, '*Doctor Faustus*, Dekker's *Old Fortunatus*, and the Morality Plays', *Modern Language Quarterly* 26.4 (1965), 501.

116 David Kathman, 'Reconsidering *The Seven Deadly Sins*', *Early Theatre* 7.1 (2004), 13–44, esp. 34.

117 See Schlueter, 'New Light', 121.

118 Murad, *The English Comedians*, 6–7.

119 Murad, *The English Comedians*, 57.

120 Examples of *fahret* (drive) occur in Act 2 (when Fortunatus tricks the Sultan), p. 141, l. 5, '*Fehret hiemit hinweg*' (translated as 'drove away with it'); the end of Act 3 (when Andelocia has been tricked out of the purse and wishes himself to Cyprus), p. 166, l. 12, '*Fähret weg*' (translated as 'drives away'); Act 4 (when Andelocia kidnaps Agrippine and wishes both of them into the woods), p. 170, l. 5, '*Fahren alßbald fort*' (translated as 'drive immediately away'); and Act 4 (when Agrippina accidentally wishes herself back to her father's court), p. 170, l. 24, '*Alßbald fähret sie weg*' ('she drives immediately away'). Examples of *gehen* (walk) occur in Act 1 (when Fortune leads Fortunatus out of the woods and they exit, only to re-enter immediately), p. 136, l. 26, '*Gehen hinein / und kommen wieder herauß*' ('walk inside / and come back again'); Act 2 (after Fortunatus tricks the Sultan out of the hat and 'drove away', the Sultan walks off-stage), p. 141, l. 15, '*Gehet hinein*' ('walks inside').

121 Albert Dessoff, 'Über englische, italienische und spanische Dramen in den Spielverzeichnissen deutscher Wandertruppen' in Max Koch, ed.,

INTRODUCTION 73

Studien zur vergleichenden Litteraturgeschichte (Berlin: Verlag von Alexander Duncker, 1901), 420–44, esp. 432.
122 The entire manuscript has been digitised and is available at the Uni Kassel Bibliothek's website: http://orka.bibliothek.uni-kassel.de/viewer/image/1296566484811/133/.
123 See Schlueter, 'New Light', 131, and the 'Ariodante and Genevra' entry in the *Lost Plays Database*. 'Robert Browne' was a particularly common name for actors in this era, though; Herbert Berry has an appendix (9) for disambiguating the various Robert Brownes in *The Boar's Head Playhouse* (Washington, DC. Folger Shakespeare Library, 1986), 191–7.
124 Paul Harms, *Die deutschen Fortunatus-Dramen und ein Kasseler Dichter des 17. Jahrhunderts* (Hamburg and Leipzig: Leopold Volz, 1892), 28–54; see Schlueter, 'New Light', 131.
125 Schlueter, 'New Light', 131–2.
126 See Carl Engel, ed., *Deutsch Puppenkomödien*, vol. 7 (Oldenburg: Schulzesche Hof-Buchhandlung und Hof-Buchdruckerei (C. Berndt & A. Schwartz), 1878), 1–48.
127 John Larpent Plays, The Huntington Library, San Marino, California; MS LA2085.
128 Donald J. Rulfs, 'Reception of the Elizabethan Playwrights on the London Stage 1776–1833', *Studies in Philology* 46.1 (1949), 68.
129 See John Genest, *Some account of the English stage, from the restoration in 1660 to 1830*, 10 vols (Bath, 1832), 8.702.
130 Henry R. Bishop, *The overture[,] song, glee, chorusses, and melo dramatic music in Fortunatus and his sons; of* [sic] *The magic purse & wishing cap:; as performed at the Theatre Royal Covent Garden* (London: Published by Goulding, Dalmaine, Potter & Co. ... & to be had at 7, Westmorland Str¹. Dublin, [1819]).
131 Bishop, *The overture*, 15.
132 I am grateful to Christopher Scobie (Music Reference Service, British Library) for providing me with a transcription of the vocal cues from Bishop's manuscript.
133 I am grateful to Matthew Lorenzon for his insightful discussion of Bishop's score (personal correspondence), which this paragraph draws on heavily.
134 Bishop, *The overture*, 6.
135 Bishop, *The overture*, 7–11.
136 Bishop, *The overture*, 12–13.
137 E. V. Lucas, ed. *The Letters of Charles Lamb to which are added those of his sister Mary Lamb* (London: J. M. Dent & Sons Ltd, 1935), 3.39.
138 James Dykes Campbell, *Samuel Taylor Coleridge: A Narrative of the Events of His Life* (London, Macmillan and Co., Ltd, 1896), 261. Lucas (*The Letters*, 40) cautiously repeats Campbell's suggestion without endorsing or refuting it.
139 Samuel Taylor Coleridge, *On the Constitution of the Church and State According to the Idea of Each*, ed. John Barrell (London: J. M. Dent & Sons Ltd, 1972), 162; Coleridge, '754. To John Brown', in *Collected Letters of Samuel Taylor Coleridge*, ed. Earl Leslie Griggs (Oxford: Clarendon Press, 1959), 3.190. Coleridge had also read J. Nott's 1812 edition of Dekker's *The Gull's Hornbook*, according to a letter from

74   INTRODUCTION

Coleridge to Nott's publisher, John M. Gutch (12 October 1815) (*Collected Letters*, ed. Griggs, 4.593–6).
140   '350. [Drama.] Outline for a play. (S MS F2.11)', E. J. Pratt Library, Victoria University in the University of Toronto.
141   A Tufts circular to participants and students urging word-of-mouth advertising reveals that a 'very considerable expense is entailed by the production, between $1,200.00 and $1,500.00 in all, including over $800.00 for costumes alone'. To put this in perspective, tickets were sold for $1 (or 50c each for groups of 10 or more). See P. M. Hayden, L. R. Lewis, R. S. Johnston, F. G. Wren, and M. A. Rogers, 'Concerning "Old Fortunatus"', Tufts University Digital Collections and Archives.
142   'Oversize Copy of The Pleasant Comedy of Old Fortunatus by Thomas Dekker', Thomas Whittemore Papers, ca. 1875–1966, MS BZ.013, Box 002, file 015, Image Collections and Fieldwork Archives, Dumbarton Oaks, Trustees for Harvard University, Washington, DC.
143   Tiffany Stern, 'Watching as Reading: The Audience and Written Text in Shakespeare's Playhouse', in *How to Do Things With Shakespeare*, ed. Laurie Maguire (Malden: Blackwell Publishing Ltd, 2008), 148–53.
144   'Final Announcement: Dekker's "Old Fortunatus" At Tufts College', undated promotional flyer produced by the English Department of Tufts College, 1906. p. 2. Tufts University Digital Collections and Archives.
145   Katharine M. Abbott, *Old Paths and Legends of the New England Border: Connecticut, Deerfield, Berkshire* (New York: G. P. Putnam's Sons, The Knickerbocker Press, 1907), 129n.
146   Undated programme notes for the production of *Old Fortunatus* (Tufts College, 1906), p. 5. Tufts University Digital Collections and Archives.
147   Undated programme notes, p. 5.
148   'Final Announcement', p. 3.
149   *Old Fortunatus* production programme notes, University of Ottawa Drama Guild, 4–5 December 1953; 'Bent on Revival of Tudor Drama', *The Evening Citizen* (Ottawa, Canada), Saturday 14 November 1953, p. 11.
150   '350-Year Old Play Staged By Ottawa U Drama Guild', *The Ottawa Journal*, Saturday 5 December 1953, p. 31.
151   Programme notes, University of Ottawa Drama Guild, 4–5 December 1953.
152   '350-Year Old Play Staged By Ottawa U Drama Guild', *The Ottawa Journal*, Saturday 5 December, 1953, p. 31.
153   'Bent on Revival of Tudor Drama', p. 11.
154   'Old Fortunatus', *La Rotonde: Journal des Étudiants de Lange Française de L'Université D'Ottawa*, 26 November 1953, p. 10. Accessed through the Internet Archive.
155   Dilke, 3.4.
156   Charles Lamb, *Specimens of English Dramatic Poets* (London: Edward Moxon, 1849), 2.87; Felix E. Schelling, *Elizabethan Drama, 1558–1642* (Boston: Houghton, Mifflin & Company, 1908), 1.391.
157   Mary Leland Hunt, *Thomas Dekker: A Study* (New York: Columbia University Press, 1911), 35.

INTRODUCTION 75

158 Anthony Trollope, MS note in Folger Shakespeare Library PR2480 1873 Cage (Shepherd, 1.174).
159 Algernon Charles Swinburne, *The Age of Shakespeare* (London: Chatto & Windus, 1908), 64, 66.
160 Swinburne, *The Age of Shakespeare*, 63.
161 Transcribed from Folger MS Y.d.1003. Contractions have been expanded, cancelled text omitted, and the text otherwise standardized for ease of reading.
162 John Woolford, ed., *Sale Catalogues of Libraries of Eminent Persons, vol. 6: Poets and Men of Letters* (London: Mansell with Sotheby Parke-Bernet Publications, 1972), 270. It was sold to Heffer for £2 16s.
163 See Woolford, ed., *Sale Catalogues*, 247–51.
164 Herford, *Studies in the Literary Relations*, 214.
165 See Richard Abrams, '"The Name of Prosper": A Philological Engagement', *RES* 66 (2014), 263.
166 Murad, *The English Comedians*, 55.
167 Moritz Fürstenau, *Zur Geschichte der Musik und des Theaters am Hofe zu Dresden* (Dresden: Rudolf Kuntze, 1861), 1.96–7.
168 Mary L. Hunt, *Thomas Dekker* (New York, 1911), 31.
169 C. F. Tucker Brooke, 'The Reputation of Christopher Marlowe', *Transactions of the Connecticut Academy of Arts and Sciences* 25 (1922), 373.
170 A. W. Ward, *History of English Dramatic Literature* (London, 1875), 2.40.
171 J. Payne Collier, ed., *The Diary of Philip Henslowe, From 1591 to 1609* (London: Shakespeare Society, 1845), 71: 'Pd unto Thomas Dickers, the 20 of Desembr 1597, for adycyons to Fostus twentie shellinges, and five shellenges for a prolog to Marloes Tamberlen, so in all I saye payde twentye five shellinges'.
172 Hoy, 1.86.
173 Hoy, 1.86.
174 Herford, *Studies in the Literary Relations*, 214.
175 Frederick Kiefer, *Fortune and Elizabethan Tragedy* (San Marino: The Huntington Library, 1983), 111.
176 Sidney R. Homan Jr, '*Doctor Faustus*, Dekker's *Old Fortunatus*, and the Morality Plays', *Modern Language Quarterly* 26.4 (1965), 498.
177 Herford, *Studies in the Literary Relations*, 214–15.
178 Homan, '*Doctor Faustus*, Dekker's *Old Fortunatus*', 499.
179 Herford made a similar observation: '[W]ith the aid of a company of Satyrs, [Fortune] drags away the body of her victim, as Faustus is carried off by Mephistophilis and his crew of devils. It is plain that a Fortunatus who ends in this way was imagined under influences wholly different from those which determined the romantic Fortunatus of the *Volksbuch*, whose death is only the natural and not unwelcome close of a career sated with success' (Herford, *Studies in the Literary Relations*, 215).
180 Kiefer, *Fortune and Elizabethan Tragedy*, 102.
181 George R. Price, *Thomas Dekker* (New York: Twayne Publishers, 1969), 49.
182 Price, *Thomas Dekker*, 45–7.
183 Conover, *Thomas Dekker*, 62.

184 Conover, *Thomas Dekker*, 62.
185 Conover, *Thomas Dekker*, 63.
186 Conover, *Thomas Dekker*, 68, 72.
187 Madeleine Doran refers to the play as a fairy tale in *Endeavors of Art: A Study of Form in Elizabethan Drama* (Madison: University of Wisconsin Press, 1954), 110; Henry Hitch Adams proposed that Dekker's play is 'almost pure domestic tragedy' in *English Domestic or Homiletic Tragedy* (New York: Columbia University Press, 1943), 81.
188 Conover, *Thomas Dekker*, 70.
189 Conover, *Thomas Dekker*, 75.
190 Conover, *Thomas Dekker*, 75.
191 Conover, *Thomas Dekker*, 76, 77.
192 Conover, *Thomas Dekker*, 77.
193 William H. Sherman, '"Gold is the strength, the sinnewes of the world": Thomas Dekker's *Old Fortunatus* and England's Golden Age', *Medieval and Renaissance Drama in England* 6 (1993), 85–102, 85.
194 Sherman, '"Gold is the strength"', 87.
195 Karl Marx, *Capital*, vol. 1, book 1 in *The Collected Works of Karl Marx and Frederick Engels. Economic Works 1857–1894*, vol. 35 (New York: International Publishers, 1996), 642.
196 Blamires, *Fortunatus in His Many English Guises*, 15.
197 Anthony Ellis, *Old Age, Masculinity, and Early Modern Drama: Comic Elders on the Italian and Shakespearean Stage* (Farnham: Ashgate, 2009), 149.
198 Ellis, *Old Age*, 142.
199 Ellis, *Old Age*, 150.
200 Ellis, *Old Age*, 154.
201 Daniel Vitkus, 'Labor and Travel on the Early Modern Stage: Representing the Travail of Travel in Dekker's *Old Fortunatus* and Shakespeare's *Pericles*', *Working Subjects in Early Modern English Drama*, ed. Michelle Dowd and Natasha Korda (Burlington: Ashgate, 2011), 228.
202 Vitkus, 'Labor and Travel', 237.
203 Lowell Duckert, 'It Grows as It Goes: Becoming Gold-Apple in Mandeville, Dekker … Beyond', *Prefix* 1.1 (2010), 8.
204 Duckert, 'It Grows as It Goes', 11, 14.
205 E.g. see Mary Floyd-Wilson, *English Ethnicity and Race in Early Modern England* (Cambridge University Press, 2003); David McInnis, *Mind-Travelling and Voyage Drama in Early Modern England* (Basingstoke: Palgrave Macmillan, 2013), 20–5.
206 On fears of cultural amorphousness and the fragility of national identity, see Nandini Das, '"Apes of Imitation": Imitation and Identity in Sir Thomas Roe's Embassy to India', in *A Companion to the Global Renaissance: English Literature and Culture in the Era of Expansion*, ed. Jyotsna G. Singh (Oxford: Wiley-Blackwell, 2009), 114–28.
207 Thomas Dekker, *The Seven Deadly Sins of London* (London: Printed by E[dward] A[llde] and S. Stafford] for Nathaniel Butter, 1606), 32.
208 Duckert, 'It Grows as It Goes', 8.
209 'Travelling Characters in Early Modern Drama', in *Travel and Drama in Early Modern England: The Journeying Play*, ed. Claire Jowitt and David McInnis (Cambridge University Press, 2018), 187–206.

INTRODUCTION 77

210 He was subsequently imprisoned for debt in 1612–19, and his second wife Elizabeth's renouncing of the administration of his estate in 1632 suggests he died in debt also – see John Twyning, 'Dekker, Thomas (c.1572–1632)', *Oxford Dictionary of National Biography* (Oxford University Press, 2004; online edn, January 2008 (www.oxforddnb.com/view/article/7428, accessed 30 January 2017)).
211 Vitkus, 'Labor and Travel', 236.
212 The travel fantasy represented by the wishing-hat has a less-well-known analogue in the anonymous MS play fragment known as 'A stately tragedy containing the ambitious life and death of the great Cham', in which the spirit Aldeboran offers Bagous the Brachman the ability to 'walke about the worlde with a wish' (Folger MS X.d.259, recto). If the lost 'Valentine and Orson' play in the Admiral's repertory in 1598 included Pacolet's horse (see 'Performance History' above), it too may have featured instantaneous travel on stage.
213 See McInnis, *Mind-Travelling*; Claire Jowitt, 'Hakluyt's Legacy: Armchair Travel in English Renaissance Drama', in *Richard Hakluyt and Travel Writing in Early Modern Europe*, ed. Daniel Carey and Claire Jowitt (Farnham: Ashgate, 2012), 295–306.
214 See McInnis, *Mind-Travelling*, 82.
215 See McInnis, 'Travelling Characters'.
216 Hillary M. Nunn, 'Playing with Appetite in Early Modern Comedy', in *Shakespearean Sensations: Experiencing Literature in Early Modern England*, ed. Katharine A. Craik and Tanya Pollard (Cambridge University Press, 2013), 104.
217 Nunn, 'Playing with Appetite', 114.
218 Nunn, 'Playing with Appetite', 114–15. Peggy Faye Shirley concurs, noting that '[h]is selection of riches is the natural reaction of a man in his situation' (*Serious and Tragic Elements in the Comedy of Thomas Dekker* (Salzburg: Universität Salzburg, 1975), 57.
219 Nunn, 'Playing with Appetite', 117.
220 Nunn, 'Playing with Appetite', 117.
221 Mulready, *Romance*, 76.
222 Mulready, *Romance*, 77.
223 Mulready, *Romance*, 54.
224 See Mulready, *Romance*, 52.
225 Mulready, *Romance*, 54.
226 R. L. Smallwood and Stanley Wells, eds, Thomas Dekker, *The Shoemaker's Holiday. Revels Plays Series* (Manchester University Press, 1979), 64.
227 Smallwood and Wells, eds, *Shoemaker's Holiday*, 64.
228 Wilfred T. Jewkes, *Act Division in Elizabethan and Jacobean Plays, 1591–1616* (Hamden, CT: The Shoestring Press, 1958), 100.
229 Henry L. Snuggs, *Shakespeare and Five Acts* (New York: Vantage Press, 1960), 36. Turning to first editions of printed playbooks from the period 1591 to 1610 – and eliminating the closet drama, and those of uncertain auspices – he found that, of the 56 divided into acts, only ten originated in the public playhouses (four of these were the product of Jonson's Classicism). By contrast, of the 75 undivided plays, 71 were produced in public playhouses (Snuggs, *Shakespeare and Five Acts*, 38).

230 On the significance of this, see Snuggs, *Shakespeare and Five Acts*, 40.
231 Snuggs, *Shakespeare and Five Acts*, 39.
232 Herford, *Studies in the Literary Relations*, 204–5.
233 Interestingly, my use of the 'movement' concept was anticipated by James H. Conover, who divides the play into 'three movements' on the basis of 'points of crisis and climax': 'a kind of exposition, the gaining of the magic powers and the establishment of the conditions of their use; ... Andelocia's first failure, in which he ignores particularly his father's warnings; ... his misuse of his second chance with the gifts and his ultimate death' (*Thomas Dekker*, 63).
234 See Jewkes, *Act Division*, 96ff.
235 Smeaton, ed., *Old Fortunatus*, xv.

OLD FORTUNATUS

Characters in the Play

1 OLD MAN, an Englishman, formerly a soldier.
2 OLD MAN, a Cypriot.
CHORUS, also delivers the prologue.
FORTUNATUS, an impoverished native of Cyprus; father of Andelocia and Ampedo. 5
ECHO (within).

Four fortunate kings:
A CARTER (Primislaus, who became King of Bohemia).
A TAILOR (John Leyden, the Dutch 'botcher' who became King of Münster). 10
A MONK (who became Pope Gregory VII).
A SHEPHERD (Viriat, who became King of Spain and Portugal).

Two nymphs, one with a globe, another with Fortune's wheel (1.71 SD). 15
FORTUNE, a goddess, 'the world's empress' (1.170).

---

1. *1 OLD MAN*] from England; a former soldier.
2. *2 OLD MAN*] from Fortunatus's homeland of Cyprus.
3. CHORUS] Appears twice to serve as Chorus 'as the story needs' (Prol.23) in addition to speaking the prologue.
4. FORTUNATUS] Dekker's Fortunatus is already an old man when the play begins. Like Prospero and Faustus, his name signifies 'prosperous one', and clearly associates him with Fortune. See Richard Abrams, '"The Name of Prosper": A Philological Engagement', *Review of English Studies* 66 (2014), 263.
6. ECHO] In Ovid, the nymph by this name repeatedly used chatter to prevent Juno from catching Jupiter fornicating; Juno deprived Echo of normal speech, leaving her with only the ability to repeat what others say. After unsuccessfully trying to court Narcissus, Echo wasted away in grief until only her voice remained (*OCD*; Ovid, *Met.* 3).
8. *Primislaus*] See 1.206–7n.
9. *John Leyden*] See 1.211–13n.
11. *Gregory*] See 1.207–8n.
12. *Viriat*] See 1.205n.

CHARACTERS IN THE PLAY

Four unfortunate kings:
HENRY V, Emperor of Germany.
FREDERICK BARBAROSSA, Holy Roman Emperor and King of Germany.
LOUIS THE MEEK, Charlemagne's son and King of France.
BAJAZETH, Emperor of the Turks.

AMPEDO, Fortunatus's elder son.
SHADOW, servant to Fortunatus and companion to Andelocia.
ANDELOCIA, Fortunatus's younger son, infatuated with Agrippine.

VICE, a female figure with gilded face and horns.
Devils (non-speaking), accompanying Vice (3.0 SD).
VIRTUE, a female figure dressed in white, wearing a coxcomb. Also called Aretë.
Nymphs (non-speaking), accompanying Virtue in scenes 3 and 10.
A PRIEST, accompanying Virtue and Vice; sings a song at 3.20–35.

The SULTAN of Babylon.
NOBLEMEN, attending the Sultan; some have speaking roles (scene 4).

---

18. HENRY V] See 1.180–1n.
19. FREDERICK BARBAROSSA] See 1.184–7n.
21. LOUIS THE MEEK] See 1.189n.
22. BAJAZETH] See 1.192n.
23. AMPEDO] In the German *Volksbuch*, Fortunatus's wife Cassandra gives birth to the couple's two sons, Ampedo and Andolosia. Fortunatus educates his sons for twelve years before yielding to his *wanderlust* and departing for Alexandria. The etymology of the name 'Ampedo' is unclear; potentially there's an allusion to his lack of desire to travel (cf. 'impede', to shackle the feet).
24. SHADOW] presumably so-named because the witty servant is a follower (and lean; see 2.118).
25. ANDELOCIA] See the note on 'Ampedo' above; this son's name is given as 'Andolosia' in the *Volksbuch*. It may recall the region of Andalusia in southern Spain, but any reason for doing so is unclear. Unlike Ampedo, Andelocia is given to travelling and spending money.
35. *Babylon*] Babylon in Egypt; see Cho.1, 35n.

82   CHARACTERS IN THE PLAY

The Three Destinies (non-speaking).
Satyrs (non-speaking).
ORLEANS, a French lord and prisoner at the English court;   40
   infatuated with Agrippine.
GALLOWAY, a lord.
A BOY, attending Orleans; carries a lute.
The PRINCE OF CYPRUS, Orleans's rival for Agrippine's love.
Princess AGRIPPINE, King Athelstan's daughter; also referred   45
   to as Agrippina.
CORNWALL, an English lord.
LONGUEVILLE, a French lord.

---

38. The Three Destinies] The Fates or Parcae of Classical mythology; these three female figures enter accompanying Fortune in scene 5 'working' (5.230.1) (i.e. spinning the 'inky thread' of Fortunatus's life, 5.259).

39. Satyrs] In Classical mythology, satyrs were half-man, half-beast (usually goat or horse), and renowned for their bestial desires and behaviour. They often accompanied Bacchus. In the English Bible, the term is applied to hairy demons who inhabit deserts (*OED*). The satyrs carry off Fortunatus's body in scene 5; in the German play, the sons perform this task.

42. GALLOWAY] The metre consistently requires the name to be disyllabic ('Gall'way').

45. AGRIPPINE] an ahistorical character (see note on Athelstan below); possibly the name, which is found in the German *Volksbuch*, recalls Julia Agrippina (AD 15–59), daughter of Tiberius and mother of Drusus Germanicus, Nero, and Caligula. Reference to her manipulation of male rulers was used in the Jacobean and Caroline periods. Anne of Denmark was referred to as 'Agrippina' in coded letters between Sir Thomas Overbury and Robert Carr (James Knowles, '"To Enlighten the Darksome Night, Pale Cinthia Doth Arise": Anna of Denmark, Elizabeth I and Images of Royalty', in *Women and Culture at the Courts of Stuart Queens*, ed. Clare McManus (Basingstoke: Palgrave Macmillan, 2003), 35). Dekker's Agrippine plays off various competing suitors against each other, and may thus bear some resemblance to her Roman namesake. 'Desire to look more fair' (9.79) leads Dekker's character to purchase and consume a magic apple that instead deforms her beauty; curiously, in the anonymous *The Tragedy of Claudius Tiberius Nero* (London, 1607), Agrippina is similarly plagued by apples: Tiberius disposes of Agrippina by offering her a poisoned apple – acceptance of the gift will result in death, refusal of the gift will result in banishment (sig. L4r).

47. CORNWALL] an English lord. Dekker also uses the name for an attendant courtier in *The Shoemaker's Holiday*.

48. LONGUEVILLE] perhaps recalling the character of this name in *Love's Labour's Lost* (1596).

CHESTER, an English lord.
LINCOLN, an English lord. 50

ATHELSTAN, King of England.
Ladies and other attendants (non-speaking), attending Athelstan.

INSULTADO, a Spanish lord and prisoner at the English court.

A Lady (non-speaking), attending Agrippine.

MONTROSE, a Scottish lord. 55
Soldiers (non-speaking), accompanying Longueville and Montrose in scene 10.

Kings (non-speaking), attending Virtue (10.267 SD).

Act and scene divisions are not given in Q; an incomplete list of characters first appeared in Dilke. 60

---

49. CHESTER] an English lord. Lisa Hopkins notes that it may not be coincidental that Dekker has an Earl of Cornwall and of Chester; the historical Athelstan was the first English king 'to fix the border between England and Wales at the Wye and England and Cornwall at the Tamar' (Hopkins, *From the Romans to the Normans on the English Renaissance Stage* (Kalamazoo: Medieval Institution Publications, West Michigan, 2017), 168).

51. ATHELSTAN] Although there were at least four kings with this name, the Athelstan in question is most likely the Athelstan who reigned as the first king of all England between 925 and 939, eldest son of Edward the Elder, and grandson of Alfred the Great. Details of his life are known from William of Malmesbury's *Gesta regum Anglorum*. The historical Athelstan never married, and did not have children, potentially making him a source of great interest to Elizabethans, but Dekker opts not to exploit the parallel with the reigning monarch, making his Athelstan a widower (6.388–9, unlike in the *Volksbuch*) and providing him with a daughter (Agrippine, who is in the *Volksbuch*).

53. INSULTADO] Possibly included in response to the apparent success of Don Armado in *Love's Labour's Lost*.

The Prologue at Court

Enter TWO OLD MEN.

1 Are you then travelling to the temple of Eliza?
2 Even to her temple are my feeble limbs travelling. Some call her Pandora; some Gloriana, some Cynthia; some Belphoebe, some Astraea: all by several names to express

4. Belphoebe] *Dilke;* Delphæbe *Q.*

The Prologue at Court] Prologues were usually spoken by a single player, but here two characters, an old man from England (1) and one from Cyprus (2), perform the opening lines which Dekker appears to have written specifically for court performance (cf. *The Shoemaker's Holiday* Prologue for performance at court on 1 January 1600, spoken by a single actor accompanied by others 'on bended knees', l. 8). There are compelling reasons to assume that the text closely resembles that of an original performance of an occasional nature, datable to 27 December 1599. See Introduction, 29.

3. *Pandora*] The association with Pandora relies on the etymological meaning of the name – Pandora having the 'gifts' (*dora*) of 'all' (*pan*) the gods – rather than anything pertaining to the evils unleashed by her opening of the jar/box, as told by Hesiod in his *Works and Days*. (Hesiod's *Theogony* describes Pandora as progenitor of the race of women, and reflects on the institution of marriage.) George Peele's Lord Mayoral pageant *Descensus Astraeae* (1591) calls Elizabeth 'Our faire *Astraea*, our *Pandora* faire' (4).

3–4. *Gloriana ... Belphoebe*] Gloriana is the chaste and powerful Fairy Queen, whom Spenser intended to embody 'glory' in general, but in particular 'the most excellent and glorious person of our soveraine the Queene'; see Spenser's 'Letter to Raleigh' prefacing *Faerie Queene*. In this 'Letter', Spenser follows the conceit of Raleigh's *The Ocean to Cynthia* and refers to Elizabeth as the moon goddess: 'For considering she beareth two persons, the one of a most royall queen or empresse, the other of a most virtuous and beautiful lady, this latter part in some places else I doe expresse in Belphoebe, fashioning her name according to your owne excellent conceit of Cynthia (Phoebe and Cynthia being both names of Diana.)'. See also *Faerie Queene* III Proem 3.

4. *Astraea*] During the Iron Age, Astraea, the virgin goddess of Justice, was the last of the immortals to leave the earth (see Ovid, *Met.* Book 1 and Spenser's *Faerie Queene* V, canto 1). Elizabeth was figured as the returned goddess in a new golden age (cf. Virgil's *Aeneid* where Rome under Augustus is celebrated as the return of Astraea to Earth); see Frances A. Yates, 'Queen Elizabeth as Astraea', *Journal of the Warburg and Courtauld Institutes* 10 (1947), 27–82.

THE PROLOGUE AT COURT 85

   several loves. Yet all those names make but one celestial   5
   body, as all those loves meet to create but one soul.
1 I am one of her own country and we adore her by the name
   of Eliza.
2 Blessed name, happy country; your Eliza makes your land
   Elizium. But what do you offer?   10
1 That which all true subjects should: when I was young, an
   armed hand; now I am crooked, an upright heart. But
   what offer you?
2 That which all strangers do: two eyes struck blind with
   admiration, two lips proud to sound her glory, two hands   15
   held up full of prayers and praises. What not, that may
   express love? What not, that may make her beloved?
1 How long is't since you last beheld her?
2 A just year. Yet that year hath seemed to me but one day,
   because her glory hath been my hourly contemplation.   20
   And yet that year hath seemed to me more than twice
   seven years, because so long I have been absent from her.
   Come, therefore, good father. Let's go faster, lest we
   come too late: for see, the tapers of the night are already
   lighted and stand brightly burning in their starry candle-   25
   sticks. See how gloriously the moon shines upon us.

---

   10. *Elizium*] a form of paronomasia or punning on the Homeric paradise of the afterlife, 'Elysium', and the 'Elysian fields' of Hesiod's Fortunate Isles (*Works and Days*), with which England is being identified as a result of Elizabeth's reign.
   11–12. *young ... crooked*] Anthony Ellis finds it significant that 'the physical condition of their old bodies resembles that of the timeworn earth', a motif that recalls the early modern belief that 'our fallen condition had worsened, that greater remoteness from Paradise translated into growing entropy in the universe' (*Old Age, Masculinity, and Early Modern Drama: Comic Elders on the Italian and Shakespearean Stage* (Farnham: Ashgate, 2009), 139, 137).
   19. *A just year*] The Admiral's Men had last performed at court on 27 December 1598.
   24. *tapers of the night*] literally wax candles; here (figuratively) the Queen's maids, who pale in comparison to the Queen as moon (see l. 20).
   25–6. *candlesticks*] support for candles/tapers; i.e. the maids have already assumed their places for the evening's entertainment.
   26. *the moon*] i.e. Cynthia (Elizabeth), the moon goddess; a particularly important name after the defeat of the Spanish Armada in 1588, when Elizabeth literally had control over the sea.

86   THE PROLOGUE AT COURT

1 Peace, fool. Tremble and kneel. The moon, sayest thou?
                                                         Both kneel.
   Our eyes are dazzled by Eliza's beams.
   See (if at least thou dare see) where she sits:
   This is the great pantheon of our goddess   30
   And all those faces, which thine eyes thought stars,
   Are nymphs attending on her deity.
   Prithee begin, for I want power to speak.
2 No, no, speak thou; I want words to begin.   *Weeps.*
1 Alack, what shall I do? Com'st thou with me   35
   And weepst now thou beholdst this majesty?
2 [*To Elizabeth*] Great landlady of hearts, pardon me.
   [*To* 1 OLD MAN] Blame not mine eyes, good father; in
      these tears
   My pure love shines, as thine doth in thy fears.
   [*To Elizabeth*] I weep for joy to see so many heads   40

---

27. SD] *Bowers*; *Q has SD at* 26.   37. hearts, pardon] *Q;* hearts, pray pardon *Daniel.*   38. Blame not mine eyes] *Dilke; given to* 1 *Old Man in* Q.   39. My pure ...] *Q returns to* 2 *Old Man here.*

---

27. SD] *Q* has the SD after the previous line due to the length of 27, but such a placement renders the first Old Man's 'kneel' redundant.

30. *pantheon*] literally a temple to all (*pan*) the gods (*theo*), it here refers to a temple consecrated to the various deistic incarnations of Elizabeth.

32. *nymphs*] in classical mythology, semi-divine spirits typically taking the form of maidens of the sea, woods, etc., and usually (in poetry) attending gods (*OED* n.1). Here, Elizabeth's maids attend her after this manner.

33. *want*] i.e., lack or need.

37. *Great landlady*] 'A woman who has tenants holding from her' (*OED* cites the present passage as its second instantiation of the term).

38. *Blame not mine eyes*] This edition follows Dilke in rejecting *Q*'s attribution of this line to 1 Old Man, as clearly it is 2 Old Man who is weeping.

40–2. *so many heads ... silver-handed age*] In the context of Elizabeth as Cynthia the moon goddess, 'silver' might be read in the sense of the hands being bathed in moonlight. It is more likely, though, that age itself is allegorized here (cf. 'grey-wingèd age' in the Epilogue at Court, 15). The description of heads clothed in the livery of silver-handed age thus suggests an image of age, personified, laying his hands on the prudent ladies' heads and 'silvering' them as it clothes them in his livery. 'Clothed' here means 'covered with, or as with, clothes' in a metaphorical sense (*OED* 'clothed, *adj.* a'), and thus pertains to hair/heads being silvered. In a rare parallel example of this specific compound, hair is silvered/aged by an allegorised figure when Shakespeare's Westmoreland (in 2*H*4) addresses the Lord Archbishop '[w]hose beard the

Of prudent ladies clothed in the livery
Of silver-handed age for serving you,
Whilst in your eyes, youth's glory doth renew.
I weep for joy to see the sun look old,
To see the moon mad at her often change,   45
To see the stars only by night to shine,
Whilst you are still bright, still one, still divine.
I weep for joy to see the world decay
Yet see Eliza flourishing like May.
Oh, pardon me, your pilgrim. I have measured   50
Many a mile to find you and have brought
Old Fortunatus and his family,
With other Cypriots (my poor countrymen),
To pay a whole year's tribute. Oh, vouchsafe,
Dread Queen of Fairies, with your gracious eyes,   55
T'accept theirs and our humble sacrifice.

---

53. Cypriots] *Dilke;* Cipriots *Bowers;* Cipnots *Q.*

silver hand of peace hath touched' (11.43). In Dekker's passage, it would be utterly appropriate if, as a marker of old age, age's livery (and not just his hands) were silver – 'livery' pertaining to the distinctive clothing or uniform of an official, by which rank or affiliation might be ascertained. The metaphor thus implies a courtly relationship between the ladies and age, as well as between the ladies and Elizabeth (by virtue of sartorial display, even if not necessarily full livery).

43. *youth's glory*] At the time of performance in 1599, Elizabeth was 66; the Prologue's praise of ideal agelessness is consonant with the monarch's iconographic portraiture (e.g. the improbably youthful 'Rainbow portrait' of c.1600).

47. *still one*] Hoy finds an allusion to Elizabeth's motto, *Semper Eadem*, which celebrates diversity in singularity, many in one.

50–1. *measured ... mile*] Perhaps recalling the wordplay on these terms from *Love's Labour's Lost* (5.2.185–98), a play performed at court at an earlier Christmas season (1597-98 or 1598–99).

53. *Cypriots*] Possibly a reference to another of Elizabeth's iconographical identities: Venus, Lady of Cyprus (her supposed birthplace). See Roy C. Strong, *The Cult of Elizabeth: Elizabethan Portraiture and Pageantry* (Berkeley: University of California Press, 1977), 47.

55. *Dread Queen of Fairies*] Another instance in which Dekker follows the Spenserian mode of address by associating Elizabeth with the figure of Gloriana, the Queen of Faery Land ('dread' as a cause of 'reverence', rather than 'fear').

1 Now I'll beg for thee too, and yet I need not:
    Her sacred hand hath evermore been known
    As soon held out to strangers as her own.
2 Thou dost encourage me: I'll fetch them in.   60
    They have no princely gifts; we are all poor.
    Our off'rings are true hearts. Who can wish more?
                                            Exeunt.

The Prologue

Of love's sweet war our timorous muse doth sing,
And to the bosom of each gentle dear
Offers her artless tunes, borne on the wing
Of sacred poesy. A benumbing fear
(That your nice souls, cloyed with delicious sounds, 5
Will loathe her lowly notes) makes her pull in
Her fainting pinions and her spirit confounds
Before the weak voice of her song begin.
Yet since within the circle of each eye
(Being like so many suns in this round sphere) 10
No wrinkle yet is seen, she'll dare to fly,
Borne up with hopes that as you oft do rear
With your fair hands those who would else sink down,
So some will deign to smile where all might frown.
And for this small circumference must stand 15

---

3. Offers] *Capell;* Offence *Q.*   10. this] *Daniel;* his *Q.*

---

1. *love's sweet war*] A surprising characterization of the play that follows; perhaps placing significant emphasis on Agrippine's suitors (Orleans, Cyprus, and Andelocia) or, as Peggy Faye Shirley suggests, the phrase may 'indicate the battle within man that arises from a conflict between what he *does* love in life and what he *should* love' (*Serious and Tragic Elements in the Comedy of Thomas Dekker* (Salzburg: Universität Salzburg, 1975), 40).
 4. *benumbing*] 'That benumbs or renders torpid; paralyzing' (*OED*, adj.); the present example predates the *OED*'s first instantiation of 1628.
 5. *nice*] fastidious, fussy; of refined tastes (*OED*, adj. and adv. 3b).
 7. *pinions*] The Prologue continues the metaphor begun with 'the wing / Of sacred poesy' (3-4). 'Pinions' refer to the terminal segment of a bird's wing (*OED*, 1a), and by extension, any of the flight feathers (*OED*, 2a).
 confounds] wastes (*OED*, *v.*, e. *Obs.*).
 12. *rear*] to cause to stand up (*OED*).
 15. *for this small*] i.e. '*because* this small ...' (*OED*).
 circumference] probably a reference to the Rose playhouse, the likely candidate for a public performance of the play by the Admiral's Men. The Rose was appreciably smaller than the Globe (for example), but importantly was circular in form. When the Admiral's Men moved to their new playhouse, the Fortune, some time prior to 1601, a reference to a 'small circumference' would no longer make sense: the Fortune was square in structure.

For the imagined surface of much land,
Of many kingdoms; and since many a mile
Should here be measured out, our muse entreats
Your thoughts to help poor art and to allow
That I may serve as Chorus to her scenes.   20
She begs your pardon, for she'll send me forth
Not when the laws of poesy do call,
But as the story needs. Your gracious eye
Gives life to Fortunatus' history.   *Exit.*

---

20. scenes] *Capell;* senses *Rhys, Smeaton;* scences *Q.*   21. me] *Q;* one *Rhys.*
23. needs. Your] *Bowers;* needes, your *Q.*

15–20. *And for ... her scenes*] Like the Chorus to Shakespeare's *Henry V*, which may or may not have been included in performances of 1599 (see Dutton, *Shakespeare, Court Dramatist* (Oxford University Press, 2016), 177 n10), the choric humility topos of apologizing for the stage's inability to present travel is a recurrent theme throughout Dekker's play, but it is somewhat unusual in its specific request for 'thoughts to help poor art' in a manner which demands an active playgoer, not a passive viewer. More than supplying missing details and thus perpetuating a unidirectional model of interaction, Dekker's Choruses actually urge playgoers to activate their imaginations in a manner conducive to mind-travelling (see Introduction). The Prologue to Jonson's *Every Man In His Humour* (printed 1616) criticizes plays in which the 'chorus wafts you o'er the seas' (15), and, when Jonson was at pains to have Mitis and Cordatus emphasize that *Every Man Out* will deploy no such scene-shifting (Ind.276–81), he probably had Dekker's play in mind.

20. *scenes*] *Q*'s spelling ('scences') admits a dual meaning of 'senses' as well as 'scenes'. The latter is adopted here chiefly on account of the metrical fit, though 'senses' (adopted by Rhys and Smeaton) would imply that the Chorus interprets the Muse's senses/perceptions for the playgoer.

22. *the laws of poesy*] Cyrus Mulready suggests a deliberate engagement with Sidney, who uses precisely this phrase in his criticism of the English stage (i.e. his *Defence of Poesy*). Dekker's shift away from the Classical use of the Chorus to bringing it onstage 'as the story needs' signals 'an important departure' from Sidney's model of a Chorus that 'narrate[s] those moments that defy representation' to one that 'serves' the story (Mulready, *Romance on the Early Modern Stage: English Expansion Before and After Shakespeare* (Basingstoke: Palgrave Macmillan, 2013), 73).

The Comedy of Old Fortunatus

[Scene 1]

Enter FORTUNATUS *meanly attired; he walks ere he speaks once or twice about cracking nuts.*

Fortunatus. So, ho, ho, ho, ho.
Echo (within). Ho, ho, ho, ho.

---

2. SP *Echo (within).*] *this ed.; Eccho* within. Q. *Echo's speech prefixes are marked in Q but Fortunatus's uses of the word 'Echo' are marked as if speech prefixes also, and Q's compositor does not use line breaks to distinguish Echo's text from Fortunatus's. 'Within' is given as part of Echo's lines rather than as a direction.*

0.1.] Smeaton adds the setting: *'A Forest in Cyprus'*.
0.1. meanly attired] poorly clothed. The SD is notable for establishing a clear contrast between Fortunatus's initial state and his appearance immediately after Fortune's visitation (see 2.141 SD below).
0.1–2. he walks ... cracking nuts] The SD is ambiguous, in that it may mean *'he walks once or twice about the Stage cracking Nuts before he speaks'* (Dilke), or that he walks about the stage before he *speaks* about cracking nuts (ll. 54–7). Rhys and Smeaton concurred with Dilke, each recasting the SD as *'he walks about cracking nuts ere he speaks'*. The SD may be read as requiring Fortunatus to commence and continue walking throughout: the long chunks of un-echoed prose make best sense if the actor delivers them at a distance from the tiring house, where the actor playing Echo is stationed 'within'; as Fortunatus reaches the rear of the stage, the words he utters are heard and repeated by Echo, and reverberate as if off the wall, but words delivered downstage are spoken to an open space which does not echo.
2. SP Echo (within)] The following passage is an example of the Wandering Wood or *selva oscura* – a reflection of the speaker's mind. Joseph Loewenstein notes that '[t]he reflections *of* this wood can only become reflections *on* this wood when the hero's wandering becomes self-consciousness .... Old Fortunatus is simply impenetrable, being both self-absorbed and un-self-conscious, and so his Echo only mocks' (*Responsive Readings: Versions of Echo in Pastoral, Epic, and the Jonsonian Masque* (New Haven: Yale University Press, 1984), 135). It is also a variant on poetic games like Philisides' 'eclogue betwixt himself and the echo' in the Second Eclogue of Sidney's *Old Arcadia*, ed. Katherine Duncan-Jones (Oxford University Press, 1985, rpt 1999), 140–2. For dramatic examples see Alan C. Dessen and Leslie Thomson, *A Dictionary of Stage Directions in English Drama, 1580–1642* (Cambridge University Press, 1999), 82.

92   THE COMEDY OF OLD FORTUNATUS   [SC. I

Fortunatus. There, boy.
Echo. There, boy.
Fortunatus. And thou be'st a goodfellow, tell me how thou   5
callst this wood.
Echo. This wood.
Fortunatus. Ay, this wood, and which is my best way out?
Echo. Best way out.
Fortunatus. Ha, ha, ha, that's true. My best way out is my   10
best way out, but how that out will come in, by this
maggot I know not. I see by this we are all worms' meat.
Well, I am very poor and very patient. Patience is a virtue.
Would I were not virtuous, that's to say, not poor, but
full of vice (that's to say, full of chinks). Ha, ha, so I am;   15
for I am so full of chinks, that a horse with one eye may
look through and through me. I have sighed long, and
that makes me windy. I have fasted long, and that makes
me chaste. Marry, I have prayed little, and that makes
me still dance in this conjuring circle. I have wandered   20
long, and that makes me weary; but for my weariness,

19–20. makes me still] *Dilke;* makes mee I still *Q.*

---

5. *goodfellow*] Dilke emends *Q*'s 'goodfellow' to 'good fellow', but *Q*'s reading permits the possibility that Fortunatus imagines himself speaking to a Robin Goodfellow-type who inhabits the woods.

12. *maggot*] with a play on 'maggot' as a strange and whimsical idea lodged in the brain (antedating *OED* n.1, 2a by some 25 years).

15–16. *chinks ... chinks*] Here used first as an echoic word imitating the sound of coins striking each other (*OED* n.3; hence 'not poor, but ... full of chinks'), then subsequently punning on the sense of a gap or crack, either in clothes or in the skin (*OED* n.1) as in Gerard's *Herball* (1597): 'The chappes and chinkes of the hands' (1.60). Shepherd finds a probable allusion to Lyly's *Grammar*, '*Effodiuntur* opes, *irritamenta* malorum', on the basis that 'as by chinks, in the first instance, money is meant, and the holes in his dress in the second'.

16. *I am so full of chinks*] Hoy traces this to Terence, *Eunuchus*, 105: '*plenus rimarum sum*'. In Terence's play, when the courtesan Thais asks if Phaedria's slave Parmeno can hold his tongue, Parmeno's reply 'I am full of cracks' refers to his inability to keep a secret if it is a lie.

17–21. *I have sighed ... weary*] cut for the Tufts performance.

19–20. *makes me still dance*] There may be a lacuna (deliberate or otherwise) in *Q*'s 'makes me I still dance'; 'I still dance' may have been intended as a new sentence or clause.

20. *conjuring circle*] Conjurors made circles to confine the spirits they would summon (see *Faustus* A-text 1.3.8); Fortunatus's endless wandering

SC. I]   THE COMEDY OF OLD FORTUNATUS   93

anon I'll lie down. Instead of fasting I'll feed upon nuts,
and instead of sighing will laugh and be lean, sirrah Echo.
Echo. Sirrah Echo.
Fortunatus. Here's a nut.   25
Echo. Here's a nut.
Fortunatus. Crack it.
Echo. Crack it.
Fortunatus. Hang thyself.
Echo. Hang thyself.   30
Fortunatus. Th'art a knave, a knave.
Echo. A knave, a knave.
Fortunatus. Ha, ha, ha, ha.
Echo. Ha, ha, ha, ha.
Fortunatus. Why so, two fools laugh at one another; I at my   35
 tittle-tattle gammer Echo, and she at me. Shortly there
 will creep out in print some filthy book of the old hoary
 wand'ring knight, meaning me. Would I were that book,
 for then I should be sure to creep out from hence. I
 should be a good soldier, for I traverse my ground rarely.   40
 Marry, I see neither enemy nor friends but popinjays, and
 squirrels, and apes, and owls, and daws, and wagtails;
 and the spite is that none of these grass-eaters can speak
 my language but this fool that mocks me and swears to
 have the last word, in spite of my teeth. Ay, and she shall   45

---

and lack of praying suggests an affinity with spirits thus confined, since his liberty is circumscribed by the wood.

23. *laugh and be lean*] an ironic inversion of the proverbial 'laugh and be fat' (Dent L91) (used by Andelocia in 10.44–5).

36. *gammer*] rustic title for an old woman, e.g. the titular character of *Gammer Gurton's Needle* (c.1553).

36–9. *Shortly ... hence*] cut for the Tufts performance.

37–8. *hoary wand'ring knight*] Fortunatus likens himself to the knight-errant figure of medieval chivalric romance, imbuing his wanderings with a quest-like quality. *Common Conditions*, a stage romance printed c.1576 (STC 5592), also opens with characters wandering in the woods. Ellis, noting the rise in vagrancy during the 1590s (leading to the Poor Law statues of 1597–98) and the disproportionate representation of the aged in their numbers, observes that Fortunatus here embodies poverty but also a 'more general decline' in Elizabethan society (*Old Age*, 152).

40. *rarely*] remarkably well.

have it because she is a woman, which kind of cattle are
indeed all echo (nothing but tongue) and are like the
great bell of St Michael's in Cyprus that keeps most
rumbling when men would most sleep. Echo, a pox on
thee for mocking me.   50
Echo. A pox on thee for mocking me.
Fortunatus. Why so, Snip-snap, this war is at an end, but
this wilderness is world without end. To see how travel
can transform: my teeth are turned into nutcrackers. A

46–9. *which kind of cattle ... sleep*] cut for the Tufts performance.
46. *cattle*] specifically in the sense of a collective term for live animals held as property (*OED*).
47–8. *the great bell ... in Cyprus*] In Peele's *The Old Wives Tale*, ll. 225–8, Lampriscus likens an incessantly chattering woman to a bell: 'By my first wife, whose tongue wearied me alive, and sounded in my ears like the clapper of a great bell, whose talk was a continual torment to all that dwelt by her, or lived nigh her'. Although there are a number of churches of the Archangel Michael in Cyprus (Fortunatus's homeland), it is unclear which (if any) might be known to Dekker and his audience. It is more likely that Dekker thought the name Michael was a good one to associate with noise because of the link with the Judgement, or (as Edward H. Sugden notes) that 'Dekker was thinking of the bell of St. M., Cornhill' (*A Topographical Dictionary to the Works of Shakespeare and His Fellow Dramatists* (Manchester University Press, 1925), 343). A further possibility is that the impoverished Fortunatus is being kept awake by the thought of money: the likeness of the Archangel Michael featured on the Elizabethan coin known as an 'angel' (see 2.37n).
49. *rumbling*] to mutter or murmur (in keeping with Fortunatus's characterization of women above). *OED* cites Munday, *Fidele and Fortunio* (1585): 'I graunt I am none of these fine *Criminadoes*, that can tumble in a Gentlewomans lap, and rumble in her eare' (sig. G.iv).
52. *Snip-snap*] Although the *OED* does not record any uses prior to 1785 of 'snip-snap' in the sense of persons given to smart repartee, Q's use of uppercase in 'Snip' encourages such an interpretation of 'Snip-snap' as an appellation for Echo here. There seems to have been a barber called 'Snipper Snapper' in the lost 'Old Joiner of Aldgate' play by Chapman (1603) (see Wiggins, #1385 or the *Lost Plays Database* entry). 'Snipper-snapper' is used by the Horse-courser in *Faustus* (A-text, 4.1.157) in the sense of a 'young insignificant of conceited fellow' (*OED*).
this war] this war of wits.
53–4. *travel can transform*] a common concern that travel could affect behaviour and identity (e.g. see Jonson, *Epigrams*, 'To William Roe'); here in a more prosaic sense of weariness.
54. *nutcrackers*] First instance provided in *OED* in the sense of 'applied *spec.* to such a device consisting of two pivoted limbs' (here, Fortunatus's teeth).

SC. I]   THE COMEDY OF OLD FORTUNATUS   95

    thousand to one I break out shortly, for I am full of nothing   55
but waxing kernels. My tongue speaks no language but
'an almond for a parrot' and 'crack me this nut'. If I hop
three days more up and down this cage of cuckoos' nests,
I shall turn wild man sure and be hired to throw squibs
among the commonalty upon some terrible day. In the   60
meantime, to tell truth, here will I lie. Farewell, fool.
Echo. Farewell, fool.
Fortunatus. Are not these comfortable words to a wise man?
All hail, Signor Tree! By your leave I'll sleep under your
leaves. I pray bow to me, and I'll bend to you, for your   65
back and my brows must, I doubt, have a game or two

---

56. waxing] *Q;* waring *Dilke.*   57. for a parrot] *Dilke;* for Parrat *Q.*

    55–60. *I break out ... day*] cut for the Tufts performance.
    55. *break out*] a person's body is said to 'break out' into boils, etc. (*OED*); l. 56 makes it clear that Fortunatus predicts breaking out into wax-kernels.
    56. *waxing kernels*] obsolete form of 'waxen-kernels' or 'wax-kernels'; hard glandular swellings, especially in the neck (*OED*), sometimes thought to be caused by an excess of melancholy (see Bolder, *Polypharmakos kai chymistes* (London, 1651) ch. CII, p. 62). Dilke's emendation, 'waring' (*OED*, obs. rare 'aware, cognisant of'), is unlikely.
    56–7. *My tongue ... a parrot*] proverbially a reward for talking (Dent A220, who dates it to c.1517); see Shakespeare *T&C* 17.186–7, 'The parrot will not do more for an almond than he for a commodious drab'. Glossing the *T&C* passage, Bevington (Ard3) notes that, parrots being fond of almonds, Thersites is implying Patroclus 'is always on the lookout for easily obtained sex'. See Introduction, 2–3.
    57. *crack me this nut*] proverbial (Dent N359), meaning something akin to 'solve this riddle'.
    58. *cage of cuckoos' nests*] Cuckoos leave their eggs in other birds' nests instead of constructing their own; perhaps Fortunatus refers to the wood's lack of sustenance.
    59–60. *throw squibs ... commonalty*] squibs (explosives) were fired or thrown; Hoy notes that pageants were 'regularly accompanied by a "wild-man" ... whose duty was to clear the way for the procession by throwing fireworks among the crowd' (95), leading Ellis to suggest that such a pageant's occurrence on some 'terrible day' has 'apocalyptic undertones', including perhaps calling to mind 'the procession of the raised souls at Judgment Day' (*Old Age*, 152). But to 'throw squibs' also means to utter remarks or quips, e.g. Dekker, *Satiromastix*, 'thou wouldst never squib out any new Salt-peter Jestes against honest Tucca' (4.2.84–5).

96 THE COMEDY OF OLD FORTUNATUS [SC. I

at noddy ere I wake again. Down, great heart, down. Hey,
ho, well, well.   *He lies down and sleeps.*

Enter a SHEPHERD, *a* CARTER, *a* MONK, *a* TAILOR,
all crowned; a nymph with a globe, another with FORTUNE'S
wheel; then FORTUNE. *After her, four* KINGS [HENRY V OF
GERMANY, FREDERICK BARBAROSSA, LOUIS THE MEEK,
and BAJAZETH] *with broken crowns and sceptres, chained in
silver gyves and led by her. The foremost come out singing.*
FORTUNE *takes her chair, the* KINGS *lying at her feet; she
treading on them as she goes up.*

The Song.

68.1. SD] *this ed.; a* Shepherd, *a* Carter, *a* Tailor, *and a* Monk *Rhys; a
Carter, a Cobler Daniel; a Gardiner, a Smith, a Monke, a Shepheard Q.*   68.3–5.
KINGS] *The names in parentheses are inferred from Fortune's lines* 180–93.

67. *noddy*] a card game (e.g. *Almond for a Parrat*, sig. F2v: 'Let not me
take you at Noddy anie more, least I present you to the parish for a gamster');
but like the lecherous subtext of the 'almond for a parrot' comment above
(56–7n), with a bawdy pun on sexual intercourse (e.g. *Blurt Master-Constable*,
sig. E2v: 'Shee'll sit up till you come, because shee'll have you play a game
at Noddie').
67–8. *Hey ... well*] Fortunatus's cue to fall asleep. At the Globe reading
in 2006, Bill Bingham yawned here for emphasis.
68.1.] Rhys emends to '*Enter a* Shepherd, *a* Carter, *a* Tailor, *and a*
Monk, *all crowned*' on the basis that the descriptions of a 'Gardener' and
'a Smith' do not tally with the description subsequently given by Fortune
at l. 207 ('carter') and l. 211 ('botcher', i.e. tailor). This edition follows
Rhys's substitution of trades, but reorders them according to Fortune's
introduction. Using the German play as evidence of Dekker's pre-court
version of *Old Fortunatus*, June Schlueter argues that this scene is much
altered for the court performance: in the 1620 play (said to correspond to
Dekker's earlier draft) only three spirits 'condemned to wander in chains
until the end of the world' appear here: 'Each had encountered Fortune,
and each, for a time, had known power, the first as King of Spain, the
second as a mighty Kaiser. (The third merely complains, anonymously, of
his misery.)' (Schlueter, 'New Light on Dekker's *Fortunati*', *MaRDiE* 26
(2013), 124).
68.9. *The Song*] The SD calls for the 'foremost' to come out singing; given
the order of procession, this would mean the Shepherd, possibly with the
Carter, Monk, and Tailor, and even the two Nymphs. As Elizabeth Ketterer
notes, Fortune's chair needs to brought on to the stage during this procession,
and the Admiral's Men often used music to cover the introduction of such
large or unwieldy props ('"Govern'd by stops, aw'd by dividing notes": The
Functions of Music in the Extant Repertory of the Admiral's Men, 1594–1621',
unpublished PhD dissertation, University of Birmingham, 2009, p. 227).

Fortune smiles, cry holiday,
Dimples on her cheeks do dwell. 70
Fortune frowns, cry welladay,
Her love is heaven, her hate is hell.
Since heaven and hell obey her power,
Tremble when her eyes do lour.
Since heaven and hell her power obey, 75
When she smiles, cry holiday.
Holiday with joy we cry
And bend, and bend, and merrily
Sing hymns to Fortune's deity,
Sing hymns to Fortune's deity. 80

All. Let us sing, merrily, merrily, merrily,
With our song let heaven resound.
Fortune's hands our heads have crowned,
Let us sing merrily, merrily, merrily.

Henry V. Accursèd queen of chance! What had we done, 85
Who having sometimes (like young Phaetons)
Rid in the burnished chariot of the sun,
And sometimes been thy minions, when thy fingers

---

74. lour] *Dilke;* lowre *Q.* 85. SP] *this ed.;* 1. King. *Q.*

69–84. *Fortune smiles ... merrily*] *Q*, like other playbooks of the period, was printed without musical scores. Although composers are often now commissioned to source or even write new music for productions (the Tufts performance specified 'Song by Coprario, published in 1614' to be used here), Ross W. Duffin has argued that 'when a playwright creates a new lyric, it is often with some recognizable song in mind', and has accordingly identified the likely tunes for almost six hundred lyrics appearing in early modern comedies. The tune 'that seems to work best' for the present song is *Dulcina* (subsequently known as *Robin Goodfellow*); for the setting, see Duffin, *Some Other Note: The Lost Songs of English Renaissance Comedy* (Oxford University Press, 2018), 300.

71. *welladay*] a sorrowful exclamation.

86. *Phaetons*] Phaeton, son of the sun god Phoebus, once drove his father's solar chariot, but could not control it and would have burnt the entire world if Jupiter hadn't killed him with a thunderbolt in order to avert disaster (Ovid, *Met.* 3). Dekker wrote a lost play called 'Phaeton' in 1598, and was paid 10s for 'his paynes' in altering it '*for* the corte' on 14 December 1600 (Foakes, 137).

87. *Rid*] i.e., ridden.

Weaved wanton love-nets in our curlèd hair,
And with sweet juggling kisses warmed our cheeks? 90
Oh, how have we offended thy proud eyes
That thus we should be spurned and trod upon,
Whilst those infected limbs of the sick world
Are fixed by thee for stars in that bright sphere
Wherein our sun-like radiance did appear? 95
All the Kings. Accursèd queen of chance, damned sorceress.
The rest. Most powerful queen of chance, dread
 sovereigness.
Fortune. No more? Curse on: your cries to me are music
And fill the sacred roundure of mine ears
With tunes more sweet than moving of the spheres. 100
Curse on! On our celestial brows do sit
Unnumbered smiles, which then leap from their throne
When they see peasants dance and monarchs groan.
Behold you not this globe, this golden bowl,
This toy called world at our imperial feet? 105

---

89. Weaved] *Rhys;* Wean'd *Q.* 95. sun-like radiance] *Rhys;* Sunne like Radiance *Q. (Occurs in uncorrected state as 'Radianee' in seven copies of Q).* 98. SP] *Q text; Fortunat. Q catchword.* 102. leap] *Dilke;* leaps *Q.*

---

89. *Weaved ... curlèd hair*] Smeaton notes that this was an 'ultra-dandified' French fashion, citing Greene's *Quip for an Upstart Courtier* (1592), 'Will you be Frenchified with a love-net down your shoulders in which you may weave your mistress's favour?'

90. *juggling*] cheating, deceptive.

93. *limbs*] perhaps in the sense of 'limb' = mischievous person, with a pun on 'limb' = the edge of the disk of a heavenly body (more usually the sun or moon), but antedating the *OED* by some 76 years if so.

95. *sun-like radiance*] *OED*'s first example of 'radiance' in the figurative context.

97. *sovereigness*] a female sovereign; *OED* first instance.

99. *roundure*] rounded form or space; *OED* first instance.

100. *moving of the spheres*] alluding to the Ptolemaic system and the belief that as they moved, the celestial bodies emitted a hum directly proportional to their size; in its perfection, this heavenly music was said to be inaudible in the sublunary world (cf. *Merchant of Venice* 5.1.57–64, where Lorenzo tells Jessica that mortals cannot hear such heavenly music).

104. *globe ... golden bowl*] Frederick Kiefer notes that this bowl 'represents not only the instability of Fortune but also the extent of her dominion' when she conflates it with the globe ('Fortune on the Renaissance Stage: An Iconographic Reconstruction' in *Fortune: 'All Is but Fortune'*, exhibition catalogue, compiled and edited by Leslie Thomson (Washington, DC: Folger Shakespeare Library, 2000), 72).

SC. I]   THE COMEDY OF OLD FORTUNATUS   99

 This world is Fortune's ball, wherewith she sports.
Sometimes I strike it up into the air
And then create I emperors and kings.
Sometimes I spurn it, at which spurn crawls out
That wild beast Multitude. Curse on, you fools!   110
'Tis I that tumble princes from their thrones
And gild false brows with glittering diadems.
'Tis I that tread on necks of conquerors
And when, like semi-gods, they have been drawn
In ivory chariots to the capitol,   115
Circled about with wonder of all eyes,
The shouts of every tongue, love of all hearts,
Being swoll'n with their own greatness, I have pricked
The bladder of their pride and made them die
As water-bubbles, without memory.   120
I thrust base cowards into honour's chair
Whilst the true-spirited soldier stands by
Bare-headed and all bare, whilst at his scars
They scoff, that ne'er durst view the face of wars.
I set an idiot's cap on Virtue's head,   125
Turn learning out of doors, clothe wit in rags
And paint ten thousand images of loam
In gaudy silken colours. On the backs

---

114. semi-gods] *Q;* demi-gods *Rhys.*

 110. *wild beast Multitude*] the general populace, a many-headed beast (cf. 5.191, 'the rank multitude', and *Lust's Dominion*, 'This py'd Camelion, this beast multitude' 3.4.22).
 112. *false brows*] usurpers (Dilke).
 114. *semi-gods*] the sense in *Q* is fine; it is not necessary to follow Rhys in emending to 'demi-gods'. An overtly half-god had appeared previously in drama at an Anglo-French court entertainment about a captive demi-god, performed at Whitehall Palace on 1 January 1582 (Wiggins, #713).
 123–4. *whilst at ... wars*] a possible echo of Romeo's 'He jests at scars that never felt a wound' (*R&J* 8.44) (Philip C. Kolin, 'A Shakespearian Echo in Dekker's "Old Fortunatus"', *N&Q* 19.4 (1972), 125).
 125. *idiot's cap*] a fool's cap. The SD calls for Virtue to enter with 'a coxcomb on her head' in 3.0.10 SD below (cf. 'motley-scorn', 3.51 below). Accordingly, I follow Rhys in assuming *Q*'s 'vertues head' is not an abstract reference but refers specifically to the figure of Virtue.
 127–8. *paint ... silken colours*] Cf. Mowbray's comment in *Richard II* that without reputation, '[m]en are but gilded loam, or painted clay' (1.1.179); Fortune may be alluding to the way she takes lowly persons and transforms them superficially in 'silken' (elegant, flattering) colours.

100   THE COMEDY OF OLD FORTUNATUS   [SC. I

    Of mules and asses I make asses ride,
    Only for sport; to see the apish world   130
    Worship such beasts with fond idolatry.
    This Fortune does and when this is done,
    She sits and smiles to hear some curse her name
    And some with adoration crown her fame.
Monk. True centre of this wide circumference,   135
    Sacred commandress of the Destinies:
    Our tongues shall only sound thy excellence.
The rest. Thy excellence our tongues shall only sound.
Barbarossa. Thou painted strumpet, that with honeyed smiles
    Openest the gates of heaven and criest, 'Come in';   140
    Whose glories being seen, thou with one frown,
    In pride, lower than hell tumblest us down.
Kings. Ever for ever will we ban thy name.
Fortune. How sweet your howlings relish in mine ears!
    Stand by. Now rise, behold: here lies a wretch.   145
                            She comes down.
    To vex your souls, this beggar I'll advance
    Beyond the sway of thought. Take instruments
    And let the raptures of choice harmony
    Through the hollow windings of his ear
                     Music a while, and he waketh.

---

131. fond idolatry] Daniel; sound idolatrie *Q.*   132. when this] *Q;* when all this *Dilke.*   139. SP] *this ed.; The second King. Q.*   149. Through] *Q;* Thorough *Daniel.*

---

    132. *when this*] Dilke emends to 'when all this' to complete the line, but this is unnecessary: other lines are irregular also, and the caesura after 'Fortune does' is a dramatically useful pause.
    144. *relish*] 'To have a specified taste, relish, or flavour; to taste in a particular way' (*OED*, citing this example).
    149. *Through*] disyllabic, 'Thorough'.
    149. SD] The Tufts production called for a 'Saraband, of Henry VIII's time' to be played here. The saraband is a slow Spanish or Moorish dance in triple time; the Tufts direction refers to the piece of music composed for said dance. The *CWBJ* editor, Joseph Loewenstein, glosses Madrigal's saraband in Jonson's *Staple of News* as 'less bawdy than bathetic', but notes that the dance and its music are 'thought to be somewhat lascivious' (4.2.112n).

  Carry their sacred sounds and wake each sense   150
  To stand amazed at our bright eminence.
Fortunatus. Oh, how am I transported? Is this earth?
  Or blessed Elizium?
Fortune.   Fortunatus, rise.
Fortunatus. Dread goddess, how should such a wretch as I
  Be known to such a glorious deity?   155
  Oh, pardon me, for to this place I came
  Led by my fate, not folly. In this wood
  With weary sorrow have I wanderèd
  And three times seen the sweating sun take rest,
  And three times frantic Cynthia naked ride   160
  About the rusty highways of the skies
  Stuck full of burning stars, which lent her light
  To court her negro paramour, grim night.
Fortune. This travel now expires: yet from this circle,
  Where I and these with fairy troops abide,   165
  Thou canst not stir, unless I be thy guide.
  I the world's empress am, Fortune my name.
  This hand hath written in thick leaves of steel
  An everlasting book of changeless Fate,
  Showing who's happy, who unfortunate.   170
Fortunatus. If every name (dread queen) be there writ
  down,

---

156. came] *Dilke;* come *Q.* 162. her light] *Q;* their light *Dilke.* 163. court] *Occurs in uncorrected state as* 'Court' *in eight copies of Q.*

---

153. *Elizium*] See Prologue at Court, l. 10.
 160. *Cynthia*] the moon goddess; cf. allusions to Elizabeth in the Prologue at Court, ll. 3 and 28.
 162. *her light*] Dilke emends to 'their light', shifting emphasis to the stars, who lend their light to Cynthia; but *Q*'s reading is retained here because it makes sense: the stars lend light *to her*, so that she can court her paramour.
 163. *negro*] literally 'dark' (because night), though in the period the term usually referred to dark-skinned people of African descent; Moors. Cf. Peele, *Battle of Alcazar*, where Muly Mahomet is referred to by this term (I.Prol.7 and elsewhere) (Charles Edelman, ed., *The Stukeley Plays: The Battle of Alcazar by George Peele and The Famous History of the Life and Death of Captain Thomas Stukeley. The Revels Plays* (Manchester University Press, 2005).
 164. *This travel now expires*] This hardship now expires (with a common pun on travel/travail).
 this circle] cf. 'conjuring circle' above, l. 20.

I am sure mine stands in characters of black.
Though happiness herself lie in my name,
I am sorrow's heir and eldest son to shame.
Kings. No, we are sons to shame and sorrow's heirs.   175
Fortune. Thou shalt be one of Fortune's minions.
Behold these four, chained like Tartarian slaves.
These I created emperors and kings
And these are now my basest underlings.
This sometimes was a German emperor,   180
Henry the Fifth, who being first deposed

---

172. *characters of black*] the sense is that, in Fortune's 'everlasting book', Fortunatus's name will be undistinguished by virtue of being entered in black-letter script (the marking of notable dates and events in red ink in prayer books, etc. goes back to antiquity). Fortunatus suggests that, despite the 'happiness' of his name, he really ought to be singled out for misfortune.

177–213. *Behold these four ... Fortune's grace.*] Against Dilke's objection to the anachronism of the persons brought together in this passage, and his claim that '[i]f these had been introduced by Fortune merely as shadowy figures ... much of the incongruity arising from their being made speakers would have been avoided' (114), it should be noted that Fortune's use of 'Tartarian' in the sense of hellish (see 177n below) indicates precisely that these *are* 'shadowy' figures from the Underworld. Hoy notes that five of the eight examples of Fortune's minions named here can be found in Pierre de La Primaudaye's *The French Academy* (1589), chapter 44 ('Of Fortune'), pp. 447–8. (The 1586 edition contains the same passage, on pp. 474–5, with Barbarossa being cited on p. 254 also, following a discussion of Tamburlaine on p. 253).

177. *Tartarian slaves*] 'Tartarian' could refer to 'Tartary' in central Asia or be a cant term for a thief (both meanings are present in Marlowe's description of Tamburlaine as 'the great Tartarian thief' (1 *Tam.* 3.3.171), but also carries the sense of the infernal, as in Orcanes' pronouncement upon Sigismond's death: 'Now scalds his soul in the Tartarian streams' (2 *Tam.* 2.3.18). This latter sense is certainly what is implied here, and Hoy notes that it is preferred by Dekker more generally in his works (97).

180–1. *German emperor, / Henry the Fifth*] Rhys suggests this is a mistake for Henry IV of Germany (1050–1106), 'brought to that extreme miserie by wars, that he asked the said *Gregory* forgiveness, & cast himselfe down at his feete. And yet before this miserable monarch could speake with him, he stood 3. days fasting and barefoote at the popes palace gate, as a poore suppliant waiting when he might have entrance & access to his holynes' (La Primaudaye (1586), 474). See also I. S. Robinson, *Henry IV of Germany* 1056–1106 (Cambridge University Press, 1999) on Henry IV's 'determination to be the master, rather than the servant, of the imperial Church' (15). Wiggins proposes the Holy Roman Emperor Henry V (1081–1125) as the intended personage here.

SC. I]   THE COMEDY OF OLD FORTUNATUS   103

    Was after thrust into a dungeon
    And thus in silver chains shall rot to death.
    This Frederick Barbarossa, Emperor
    Of Almaine once, but by Pope Alexander   185
    Now spurned and trod on when he takes his horse,
    And in these fetters shall he die his slave.
    This wretch once wore the diadem of France:
    Louis the Meek, but through his children's pride
    Thus have I caused him to be famishèd.   190
    Here stands the very soul of misery,
    Poor Bajazeth, old Turkish emperor
    And once the greatest monarch in the East.
    [*To* BAJAZETH] Fortune herself is sad to view thy fall
    And grieves to see thee glad to lick up crumbs   195
    At the proud feet of that great Scythian swain,
    Fortune's best minion, warlike Tamburlaine.

---

189. Louis] *this ed.;* Lewis *Q.*   194. sad] *Dilke;* said *Q.*

184–7. *Frederick Barbarossa ... Pope Alexander ... his slave.*] La Primaudaye (1586) writes of Pope Alexander's treatment of Barbarossa (1120–90): 'He that trode upon the emperor *Frederike Barbarossa* his necke, and pusht him twise with his foote when he had him at his devotion' (254). Hoy cites a woodcut showing this incident in Foxe's *Actes and Monuments* (1563), p. 41.

    189. *Louis the Meek*] Louis I (778–840), son of Charlemagne: 'Lewes the Meeke, emperour, & king of France, was constrained to give over his estate, & to shut himself up in a monasterie, through the conspiracie of his own children' (La Primaudaye (1586), 474).

    192. *Poor Bajazeth*] the Ottoman Sultan Bayazid (1354–1403), captured by the Tartarian Timur in 1402, dramatized by Marlowe as Bajazeth, Emperor of the Turks, in *Tamburlaine* (1587), where he famously dashed his brains out against the iron cage in which he was held captive (5.1.304). Samuel Chew notes that 'Dekker stands quite alone in his sense of the pathos of [Bajazeth's] hapless situation' (*The Crescent and the Rose: Islam and England During the Renaissance* (New York: Oxford University Press, 1937), 470). Hoy suggests that the 'crumbs' specified in l. 198 demonstrate Dekker's indebtedness not to Marlowe or La Primaudaye but to Thomas Fortescue's translation of Pedro Mexia's *The Foreste or Collection of Histories* (1571), which is unique in describing Tamburlaine pestering Bajazeth with 'the croomes, that fell from hys table' (85).

    196. *Scythian*] the ancient nomadic race inhabiting a large part of Russia, as exemplified by Marlowe's Tamburlaine (1. 196).

104   THE COMEDY OF OLD FORTUNATUS   [SC. I

>   Yet must thou in a cage of iron be drawn
>   In triumph at his heels, and there in grief
>   Dash out thy brains.
> *Bajazeth.*   Oh, miserable me.   200
> *Fortune.* No tears can melt the heart of destiny.
>   These have I ruined, and exalted those.
>   These hands have conquered Spain, these brows fill up
>   The golden circle of rich Portugal.
>   Viriat, a monarch now but born a shepherd.   205
>   This, Primislaus (a Bohemian king),
>   Last day a carter. This monk Gregory,
>   Now lifted to the Papal dignity.
>   Wretches, why gnaw you not your fingers off
>   And tear your tongues out, seeing yourselves trod
>   down?   210

---

200. SP] *this ed.;* 4 *King. Rhys;* 3 *King. Dilke; The third King. Q.* 202. ruined] *Dilke;* rain'd *Q.* 202. those] *Q;* these *Daniel.* 210. down?] *Bowers;* down, *Q.*

---

204. *golden circle*] a band encircling the head, a crown (*OED*, citing this example).

205. *Viriat ... shepherd*] The King of Spain and Portugal, and a shepherd by birth, Viriatus or Viriathus (d. 139 BC) rose to a position of military power, leading the Lusitanian resistance against the Romans. His story is related in a number of early modern texts, but Hoy draws attention to the fact that, like the detail of Bajazeth being offered crumbs to eat, an account of Viriat (and of Primislaus, see below), occurs in Mexía's *The Foreste* (1571), fols 99r-v.

206–7. *Primislaus ... a carter*] Hoy notes that there is an account of Primislaus, King of Bohemia (d. 745 BC), in *The Foreste,* fol. 101v (where a comparison is made between the rise of Primislaus the carter and of Tamburlaine the shepherd). Mexía relates that the Bohemians let an unbridled horse guide their decision about who would be their next king; Primislaus was the first to calm the horse.

207–8. *monk Gregory ... Papal dignity*] Hildebrande (Hellebrand) or Pope Gregory VII (c.1020–85) was born of humble origin and became a Benedictine monk in Rome, becoming chaplain to Gregory VI and pope in 1073 during the reign of Henry IV of Germany (see 183–4n above). Wiggins disagrees with Hoy's identification of Gregory as Pope Gregory VII, noting that Gregory the Great (d. 604) was the first monk to become pope. This is a plausible identification, though the text does not require the Gregory to be the *first* monk to be crowned pope.

And this Dutch botcher wearing Münster's crown,
John Leyden, born in Holland poor and base,
Now rich in empery and Fortune's grace.
As these I have advanced, so will I thee.
Six gifts I spend upon mortality: 215
Wisdom, strength, health, beauty, long life, and riches.
Out of my bounty, one of these is thine.
Choose then which likes thee best.
Fortunatus. Oh, most divine!
Give me but leave to borrow wonder's eye,
To look, amazed, at thy bright majesty. 220
Wisdom, strength, health, beauty, long life, and riches?

---

211. crown,] *Bowers;* crown? *Q.*

    211–13. *Dutch botcher ... grace*] The Anabaptist John Leyden was a tailor ('botcher') in Holland in the early sixteenth century (c.1510–36); he briefly ruled Münster as king after leading a Protestant rebellion there and seizing the city, but his good fortune was short-lived and he was ultimately put to death, as numerous early modern commentators observed. In the context of 'fortune, desirous of change', one author writes: '*John Leyden* a butchers sonne of *Holland* was proclaimed King, and raigned three yeares in great prosperite, and then subverted' (H. R., *A Defiance to Fortune Proclaimed by Andrugio, Noble Duke of Saxony* ... (1590), sigs M2r–v). Hoy gives the alternative names Jan Beuckelson, Bockelson or Bockold, and notes that Nashe gave a lengthy account of Leyden's story in *The Unfortunate Traveller* (1594), sigs D3r–Ev.
    213. *empery*] an emperor's territory (see also l. 240 below).
    215–318. *Six gifts ... quickly die.*] This entire passage on 'Fortune giving Fortunatus his choice of goods' (except ll. 262–3) was extracted by Thomas Campbell, *Specimens of the British Poets*, vol. 3 (London: John Murray, 1819), 210–14.
    216. *Wisdom ... riches*] As Phoebe S. Spinrad has noted, '[t]he audience that knows its old Moralities will immediately be alerted to the trap here: except for wisdom, all the proffered gifts are illusory and transitory' (*The Summons of Death on the Medieval and Renaissance Stage* (Columbus: Ohio State University Press, 1987), 112). The choice is a typical folklore test, other examples of which include the testing of King Solomon (1 Kings 3: 5–14) and of Paris (see 266n below), not to mention Portia's casket-test in *Merchant of Venice* (which may have been in the Chamberlain's Men's repertory about the time that the lost '1 Fortunatus' play was in the Admiral's Men's repertory).

Fortune. Before thy soul at this deep lottery
    Draw forth her prize, ordained by destiny,
    Know that here's no recanting a first choice.
    Choose then discreetly, for the laws of Fate,   225
    Being graven in steel, must stand inviolate.
Fortunatus. Daughters of Jove and the unblemished night,
    Most righteous Parcae: guide my genius right.
    Wisdom, strength, health, beauty, long life, and riches?
Fortune. Stay, Fortunatus, once more hear me speak.   230
    If thou kiss wisdom's cheek and make her thine,
    She'll breathe into thy lips divinity
    And thou (like Phoebus) shalt speak oracle.
    Thy heaven-inspired soul, on wisdom's wings,
    Shall fly up to the parliament of Jove   235
    And read the statutes of eternity,
    And see what's past and learn what is to come.
    If thou lay claim to strength, armies shall quake
    To see thee frown; as kings at mine do lie,
    So shall thy feet trample on empery.   240
    Make health thine object, thou shalt be strong proof

---

228. Parcae] *Dilke;* Parce *Q.*   233. Phoebus] *Dilke;* Phebus *Q.*

222–98. *Before ... rich.*] Selected by Charles Lamb for reproduction in his *Specimens of English Dramatic Poets* (London, 1808), 56–8. (Lamb omits ll. 259–63.)

    223. *ordained by destiny*] An ambiguous comment: if it applies to the drawing forth of the prize, it would seem to suggest that Fortunatus never really had a choice and was bound to choose riches; alternatively, it might apply to the inability to recant a first choice.

    225–6. *the laws of Fate ... inviolate*] This passage was noted under the rubric 'Fate' by Robert Allott in *Englands Parnassus* (London, 1600), p. 87.

    227–8. *Daughters of Jove ... Parcae*] The Parcae are the three Fates of Latin poetry; Hesiod (*Theogony*) identifies them as daughters of Zeus (i.e. Jove) (*OCD*, 'Fate'). Rhys conjectured that Fortunatus addresses Fortune and her two nymphs, but he may equally be apostrophizing the absent Destinies.

    228. *genius*] In pagan belief, the guardian spirit who guides an individual's fortunes, for better or worse.

    233. *Phoebus ... oracle*] The sun god Phoebus/Apollo (cf. 86n above) presided over the Delphic oracle and was thus associated with predictions and advice.

    239. *at mine do lie*] i.e. lie at Fortune's feet (cf. l. 243, 'So shall thy feet ...').

SC. 1]   THE COMEDY OF OLD FORTUNATUS   107

  'Gainst the deep-searching darts of surfeiting,
  Be ever merry, ever revelling.
  Wish but for beauty and within thine eyes
  Two naked Cupids amorously shall swim,   245
  And on thy cheeks I'll mix such white and red
  That Jove shall turn away young Ganymede
  And with immortal arms shall circle thee.
  Are thy desires long life? Thy vital thread
  Shall be stretched out, thou shalt behold the change 250
  Of monarchies and see those children die
  Whose great-great-grandsires now in cradles lie.
  If through gold's sacred hunger thou dost pine,
  Those gilded wantons which in swarms do run
  To warm their slender bodies in the sun   255
  Shall stand for number of those golden piles
  Which in rich pride shall swell before thy feet;
  As those are, so shall these be infinite.
  Awaken then thy soul's best faculties
  And gladly kiss this bounteous hand of Fate,   260
  Which strives to bless thy name of Fortunate.
The Kings. Old man, take heed, her smiles will murder
  thee.

  244–5. *within thine eyes ... swim*] Rhys proposes that this image may be indebted to an anonymous poem, 'A praise of his Lady', in *Tottel's Miscellany* (1557), which contains the lines, 'In each of her two crystal eyes / Smileth a naked boy'.
  246. *such white and red*] A commonplace image of beauty derived from the Petrarchan blazon.
  247. *young Ganymede*] The name Ganymede came to stand for a catamite, and carries overt homosexual overtones: on account of his childish beauty, Ganymede was kidnapped by an eagle (or by Jove disguised as an eagle, in Ovid, *Met.* 10.154–60), and became Jove's cup-bearer. If Fortunatus chooses the gift of beauty, he will exceed even Ganymede, and Jove will embrace him with his 'immortal arms' (l. 248). See also 2 *Honest Whore* 1.1.7.
  253. *sacred*] accursed. See *OED*, '[After Latin *sacer*; frequently translating or in allusion to Virgil's *auri saca fames* (Æn. iii. 57).] Now rare', citing this example. Cf. *Titus* 1. 616: 'our empress, with her sacred wit'.
  254–8. *gilded wantons ... infinite*] Fortune's simile of gold being as plentiful as flies are numerous may also contain an oblique suggestion of the ephemeral nature of the riches, as James Russell Lowell notes (*The Complete Works of James Russell Lowell. Latest Literary Essays and Addresses: The Old Dramatists* (Boston, 1905), 205).

108   THE COMEDY OF OLD FORTUNATUS   [SC. I

The Others. Old man, she'll crown thee with felicity.
Fortunatus. Oh, whither am I rapt beyond myself?
More violent conflicts fight in every thought   265
Than his whose fatal choice Troy's downfall wrought.
Shall I contract myself to wisdom's lore?
Then I lose riches, and a wiseman poor
Is like a sacred book that's never read:
To himself he lives and to all else seems dead.   270
This age thinks better of a gilded fool
Than of a threadbare saint in wisdom's school.
I will be strong. Then I refuse long life,
And though mine arm should conquer twenty worlds,

---

263. SP] *this ed.; Th'other. Q.*   264. rapt] *Dilke;* wrap't *Q.*

264–89. *Oh ... tribulation*] Cf. Faustus's deliberations in the opening of Marlowe's play, A-text 1.1.1–65.

266. *his whose fatal choice*] The allusion here is to another choice-based folktale, the Judgement of Paris, in which love is selected from the offerings available. Eris, the figure of strife, started a quarrel between Hera, Athena, and Aphrodite by throwing amongst them a golden apple (the 'apple of discord') bearing the inscription, 'To the fairest' (cf. 'The ball of gold that set all Troy on fire', 4.44 below). To settle their dispute over who is the most beautiful, the goddesses appeared naked before Paris, but he was unable to judge. Consequently, they each attempted to bribe him: Athena offered Paris wisdom and the skill of a warrior; Hera offered political power and kingship; Aphrodite offered him the love of Helen of Troy, which of course he accepted, thus in one sense precipitating 'Troy's downfall'. (A comparable parable of choice is Solomon's selection of wisdom from God's offering of wisdom, long life, riches, or the destruction of his enemies; see 1 Kings 3: 5–14.)

267. *lore*] Dilke was the first to emend *love* to *lore*; Bowers notes that the phrase appears both here and in Cho.1, 25 below, and that consistency is required. Noting that the present example is part of a couplet, and hence the need for the final word of 267 to rhyme with 'poor' in 268, Bowers adopts the emendation to *lore*. This edition follows Bowers's justification.

268–72. *a wiseman poor ... wisdom's school*] Noted by Allott in *Englands Parnassus* under 'Wisdom' (p. 303). Dilke cites Ecclesiastes 9: 14ff, and Hoy (citing Charles Crawford's 1913 Oxford edition of *England's Parnassus*) notes that an altered version of these lines appears in *Love's Garland, or Poesies for Rings, &c* (1624). The unique extant copy of the first edition of *Love's Garland* lacks the final pages, but the 1648 edition prints the following under the heading, 'On a good man': 'A wise man poore, is like a sacred booke that's never read: / To himselfe he lives, though to the world seems dead: / Yet this age counts more of a golden foole, / Than of a threed-bare Saint, nurst up in wisedomes Schoole' (sig. B4r). The 1674 third edition alters the title to 'On a good woman' (sig. B4r).

There's a lean fellow beats all conquerors: 275
The greatest strength expires with loss of breath,
The mightiest in one minute stoop to Death.
Then take long life or health. Should I do so,
I might grow ugly, and that tedious scroll
Of months and years, much misery may enrol. 280
Therefore I'll beg for beauty. Yet I will not:
The fairest cheek hath oftentimes a soul
Leprous as sin itself, than hell more foul.
The wisdom of this world is idiotism,
Strength a weak reed; health, sickness' enemy, 285
And it at length will have the victory.
Beauty is but a painting and long life
Is a long journey in December gone,
Tedious and full of tribulation.
Therefore, dread sacred empress, make me rich. 290
     Kneel down.
My choice is store of gold. The rich are wise.
He that upon his back rich garments wears
Is wise, though on his head grow Midas' ears.

---

275. *lean fellow*] i.e. the allegorical persona of Death, often represented in skeletal form in art; cf. 'that lean, tawny-faced tobacconist Death' (l. 345, below).

282–3. *The fairest ... foul*] Noted by Allott in *Englands Parnassus* under 'Beauty' (p. 18). According to the Renaissance conception of Neo-Platonic thought, outward appearance was indicative of inner moral fibre (Caliban's physical deformity is thus symptomatic of his alleged moral turpitude); Fortunatus here suggests the opposite, and in positing the potential for looks to be deceiving, implicitly suggests that Fortune's bestowal of beauty is superficial, like cosmetics.

290. SD] The use of the imperative here ('Kneel down', not 'He kneels down') may suggest that the manuscript behind *Q* had been marked up for performance. See also Cho.2, 32 SD and 7.0.1 SD below.

291. *My choice ... gold*] Shirley defends the hungry and destitute wanderer's choice: 'What is most important to him at the time is the resolution of his immediate problems; he can see how wealth would supply that resolution, and the other gifts more or less lose their value in the light of the potential good the money will do for him' (*Serious and Tragic Elements*, 57).

293. *Midas' ears*] The relevance of the Phrygian King Midas here is not his golden touch, but his foolishness (or lack of wisdom), which Fortunatus fails to perceive or wilfully ignores. Ovid relates that, after Bacchus restored Midas to his original condition, Midas stumbled upon Pan and Apollo engaged in a musical contest on the mountain of Tmolus. Tmolus declared Apollo's lyre was greater than Pan's pipes, but Midas objected. Apollo, refusing to suffer such foolish human ears, punished Midas by making ass's ears grow on his head (*Met.* 11.151–80).

110   THE COMEDY OF OLD FORTUNATUS   [SC. I

> Gold is the strength, the sinews of the world;
> The health, the soul, the beauty most divine.   295
> A mask of gold hides all deformities.
> Gold is heaven's physic, life's restorative.
> Oh, therefore make me rich. Not as the wretch
> That only serves lean banquets to his eye,
> Has gold, yet starves; is famished in his store.   300
> No, let me ever spend, be never poor.

Fortune. Thy latest words confine thy destiny.
> Thou shalt spend ever and be never poor.
> For proof receive this purse, with it this virtue:
> Still when thou thrusts thy hand into the same,   305
> Thou shalt draw forth ten pieces of bright gold,
> Current in any realm where then thou breathest.
> If thou canst dribble out the sea by drops,
> Then shalt thou want: but that can ne'er be done,
> Nor this grow empty.

Fortunatus.   Thanks, great deity.   310

Fortune. The virtue ends when thou and thy sons end.
> This path leads thee to Cyprus: get thee hence.
> Farewell, vain covetous fool. Thou wilt repent

298–300. *the wretch ... his store*] The identity of this figure of greed is probably 'Septitius', emblematized as '*In avaros*' (Emblem 85) by Andrea Alciato in his *Book of Emblems* (*Emblematum liber*), a collection of 220 Latin poems which went through some 170 or more editions in the sixteenth and seventeenth centuries. It was first printed in English by Whitney in *A choice of emblems* (1586), p. 18, and the specific emblem in question was later incorporated into a discussion of avarice by Thomas Heywood in *The hierarchie of the blessed angells* (London, 1635), book 9, p. 597.

307. *Current in any realm*] The fact that the riches will be in the appropriate currency for wherever Fortunatus is located when he draws gold from his purse suggests that an expectation of travel is inextricably bound up in the fantasy of wealth (see McInnis, *Mind-Travelling*, 76–7).

308. *dribble out the sea by drops*] a proverbially impossible feat (Dent S183).

312. *This path ... Cyprus*] If taken literally, Dekker is guilty of a geographical error akin to Shakespeare's coast of Bohemia: Cyprus is an island and cannot be reached by path. The wandering wood where this conversation takes place seems to be located outside of time and place though, so 'Cyprus' here stands for 'civilization' and Fortune is helping Fortunatus find his way out of the wood.

313. *Farewell, vain covetous fool*] Fortune and Fortunatus part ways, but although Fortune's line seemingly implies that Fortunatus will depart first, he lingers after she and her entourage exit. If her lines beginning 'Thou wilt repent' are intended as an aside, Fortunatus nevertheless overhears the final line at least, for her repeats it verbatim at l. 319 below.

That for the love of dross thou hast despied
Wisdom's divine embrace. She would have borne thee   315
On the rich wings of immortality.
But now go dwell with cares and quickly die.
Kings. We dwell with cares, yet cannot quickly die.

Exeunt all singing. FORTUNATUS *remains.*

Fortunatus. 'But now go dwell with cares and quickly die'?
How quickly? If I die tomorrow, I'll be merry today; if   320
next day, I'll be merry tomorrow. Go dwell with cares?
Where dwells Care? Hum ha, in what house dwells Care,
that I may choose an honester neighbour? In princes'
courts? No. Among fair ladies neither, there's no care
dwells with them but care how to be most gallant. Among   325
gallants then? Fie, fie, no. Care is afraid sure of a gilt
rapier. The scent of musk is her poison, tobacco chokes
her, rich attire presseth her to death. Princes, fair ladies,
and gallants have amongst you then, for this wet-eyed
wench Care dwells with wretches. They are wretches that   330
feel want. I shall feel none if I be never poor, therefore
Care I cashier you my company. I wonder what blind

318.1. SD] *this ed.; manet* Fortunatus *Q.*   324. No. Among] *Rhys;* No, among *Q.*   326. gilt] *Dilke;* guilt *Q.*   327. scent of musk] *Dilke;* sent of Muske *Q.*   327. poison] *Dilke;* prison *Q.*   331. shall feel none] *Q; Dilke claims Q's reading is* 'I feel none', *and amends to* 'shall feel none'.

---

317. *go dwell with cares*] In ll. 319–32 below, it is clear that Fortunatus has missed the point of Fortune's injunction, and laughs off the ominous command by resorting to wordplay. Fortunatus interprets 'dwell with' as 'live with, alongside', but Fortune's ambiguous line turns on a pun, wherein 'dwell' = 'to dwell on, upon'. Dekker apparently alludes to Juvenal's tenth satire, in which he declaimed against foolish men whose excessive care for wealth leads to their untimely demise.
318. SD Exeunt all singing] The Tufts production specified a reprisal of the Coprario from 1.69–84.
327–8. *The scent of musk ... tobacco ... rich attire*] These items are each notable as luxury goods of sorts: the sweet smell of musk (either the glandular excretion of animals or the smell of musk-roses) was prized in perfumes; tobacco was still a new trend and conspicuously consumed good; and rich attire (clothing) is evidently more about sartorial splendour than utilitarian function.
332. *I cashier you*] I discharge / dismiss you from.

gossip this minx is, that is so prodigal? She should be a
good one by her open dealing. Her name's Fortune. It's
no matter what she is, so she does as she says. 'Thou   335
shalt spend ever and be never poor'. [*Feels inside the bag.*]
Mass, yet I feel nothing here to make me rich. Here's no
sweet music with her silver sound. Try deeper. Ho! God
be here! Ha, ha, one, two, three, four, five, six, seven,
eight, nine, and ten. Good, just ten. It's gold sure, it's so   340
heavy. Try again. One, two, &c. Good again, just ten,
and just ten. Ha, ha, ha! This is rare. A leather mint,
admirable! An Indian mine in a lamb's skin, miraculous!
I'll fill three or four bags full for my sons, but keep this
for myself. If that lean, tawny-faced tobacconist Death,   345
that turns all into smoke, must turn me so quickly into

339–40. one, two, ... ten,] *Dilke;* 1, 2, ... 10, *Q.*   341. One, two,] *this ed.;*
1, 2, *Q.*   345. tawny-faced] *Dilke;* tawnie face *Q.*

333. *gossip*] 'A person, mostly a woman, of light and trifling character, esp.
one who delights in idle talk; a newsmonger, a tattler' (*OED*, citing this example).
338. *sweet music ... silver sound*] proverbial (Dent M1319.1); literally the
sound of coins (cf. 'gold's sweet music', 2.169 below); also a direct quotation
from 'In commendation of Musick' (item 53 in Richard Edwards, *The
paradyse of dayntie devises* (1576), p. 55), the same song that Peter quotes in
R&J (21.148–9 and 158–9). See also 6.396 below.
341. &c.] Clearly the '&c.' signifies that the character continues to count,
not that he literally says 'et cetera'; possibly this indicates a reader's rather than
an actor's text, and thus that the copy-text was Dekker's own manuscript rather
than a document that had been marked up significantly for performance.
343. *Indian*] i.e. the East Indies (cf. 2.79–80), source of fabled gold.
lamb's skin] clearly a reference to the 'Sweet purse' of ll. 349–50 (cf.
2.77–84 below), and Dekker uses 'lamb-skins' thus in *Shoemaker's Holiday*
10.10–11 ('Hang these penny-pinching fathers, that cram wealth in innocent
lamb-skins') but the Revels editors gloss that passage by citing the present
passage, and the *OED* does not record this meaning. A wolf dressed in
lamb's skin was a commonplace, however, and it may be that the specific
association of 'lamb's skin' with concealment is what Dekker had in mind
when Fortunatus comments on the unlikelihood of an Indian mine being
concealed in a humble casing.
345. *lean, tawny-faced tobacconist Death*] Cf. ll. 275–7 above. Here, 'tobacconist' is used in the obsolete sense of one who is addicted to tobacco rather
than a purveyor of tobacco. Depictions of tobacco on stage typically match
this description: in Thomas Tomkis's university play *Lingua* (1607), Tobacco
is 'apparelled in a taffata mantle, his armes browne and naked ... his necke
bare, hung with Indian leaves, his face browne painted with blewe stripes'
(sig. H4r). In his preface to *News from Hell* (1606), Dekker describes '*Don
Pluto*' as 'that great *Tobaconist* the Prince of smoake & darknes' (sig. A4v).

SC. 2]   THE COMEDY OF OLD FORTUNATUS   113

    ashes, yet I will not mourn in ashes but in music. Hey
old lad, be merry! Here's riches, wisdom, strength,
health, beauty, and long life (if I die not quickly). Sweet
purse, I kiss thee. Fortune, I adore thee. Care, I despise   350
thee. Death, I defy thee!   [*Exit.*]

[Scene 2]

    Enter AMPEDO, SHADOW *after him, both sad;*
        ANDELOCIA *after them.*

Andelocia. S'heart! Why, how now? Two knights of the post?
Shadow. Ay, master, and we are both forsworn, as all such
    wooden knights be; for we both took an oath – marry it

---

349. quickly). Sweet] *this ed.;* quickly) sweete *Bowers;* quickly, sweet *Q.*

    349. *life (if ... quickly). Sweet*] Noting the ambiguous punctuation in *Q* ('... *life. (If I die not quickly, sweete...*'), Bowers observes that all editors have associated the parenthetical clause with the sentence ending with 'life', and claims that this interpretation 'does violence to the sense, for, if Fortunatus has thus qualified the purse's promise of long life, it is scarcely probably he would then defy death so confidently'. His solution is to substitute the missing bracket for the comma after 'quickly'. But Fortunatus has just expressed concern that the 'tawny-faced tobacconist Death' will turn him 'so quickly into ashes' that he won't be able to enjoy his newfound riches for long (1.345–7), and the purse hasn't promised long life, it has promised riches – which Fortunatus exuberantly claims can provide the means for wisdom, strength, health, beauty, and long life (the latter, he quips, only if he doesn't die quickly).

    0.1.] Smeaton adds the setting: '*Near the House of Fortunatus*'.
    1. *S'heart*] a mild profanity ('God's heart').
    knights of the post] Andelocia refers to the impoverished appearance of his brother and Shadow. 'Knights of the post' were notorious perjurers who made their livings by providing false depositions (*OED*); William Fisher explains in *A godly sermon preached at Paules Crosse* ... (1592) that it 'is thought they have no more conscience what they sweare many times, than a verye poste' (sig. A7v). In some copies of *Pierce Penilesse* (1592), Nashe defines 'A knight of the Post' as 'a fellowe that will sweare you any thing for twelve pence' (sig. A4r, Huntington copy, STC (2nd ed.) / 18373).

    2–11. *and we are both ... bull beef.*] cut for the Tufts performance.
    2. *both forsworn*] have both perjured ourselves, broken our oaths. Shadow and Ampedo had apparently declared their commitment to continual eating ('we would not fast twenty-four hours') but have grown hungry and lack food in their poverty.
    3. *wooden*] in the sense of lacking liveliness (on account of their hunger).

was not corporal, you may see by our cheeks – that we
would not fast twenty-four hours to amend, and we have 5
tasted no meat since the clock told two dozen.
Andelocia. That lacks not much of twenty-four, but I wonder
when that half-faced moon of thine will be at the full?
Shadow. The next quarter, not this. When the sign is in
Taurus. 10
Andelocia. Ho, that's to say, when thou eatst bull beef. But
Shadow, what day is today?
Shadow. Fasting day.
Andelocia. What day was yesterday?
Shadow. Fasting day too. 15
Andelocia. Will tomorrow be so too?
Shadow. Ay, and next day too.
Andelocia. That will be rare, you slave, for a lean diet makes
a fat wit.
Shadow. I had rather be a fool and wear a fat pair of cheeks. 20
Andelocia. Now am I prouder of this poverty, which I know

---

4. *Q places closing parenthesis after* corporal.   5. to amend] *Q;* to an end
Dilke.   18. slave, for] *this ed.;* 2 *lines in Q (*slave: / For*).*

---

4. *not corporal*] A corporal oath is an oath ratified by corporally touching a sacred object (*OED*); Shadow uses 'corporal' to refer to his exaggeratedly emaciated body rather than in the sense of the oath-swearer's physical contact with a bible (or similar object).

5. *to amend*] Dilke thinks this is erroneous, and proposes 'to an end' as a plausible alternative (though he does not adopt the emendation himself), but Shadow's line below, 'here follows no amendment' (29), suggests that 'amend' is indeed the correct reading.

10. *Taurus*] the sign of the bull in the zodiac, corresponding to approximately 21 April; if taken literally, Shadow's reference to its occurrence in the 'next quarter' would indicate that the current action takes place in winter.

11. *eatst bull beef*] proverbial, cf. Dent B719*, citing this example: 'He looks as big as if he had eaten (TO eat, look like) BULL BEEF'.

13. *Fasting day*] a holy day or day of fasting; not an optional observance or real holiday for the food-deprived Shadow, however.

18–19. *a lean diet makes fat wit*] proverbial, cf. Dent (?)D329 'The sparing DIET is the spirit's feast'.

20. *fool ... cheeks*] To be 'as fat as fools' was proverbial (Dent F443; cf. *Northward Ho* 1.3.34–5).

21–9. *Now am I prouder ... livery.*] cut for the Tufts performance.

is mine own, than a waiting gentlewoman is of a frizzled groatsworth of hair that never grew on her head. Sirrah Shadow, now we can all three swear like Puritans at one bare word. This want makes us like good bowlers: we are 25 able to rub out and shift in every place.
Shadow. That's not so. We have shifted ourselves in no place this three months. Marry, we rub out in every corner, but here follows no amendment either of life or of livery.
Andelocia. Why, brother Ampedo, art thou not yet tired with 30 riding post? Come, come, light from this logger-headed jade and walk afoot, and talk with your poor friends.
Shadow. Nay, by my troth, he is like me; if his belly be empty, his heart is full.

22–3. *frizzled groatsworth of hair*] The sense is of a balding yet vain gentlewoman who is inordinately proud of her cheap, fashionable wig. Hair or wigs that were frizzled ('consisting of or covered with crisp curls', *OED*) seem to have been in vogue; consider Austin Saker's comment in *Narbonus: The laberynth of libertie* (1580): 'then must his haire bee curled after the cutte, or frizled after the finest fashion', p. 50). A groat was an English silver coin of little value (4d), often used in reference to something disparagingly cheap (Sandra K. Fischer, *Econolingua: A Glossary of Coins and Economic Language in Renaissance Drama* (Newark: University of Delaware Press, 1985), 84). Cf. Hodge's joke at Margery's expense in *Shoemaker's Holiday*, 10.42–55.

23. *Sirrah*] archaic term of address expressing contempt, used attributively with proper nouns.

24. *swear like Puritans*] Puritans generally abstained from swearing oaths; cf. *Every Man In His Humour (Q)*, ed. Bevington, *CWBJ* 3.1.73, where Thorello, puzzled by what he takes to be Piso's refusal to swear, discounts Puritanism as a possible explanation.

26. *rub out and shift*] In the game of bowls, to 'rub out' and 'shift' is to make an effort ('make shift') to ensure the bowl continues on its course without encountering impediments ('rubs') which might divert it. Shadow and Ampedo are dismayed that, despite their best efforts, their course hasn't run smooth.

31. *riding post*] to ride with haste, in the manner of a courier.

31–2. *logger-headed jade*] 'logger-headed' = having a large head (of animals), or meaning thick-headed, stupid when applied to humans. Cf. Nicholas Breton, *Pasquils mad-cap* (1600), 'Who hath not seene a logger-headed Asse, / That hath no more wit than an olde join'd stoole' (p. 5). 'Jade' is used contemptuously of horses (e.g. Tamburlaine's infamous 'Holla, ye pampered jades of Asia' in *2 Tam.* 4.3.1); here it is used figuratively to refer to Ampedo's hunger (which according to Shadow, ll. 2–6, is self-imposed, but cf. Andelocia's retort at ll. 35–6).

33–4. *if his belly ... full*] Cf. ll. 18–19 above.

Andelocia. The famine of gold gnaws his covetous stomach 35
  more than the want of good victuals. Thou hast looked
  very devilishly ever since the good angel left thee. Come,
  come, leave these broad-brim fashions. Because the
  world frowns upon thee, wilt not thou smile upon us?
Ampedo. Did but the bitterness of mine own fortunes 40
  Infect my taste, I could paint o'er my cheeks
  With ruddy-coloured smiles. 'Tis not the want
  Of costly diet or desire of gold
  Enforces this rupture in my wounded breast.
  Oh no, our father (if he live) doth lie 45
  Under the iron foot of misery
  And (as a dove gripped in a falcon's claw)
  There pant'th for life, being most assured of death.
  Brother, for him my soul thus languisheth.
Shadow. 'Tis not for my old master that I languish. 50

---

38. these broad-brim fashions.] *Dilke;* this broad brim fashions, *Q.*   41.
o'er] *Dilke;* ore *Q.*   44. Enforces] *Rhys;* Inforce *Q.*

36–9. *Thou hast looked ... us?*] cut for the Tufts performance.

37. *good angel*] Andelocia alludes to his brother's poverty by punning on the Elizabethan gold coin of that name (see 1.47–8n). Ampedo picks up the image in l. 42 ('ruddy-coloured smiles'), and it is repeated by Andelocia ('ruddy lips of angels') in l. 92. Fischer explains 'ruddy' as an example of 'ruddock', slang for reddish gold coin (*Econolingua*, 41, 117).

38. *broad-brim fashions*] not merely the sign of 'a dejected lover', as Hoy has it; rather, a sign of discontent and melancholy more generally – including as occasioned by poverty, as in Richard Brathwaite's example of the Gamester (gambler) who is down on his luck: 'Suppose him then walking like a second *Malevolo* with a dejected eye, a broad-brim'd hat or'e-pentising his discontented looke, an enwreathed arme like a dispassionate Lover, a weake yingling spurre guiltlesse of gold, with a winter suite, which must of necessitie suite him all Summer' (*Whimzies: or, a new cast of characters* (1631), p. 56). Ampedo's looking 'very devilishly' and the world frowning upon him support this reading.

41. *o'er*] *Q*'s 'ore' may preserve a sense of 'gold' in keeping with the dialogue here.

48. *pant'th*] Dilke emends to 'panteth'; I retain 'pant'th' to assist with scansion.

Ampedo. I am not enamoured of this painted idol,
   This strumpet world, for her most beauteous looks
   Are poisoned baits hung upon golden hooks.
   When fools do swim in wealth, her Cynthian beams
   Will wantonly dance on the silver streams. 55
   But when this squint-eyed age sees virtue poor,
   And by a little spark sits shivering,
   Begging at all, relieved at no man's door,
   She smiles on her (as the sun shines on fire)
   To kill that little heat, and with her frown 60
   Is proud that she can tread poor virtue down.
   Therefore her wrinkled brow makes not mine sour;
   Her gifts are toys and I deride her power.
Shadow. 'Tis not the crab-tree-faced world neither that
   makes mine sour. 65
Andelocia. Her gifts toys? Well, brother virtue, we have let slip
   the ripe plucking of those toys so long that we flourish

51–60. *I am not enamoured ... heat*] In the context of Dekker's biography and time spent in the King's Bench prison, Campbell comments on Dekker's poetry and cites the present passage: 'No wonder poor Dekker could rise a degree above the level of his ordinary genius in describing the blessings of Fortunatus's inexhaustible purse: he had probably felt but too keenly the force of what he expresses in the misanthropy of Ampedo, "I'm not enamour'd of this painted idol"' (*Specimens*, 210).

53. *golden hooks*] Not in *OED*, but Fischer explains it as '[f]rom a fishing analogy, economically something beautiful or enticing that lures a man to seek wealth or entraps him into parting with his money. This could also refer to a prostitute' (*Econolingua*, 81). This latter sense is consonant with Ampedo's 'painted idol' (l. 51) and 'strumpet world' (l. 52).

54–63. *When fools ... her power,*] cut for the Tufts performance.

56. *squint-eyed*] Dekker uses the phrase often, as for example in *Lust's Dominion* 2.3.119. As Ellis notes, 'the depraved condition of the aged Fortunatus seems to parallel a more universal affliction ... . [A]ll of human society resembles an old man whose failing eyesight causes him to lose his way' (*Old Age*, 151). Whereas in the present example, 'squint-eyed' describes 'an aging, corrupt world', in Cho.1, 24 the exact same phrase is used 'to portray the comparably decrepit Fortunatus' (*Old Age*, 154).

64. *crab-tree-faced*] frowning; resembling a crab-tree (wild apple) in being crooked or knotted, e.g. Inigo Jones's prefatory verses to Coryate, *The Odcombian Banquet* (1611): 'when thou drink'st / Thou makst a crab-tree face, shakst head, and winkst' (sig. H4v). The marginal note explains: 'The modesty of the Author being such, & his temperance in drinking, that hee sometimes frowneth when a health is drunke unto him'.

118   THE COMEDY OF OLD FORTUNATUS   [SC. 2

          like apple trees in September, which, having the falling
          sickness, bear neither fruit nor leaves.
Shadow. Nay, by my troth, master; none flourish in these   70
    withering times but ancient bearers and trumpeters.
Andelocia. Shadow, when thou provest a substance, then the
    tree of virtue and honesty and such fruit of heaven shall
    flourish upon earth.
Shadow. True, or when the sun shines at midnight, or women   75
    fly; and yet they are light enough.
Andelocia. 'Twas never merry world with us since purses and
    bags were invented, for now men set lime-twigs to catch
    wealth, and gold, which riseth like the sun out of the East
    Indies to shine upon every one, is like a cony taken   80
    napping in a purse net and suffers his glist'ring yellow-
    faced deity to be lapped up in lambskins, as if the

81–2. yellow-faced] *Dilke;* yellow face *Q.*

68–87. *which ... execution.*] cut for the Tufts performance.

68–9. *falling sickness*] A common name for epilepsy (cf. *Julius Caesar* 1.2.248, where Brutus explains that Caesar 'hath the falling sickness'); here meant more literally as the tree has let fall its fruit and leaves.

70–1. *none flourish ... trumpeters*] with a pun on 'flourish' = thrive and 'flourish' = to sound a fanfare on the trumpet (hence accompanied by an 'ancient bearer', an ensign or one who bears the banner/standard; with an additional pun on 'flourish' and 'bearer' in the sense of child-bearing. As Ellis notes, these lines indicate that 'destitution is not unusual' in this society, and that Fortunatus's family and servant are not unique in their impoverishment (*Old Age*, 152).

76. *they are light enough*] in the context of women, 'light' here connotes being wanton or unchaste (*OED* 14b).

78–9. *lime-twigs to catch wealth*] Twigs smeared with lime (from the Latin for mud or loam; a sticky substance derived from the bark of holly) were used to catch birds. The phrase is applied figuratively here, as in *Sir Thomas Wyatt*, 'Catch Fooles with Lime-twigs dipt with pardons' (4.1.50).

80–1. *like a cony ... purse net*] figuratively speaking, to be caught out like a rabbit or 'cony' (by extension applied to the dupe or victim of the cony-catcher). A purse net was a bag-shaped drawstring net used for rabbit catching or for fishing. This example of 'purse net' antedates the *OED*, which cites Dekker and Webster's *Westward Ho* (1607) as its earliest instantiation of the obsolete figurative sense.

82. *lambskins*] Cf. 1.343n above.

innocency of those leather prisons should dispense with
the cheverel consciences of the iron-hearted jailers.

Shadow. Snudges may well be called jailers: for if a poor   85
wretch steal but into a debt of ten pound, they lead him
straight to execution.

Andelocia. Doth it not vex thee, Shadow, to stalk up and
down Cyprus and to meet the outside of a man, lapped
all in damask, his head and beard as white as milk, only   90
with conjuring in the snowy circles of the field argent,
and his nose as red as scarlet, only with kissing the ruddy
lips of angels, and such an image to wear on his thumb,
three men's livings in the shape of a seal ring, whilst my
brother virtue here –   95

Shadow. And you his brother vice.

Andelocia. Most true, my little lean iniquity; whilst we three,
if we should starve, cannot borrow five shillings of him
neither in word nor deed? Does not this vex thee, Shadow?

---

84. *cheverel consciences*] cheverel- or kid-leather was extremely pliable; the term appeared in conjunction with 'conscience' in proverbial use, for example in Lyly's anti-Martinist tract *Pap with a Hatchet* (1589): 'if they make their consciences stretch like chiverell in the raine' (sig. D2r). Cf. Dent C608*.

85. *Snudges*] misers; cf. Dekker's *Seven Deadly Sins* (1606), '*those snudges & miserable cormorants that now feede upon thee*' (sig. Gv). See also 5.375 below, 'that snudge, his destiny', cited by *OED* as an example of the transferred sense of the noun.

85–7. *if ... execution*] the pun is on 'execution' = death, but the literal meaning is the execution (enforcement) of a writ against a debtor (Fischer, *Econolingua*, 74). Ellis suggests instead that Shadow's lines reflect 'an anxious reality [of the 1590s] – that judicial sentences had stiffened with the decade's rise in English crime rates' (*Old Age*, 153). A more personal concern may also register in these lines: Shirley suggests that Dekker was 'strongly aware of the debtor's plight' (*Serious and Tragic Elements*, 47), noting that on 30 January 1599 (months before writing *Fortunatus*) Henslowe lent Dekker £3 10s to discharge him from arrest by the Lord Chamberlain's Men (Foakes, 104).

88–94. *Doth it not ... ring*] As Ellis notes, shortly hereafter 'Fortunatus and Andelocia become unremitting spendthrifts, images of the very greed they once abhorred in the upper class', as in this passage (*Old Age*, 154).

89–90. *lapped all in damask*] wrapped up (*OED*, citing no examples) in rich silken cloth owing its name to Damascus, where it was originally produced.

90–3. *his head ... angels*] cut for the Tufts performance.

91. *field argent*] from heraldry, referring to the background of the shield being silver.

Shadow. Not me. It vexes me no more to see such a picture than to see an ass laden with riches, because I know when he can bear no longer, he must leave his burden to some other beast.

Andelocia. Art not thou mad, to see money on goldsmiths' stalls and none in our purses?

Shadow. It mads not me, I thank the Destinies.

Andelocia. By my poverty (and that's but a threadbare oath), I am more than mad to see silks and velvets lie crowding together in mercers' shops, as in prisons, only for fear of the smell of wax (they cannot abide to see a man made out of wax). For these satin commodities have such smooth consciences that they'll have no man give his word for them or stand bound for their coming forth, but vow to lie till they rot in those shop counters, except Monsieur Money bail them. Shadow, I am out of my little wits to see this.

Shadow. So is not Shadow. I am out of my wits to see fat gluttons feed all day long, whilst I that am lean fast every day. I am out of my wits to see our Famagusta fools turn half a shop of wares into a suit of gay apparel, only to

---

100–3. *It vexes me ... beast.*] cut for the Tufts performance. Shadow's meaning is simply that an ass with riches must eventually die and part with its gold. Hoy compares with Tilley A352 and A360, but the point of each of those proverbs is that an ass is still an ass even if it carries gold (cf. ll. 163–5 below), hence neither proverb quite captures the sense of Dekker's lines. Dilke finds an echo of these lines in Shakespeare's *Measure for Measure*: 'If thou art rich, thou'rt poor, / For like an ass whose back with ingots bows, / Thou bear'st thy heavy riches but a journey, / And death unloads thee' (3.1.24–7).

107–30. *By my poverty ... mad.*] cut for the Tufts performance.

108–15. *to see silks ... Monsieur Money bail them*] Andelocia laments being unable to buy the mercer's rich wares, the purchase of which requires cash ('Monsieur Money'). In his poverty, his only option for payment would be bonds, which usually consist of parchment and 'wax', and which the mercer will not accept ('they'll have no man give his word for them').

110–11. *a man made out of wax*] Hoy notes the unclear origin of this expression in the *OED* and suggests that, rather than meaning 'as faultless as if modelled in wax', an instructive comparison can be made with *Seven Deadly Sins*: 'is now a new man made out of wax, thats to say, out of those bonds, whose seales he most dishonestly hath canceld' (p. 6).

119. *Famagusta*] a port city on the east coast of Cyprus, home to Fortunatus and his sons.

SC. 2]   THE COMEDY OF OLD FORTUNATUS   121

    make other idiots laugh and wise men to cry, 'Who's the
    fool now?'. I am mad to see soldiers beg and cowards
    brave. I am mad to see scholars in the broker's shop and
    dunces in the mercer's. I am mad to see men that have
    no more fashion in them than poor Shadow, yet must   125
    leap thrice a day into three orders of fashions. I am mad
    to see many things, but horn-mad that my mouth feels
    nothing.
Andelocia. Why, now Shadow, I see thou hast a substance! I
    am glad to see thee thus mad.   130
Ampedo. [*Aside*] The sons of Fortunatus had not wont
    Thus to repine at others' happiness.
    But fools have always this loose garment wore:
    Being poor themselves, they wish all others poor.
    [*To* ANDELOCIA] Fie, brother Andelocia, hate this
        madness.   135
    Turn your eyes inward and behold your soul,
    That wants more than your body. Burnish that
    With glittering virtue and make idiots grieve
    To see your beauteous mind in wisdom shine,
    As you at their rich poverty repine.   140

            Enter FORTUNATUS *gallant.*

---

129. now Shadow] *Dilke;* now shadow *Q.*

    121–2. *'Who's the fool now?'*] proverbial, Dent F513.11; Hoy attributes this line specifically to the ballad, 'Martyn said to his man, whoe is the foole nowe', entered in the Stationers' Register on 9 November 1588. The ballad was frequently reprinted, especially by Thomas Ravenscroft, e.g. song 16 in his *Deuteromelia* (London, 1609), sig. D?r, where it is set to music. Duffin suggests that Shadow's line may have been sung, and delivered to that melody (Duffin, *Some Other Note,* 303).
    125–6. *must leap ... fashions*] Perhaps in the vein of the smartly dressed courtier Fastidious Brisk or his apish imitator Fungoso in Jonson's *Every Man Out of His Humour* (1599, printed 1600).
    127. *horn-mad*] enraged like a horned animal, a bull.
    140.1. *gallant*] i.e. gallantly attired. This early transformation from being 'meanly attired' (0.1 SD) may well explain the Stationers' Register entry for Dekker's play as 'A commedie called old Fortunatus in his newe lyuerie' (*SR* 3.156). If so, it would largely dispel the notion, advanced by Chambers (3.291), that Dekker was merely dressing-up the older 'Fortunatus, part 1' play recorded by Henslowe. See Introduction, 5.

Andelocia. Peace, good virtue. Shadow, here comes another shadow.
Shadow. It should be a chameleon, for he is all in colours.
Ampedo. Oh, 'tis my father! With these tears of joy,
My love and duty greet your fair return.   145
A double gladness hath refreshed my soul;
One, that you live, and one, to see your fate
Looks freshly, howsoever poor in state.
Andelocia. My father Fortunatus, and thus brave?
Shadow. 'Tis no wonder to see a man brave, but a wonder   150
how he comes brave.
Fortunatus. Dear Andelocia and son Ampedo,
And my poor servant Shadow: plume your spirits
With light-winged mirth, for Fortunatus' hand
Can now pour golden showers into their laps   155
That sometimes scorned him for his want of gold.
Boys, I am rich, and you shall ne'er be poor!
Wear gold, spend gold, we all in gold will feed.
Now is your father fortunate indeed.
Andelocia. Father, be not angry if I set open the windows of   160
my mind. I doubt for all your bragging you'll prove like
most of our gallants in Famagusta that have a rich outside
and a beggarly inside, and, like mules, wear gay trappings
and good velvet foot-cloths on their backs, yet champ on
the iron bit of penury (I mean, want coin). You gild our   165
ears with a talk of gold, but I pray dazzle our eyes with
the majesty of it.

141–2. another shadow.] *Dilke;* another Shadow *Q.*   165. gild] *Q;* glad *Dilke.*

---

143. *chameleon*] The chameleon's ability to change the colour of its skin is one of its distinguishing features.

149. *brave*] finely dressed (*OED*).

155. *pour golden showers into their laps*] According to Apollodorus, when Perseus locked his daughter Danaë in a bronze chamber (following a prediction that her son would kill him), Zeus visited her by disguising himself as a golden shower of coins which poured into her lap and impregnated her (*OCD*; see also Arachne's tapestry in Ovid, *Met.* 6.113–14). On the mobility of gold (physical and social) and the 'liquid copulation myth', see Lowell Duckert, 'It Grows as It Goes: Becoming Gold-Apple in Mandeville, Dekker ... Beyond', *Prefix* 1.1 (2010), 4–5.

164. *foot-cloths*] richly ornamented clothes covering a horse's back and hanging down to the ground; a marker of status (*OED*).

165. *gild*] Dilke emends to 'glad', but to gild with (talk of) gold makes perfect sense.

SC. 2]   THE COMEDY OF OLD FORTUNATUS   123

Fortunatus. First will I wake your senses with the sound
    Of gold's sweet music. Tell me what you hear.
                                             [*Shakes purse.*]
Ampedo. Believe me, sir, I hear not anything.   170
Andelocia. Ha, ha, ha. S'heart, I thought as much. If I hear
    any jingling, but of the purse strings that go flip, flap, flip,
    flap, flip, flap, would I were turned into a flip-flap and
    sold to the butchers.
Fortunatus. Shadow, I'll try thine ears. Hark, does't rattle?   175
                                        [*Shakes purse again.*]
Shadow. Yes, like three blue beans in a blue bladder: rattle,
    bladder, rattle. Your purse is like my belly; th' one's
    without money, th' other without meat.
Fortunatus. Bid your eyes blame the error of your ears,
    You misbelieving pagans. See, here's gold.   180
    Ten golden pieces. Take them, Ampedo.
    Hold, Andelocia, here are ten for thee.
Ampedo. Shadow, there's one for thee; provide thee food.
Fortunatus. Stay, boy, hold. Shadow, here are ten for thee.
Shadow. Ten, master? Then defiance to fortune and a fig for   185
    famine!

---

173. flip-flap] *Q;* flie-flap *Daniel.*

---

169. *gold's sweet music*] Cf. 1.338n above. The Covent Garden text explicitly directs Fortunatus to shake his purse here (p. 17).
  172. *purse strings*] strings drawing a purse closed (*OED*, citing this example).
  173. *a flip-flap*] literally, something that goes 'flip-flap', e.g. a fan or strip of cloth, often as a deterrent against flies (*OED*, citing this example). Daniel's suggestion 'flie-flap' (i.e. 'fly-flap') does not differ substantively in meaning but loses the playful engagement with the preceding lines' 'flip, flap'.
  176–7. *three blue beans ... rattle*] proverbial (Dent B124) and a tongue-twister, referring to a rattle made from a bladder (*OED*). Cf. Zantippa's line in Peele's *Old Wives Tale* (1595), 'Three blue beans in a blue bladder – rattle, bladder, rattle!' (ed. Binnie, ll. 686–7). Hoy compares with the Alleyn manuscript of Greene's *Orlando Furioso*, 'let him put his arme into my bagg thus deep: yf he will eate, go ... he shall have it. thre blew beans ... a blewe bladder; rattle, bladder rattler'.
  185–6. *a fig for famine*] an expression of contempt, where 'fig' = anything small or valueless (*OED*). The Covent Garden production exemplified Shadow's newfound ability to satisfy his appetite by having him yearn 'for a hot dish of stewed trotter now' and offer 'golden sauce' to 'a man with a hot smoking cover, or chafing-fire' who crosses the stage apparently selling precisely such dishes. Shadow runs after the vendor, only to return fifteen lines later 'with a bowl and spoon, eating voraciously' (18–20). The bowl is retained for his next entrances also.

Fortunatus. Now tell me, wags: hath my purse gold or no?
Andelocia. We the wags have gold, father; but I think there's
not one angel more wagging in this sacred temple. Why,
this is rare. Shadow, five will serve thy turn. Give me th'   190
other five.
Shadow. Nay, soft, master; liberality died long ago. I see some
rich beggars are never well but when they be craving. My
ten ducats are like my ten fingers; they will not jeopard
a joint for you. I am yours and these are mine; if I part   195
from them, I shall never have part of them.
Ampedo. Father, if heaven have blessed you once again,
Let not an open hand disperse that store,
Which gone, life's gone: for all tread down the poor.
Fortunatus. Peace, Ampedo, talk not of poverty.   200
Disdain, my boys, to kiss the tawny cheeks
Of lean necessity. Make not inquiry
How I came rich: I am rich, let that suffice.
There are four leathern bags trussed full of gold;
Those spent, I'll fill you more. Go lads, be gallant.   205
Shine in the streets of Cyprus like two stars
And make them bow their knees that once did spurn you,
For to effect such wonders gold can turn you.

190. Shadow] *Dilke;* Saddow *Q.*

---

187. *wags*] mischievous boys (*OED*); e.g. in Jonson's *Poetaster* (1601), where Crispinus describes Venus's son Cupid as the 'wag' (*CWBJ* 4.3.67).

189. *sacred temple*] The figurative use of 'temple' for 'purse' is noted by Fischer (*Econolingua*, 127) but not the *OED*.

190. *rare*] splendid, uncommonly good. Cf. 3.94.

194. *ten ducats*] if meant literally, not a sizeable amount; as Fischer notes, in drama 'a single ducat or three odd ducats is a small, trifling sum; forty ducats can buy enough poison for suicide or a beautiful ring; one thousand ducats is a substantial fee; two thousand ducats is the price of a diamond or, per annum, a good marriage settlement' (*Econolingua*, 69). However, 'ducat' could also refer generically to any coin, and Fortunatus's specification of 'golden pieces' at l. 181, plus Andelocia's reference to an 'angel' in l. 189 suggests that a substantial, rather than a trifling, sum is implied here. A gold ducat (9s) was worth about the same as an angel (10s).

194. *jeopard*] The alliterative phrase 'jeopard a joint' means to put a section of a finger (rather than the whole body) in jeopardy (*OED*, citing this example).

206–8. *Shine ... turn you*] As Duckert notes, 'gold has the power to transform social status' as well as enable travel, and Fortunatus's advice here 'smacks of class revenge' (5).

SC. 2] THE COMEDY OF OLD FORTUNATUS 125

    Brave it in Famagusta, or elsewhere.
    I'll travel to the Turkish emperor, 210
    And then I'll revel it with Prester John
    Or banquet with great Cham of Tartary,
    And try what frolic court the Sultan keeps.
    I'll leave you presently. Tear off these rags.
    Glitter, my boys, like angels, that the world 215
    May (whilst our life in pleasure's circle runs)
    Wonder at Fortunatus and his sons.
Andelocia. Come, Shadow, now we'll feast it royally.
Shadow. Do, master, but take heed of beggary.   *Exeunt.*

---

216. runs] *Dilke;* ronnes *Bowers;* roams *Rhys;* romes *Q.*

210–13. *I'll travel ... Sultan keeps*] In the 'Epistle Dedicatory' of *News from Grave's End* (1604), Dekker maps a virtually identical journey when he engages in fanciful mind-travelling via the universal maps of Mercator and Plancius, imagining himself travelling 'to the great Turkes *Serraglio*' to visit '*Prester Iohn*, and the *Sophy*' and the 'Soldan of Egipt' (sig. A3v) (see *N&Q* 62.4 (2015), 554). Fortunatus, initially by virtue of the possibilities his new-found wealth affords, then subsequently by the magical properties of the wishing-cap, is able to physically enact these fantasies of transportation to exotic climes.

    211. *Prester John*] legendary Christian king, variously said to rule in Asia (where his kingdom was ultimately overrun by Genghis Khan) or in Africa (as in Mercator's 1595 map, which depicts Prester John in Ethiopia).

    212. *great Cham of Tartary*] probably Genghis Khan. In *The Generall Historie of the Turkes* (1603), Knolles writes: 'the Tartars ... stirred up by their owne wants, and the persuasion of one Zingis (or as some call him, Cangis) holden amongst them for a great prophet, and now by them made their leader, and honoured with the name of Vlu-Chan, that is to say, the Mightie king (commonly called the great Cham)' (p. 75). On the London stage, the Strange's Men produced a pair of 'Tamar Cham' plays, with Part 2 being performed on 28 April 1592 (marked 'ne' by Henslowe). The plays were acquired by the Admiral's Men by 1596, when Part 1 was revived on 6 May and Part 2 on 11 June. The Admiral's Men subsequently bought the book of the plays from Alleyn in 1602, and, although the plot for a revival of Part 1 survived just long enough to be transcribed by Steevens and printed in 1803, the plays themselves are lost. The name Velruus (or Velraus) for the Great Cham was also used in the manuscript fragment of *A stately tragedy containing the ambitious life and death of the great Cham ... ca.* 1590 (Folger MS. X.d.259).

126 THE COMEDY OF OLD FORTUNATUS [SC. 3

[Scene 3]

Music sounds.

Enter VICE *with a gilded face and horns on her head, her garments long, painted before with silver half-moons, increasing by little and little till they come to the full. In the midst of them in capital letters, this written:* Crescit Eundo. *Her garment painted behind with fools' faces and devils' heads and underneath in the midst this written:* Ha, Ha, He. *She and*

0.1.] Smeaton adds the setting: '*A Forest in Cyprus*'. The Virtue–Vice scene here helps establish the lapsing of time between when Fortunatus appears previously in scene 2 and where he is seen next (in scene 4, after the Chorus summarizes his far-flung travels) (James H. Conover, *Thomas Dekker: An Analysis of Dramatic Structure* (The Hague: Mouton, 1969), 70).

0.1. Music sounds] Ketterer notes that 'musical performance works almost like an annunciatory signal: it marks the entry of the superhuman figures into an imaginative space' (228), and observes that the appearance of the allegorical figures is accompanied by music throughout the play (cf. the singing accompanying the procession at 1.68.6 above). The Tufts production called for 'Dance, from an entertainment given to the King by the Earl of Cumberland. Printed in 1618' at this point. See George Mason, *The ayres that were sung and played, at Brougham Castle in Westmerland, in the Kings entertainment* (London, 1618), STC (2nd ed.) / 17601.

0.2. VICE] Hoy compares Vice's garments to Pliny's description of the skin of panthers (with moonlike shapes waxing and waning), but surely the significance of the symbolism lies elsewhere. The association between the moon/stars and fate was commonplace (e.g. 'The star-crossed son of Fortunatus' below, Cho.2, 6; or Shakespeare's 'star-crossed lovers', *R&J* 1.6), and Vice's role is to influence decision making by offering temptation (see 0.13–14n below). The moon's horns are also apposite in that, like the 'horns on her head', they connote both devilry (cf. the '*devils' heads*' on the back of her garment) and the punishment for foolishness (see the note for 93 SD below).

0.5. *Crescit Eundo*] 'increasing as it goes', like the half-moons surrounding it on Vice's garments. The phrase is derived from Virgil's depiction of the Fame monster (Rumour) in *Aeneid* 4, 'Fama crescit eundo'. Dekker invokes the phrase again in the context of 'Lying' and the spreading of untruths in *The Seven Deadly Sins* (1606): 'for though a Lye have but short legs (like a Dwarfes) yet it goes farre in a little time, *Et crescit eundo*, and at last prooues a tall fellow' (14). Duckert suggests an alternative source: Lucretius's *De Rerum Natura*, Book 6, where the phrase is applied to a thunderbolt's progress across the sky, or 'matter in constant movement': 'For a playwright interested in gold's mobility and its liquid effects, "growing and going" is a powerful expression for the mobilized golden apples as well' (Duckert, 12–13).

others wearing gilded vizards and attired like devils bring out a fair tree of gold with apples on it. After her comes VIRTUE, *a coxcomb on her head, all in white before and this written about the middle:* Sibi sapit. *Her attire behind painted with crowns and laurel garlands, stuck full of stars held out by hands thrust out of bright clouds and among them thus written:* Dominabitur astris. *She and other nymphs all in white, with coxcombs on their heads, bring a tree with green and withered leaves mingled*

0.8. vizards] masks (*OED*, citing this example).

0.9–15. fair tree ... withered leaves] Perhaps recalling the fourth pageant of the Royal Entry of Queen Elizabeth I into London on the day before her coronation (1559; STC 7590), which featured two male youths offering allegorical choices: Ruinosa Respublica (signifying a decayed commonweal) attended a 'withered and deadde' tree on a 'cragged, barreyn, and stonye' hill, whilst Respublica Bene Instituta (signifying a flourishing commonweal) attended a 'very freshe and fayre' tree on a 'fayre, freshe, grene, and beautifull' hill (sigs C3v–C4r).

0.9. tree of gold with apples] Henslowe's inventory of stage properties, dated 10 March 1598, includes 'j tree of gowlden apelles' (Foakes, 320), but this property is more likely to have belonged to the lost two-part 'Hercules' plays (Admiral's Men, 1595) than to the lost '1 Fortunatus' play; see *N&Q* 58.2 (2011), 270–2. Henslowe's is a tree with golden apples, not a golden tree with apples (which is what Vice brings on stage); but note that, when Agrippine and Andelocia encounter Vice's tree, it does have 'apples like gold' (7.74).

0.10. coxcomb] a fool's cap, cf. 'motley-scorn', l. 51 below, and 'I set an idiot's cap on virtue's head', 1.125 above.

0.11. *Sibi sapit*] 'she is wise for herself'; variations on this were commonplace, e.g. 'he is not wise that is not wise for himself' (Dent W532*). Cf. George Wapull, *The Tide Tarrieth No Man* (1576), '*Ne quisque sapit, qui sibi non sapit*, / This saying I redde, when as I went to schoole, / One not wise for himselfe, is but a very foole' (sig. B1). See also l. 59 below.

0.13–14. *Dominabitur astris*] Virtue's aspirational motto alludes to the wise man's ability to defy Fortune and control his fate (dominate the stars), as Bartholomeu Filippe explains: 'it is commonlie said, *Uir sapiens dominabitur astris*, Every wise man may commaund the starres, and beare rule over them. For though the starres and Planets encline to one thing or other, yet can they not force men to it that be wise and circumspect, and of judgement howe to governe themselves. No inclination of starre or Planet; can force such men to doo that which they will not, nor take away from them & deprive them of the free-will that God hath given them' (*The counseller a treatise of counsels and counsellers of princes* (1589), fol. 50). The phrase and concept seem to have been a favourite of Robert Greene's; see his *Planetomachia* (1585), sig. G2r, his *Euphues his censure to Philautus* (1587), sig. F2v, and his *Greenes mourning garment* (1590), p. 40.

together and little fruit on it. After her FORTUNE, *one* [*nymph*]
bearing her wheel, another her globe; and last, the PRIEST.

Fortune. You ministers of Virtue, Vice, and Fortune:
    Tear off this upper garment of the earth
    And in her naked bosom stick these trees.
Virtue. How many kingdoms have I measured,
    Only to find a climate apt to cherish   5
    These withering branches? But no ground can prove
    So happy. Ay me, none do Virtue love.
    I'll try this soil; if here I likewise fade,
    To heaven I'll fly, from whence I took my birth,
    And tell the gods I am banished from the earth.   10
Vice. Virtue, I am sworn thy foe: if there thou plant,
    Here opposite to thine my tree shall flourish
    And (as the running woodbine) spread her arms
    To choke thy withering boughs in their embrace.
    I'll drive thee from this world: were Virtue fled,   15
    Vice as an angel should be honourèd.

---

13. woodbine] *Dilke;* wood-bind *Q.*

---

3. *bosom stick*] used in a comparable sense in the passage attributed to Dekker by Robert Allott in *Englands Parnassus*, under the heading 'Grove' (cf. l. 42's 'grove', below), where the Earth is referred to as 'the lap of that greene meade, / Whose bosome stucke with purple Violets' (p. 478).

8–10. *if here ... the earth*] Astraea (Justice) was the last immortal to leave the Earth during the Iron Age (Ovid, *Met.* 1; see Prologue at Court 4n above); Virtue here anticipates a similar need to depart the debauched earthly world.

13. *running woodbine*] As a kind of climbing plant, the woodbine (like the honeysuckle, or ivy) is frequently used as a poetic device for a lover's embrace (cf. *Midsummer Night's Dream* 5.498) or, as in the current use, a kind of suffocating strangulation of the host plant by the parasite. The phrase 'yoong Musk-rose trees, / About whose waste the amorous woodbine twines, / Whilst they seeme maidens in a lovers armes', also appears in the passage attributed to Dekker by Robert Allott in *Englands Parnassus* under the heading 'Grove' (cf. 3n above).

SC. 3]   THE COMEDY OF OLD FORTUNATUS   129

Fortune. Servants of this bright devil and that poor saint,
  Apply your task. Whilst you are labouring,
  To make your pains seem short, our priest shall sing.

The Song.

Whilst he sings, the rest set the trees into the earth.

Priest. Virtue's branches wither, Virtue pines,   20
  Oh, pity, pity and alack the time.
  Vice doth flourish, Vice in glory shines,
  Her gilded boughs above the cedar climb.
  Vice hath golden cheeks. Oh, pity, pity.
  She in every land doth monarchize.   25
  Virtue is exiled from every city,
  Virtue is a fool, Vice only wise.
  Oh, pity, pity. Virtue weeping dies.
  Vice laughs to see her faint (alack the time).

---

18. task. Whilst ... labouring,] *this ed.;* taske ... labouring: *Q.*

---

18. *Apply*] to ply, practise, or perform one's task; cf. Dekker's *Shoemaker's Holiday*, 'Ply your business, Hodge' (10.143).

18–19. *Whilst ... sing*] Another instance (cf. the introduction of Fortune's chair above at 1.68.7) of the 'use of music to accomplish demanding staging practices' (Ketterer, 229); here to cover the planting of the trees. See also the removal of Fortunatus's body by satyrs at 5.349 SD below.

19.1. *The Song*] Regarding the tune for these lyrics, Duffin notes that '[p]entameters are rare in popular music' and that 'among a handful of eight-line pentameters, the best match seems to be *I am a lover* from [Alfonso] Ferrabosco's 1609 *Ayres*' (see Duffin, *Some Other Note*, 301). The Tufts production called for 'Partly an old ballad, "Titus Andronicus," and partly a song of Robert Jones, "My love bound me," published in 1601'. Numerous ballads about Titus Andronicus have survived from the seventeenth century; for the Robert Jones song, see his *The second booke of songs and ayres* (1601), STC (2nd ed.) / 14733.

19.2.] The 'he' is the priest mentioned in l. 19. Dessen and Thomson (82) note that 'earth' is a rarely used term for the main platform, and suggest the use of the trapdoor for the setting of these trees in the earth.

23. *cedar*] The cedar was proverbially straight/tall (Dent (?)C207*), though also thus precarious: 'High Cedars fall, when lowe shrubs safe remaine' (*Patient Grissil*, 2.2.122). Cf. 5.247 below.

25. *monarchize*] Obs. to predominate or be pre-eminent; to have power, hold sway (i.e. Vice rules absolutely). (*OED* cites this as its first example of the intransitive extended use). Cf. *Richard II*: 'Allowing him a breath, a little scene, / To monarchize, be feared, and kill with looks' (3.2.160–1).

            This sinks; with painted wings the other flies,   30
            Alack that best should fall and bad should climb.
            Oh, pity, pity, pity. Mourn, not sing;
            Vice is a saint, Virtue an underling.
            Vice doth flourish, Vice in glory shines,
            Virtue's branches wither, Virtue pines.   35
Fortune. Flourish or wither, Fortune cares not which.
            In either's fall or height, our eminence
            Shines equal to the sun. The queen of chance
            Both virtuous souls and vicious doth advance.
            These shadows of your selves shall (like yourselves)   40
            Strive to make men enamoured of their beauties.
            This grove shall be our temple and henceforth
            Be consecrated to our deities.
Virtue. How few will come and kneel at Virtue's shrine?
Vice. This contents Virtue, that she is called divine.   45
Fortune. Poor Virtue. Fortune grieves to see thy looks
            Want cunning to entice. Why hang these leaves
            As loose as Autumn's hair, which every wind
            In mockery blows from his rotten brows?
            Why, like a drunkard, art thou pointed at?   50
            Why is this motley-scorn set on thy head?
            Why stands thy court wide open, but none in it?
            Why are the crystal pavements of thy temple

---

49. from his] *Q; from off his* Deighton.

---

44. *How few ... Virtue's shrine*] Virtue recognizes that she has few followers left on Earth. Bowers queries whether the speech prefixes of ll. 44 and 45 have been transposed but retains *Q*'s reading and assumes Vice is offering 'sarcastic commentary on line 44'.

47–9. *Why hang ... rotten brows*] Fortune, appropriately, evokes a cyclical metaphor (the seasons) to describe Virtue's fallen state, but it is a singularly circular metaphor: the withered leaves on Virtue's tree (the tenor) hang as loosely as personified Autumn's loose hair (the vehicle) – but this vehicle is itself an image of loose autumnal leaves, and thus the original tenor. Hoy compares these lines with the following passage from Dekker's *The Dead Term* (1608): 'The unwholesome breath of Autumne, who is so full of diseases, that his very blowing uppon trees, makes theyr leavs to fal off' (sig. Cr). Kenneth Deighton's conjectural emendation to l. 49 ('from *off* his') is extra-metrical and unnecessary.

51. *motley-scorn*] *OED* has 'n. Obs. rare = cock's-comb', citing this as its only example. Cf. SD 0.9–10 above.

SC. 3]   THE COMEDY OF OLD FORTUNATUS   131

    Not worn, not trod upon? All is for this:
    Because thy pride is to wear base attire,   55
    Because thine eyes flame not with amorous fire.
Virtue. Virtue is fairest in a poor array.
Fortune. Poor fool, 'tis not this badge of purity,
    Nor *sibi sapit* (painted on thy breast),
    Allures mortality to seek thy love.   60
    No: now the great wheel of thy globe hath run
    And met his first point of creation.
    On crutches went this world but yesterday;
    Now it lies bed-rid and is grown so old
    That it's grown young, for 'tis a child again.   65
    A childish soul it hath; 'tis a mere fool,
    And fools and children are well pleased with toys.
    So must this world: with shows it must be pleased.
    Then Virtue, buy a golden face like Vice
    And hang thy bosom full of silver moons   70
    To tell the credulous world as those increase,
    As the bright moon swells in her pearlèd sphere,
    So wealth and pleasures them to heaven shall rear.
Virtue. Virtue abhors to wear a borrowed face.
Vice. Why hast thou borrowed then that idiot's hood?   75
Virtue. Fools placed it on my head that knew me not,
    And I am proud to wear the scorn of fools.
Fortune. Mourn in that pride and die. All the world hates
    thee.
Virtue. Not all. I'll wander once more through the world.
    Wisdom, I know, hath with her blessèd wings   80
    Fled to some bosom. If I meet that breast,
    There I'll erect my temple and there rest.

---

57. *Virtue ... array*] misquoted as 'Vertue is fayrest in a poore art aye' and attributed to Dekker by Allott in *Englands Parnassus* under 'Virtue' (p. 290).
61–8. *No ... pleased.*] cut for the Tufts performance.
63–6. *On crutches ... fool*] Ellis notes that 'this vision of time adopts an image of senescence, of the earth as a rapidly aging human body' (*Old Age*, 151); in other words, another image of the world as macrocosm corresponding to Fortunatus's aged body as microcosm.
66. *mere*] pure, absolute.
74. *Virtue abhors ... borrowed face*] Noted by Allott in *Englands Parnassus* under 'Virtue' (p. 290).
75. *idiot's hood*] obs. term for a fool's cap (*OED* first instance).

132   THE COMEDY OF OLD FORTUNATUS   [SC. 3

    Fortune nor Vice shall then e'er have the power
    By their loose eyes to entice my paramour.
    Then will I cast off this deformity   85
    And shine in glory and triumph to see
    You conquered at my feet, that tread on me.
Fortune. Virtue begins to quarrel. Vice, farewell.
Vice. Stay, Fortune, whilst within this grove we dwell.
    If my angelical and saint-like form   90
    Can win some amorous fool to wanton here
    And taste the fruit of this alluring tree,
    Thus shall his saucy brows adornèd be,   *Makes horns.*
    To make us laugh.
Fortune.   It will be rare. Adieu.
Virtue. Foul hell-bred fiend, Virtue shall strive with you.   95
    If any be enamoured of thine eyes,
    Their love must needs beget deformities.
    Men are transformed to beasts, feasting with sin;

    83–4. *Fortune ... paramour.*] cut for the Tufts performance.
    85. *deformity*] the fool's cap (coxcomb).
    93. SD.] Horns are conventionally the sign of a cuckold (a man with an unfaithful wife) because they represent something that everyone but the deceived husband can see. Here, in a less sexualized sense, Vice plans to mark her victim for public ridicule; the fate that ultimately befalls Andelocia, Agrippine, Montrose, and Longueville when they eat her apples.
    93. *saucy brows*] The adjective 'saucy' here refers not to insolence but to 'saucefleme', a swelling or inflammation of the face said to result in redness, which in turn suggests blushing or the embarrassment of the 'amorous fool' seduced by Vice. This swelling leads on to Vice's suggestion of horns sprouting from the fool's head.
    94. *rare*] splendid, uncommonly good.
    95. *strive*] quarrel, fight with.
    96–7. *If any ... beget deformities*] In a chapter 'Of monsters which take their cause and shape by imagination' in his *Des Monstres et prodiges* (1573), Ambroise Paré describes the aetiology of monsters and monstrous births, noting that the ancients 'soon perswaded themselves that the faculty which formeth the infant may be led and governed by the firme and strong cogitation of the Parents begetting them (often deluded by nocturnall and deceitfull apparitions) or by the mother conceiving them, and so that which is strongly conceived in the mind, imprints the force into the infant conceived in the wombe' (*The workes of that famous chirurgion Ambrose Parey* (1634), 978).
    98. *Men are transformed ... sin*] Probably an allusion to Circe, the witch who changes men to wild beasts (*Odyssey* 10) or, more particularly, to swine (*Aeneid* 7).

But if, in spite of thee, their souls I win
To taste this fruit, though thou disguise their head, 100
Their shapes shall be re-metamorphosèd.
Vice. I dare thee do thy worst.
Virtue. My best I'll try.
Fortune. Fortune shall judge who wins the sovereignty.
                                                    Exeunt.

[Chorus 1]

                    Enter CHORUS.

Chorus. The world to the circumference of heaven
    Is as a small point in geometry,
    Whose greatness is so little that a less
    Cannot be made. Into that narrow room
    Your quick imaginations we must charm   5
    To turn that world, and turned again to part it
    Into large kingdoms, and within one moment
    To carry Fortunatus on the wings
    Of active thought many a thousand miles.
    Suppose, then, since you last beheld him here 10
    That you have sailed with him upon the seas
    And leapt with him upon the Asian shores,

99–101. *But if ... re-metamorphosèd*] The restorative property of Virtue's apples becomes important in scene 9, when Andelocia disguises himself as a French doctor and cures Montrose and Longueville whilst trying to retrieve the wishing-cap from King Athelstan's court.

1–9. *The world ... thousand miles*] An example of what Henry S. Turner refers to as 'the mimetic capacity shared between stage and practical geometry'. Dekker asserts 'a fundamental congruence between stage and map' and proposes 'geometrical projection as a kind of poetic projection that is somehow necessary to stage performance' (*The English Renaissance Stage: Geometry, Poetics, and the Practical Spatial Arts, 1580–1630* (Oxford: Oxford University Press, 2006, rpt 2010), 195, 6). The 1620 German play, which seems to correspond to Dekker's earlier draft (prior to alterations for the performance at court), does not have such choric moments.

1–4. *The world ... made*] noted by Allott in *Englands Parnassus* under 'World' (p. 319).

5. *quick imaginations*] lively imaginations (the wings of *active* thought below, l. 9). See McInnis, *Mind-Travelling*, 38–50.

>   Been feasted with him in the Tartar's palace
>   And all the courts of each Barbarian king.
>   From whence (being called by some unlucky star,   15
>   For happiness never continues long),
>   Help me to bring him back to Aragon,
>   Where for his pride (riches make all men proud),
>   On slight quarrel, by a covetous earl
>   Fortune's dear minion is imprisoned.   20
>   There think you see him sit with folded arms,
>   Tears dropping down his cheeks, his white hairs torn,
>   His legs in rusty fetters and his tongue
>   Bitterly cursing that his squint-eyed soul
>   Did not make choice of wisdom's sacred lore.   25
>   Fortune (to triumph in unconstancy)
>   From prison bails him. Liberty is wild,
>   For being set free, he like a lusty eagle
>   Cuts with his vent'rous feathers through the sky
>   And lights not till he find the Turkish court.   30

14. king] *Capell;* kings *Q.*   25. lore] *Capell;* loue, *Q.*

---

13. *Tartar's palace*] as predicted in 2.212 above.

17. *Aragon*] It is not clear why the Chorus brings Fortunatus *back* to Aragon; none of the action thus far in the present play has taken place there. Presumably the Chorus here summarizes events (like the episode in Cho.2 and scene 7 when Andelocia has apparently disguised himself as a jeweller) that were cut from Dekker's earlier draft to make room for an enlarged supernatural plot for the performance at court.

19. *covetous earl*] In the *Volksbuch*, the young Fortunatus works for a time for the Earl of Flanders until the other servants conspire against him out of jealousy, forcing Fortunatus to flee. These episodes may be being conflated in the Chorus's reference to a 'covetous earl'.

21. *sit with folded arms*] a conventional sign of sorrow, e.g. Ferdinand in *The Tempest*, 'sitting, / His arms in this sad knot' (1.2.222–3).

24. *squint-eyed soul*] Fortunatus laments that his soul apprehends the world obliquely, distorting it rather than evaluating it clearly. Cf. 2.56n above.

25. *lore*] Dilke emends to 'lore', a reading that is followed here on the basis of Bowers's justification (see 1.267n above).

26. *unconstancy*] Rhys emends this obsolete form to the modern *inconstancy*, but the sense is clear and 'in inconstancy' creates an undesirable jarring in delivery.

28. *eagle*] Andelocia will later liken gold to an eagle that permits travel to any destination (5.419).

29. *vent'rous*] aphetic form of 'adventurous'.

30. *lights*] 'descends', in the sense of 'alight' (usually in the context of horse travel; here, more generally, to end his journey).

[SC. 4]   THE COMEDY OF OLD FORTUNATUS

    Thither transport your eyes and there behold him,
    Revelling with the Emperor of the East.
    From whence (through fear) for safeguard of his life,
    Flying into the arms of ugly night,
    Suppose you see him brought to Babylon   35
    And that the sun, clothed all in fire, hath rid
    One quarter of his hot celestial way
    With the bright morning, and that in this instant,
    He and the Sultan meet – but what they say,
    Listen you, the talk of kings none dare bewray.   *Exit.*   40

[Scene 4]

    Enter the SULTAN, *his* NOBLEMEN, *and* FORTUNATUS.

Sultan. Art thou that Fortunatus whose great name,
    Being carried in the chariot of the winds,
    Has filled the courts of all our Asian kings
    With love and envy? Whose dear presence ties
    The eyes of admiration to thine eyes?   5
    Art thou that Jove that in a shower of gold
    Appearedst before the Turkish emperor?
Fortunatus. I am that Fortunatus, mighty Sultan.
Sultan. Where is that purse which threw abroad such
    treasure?

---

    3. filled] *Rhys;* fild *Q.*

---

    35. *Babylon*] Babylon was the name of a Roman citadel proximate to modern-day Cairo (which was sometimes referred to as 'Babylon the Less' to distinguish it from the more famous Babylon in Assyria – see Chew, *Crescent and the Rose*, 24n). In the legend, Fortunatus travels to Cairo, and Dekker appears to be referring to 'Babylon of Egypt' here. In the Covent Garden adaptation, Fortunatus visits the Caliph in Alexandria instead.
    40. *bewray*] to divulge or reveal (*OED*, citing this example) (see also 5.329 below).
    0.1. SD] Rhys adds the setting: 'The Court at Babylon'.
    3. *filled*] *Q*'s 'fild' may carry the dual sense of 'filled' and 'filed' (in the sense of 'defiled'), but the more positive reading is adopted here as the more likely.
    6. *Jove ... gold*] Cf. 2.155n above.
    7. *Appearedst*] The metre requires it to be disyllabic.

Fortunatus. I gave it to the Turkish Suleiman. 10
   A second I bestowed on Prester John,
   A third the great Tartarian Cham received:
   For with these monarchs have I banqueted,
   And rid with them in triumph through their courts
   In crystal chariots drawn by unicorns. 15
   England, France, Spain, and wealthy Belgia,
   And all the rest of Europe's blessed daughters
   Have made my covetous eye rich in th'embrace
   Of their celestial beauties. Now I come
   To see the glory of fair Babylon. 20
   Is Fortunatus welcome to the Sultan?
   For I am like the sun: if Jove once chide,
   My gilded brows from amorous heaven I hide.
Sultan. Most welcome and most happy are mine arms
   In circling such an earthly deity! 25
   But will not Fortunatus make me blessed
   By sight of such a purse?

---

10. Suleiman] *this ed.;* Soliman *Q.*

---

10. *I gave it*] At the Globe reading in 2006, Bill Bingham paused here as Fortunatus decided to lie about the purse's whereabouts. The character's decision may suggest that Fortunatus perceives a threat to his safety at this point; the offer at ll. 27–32 below to manufacture a purse for the Sultan (which Fortunatus cannot really do) may be a prudent attempt to maintain safety by creating the perception that the Sultan depends on him. Withholding the promised purse may also be intended to encourage the Sultan to lavish him with luxuries as the other monarchs have reputedly done.

10. *Turkish Suleiman*] the Ottoman emperor Suleiman (or Solyman) the Magnificent (reigned 1520–66) (Chew, *Crescent and the Rose*, 252), the subject of the anonymous play *Soliman and Perseda*, which purports to dramatize the siege of Rhodes. Apart from this and his territorial expansion into Europe, Suleiman was known chiefly for filicide; see Heywood, *Troia Britanica* (1609): 'The *Turkish Solyman* with his owne hands / Slew his sonne Mustapha' (462).

11. *Prester John*] See 2.211n above.

12. *Tartarian Cham*] See 2.212n above.

16. *Belgia*] loose appellation for the Netherlands and low Germany (*OED*).

22. *Jove*] Jove was both king of the gods (hence an appropriately respectful term for the Sultan in this metaphor) and god of the sky, as recalled by his frequent association with the thunderbolt. His (and thus the Sultan's) chiding of the sun (i.e. Fortunatus) would see the sun retreat and withdraw his favours. See also 1.227–8n and 247n above for other references to Jove.

Fortunatus. Ere I depart,
The Sultan shall receive one at my hands:
For I must spend some time in framing it
And then some time to breathe that virtuous spirit   30
Into the heart thereof, all which is done
By a most sacred inspiration.
Sultan. Welcome, most welcome, to the Sultan's court.
Stay here and be the King of Babylon.
Stay here and I will more amaze thine eyes   35
With wondrous sights than can all Asia.
Behold yon tower; there stands mine armoury,
In which are corslets forged of beaten gold
To arm ten hundred thousand fighting men,
Whose glittering squadrons when the sun beholds,   40
They seem like to ten hundred thousand Joves,
When Jove on the proud back of thunder rides,
Trapped all in lightning flames. There can I show thee
The ball of gold that set all Troy on fire.
There shalt thou see the scarf of Cupid's mother,   45
Snatched from the soft moist ivory of her arm,
To wrap about Adonis' wounded thigh.
There shalt thou see a wheel of Titan's car
Which dropped from heaven when Phaeton fired the world.

---

48. car] *Dilke;* care *Q.*

---

32. *sacred inspiration*] 'Inspiration' (from the Latin *inspīrāre*, to breathe into) possibly alludes to the divine creation of Man (Genesis 2: 7), and may therefore be anticipated by a pun on 'breathe' in l. 30.

37. *tower*] Rhys's emendation to 'town', presumably made for the purposes of metre, makes little sense – why would the Sultan point from his court to another town? – whereas 'tower' (i.e. a keep, fortification) would be an appropriate stronghold to protect the treasures he proceeds to describe. 'Tower' should be monosyllabic here.

38. *corslets*] a piece of defensive body armour (*OED*).

44. *ball ... fire*] Another reference to the golden apple inscribed 'To the fairest', which Eris threw between Hera, Athena, and Aphrodite, leading to the Judgement of Paris and thereafter the downfall of Troy (cf. 1.264n above).

45–7. *scarf ... wounded thigh*] A reference to Adonis being killed by the wild boar he had hunted, and Venus attempting to tend to his wound with an article of her own clothing (here specified as a scarf).

48–9. *Titan's car ... world*] Cf.1.86n above.

I'll give thee (if thou wilt) two silver doves	50
Composed by magic to divide the air,	
Who, as they fly, shall clap their silver wings	
And give strange music to the elements.	
I'll give thee else the fan of Proserpine	
Which in reward for a sweet Thracian song,	55
The black-browed empress threw to Orpheus,	
Being come to fetch Eurydice from hell.	

Fortunatus. Hath ever mortal eye beheld these wonders?
Sultan. Thine shall behold them and make choice of any,
    So thou wilt give the Sultan such a purse.   60
Fortunatus. By Fortune's blessèd hand (who christened me),
    The mighty Sultan shall have such a purse,

---

51. air] *Dilke;* ayre *Q.*

---

51. *divide the air*] *Q*'s 'ayre' is suggestive of the more frequent early modern spelling of 'air' in the sense of a tune or melody (hence the 'strange music' of l. 53).

54–7. *fan of Proserpine ... Eurydice from hell*] When Orpheus descended to the underworld (Ovid, *Met.* 10), he negotiated with Pluto and Proserpine in the hope of retrieving his wife, Eurydice. He played his lyre with such beauty that the king and queen could not refuse his request, and he succeeded in winning Eurydice's conditional release. In some accounts, Proserpine's sympathy for Orpheus's loss of Eurydice (so much like her own sudden transportation to the Underworld) contributes to this decision; Dekker here adds a detail of Proserpine bestowing a favour on Orpheus, in the form of her fan. Ladies did sometimes have feathered fans (e.g. Jonson, *Cynthia's Revels* (*Q*), *CWBJ*: 'the least feather in her bounteous fan' (3.4.45)) but the 'fan' more likely refers to the Greek *liknon*, a basket- or shovel-like instrument for winnowing grain (*OED* n1, the primary meaning of 'fan' in the period). In Orphic mysticism, such fans were sometimes included in marriage rituals as symbols of purification, and would thus constitute an appropriate gift to Orpheus as he reclaims his wife. As a symbol of fertility (bearing fruit), they might also be used as a cradle, and thus become a symbol for new birth or rebirth/resurrection; again, an appropriate image for Eurydice's release from the Underworld. Proserpine, whose return to Earth is associated with the spring, and whose departure back to the Underworld coincides with the harvest, might be expected to have such a fan. Bernard Ashmole categorically states that '[t]he liknon belongs to the gods of fertility-Demeter, Persephone, Dionysus' ('Kalligeneia and Hieros Arotos', *Journal of Hellenic Studies* 66 (1946), 9). On the fans themselves, see Jane Ellen Harrison, *Prolegomena to the Study of Greek Religion*, 2nd ed. (Cambridge: Cambridge University Press, 1907), 517–34, esp. 526ff.

SC. 4]   THE COMEDY OF OLD FORTUNATUS   139

    Provided I may see these priceless wonders.
Sultan. Leave us alone.   *Exeunt Nobles.*
    Never was mortal ear
    Acquainted with the virtue of a jewel   65
    Which now I'll show (out-valuing all the rest).
Fortunatus. It is impossible.
Sultan.   Behold this casket –
                                      Draws a curtain.
    Fettered in golden chains, the lock pure gold,
    The key of solid gold, which myself keep.
    And here's the treasure that's contained in it.   70
                                      Takes out the hat.
Fortunatus. A coarse felt hat? Is this the precious jewel?
Sultan. I'll not exchange this for ten diadems.
    On pain of death, none listen to our talk!
Fortunatus. What needs this solemn conjuration?
Sultan. Oh, yes; for none shall understand the worth   75
    Of this inestimable ornament
    But you: and yet not you, but that you swear
    By her white hand, that lent you such a name,
    To leave a wondrous purse in Babylon.
Fortunatus. What I have sworn, I will not violate.   80
    But now uncover the virtues of this hat.
Sultan. I think none listen; if they do, they die.
Fortunatus. None listen. Tell, what needs this jealousy?
Sultan. You see 'tis poor in show; did I want jewels,
    Gold could beget them, but the wide world's wealth   85

---

63. priceless] *Rhys;* prizelesse *Q.*

---

    63. *priceless wonders*] *Q*'s 'prizeless' is an early modern spelling of the modern 'priceless' (e.g. Shakespeare, *Lucrece* (1594), 'What priselesse wealth the heauens had him lent', sig. B1v; the *OED* does not record 'prizeless' before 1856).
    66. *out-valuing*] surpassing in value (*OED* first instance).
    67–71. *casket ... jewel*] perhaps recalling the fairytale motif of Portia's casket test in *Merchant of Venice*, where the seemingly least valuable item is actually to be most prized. Michael Haldane (writing about the Fortunatus legend more generally) notes that the Sultan's possession of the hat 'points to a literary precursor: the flying-carpet of Oriental legend' ('The Translation of the Unseen Self: Fortunatus, Mercury and the Wishing-Hat', *Folklore* 117.2 (2006), 174).
    73. *On pain... talk!*] This outburst is directed to the offstage noblemen, whom the Sultan suspects of eavesdropping after their exit at l. 64 above.

140   THE COMEDY OF OLD FORTUNATUS   [SC. 4

Buys not this hat. This, clapped upon my head,
I (only with a wish) am through the air
Transported in a moment over seas
And over lands to any secret place.
By this I steal to every prince's court   90
And hear their private counsels and prevent
All dangers which to Babylon are meant.
By help of this I oft see armies join,
Though when the dreadful *alvarado* sounds
I am distant from the place a thousand leagues.   95
Oh, had I such a purse and such a hat,
The Sultan were, of all, most fortunate.
Fortunatus. [*Aside*] Oh, had I such a hat, then were I brave.
[*To* SULTAN] Where's he that made it?
Sultan.   Dead, and the whole world
Yields not a workman that can frame the like.   100
Fortunatus. No does? [*Aside*] By what trick shall I make this
mine?

101. SD] Q *places at the margin.*

---

87. *a wish*] Cited by the *OED* as an 'instance of wishing'.
90–5. *By this ... leagues.*] The cutting of these lines from the Tufts performance is quite significant, in that it eliminates the Sultan's prudent use of the wishing-cap for statecraft purposes.
94. alvarado] obs. (from Spanish) term for a signal given in the morning to discharge the night watch (*OED*, citing this as one of only two examples). The implication is that the army is readying for battle.
99–100. *Where's he ... Dead*] Haldane notes that an important difference between the two magical items is their respective lifespans: the purse's charm ends when Fortunatus's sons die; the hat's powers are eternal, as this passage indicates with the acknowledgement that its maker died long ago ('The Translation of the Unseen Self', 173).
101. *No does?*] 'Does it not?' Dilke emends to 'None does?'; Rhys emends to 'No, does't?' (explaining in his note that it implies 'No, does it not?'). Hoy, following Scherer, leaves the text unaltered, finding a comparable construction in *King John*, 'No had, my lord?', where the sense is 'had I not, had I none' (*King John*, ed. A. R. Braunmuller (Oxford University Press, 1989), 4.2.207n; the *New Oxford Shakespeare* emends to 'My hand, my lord?', 4.2.206).
101–8. *By what trick ... sons*] The Caliph of the Covent Garden production is more greedy than naive; he keeps the cap 'at a distance from Fortunatus', who makes the light cap heavy by filling it 'to the brim / With gold' until the Caliph can no longer hold it and is forced to place it on a table. Fortunatus then 'lays hold of the cap, upsets the gold in it, puts the cap on', and wishes himself away (29–30).

[*To* SULTAN] Methinks, methinks, when you are borne
o'er seas
And over lands, the heaviness thereof
Should weigh you down, drown you, or break your
neck.
Sultan. No, 'tis more light than any hat beside: 105
Your hand shall peise it.
Fortunatus.   Oh, 'tis wondrous heavy.
Sultan. Fie, you're deceived. Try it upon your head.
Fortunatus. Would I were now in Cyprus with my sons.
                                                                Exit.
Sultan. Stay, Fortunatus, stay! I am undone.
Treason, lords, treason! Get me wings, I'll fly 110
After this damnèd traitor through the air.

Enter NOBLES.

Nobles. Who wrongs the mighty king of Babylon?
Sultan. This Fortunatus, this fiend wrongs your king.
Nobles. Lock the court gates! Where is the devil hid?
Sultan. No gates, no grates of iron imprison him. 115
Like a magician breaks he through the clouds,
Bearing my soul with him; for that jewel gone,
I am dead and all is dross in Babylon.

---

106. *peise*] *OED* has '[t]o estimate or assess the weight of by lifting or holding in the hand' (e.g. Holland's translation of Camden's *Britain* (1610), 'Pearles, the bignesse and weight whereof he was wont to peise and trie by his hand').

108–15. *Would I were ... imprison him*] Marston appears to recall this passage in his *Antonio's Revenge* (late 1600 or early 1601), when Pandulpho boasts: 'Hadst thou a jail /With treble walls like antique Babylon, / Pandulpho can get out. I tell thee, Duke, / I have old Fortunatus' wishing-cap, / And can be where I list, even in a trice' (ed. Gair, 2.2.76–80).

116. *Like a magician ... clouds*] It is unclear how characters using the wishing-cap made their sudden exits. Breaking through the clouds sounds like transvection (the flight of witches), which was often reputedly accompanied by fog and filthy air. It is possible that a lifting machine may have been deployed but these were typically accompanied by music to cover the creaking sound of the mechanics, and there is no cue for music here. On transvection and stage representations of witches in flight, see Roy Booth, 'Witchcraft, Flight and the Early Modern English Stage', *Early Modern Literary Studies* 13.1 (May 2007), 3.1–37.

142   THE COMEDY OF OLD FORTUNATUS   [SC. 5

Fly after him? 'Tis vain. On the wind's wings
He'll ride through all the courts of earthly kings.   120
Nobles. What is the jewel that your grace hath lost?
Sultan. He dies that troubles me. Call me not king,
For I'll consume my life in sorrowing.   *Exeunt.*

[Scene 5]

Enter ANDELOCIA *very gallant, and* SHADOW.

Andelocia. Shadow, what have I lost today at dice?
Shadow. More than you will win again in a month.
Andelocia. Why sir, how much comes it to?
Shadow. It comes to nothing, sir, for you have lost your wits
and when a man's wits are lost, the man is like twenty   5
pounds' worth of tobacco, which mounts into th'air and
proves nothing but one thing.
Andelocia. And what thing is that, you ass?
Shadow. Marry sir, that he is an ass that melts so much money
in smoke.   10
Andelocia. 'Twere a charitable deed to hang thee a smoking.
Shadow. I should never make good bacon, because I am not
fat.
Andelocia. I'll be sworn thy wit is lean.
Shadow. It's happy I have a lean wit. But master, you have   15
none; for when your money tripped away, that went after
it and ever since you have been mad. Here comes your
brother.

Enter AMPEDO.

Borrow a dram of him, if his be not mouldy, for men's wits
in these days are like the cuckoo, bald once a year; and   20

18.1. SD] *Rhys; placed after* dram of him *in Q.* 19–20. Borrow... if ... are] *Q lines:* borrow ... him. / If ... daies, / A're ...

0.1. SD] Rhys adds the setting, 'Outside the House of Fortunatus'.
7. *proves*] with a pun on 'turn out to be' (*OED* v 3d) and 'establish or demonstrate an argument' (*OED* v 1a).
19. *Borrow a dram ... mouldy*] Shadow urges Andelocia to borrow a little ('a dram') of his brother's wit if it's not worn out with age (*OED*).

SC. 5] THE COMEDY OF OLD FORTUNATUS 143

    that makes motley so dear and fools so good cheap.
Andelocia. Brother, all hail.
Shadow. There's a rattling salutation.
Andelocia. You must lend me some more money. Nay, never
    look so strange, an you will come off, so. If you will bar   25
    me from square play, do. Come, come, when the old
    traveller my father comes home like a young ape full of
    fantastic tricks, or a painted parrot stuck full of outland-
    ish feathers, he'll lead the world in a string and then (like
    a hotshot) I'll charge and discharge all.   30
Shadow. I would be loath, master, to see that day: for he leads
    the world in a string that goes to hanging.

---

25. an] *Dilke;* and *Q.*

    19–21. *for men's wits ... good cheap.*] cut for the Tufts performance. A cuckoo is usually invoked when ridiculing someone for being monotonous (*OED* n.3), and this seems to be the criticism of men's wits 'in these days'; Hoy suggests an analogue in *Satiromastix*, where he identifies 'the bird's traditional moulting period' as the subject of Dekker's references (*Sat.* 3.1.128n). Shadow may therefore be punning on the figurative meaning of 'bald' as 'meagre, trivial, paltry' or otherwise bare of meaning (*OED* n.II. fig.6, citing Nashe's *Christ's Teares* 63b: 'Had rather heare a jarring black-sant, then one of theyr balde sermons').
    21. *motley*] the multicoloured costume of a fool (dear because demand is high: fools are abundant).
    22–3. *all hail ... rattling salutation*] 'all-hail' is a welcome or greeting (originally 'all health'); Shadow, like the Princess in *Love's Labour's Lost* (5.2.341–2) or Theseus in *Two Noble Kinsmen* (3.5.101), wilfully misconstrues it as an unwelcoming demand for a hailstorm.
    25. *an you will come off, so*] If Ampedo wants to avoid an argument, he should loan Andelocia the money (if you want to not argue ['come off' = desist, retire], give me the money [so]).
    25–34. *an you ... wilt be?*] cut for the Tufts performance.
    26. *square*] fair, honest, just (*OED*).
    27–9. *young ape ... feathers*] Cf. Dekker's *The Seven Deadly Sinnes of London* (1606): '*Apishnesse* rides in a Chariot made of nothing but cages, in which are all the strangest out-landish Birds that can be gotten: the Cages are stucke full of Parats feathers' (32).
    29. *lead the world in a string*] Proverbially, to lead in a string or to have on a string is to have under control (*OED*; Dent W886).
    30. *hotshot*] one who is eager to shoot, hence a pun on charge and discharge in terms of loading and using a firearm (*OED* I 5. spec.) and to lay or place goods as a loan upon (*OED* I†2). Andelocia is keen to acquire his father's wealth, which he offers as a surety against any sum his brother might advance him presently.

144   THE COMEDY OF OLD FORTUNATUS   [SC. 5

Andelocia. Take heed I turn not that head into the world and
  lead you so. – Brother wilt be? Ha' ye any ends of gold
  or silver?   35
Ampedo. [*Aside*] Thus wanton revelling breeds beggary.
  – Brother, 'twere better that you still lived poor.
  Want would make wisdom rich, but when your coffers
  Swell to the brim, then riot sets up sails,
  And like a desperate unskilled mariner   40
  Drives your unsteady fortunes on the point
  Of wrack inevitable. Of all the wealth
  Left by our father when he left us last,
  This little is unspent and this being wasted,
  Your riot ends; therefore consume it all.   45
  I'll live; or dying, find some burial.
Andelocia. Thanks for my crowns. Shadow, I am villainous
  hungry to hear one of the seven wise masters talk thus
  emptily.
Shadow. I am a villain, master, if I am not hungry.   50
Andelocia. Because I'll save this gold, sirrah Shadow, we'll
  feed ourselves with paradoxes.

34. Ha' ye] *Rhys;* Hay *Q.*   47. Thanks for my crowns] *Dilke; given to Ampedo in Q.*

34–5. *Ha' ye any ends ... silver?*] Hoy notes that this is a street vendor's cry, e.g. *Welsh Embassador* 1.3.35: 'myne Aunt cryd ends of gold and silver'.

42. *wrack*] fig., the disablement or destruction of a vessel by accident of navigation (*OED*, citing this example).

48. *seven wise masters*] 'The Seven Wise Masters of Rome' was a Middle English romance, in which the wise men successfully confute the baseless allegations made by the empress against her stepson. It was printed as *The Seven Sages of Rome* at least six times between the mid-sixteenth century and 1602. Henslowe bought a 'boocke called the vij wisse masters' from Chettle, Dekker, Haughton, and Day in various instalments from 1 to 8 March 1600. As Knutson notes, the subsequent expenditure, on 25 March, of 40os on apparel and 36os on related purchases suggests the play was to be 'a spectacular offering' (Roslyn L. Knutson, 'Toe to Toe Across Maid Lane: Repertorial Competition at the Rose and Globe, 1599–1600', in *Acts of Criticism: Performance Matters in Shakespeare and His Contemporaries*, ed. June Schlueter and Paul Nelsen (Madison and Teaneck: Fairleigh Dickinson University Press, 2005), 30).

51–62. *Because... do it.*] cut for the Tufts performance.

52. *paradoxes*] In a note on *Satiromastix* 4.3.68.1, Hoy notes Dekker's delight in such philosophical set pieces as the 'paradox in commendation of hunger' that follows (60–1), listing ten explicit instances of paradox elsewhere in the author's works.

Shadow. Oh, rare! What meat's that?
Andelocia. Meat, you gull? 'Tis no meat. A dish of paradoxes is a feast of strange opinion; 'tis an ordinary that our greatest gallants haunt nowadays, because they would be held for statesmen.
Shadow. I shall never fill my belly with opinions.
Andelocia. In despite of swag-bellies, gluttons, and sweet-mouthed epicures, I'll have thee maintain a paradox in commendation of hunger.
Shadow. I shall never have the stomach to do it.
Andelocia. See'st thou this *crusado*? Do it and turn this into a feast.
Shadow. Covetousness and lechery are two devils; they'll tempt a man to wade through deep matters. I'll do it, though good cheer conspire my death for speaking treason against her.
Andelocia. Fall to it then with a full mouth.
Shadow. O famine, inspire me with thy miserable reasons. I begin, master.
Ampedo. Oh, miserable invocation!
Andelocia. Silence.
Shadow. There's no man but loves one of these three beasts: a horse, a hound, or a whore. The horse, by his goodwill, has his head ever in the manger; the whore, with your ill will, has her hand ever in your purse; and a hungry dog eats dirty puddings.

---

61. commendation] *Dilke;* commendations *Q.*

55. ordinary] an inn or tavern where fixed-price meals are available.

59. *swag-bellies*] As Bowers notes, *Q*'s attractive *hapax legomenon* 'sway-bellies' is a misreading for 'swag-bellies'; a term Dekker uses often, e.g. *Shoemaker's Holiday* 4.6, 20.23. The *Shoemaker's Holiday* examples and the *Fortunatus* example (once emended) antedate the *OED* by 11 years.

60. maintain] to uphold in speech or argument (i.e. to maintain a position; here, one which Shadow opposes).

63. crusado] a Portuguese coin named for the short or long cross on its reverse; the first coin struck from New World gold, it was valued at approximately 6s 8d (Fischer, *Econolingua*, 64).

65–111. *Covetousness ... little urchins.*] cut for the Tufts performance.

69. *with a full mouth*] delivered with utmost force (*OED*).

76–7. *whore...purse*] perhaps with a codpiece subtext (as played by Jen Waghorn in the Shakespeare Institute reading in 2016).

77–8. *a hungry dog eats dirty puddings*] Dent D538*.

Andelocia. This is profound. Forward: the conclusion of this now. 80

Shadow. The conclusion is plain: for since all men love one of these three monsters, being such terrible eaters, therefore all men love hunger.

Ampedo. A very lean argument.

Shadow. I can make it no fatter. 85

Andelocia. Proceed, good Shadow; this fats me.

Shadow. Hunger is made of gunpowder.

Andelocia. Give fire to that opinion.

Shadow. Stand by, lest it blow you up. Hunger is made of gunpowder, or gunpowder of hunger; for they both eat 90 through stone walls. Hunger is a grindstone, it sharpens wit. Hunger is fuller of love than Cupid, for it makes a man eat himself. Hunger was the first that ever opened a cook's shop; cooks the first that ever made sauce; sauce being lickerish, licks up good meat; good meat preserves 95 life: hunger therefore preserves life.

Ampedo. By my consent thou shouldst still live by hunger.

Shadow. Not so, hunger makes no man mortal. Hunger is an excellent physician, for he dares kill anybody. Hunger is one of the seven liberal sciences. 100

Andelocia. Oh, learned? Which of the seven?

---

82. *terrible eaters*] probably in the sense of *OED* †d. fig., 'To submit to, "swallow" (an insult, an injury)'; e.g. *Sir Thomas Wyatt*, 'Ile eate no wrongs' (4.4.21). Men, in other words, are gluttons for punishment ('love hunger').

89–91. *Hunger ... stone walls*] Dent H811*, cf. Marston, *Antonio's Revenge*: 'They say hunger breaks through stone walls' (ed. Gair, 5.2.2).

94. *cook's shop*] a shop where cooked food is sold and eaten (now more commonly 'cook-shop') (*OED*).

95. *lickerish*] pleasant to the palate, tempting (*OED*). The subsequent pun on '*licks* up good meat' would be weakened for the modern reader if the alternative spelling ('liquorish') were used here.

100. *seven liberal sciences*] an interchangeable term ('science' = branch of knowledge) for the seven liberal arts, i.e. the classical *Trivium* (grammar, logic, rhetoric) and the medieval *Quadrivium* (arithmetic, music, geometry, and astronomy).

101. *Oh, learned?*] It is not necessary to discard *Q*'s punctuation in favour of the exclamation adopted by Dilke, Rhys, and Smeaton; rather than mock-praise ('Oh, learned!') Andelocia's sarcasm might just as well take the form of a mocking question (sarcastically dubbing Shadow 'learned').

Shadow. Music, for she'll make a man leap at a crust. But, as few care for her six sisters, so none love to dance after her pipe. Hunger, master, is hungry and covetous; therefore the *crusado*. 105
Andelocia. But hast thou no sharper reasons than this?
Shadow. Yes one: the Dagger in Cyprus had never stabbed out such sixpenny pies, but for hunger.
Andelocia. Why, you dolt, these pies are but in their minority.
Shadow. My belly and my purse have been twenty times at 110 daggers drawing, with parting the little urchins.

107. Dagger] *this ed.;* dagger *Q*.   108. pies] *Scherer;* pipes *Q*.

102–4. *leap at a crust ... dance after her pipe*] Hunger proverbially makes one leap for a crust (Dent C870); the pun here is on 'leap' as 'dance' (*OED* 3), hence the substitution of 'music' for 'hunger'. Shadow's declaration that 'none love to dance' affirms that being hungry is undesirable – which leads him to reiterate his request for the *crusado*. 'Dance after my pipe' was the alternative title to a bawdy ballad containing a *dance macabre*, 'The Shaking of the Sheets, or The Dance of Death', and seems to be a commonplace injunction made by Death. In Middleton's *The Black Book*, Lucifer says 'I am not a little proud, I can tell you, Barnaby, that you dance after my pipe so long' (ed. G. B. Shand in *Thomas Middleton: The Collected Works*, gen. eds Gary Taylor and John Lavagnino (Oxford: Clarendon Press, 2007), ll. 780–1); and in Middleton's *Friar Hubburd's Tales, or The Ant and the Nightingale*, it is again 'the old devourer of virtue ... Death' who makes 'our landlord dance after his pipe' (ed. Adrian Weiss in Taylor and Lavagnino, l. 310). Shadow probably means he'd rather not die of hunger.

107–8. *Dagger in Cyprus ... sixpenny pies*] Dilke was the first to suggest 'pies' in lieu of *Q*'s 'pipes' but did not adopt the emendation himself. Confusion stems from the reference to both 'pipe' (104) and 'pies' (109) on either side of l. 108's ambiguous noun, but 'sixpenny pies' is clearly correct. 'The Dagger' was the name of a tavern in Holborn and another in Cheapside on the corner of Foster Lane (see Sugden, 'Dagger'; *OED* n1 †11; Hoy, *Satiromastix* 1.2.304–5n). Both taverns were known for their 'dagger-pies', which must have been inexpensive judging from Tucca's exclamation, 'ile not take thy word for a dagger Pye' (*Satiromastix* 1.2.304–5). Fischer notes that sixpence is a small sum, 'the price of a small pie or pastry' (*Econolingua*, 104). The 'stabbing out' is probably just a pun on 'dagger', but may refer to the pies' crusts, which would be stabbed during preparation. Perhaps such menial work on cheap baked goods was undertaken only out of necessity (i.e. hunger).

109. *in their minority*] in their youth, still in the state of being a minor (i.e. the metaphorical pies are not ready). Possibly with a pun on 'pie' = a heap/pile of manure stacked for maturing (*OED* n.2), and thus a double-edged insult in which Shadow's attempts at wit are manure *and* they are not matured.

111. *daggers drawing*] on the brink of fighting, in a state of open hostility (*OED*).

THE COMEDY OF OLD FORTUNATUS   [SC. 5

                    Enter FORTUNATUS.

Ampedo. Peace, idiot, peace! My father is returned.
Fortunatus. Touch me not, boys, I am nothing but air! Let
    none speak to me, till you have marked me well.
Shadow. [*Chalking* FORTUNATUS'S *back*] Now speak your   115
    mind.
Ampedo. Villain, why hast thou chalked my father's back?
Shadow. Only to mark him and to try what colour air is of.
Fortunatus. Regard him not, Ampedo. Andelocia, Shadow:
    view me. Am I as you are, or am I transformed?   120
Andelocia. I thought travel would turn my father madman or
    fool.
Ampedo. How should you be transformed? I see no change.
Shadow. If your wits be not planet-stricken, if your brains lie
    in their right place, you are well enough; for your body   125
    is little mended by your fetching vagaries.
Andelocia. Methinks, father, you look as you did, only your
    face is more withered.

124. planet-stricken] *Rhys;* planet strucken *Q.*   126. vagaries] *this ed.;* fegaries *Q.*

113–230. *Touch me not ... Italianate.*] This lengthy passage, with many lines cut, was selected by Charles Lamb for inclusion in his *Specimens of English Dramatic Poets* (London, 1808), 58–60.

113. *nothing but air*] Hoy finds an allusion to the four elements and provides quotations analogous in meaning to regal Cleopatra's 'I am fire and air' (*Antony and Cleopatra* 43.278). Although Fortunatus might be full of self-importance, the more likely explanation is that he refers to having just 'cut through the air like a falcon' (l. 142 below).

113–19. *Let none ... Ampedo.*] cut for the Tufts performance.

114. *marked me well*] taken notice of me properly; this example antedates *OED* 25b by some 25 years.

120. *transformed*] See 1.53–4n above on 'how travel can transform'. Ellis suggests that Fortunatus 'boasts that he has achieved a kind of personal alchemy, the transmutation of his own base substance into something ethereal' (*Old Age,* 153).

124–6. *If your wits ... vagaries.*] cut for the Tufts performance.

124. *planet-stricken*] To strike as a malignant influence; to blast (*OED* first instance); cf. Puntarvolo's declamation, 'I am planet-struck', which Carlo Buffone glosses favourably as 'an ecstasy' (*Every Man Out* 2.1.309, 312) but which Deliro invokes as a malignant confrontation with fate ('Some planet strike me dead!', 5.3.522).

126. *vagaries*] *Q*'s fegaries (*dial.* and *colloq.*, a vagary, prank, freak; a whim, eccentricity) is the *OED*'s first instance.

SC. 5]   THE COMEDY OF OLD FORTUNATUS   149

Fortunatus. That's not my fault. Age is like love, it cannot be
   hid.   130
Shadow. Or like gunpowder a-fire, or like a fool, or like a
   young novice new come to his lands; for all these will
   show of what house they come. Now, sir, you may amplify.
Fortunatus. Shadow, turn thy tongue to a shadow: be silent.
   Boys, be proud. Your father hath the whole world in this   135
   compass. I am all felicity, up to the brims. In a minute
   am I come from Babylon; I have been this half hour in
   Famagusta.
Andelocia. How? In a minute, father? Ha, ha, I see travellers
   must lie.   140
Shadow. 'Tis their destiny, the Fates do so conspire.
Fortunatus. I have cut through the air like a falcon; I would
   have it seem strange to you.
Shadow. So it does, sir.
Fortunatus. But 'tis true. I would not have you believe it   145
   neither.
Shadow. No more we do not, sir.
Fortunatus. But 'tis miraculous and true. Desire to see you
   brought me to Cyprus. I'll leave you more gold and go
   visit more countries.   150
Shadow. Leave us gold enough and we'll make all countries
   come visit us.

---

151. SP] Dilke suggests assigning this to Andelocia (but leaves it with Shadow).

129–30. *Age is like love, it cannot be hid*] 'Love cannot be hid' is proverbial (Dent L500*); Fortunatus happily wears the outward signifiers of age as a badge of honour acquired through his exploits.

131–4. *Or like ... silent.*] cut for the Tufts performance.

135–6. *in this compass*] Ambiguous – either 'in this limited space' (an echo of Cho.1, 1–4), or more specifically, the purse (see l. 300 below).

139–40. *travellers must lie*] Travellers could proverbially lie with authority, since the travel/travail required to prove them wrong was so considerable (Dent T476*).

142. *falcon*] Another instance of bird of prey imagery in the play (cf. the 'lusty eagle' of Cho.1, 28–9). The eagle travels far but the peregrine falcon travels fastest of all creatures.

151–2. *Leave us gold ... us*] Dilke stopped short of reassigning this speech but noted that it 'agrees better with the station and temper of Andelocia; and the next speech of Ampedo's forms then a proper rejoinder'. No editor has accepted Dilke's proposed re-assignment, however.

150   THE COMEDY OF OLD FORTUNATUS   [SC. 5

Ampedo. The frosty hand of age now nips your blood
  And strews her snowy flowers upon your head,
  And gives you warning that within few years   155
  Death needs must marry you. Those short-lived
     minutes
  That dribble out your life must needs be spent
  In peace, not travel. Rest in Cyprus then.
  Could you survey ten worlds, yet you must die;
  And bitter is the sweet that's reaped thereby.   160
Andelocia. Faith, father, what pleasure have you met by
  walking your stations?
Fortunatus. What pleasure, boy? I have revelled with kings,
  danced with queens, dallied with ladies, worn strange
  attires, seen fantasticoes, conversed with humorists,   165
  been ravished with divine raptures of Doric, Lydian, and

---

154 strews] strowes *Q*.   155. gives] *Dilke;* giue *Q*.   156. short-lived] *Dilke;* short liues *Shepherd;* short lines *Q*.

153–4. *frosty hand of age ... your head*] Cf. 'silver-handed age' in the Prologue at Court (42), and 'grey-wingèd age' in the Epilogue at Court (15).

154. *strews*] *Q*'s 'strowes' (arch. and *dial.* form of the verb) encourages assonance with 'snowy flowers'.

158. *travel*] a common pun on travel/travail.

160. *bitter ... thereby*] a variation of the proverbial 'after sweet the sour comes' (Dent S1034.11, citing the 1559 *Mirror for Magistrates*, 152: 'But soone is sowre the sweete that Fortune sendes').

162. *walking your stations*] Andelocia is likening his father's journey to a secularized pilgrimage devoted to pleasure, which English travellers were beginning to undertake around the time Dekker was writing (see McInnis, *Mind-Travelling*, 23) (*OED* n P2 b. 'to perform a series of (prescribed) devotions at a holy place or succession of holy places, *spec.* at the Stations of the Cross').

165. *fantasticoes*] A fantastico is an obsolete term for an absurd and irrational person (*OED*, citing only one other example, from *R&J* Q1 (1597), sig. E1v: 'Limping antique affecting fantasticoes'. In her Oxford edition of *R&J*, Jill L. Levenson cites Nashe, *Saffron-Walden*, 1596 as an earlier illustration, however).

166–7. *Doric, Lydian, and Phrygian harmonies*] John Birchensha's translation of *Templum musicum* (1664) provides a succinct account of the perceived differences in these forms of music in its description of 'the querulous *Lydian*, or the religious *Phrygian*, or Warlike *Dorian*' (40). Greek music was melodic, 'harmonies' referring more to the underlying structures. Seven attunements can be formed from the intervals within a single genus; they are referred to collectively as *harmoniai* and individually by their ethnic names: Mixolydian, *Lydian, Phrygian, Dorian,* Hypolydian, Hypophrygian and Hypodorian (my emphasis; *OCD,* 'music', 6 'Melodic Structure').

SC. 5]   THE COMEDY OF OLD FORTUNATUS   151

 Phrygian harmonies. I have spent the day in triumphs
 and the night in banqueting.
Andelocia. Oh, rare! This was heavenly.
Shadow. Methinks 'twas horrible.   170
Andelocia. He that would not be an Arabian phoenix to burn
 in these sweet fires, let him live like an owl for the world
 to wonder at.
Ampedo. Why, brother, are not all these vanities?
Fortunatus. Vanities? Ampedo, thy soul is made of lead; too   175
 dull, too ponderous to mount up to the incomprehensible
 glory that travel lifts men to.
Shadow. My old master's soul is cork and feathers, and being
 so light doth easily mount up.
Andelocia. Sweeten mine ears, good father, with some more.   180
Fortunatus. When in the warmth of mine own country's arms

---

170. SP] Dilke and Scherer assign this speech to Ampedo.

 170. SP] Bowers defends Q's allocation of this line to Shadow rather than Ampedo (Dilke and Scherer's choice of emendation), citing Shadow's dislike of travel in 5.426ff below.
 171-2. *Arabian phoenix ... owl*] Andelocia embraces his father's indulgent lifestyle and casts scorn on those who would oppose it. The unique phoenix must self-immolate in order to regenerate and is admired as an exotic marvel; the owl typically elicits a decidedly more prosaic response, being strange and wondered at, as for example in Jonson's *The Case Is Altered*, where Paolo tells Angelo, 'The very owl, / Whom other birds do stare and wonder at, / Shall hoot at thee' (*CWBJ* 5.4.68-70). The two birds are compared in the anonymous *Lamentatio civitatis, or, Londons complaint against her children in the countrey* (1665): 'poor, distressed, rejected, diseased *London*, once the *Phoenix*, now the *Owle*; once the *Paragon of beauty*, now a *Pattern of deformity*' (1).
 175-7. *Vanities? ... lifts men to*] These lines provide an unusually forthright defence of the benefits of pleasurable travel in terms of spiritual nourishment; Fortunatus doesn't simply suggest that travel is an idle but harmless pursuit — he rather presents it as positively beneficial (McInnis, *Mind-Travelling*, 79).
 181-6. *When ... so clear*] In his *A direction for travailers ...* (1592), Justus Lipsius similarly observes that only the base-minded 'content their poore thoughts with their owne countries knowledge, and being glued to their home they carrie (with the sluggishe and slowfooted snaile) their howses on theyr backs' whereas the 'heavenlie spirited men' are 'never well but when they imitate the hevens, which are in perpetuall motion' (sig. A2v). In a tract written in 1598 but not published until 1605, Robert Dallington expresses comparable sentiments: 'Base and vulgar spirits hover still about home: those are more noble & divine, that imitate the *Heavens*, and joy in motion' (*A Method for Travell. Shewed by taking the view of France. As it stoode in the yeare of our Lord* 1598 (London, 1605), sig. Br).

We yawned like sluggards, when this small horizon
Imprisoned up my body, then mine eyes
Worshipped these clouds as brightest. But, my boys,
The glist'ring beams which do abroad appear   185
In other heavens — fire is not half so clear.
Shadow. Why, sir, are there other heavens in other countries?
Andelocia. Peace, interrupt him not upon thy life.
Fortunatus. For still in all the regions I have seen,
 I scorned to crowd among the muddy throng   190
Of the rank multitude, whose thickened breath,
Like to condensed fogs, do choke that beauty
Which else would dwell in every kingdom's cheek.
No, I still boldly stepped into their courts,
For there to live, 'tis rare. Oh, 'tis divine!   195
There shall you see faces angelical.
There shall you see troops of chaste goddesses
Whose star-like eyes have power (might they still shine)
To make night day and day more crystalline.
Near these you shall behold great heroes,   200
White-headed counsellors and jovial spirits,
Standing like fiery cherubims to guard
The monarch, who in Godlike glory sits
In midst of these, as if this deity
Had with a look created a new world,   205
The standers by being the fair workmanship.

---

187. *other heavens ... countries*] In the previous line, Fortunatus used 'heavens' to refer to the sky, but Shadow's religious relativism here anticipates the concerns of (for example) William Percy's *Mahomet and His Heaven* (1601).

191–3. *the rank multitude ... kingdom's cheek*] In his disdain for the general populace (cf. the 'wild beast Multitude' in 1.110) and penchant for dining with royalty, Fortunatus demonstrates an unashamedly elitist sensibility. He is undoubtedly privileged, and part of the appeal to the average playgoer might well be the extraordinariness of his travels (much like Faustus's travels). Accordingly, these lines were an important cut for the Tufts performance; their absence eliminates Fortunatus's elitism.

194–206. *No ... fair workmanship*] Richard Dutton asks (personal correspondence) whether these lines might have been inserted specially for the court performance, as a cheeky 'flattering' of the elite audience.

201. *White-headed*] white-haired, especially from age (*OED*, citing this example).

Andelocia. Oh, how my soul is rapt to a third heaven!
I'll travel sure and live with none but kings.
Shadow. Then Shadow must die among knaves. And yet why
so? In a bunch of cards, knaves wait upon the kings. 210
Andelocia. When I turn king, then shalt thou wait on me.
Shadow. Well, there's nothing impossible: a dog has his day
and so have you.
Ampedo. But tell me, father, have you in all courts
Beheld such glory, so majestical 215
In all perfection? No way blemishèd?
Fortunatus. In some courts shall you see Ambition
Sit piecing Daedalus' old waxen wings,
But being clapped on and they about to fly,
Even when their hopes are busied in the clouds, 220
They melt against the sun of majesty
And down they tumble to destruction.
For since the heavens' strong arms teach kings to stand,

---

207. *rapt to a third heaven*] The third heaven is a place of supreme bliss, the abode of God (*third* because it is said to be beyond the visible sky *and* the space adjacent to that; *OED*, 'third adj. and n. Additions'). Andelocia is likening himself to Paul, who was rapt to the third heaven and saw what mortals could not see during their time on earth (see Romans 8: 18).

212. *a dog has his day*] Dent D464*.

217-22. *In some courts ... destruction*] Noted by Allott in *Englands Parnassus* under 'Ambition' (p. 5).

217-25. *In some courts ... trait'rous hands.*] On the cancellation of the leaf in *Q* containing this passage, probably on account of this passage and its possible relevance to the Essex rebellion, see Introduction, 8-11.

218. *piecing Daedalus' old waxen wings*] Daedalus built the labyrinth in Crete to conceal the minotaur born of Pasiphae. When Theseus killed the minotaur, Daedalus decided to flee the island with his son Icarus. He built wings to facilitate their escape, but Icarus did not heed his father's advice and flew too close to the sun. The wax in his wings melted, and Icarus plummeted to his death (Ovid, *Met.* 8). Rhys emends 'piecing' to 'piercing', perhaps opting for the more violent option in anticipation of the disaster that befell Daedalus's son, but, as the next line makes clear ('about to fly'), the correct reading should be *Q*'s 'piecing' (= the action of joining pieces together, *OED*). Ambition tries to reuse Daedalus's wings but repeats Icarus's mistake. Hoy finds an echo of the anonymous *King Leir*, 'I would he had old Dedalus waxen wings, / That he might flye, so I might stay behind' (ll. 416-17); Faustus's 'waxen wings' (Prol.21) is a more memorable example.

220. *busied*] busily occupied or engaged (*OED*).

223-5. *since the heavens' ... trait'rous hands*] noted by Allott in *Englands Parnassus* under 'Kings' (p. 156), but in Allott's reproduction there is only *one* throne and *one* traitorous hand. See Introduction, 8-11.

154　　　THE COMEDY OF OLD FORTUNATUS　　　[SC. 5

 Angels are placed about their glorious throne
 To guard it from the strokes of trait'rous hands.　　225
 By travel, boys, I have seen all these things.
 Fantastic complement stalks up and down,
 Tricked in outlandish feathers; all his words,
 His looks, his oaths, are all ridiculous,
 All apish, childish, and Italianate.　　230
  Enter FORTUNE, *after her three* Destinies *working.*
Shadow. I know a medicine for that malady.
Fortunatus. By travel, boys, I have seen all these things.
Andelocia. And these are sights for none but gods and
 kings.

224–5. *Angels ... guard it*] Cf. *Lust's Dominion*, 'Angels of heaven, / Stand like his guard about him' (2.2.14–15).
226–34. *By travel ... blind.*] These sentiments about the pleasure of travel were cut for the Tufts performance.
227. *Fantastic complement*] 'complement' most likely refers in an obsolete sense to a quality or personal accomplishment (*OED* II. †7.), e.g. Jonson, *Every Man Out*, 'all the rare qualities, humours, and complements of a gentleman' (*CWBJ* 1.2.20–1). Here, such a quality is personified as a returned traveller who has acquired the worst of foreign characteristics and traits, dressing and speaking in outlandish Continental fashion. If there is a pun on 'complement' = the full moon (*OED* †2.b, from heraldry; cf. 'increment' and 'decrement'), then there may also be a deliberate contrast here with the 'sun of majesty' in 221 above.
227. *stalks*] to walk with stiff, high, measured steps, implying haughtiness (*OED* 4a).
228. *Tricked in*] dressed up in (*OED* b).
230. *apish, childish, and Italianate*] An 'English man Italianated' is '[h]e, that by living, & traveling in Italie, bringeth home into England out of *Italie*, the Religion, the learning, the policie, the experience, the maners of *Italie*', according to Roger Ashcam in *The Scholemaster* (1570); he adds that '[t]hese be the inchantementes of *Circes*, brought out of *Italie*, to marre mens maners in England' (sig. I.iiv). The stereotypical proof of an unprofitable voyage was the voyager's adoption of apish affectations and clothing (or even Catholicism) to the exclusion of any genuinely beneficial transformations; on the *ars apodemica* and warnings against such affectations, see Daniel Carey, *Continental Travel and Journeys Beyond Europe in the Early Modern Period: An Overlooked Connection* (London: Hakluyt Society, 2009), 8–9, and McInnis, *Mind-Travelling*, 24–5, 85–6.
230.1. SD] Rhys specified 'in the background' for Fortune's entrance, as she remains unnoticed until she addresses Fortunatus in l. 242. 'Working' presumably refers to the passing back and forth of the 'inky thread' of Fortunatus's life, mentioned in l. 259.

SC. 5]   THE COMEDY OF OLD FORTUNATUS   155

Shadow. Yes, and for Christian creatures, if they be not
   blind.
Fortunatus. In these two hands do I grip all the world.   235
   This leather purse and this bald woollen hat
   Make me a monarch: here's my crown and sceptre.
   In progress will I now go through the world.
   I'll crack your shoulders, boys, with bags of gold
   Ere I depart. On Fortune's wings I ride,   240
   And now sit in the height of human pride.
Fortune. [*Stepping forward*] Now, fool, thou liest. Where thy
   proud feet do tread,
   These shall throw down thy cold and breathless head.
Fortunatus. O sacred deity, what sin is done,   *All kneel.*
   That Death's iron fist should wrestle with thy son?   245
Fortune. Thou art no son of Fortune, but her slave.
   Thy cedar hath aspired to his full height.
   Thy sun-like glory hath advanced herself
   Into the top of pride's meridian
   And down amain it comes. From beggary   250
   I plumed thee like an ostrich; like that ostrich,
   Thou hast eaten metals and abused my gifts,
   Hast played the ruffian, wasted that in riots
   Which as a blessing I bestowed on thee.

---

241. human] *Dilke;* humane *Q*.

238. *progress*] an official journey made by a monarch (*OED* II.5).
243. *These*] i.e. the Destinies.
247. *cedar ... height*] Cedars were renowned for attaining great heights (cf. 3.23n, where Vice's gilded boughs surpass even the cedar). As Hoy notes, the cedar is an emblem of ambitious pride.
250. *amain*] with full force or speed (*OED* 2a).
251. *I plumed thee like an ostrich*] Another explicit reference to Fortunatus '*in his newe lyuerie*' (*SR* 3.156); see also 2.140.1 SD and Introduction, 5. The plumage of ostriches was often remarked upon, e.g. *Welsh Ambassador* 2.1.15–17: 'Of gallants that come briske into the feild, / Of scarlett larded tick with glitteringe lace / And feathers that plumed estriges out face'.
251-2. *like that ostrich ... eaten metals*] Ostriches supposedly had stomachs strong enough to digest metal; see *OED* 'metal-maw'. As Hoy notes, Dekker uses the image often (e.g. *Noble Spanish Soldier* 4.1.32–3, 'Estrige-like, / To digest Iron and Steele!'; *London's Tempe* 139–40, 'The third show is an Estridge ... biting a horse-shoe').
253. *in riots*] in debauched, extravagant living (*OED* 21a).

Fortunatus. Forgive me, I will be more provident. 255
Fortune. No, endless follies follow endless wealth.
   Thou hadst thy fancy, I must have thy fate,
   Which is to die when th'art most fortunate.
   This inky thread thy ugly sins have spun:
   Black life, black death. [*To the Destinies*] Faster, that it
      were done. 260
Fortunatus. Oh, let me live but till I can redeem.
Fortune. The Destinies deny thee longer life.
Fortunatus. I am but now lifted to happiness.
Fortune. And now take I most pride to cast thee down.
   Hadst thou chosen wisdom, this black had been white, 265
   And Death's stern brow could not thy soul affright.
Fortunatus. [*Offering the purse*] Take this again; give wisdom
   to my sons.
Fortune. No, fool, 'tis now too late. As death strikes thee,
   So shall their ends sudden and wretched be.
   Jove's daughters (righteous Destinies), make haste: 270
   His life hath wasteful been and let it waste.
         Exeunt [FORTUNE *and the three* Destinies].
Andelocia. Why the pox dost thou sweat so?
Shadow. For anger to see any of God's creatures have such
   filthy faces as these sempsters had that went hence.
Andelocia. Sempsters? Why, you ass, they are Destinies. 275
Shadow. Indeed, if it be one's destiny to have a filthy face, I
   know no remedy but to go masked and cry, 'Woe worth
   the Fates'.

---

264. most] *Dilke;* must *Q.*

---

259. inky thread] presumably the three Destinies who enter '*working*' (230.1 SD) are working on this inky thread of Fortunatus's life. Kiefer suggests that Fortune may herself handle the black thread: 'it would be theatrically appropriate if the deity who earlier handed to Fortunatus the magic purse were now to hold out to him the thread of his own misspent life' ('Fortune on the Renaissance Stage', 73).
   270. *Jove's daughters*] see 1.227–8n.
   271. *waste*] decay, deteriorate; waste away.
   275. *Sempsters*] The early modern term 'sempster' (or 'seamster') corresponds to the modern 'seamstress', i.e. one who sews (used here because the Destinies spin the threads of life) (*OED*).
   277. *Woe worth*] cursed be, may evil befall or light upon (*OED* II.4a).

SC. 5]   THE COMEDY OF OLD FORTUNATUS   157

Ampedo. Why droops my father? [*To* FORTUNATUS] These
    are only shadows,
    Raised by the malice of some enemy   280
    To fright your life, o'er which they have no power.
Shadow. Shadows? I defy their kindred.
Fortunatus. O Ampedo, I faint. Help me, my sons.
Andelocia. Shadow, I pray thee run and call more help.
Shadow. If that desperate Don Dego Death hath ta'en up the   285
    cudgells once, here's never a fencer in Cyprus dare take
    my old master's part.
Andelocia. Run, villain, call more help.
Shadow. Bid him thank the Destinies for this.   *Exit.*
Fortunatus. Let him shrink down and die between your
    arms,   290
    Help comes in vain. No hand can conquer Fate.
    This instant is the last of my life's date.
    This goddess (if at least she be a goddess)
    Names herself Fortune. Wand'ring in a wood,
    Half-famished, her I met. 'I have', quoth she,   295
    'Six gifts to spend upon mortality:
    Wisdom, strength, health, beauty, long life, and riches.
    Out of my bounty, one of these is thine'.
Ampedo. What benefit did from your choice arise?

---

289. him] *Q;* me *Dilke.*

---

285. *Don Dego*] Dekker's preferred spelling (retained here for the purposes of metre) for 'Don Diego', i.e. a Spaniard (in a pejorative sense). See *Sir Thomas Wyatt*, 4.2.51–8, esp. 52: 'A Dondego is a kinde of Spanish Stockfish, or poore John'.

285–6. *ta'en up the cudgels*] to play a contest with cudgels/short sticks, e.g. Richard Stubbes's argument that a man is not a fencer if he only '*sometime taketh up the cudgells to play a venny*' (i.e. a bout of fencing) (*Th'overthrow of stage-playes* (1599), 73) (both examples antedate *OED* 1.b by 30 years).

290. *Let him shrink*] Dilke emends to 'Let me shrink', but Fortunatus, although indeed referring to himself, uses the third person because he is responding directly to Shadow's injunction, 'Bid *him* thank the Destinies'.

299. *What benefit ... arise?*] Ampedo can't be making a glib judgement about the real 'benefit' of the choice, since Fortunatus finds it necessary to reveal in the next line that he chose riches. Ampedo is simply asking which gift his father chose.

Fortunatus. Listen, my sons. In this small compass lies 300
  Infinite treasure. This she gave to me,
  And gave to this, this virtue: 'Take', quoth she,
  'So often as from hence thou drawst thy hand,
  Ten golden pieces of that kingdom's coin
  Where'er thou liv'st, which plenteous sure shall last 305
  After thy death, till thy sons' lives do waste'.
Andelocia. Father, your choice was rare, the gift divine.
Fortunatus. It had been so, if riches had been mine.
Ampedo. But hath this golden virtue never failed?
Fortunatus. Never.
Andelocia.   Oh, admirable! Here's a fire 310
  Hath power to thaw the very heart of death
  And give stones life, by this most sacred breath.
  See brother, here's all India in my hand.
Fortunatus. Inherit you, my sons, that golden land.
  This hat I brought away from Babylon. 315
  I robbed the Sultan of it; 'tis a prize
  Worth twenty empires. In this jewel lies –

---

308. riches] *Q;* wisdom *Dilke.*   312. breath] *Rhys;* death *Q.*   317. empires. In this jewel lies –] *Bowers;* empires in this jewel lies *Dilke;* Empires. In this Jewell lies. *Q.*

---

300. *small compass*] That 'small compass' here explicitly refers to the purse ('This she gave to me', 301) suggests that the purse is also the subject of Fortunatus's announcement in 136 above. As with Barabas's 'Infinite riches in a little room' (*Jew of Malta* 1.1.37), the idea of a small or humble vessel for tremendous wealth is proverbial (Dent W921).

308. *riches had been mine*] Editors since Dilke have substituted 'wisdom' for *Q*'s 'riches', observing that the context demands the change. This is intuitively correct, but it is difficult to comprehend how a scribal error would produce such a mistake, and Ampedo's next line is consonant with 'riches' rather than 'wisdom'. Moreover, as Bowers notes, the emendation loses the irony and ignores the fact that Ampedo's question in the next line depends on wordplay.

313. *India*] i.e. the East Indies (cf. 1.343n above).

317. *empires. In this jewel lies –*] Bowers challenges the emendation of all editors since Dilke, who ignore the capitalization and punctuation and add 'in this jewel lies' to the preceding sentence. He notes the parallel construction in ll. 301–2 where the value of the purse is described; here, he is in the process of describing the value of the hat, but is interrupted.

SC. 5]   THE COMEDY OF OLD FORTUNATUS   159

Andelocia. How, father? Jewel? Call you this a jewel? It's
   coarse wool, a bald fashion and greasy to the brim. I have
   bought a better felt for a French crown forty times. Of   320
   what virtuous block is this hat, I pray?
Fortunatus. Set it upon thy head and with a wish,
   Thou in a moment, on the wind's swift wings
   Shalt be transported into any place.
Andelocia. A wishing-hat and a golden mine?   325
Fortunatus. O Andelocia, Ampedo! Now Death
   Sounds his third summons. I must hence. These jewels
   To both I do bequeath. Divide them not,
   But use them equally. Never bewray
   What virtues are in them, for if you do,   330
   Much shame, much grief, much danger follows you.
   Peruse this book; farewell. Behold in me
   The rotten strength of proud mortality.   *Dies.*
Ampedo. His soul is wand'ring to the Elizium shades.

---

323. a moment] *Dilke;* the moment *Q.*

319–20. *bald fashion … French crown*] Andelocia disparages the plain ('bald') hat with a pun on 'French crown' = baldness caused by syphilis (*OED* 2) (rather than = a French coin worth about 4s).

321. *block*] mould for a hat (*OED* 4a), e.g. 2 *Honest Whore,* 'Mine is as tall a felt as any is this day in *Millan,* and therefore I love it, for the blocke was cleft out for my head, and fits me to a haire' (1.3.15–17).

326–7. *Death … third summons*] Hoy suggests an allusion to the sounding of the trumpet three times in a playhouse to signify the commencement of a play.

329. *bewray*] See Cho.1, 40 above.

332. *Peruse this book*] Fortunatus has kept a diary of his travels, which he now bequeaths to his sons. The English traveller Thomas Coryate desperately sought the approval of the London elite through publishing various accounts of his travels (often at a loss); Fortunatus, by contrast, appears to have concealed his travelogue from others until the moment of his death. It would therefore appear to serve an altogether more personal purpose, of remembrance and perhaps mind-travelling (see McInnis, *Mind-Travelling,* 81).

333. SD] As Shirley notes, 'Fortunatus dies quietly, but the occurrence of even this type of death is an event which seems to belong outside the usual realm of comedy' (*Serious and Tragic Elements,* 51).

334. *Elizium*] The primary sense is clearly 'Elysian' but see 1.153 and Prologue at Court 10 for puns on Elizabeth's name during the performance at Richmond. *Q's* spelling is retained here because it may be of a piece with the puns listed above, which are so clearly deliberate and occasional.

160   THE COMEDY OF OLD FORTUNATUS   [SC. 5

Andelocia. The flower that's fresh at noon at sunset fades.   335
   Brother, close you down his eyes, because you were his
   eldest; and with them close up your tears, whilst I (as all
   younger brothers do) shift for myself. Let us mourn
   because he's dead, but mourn the less because he cannot
   revive. The honour we can do him is to bury him royally.   340
   Let's about it then, for I'll not melt myself to death with
   scalding sighs, nor drop my soul out at mine eyes, were
   my father an emperor.
Ampedo. Hence, hence. Thou stopst the tide of my true tears.
   True grief is dumb, though it hath open ears.   345
Andelocia. Yet God send my grief a tongue, that I may have
   good utterance for it. Sob on, brother mine; whilst you
   sigh there, I'll sit and read what story my father has
   written here.

   They both fall asleep. FORTUNE *and a company of satyrs
   enter with music, and playing about* FORTUNATUS'S *body,
   take it away. They gone,* SHADOW *enters running.*

349.3. SD *it*] Dilke; *them* Q.   349.3. SD SHADOW] Dilke; Saddow Q.

---

335. *The flower ... fades*] a variant of the proverbial 'It fades (withers) like a flower' (Dent F386), which usually entails a short life, or withering at the peak of (metaphorical) summer.

337–40. *whilst I ... revive.*] The cutting of these lines for the Tufts performance reduces Andelocia's pragmatism.

338. *shift for myself*] First-born sons inherited their father's wealth; younger sons were generally not the recipient of such financial support, and had to provide ('shift') for themselves.

339–40. *mourn the less ... cannot revive*] Proverbially, tears cannot bring back the dead (Dent (?)T82.12).

342. *drop my soul out at mine eyes*] Andelocia refers to excessive weeping. Tears are the proverbial blood of the soul (Dent (?)T82.11), e.g. Ludwig Lavater, *The book of Ruth expounded in twenty eight sermons* (1584): 'sorrow bringeth forth tears: as bloud springeth out of the body if it be wounded: so if the soule be wounded teares break forth. Wherefore some do call teares the bloud of the soule' (fol. 34). Hoy compares with 6.85–7.

345. *True grief...ears*] An allusion to Seneca, *Hippolytus*, l. 607 ('*Curae leves loquuntur, ingentes stupent*'); cf. Chapman, *The Widow's Tears* (1605), sig. G4v: 'These / Grieves that sound so lowd, prove alwaies light'; or *Macbeth* 4.3.209–10: 'The grief that does not speak / Whispers the o'erfraught heart and bids it break'.

349.1. *a company of satyrs*] The inclusion of satyrs to clear the stage of Fortunatus's body appears to be occasional, perhaps unique to the performance at court. Their cloven feet may be suggestive of the diabolic. The sons

SC. 5]   THE COMEDY OF OLD FORTUNATUS   161

Shadow. I can get none, I can find none. [*To* ANDELOCIA]   350
   Where are you, master? Have I ta'en you napping? [*To*
   AMPEDO] And you too? I see sorrow's eyelids are made
   of a dormouse skin – they seldom open. Or of a miser's
   purse – that's always shut. Soho, master!
Andelocia. Shadow, why how now? What's the matter?   355
Shadow. I can get none sir, 'tis impossible.
Ampedo. What is impossible? What canst not get?
Shadow. No help for my old master.
Andelocia. Hast thou been all this while calling for help?
Shadow. Yes sir. He scorned all Famagusta when he was in   360
   his huffing, and now he lies puffing for wind, they say
   they scorn him.
Ampedo. The poison of their scorn infects not him;
   He wants no help. See where he breathless lies.
   [*To* ANDELOCIA] Brother, to what place have you
   borne his body?   365
Andelocia. I bear it? I touched it not.
Ampedo. Nor I. A leaden slumber pressed mine eyes.

---

remove the body in every other version of the play and legend (see Introduction, 50–51). Conover suggests that the actors who play the satyrs and dance in this scene were probably the same dancers who perform in the following scene (*Thomas Dekker*, 71).

349.2. with music] Presumably the music is solemn, for, in ll. 371–2 below, Ampedo thinks he 'heard the tunes / Of sullen passions apt for funerals'. The Tufts performance used Francis Pilkington's song 'Rest, sweet Nymphs' (1605) and marked the entry of the satyrs with 'The Short Measure of My Lady Wynkfield's Round' (date unknown).

353. *dormouse*] small rodent noted for its hibernation (*OED*) or sleepiness, e.g. *Twelfth Night*, 3.2.15: 'awake your dormouse valour'.

354. *Soho, master!*] 'Soho' is a hunter's call, drawing attention to a hare, and hence used to announce any discovery (*OED*).

361. *huffing*] Blustering, hectoring, bullying (*OED* n.2, citing this example as its first instance).

367. *A leaden slumber*] A heavy sleep, which prevented him noticing an important event (and thus perhaps recalling Richmond's 'Lest leaden slumber peise me down tomorrow / When I should mount with wings of victory', *Richard III* 5.4.85–6). cf. the 'golden slumbers' of the lullaby in *Patient Grissil* (4.2.99) and the 'iron slumber' of Detraction and Oblivion in *The Magnificent Entertainment* (833).

Shadow. Whether it were lead or latten that hasped down
those winking casements, I know not, but I found you
both snorting. 370
Ampedo. And in that sleep methought I heard the tunes
Of sullen passions apt for funerals
And saw my father's lifeless body borne
By satyrs. Oh, I fear that deity
Hath stolen him hence; that snudge, his destiny. 375
Andelocia. I fear he's risen again; didst not thou meet him?
Shadow. I, sir? Do you think this white and red durst have
kissed my sweet cheeks if they had seen a ghost? But,
master, if the Destinies, or Fortune, or the Fates, or the
fairies have stolen him, never indict them for the felony. 380
For by this means the charges of a tomb is saved and
you, being his heirs, may do as many rich executors do:
put that money in your purses and give out he died a
beggar.
Andelocia. Away, you rogue! My father die a beggar? 385
I'll build a tomb for him of massy gold.

---

368. *latten*] 'A mixed metal of yellow colour, either identical with, or closely resembling, brass; often hammered into thin sheets' (*OED* 'latten, n.*1*a', citing this example).
   hasped] fastened, as with a hasp (usually a hinged clasp of metal; *OED*).
   375. *snudge*] See 2.85n above.
   376. *risen again*] Possibly an allusion to Matthew 28: 6–10 and the women meeting Jesus after he has risen from the tomb, but more likely an allusion to Lazarus, who Lisa Hopkins shows was 'an important aspect of Cyprus's cultural identity' ('Love and War on Venus' Island: *Othello* and *The Lover's Melancholy*', *Journal of Mediterranean Studies* 25.1 (2016), 50). Hopkins cites a passage from Allott's *Wits theater of the little world* (1599) which specifies that 'Lazarus, whom Christ raysed from death, was the first Bishop of Cyprus' (Hopkins, 50).
   378–89. *But, master ... alabaster.*] This discussion of the memorial for their father, with implications about the importance of status, was cut for the Tufts performance.
   380. *fairies*] possibly referring to folklore tradition, popular in medieval romance, where fairies were thought to *take* mortals rather than the mortals *dying*.
   386. *massy gold*] solid and weighty, occurring in mass (*OED*); e.g. Theridamus's mention of 'costly cloth of massy gold' in *2 Tam.* 4.2.40.

SC. 5]   THE COMEDY OF OLD FORTUNATUS   163

Shadow. Methinks, master, it were better to let the memory
 of him shine in his own virtues – if he had any – than in
 alabaster.
Andelocia. I shall mangle that alabaster face, you whoreson   390
 virtuous vice.
Shadow. He has a marble heart that can mangle a face of
 alabaster.
Andelocia. Brother, come, come, mourn not. Our father is but
 stepped to agree with Charon for his boat hire to Elizium.   395
 See, here's a story of all his travels. This book shall come
 out with a new addition: I'll tread after my father's steps.
 I'll go measure the world. Therefore let's share these
 jewels. Take this, or this.
   [*He gestures to the hat and purse.*]

   389–90. *in alabaster ... alabaster face*] punning on (1) an ornamental stone used for carving (*OED* A.n.1, citing this example) and (2) smooth white alabaster-like skin (*OED* 2. fig.).
   395. *agree with*] to negotiate the price; in this case, of hiring the boat from Charon, the ferryman of Hades, to cross the river to the Underworld. Once there, Fortunatus, like Aeneas, will face a fork in the road: Elysium to the right, Tartarus to the left (see *Aeneid* 6). Andelocia suggests that Fortunatus is destined for paradise rather than torment, but he may be optimistic, given the devil-like satyrs that bear away his father's body.
   395. *Elizium*] See Prologue at Court, l.11n and 5.334n.
   396. *story ... book*] The German play contains greater detail of the contents of Fortunatus's book: 'unter dessen habe ich unsers Vatern Bibliothec gar durch gesuchet / und ein Buch gefunden / worin er alle seine Reisen die Zeit seines Lebens eingeschrieben / und finde wie er in seiner Jugendt die halbe Welt / alle Christliche Königreiche durchzogen / und da er unser Fraw Mutter schon gehabt / ist er noch in die Heidenschafft gezogen / derhalben lieber was wollen wir anfahen / laß uns unsers Vatern Fußstapffen auch nachtreten / laß uns ziehen und nach Ehren streben / wie unser Vater gethan / hastu es nicht gelesen / so liß es noch / ich weiß du wirst in eine Anmuth dadurch kommen' (*Von Fortunato*, Act 3, p. 148, ll. 11–21; 'in the meantime I have searched through our dear father's library / and found a book / in which he noted down all of the travels he has done throughout his lifetime / and found out how in his youth he went through half the world / through all Christian kingdoms / and even though he had our dear mother already / he still went to heathendom / because of this what shall we embark upon / let's follow in our dear father's footsteps / let's go and strive for honours / in the way our dear father has done / did you not read it / so read it now / I know you will get into its charm'). All translations fom this source are by Elena Benthaus.
   398–9. *let's share these jewels*] Andelocia explicitly disobeys their father's dying wish above (5.328), as Ampedo notes in the next line.

164   THE COMEDY OF OLD FORTUNATUS   [SC. 5

Ampedo. Will you then violate our father's will? 400
Andelocia. A Puritan? Keep a dead man's will? Indeed, in the old time, when men were buried in soft churchyards that their ghosts might rise, it was good. But brother, now they are imprisoned in strong brick and marble, they are fast. Fear not. Away, away! These are fooleries, gulleries, 405 trumperies. Here's this or this, or I am gone with both.
Ampedo. Do as you please, the sin shall not be mine. Fools call those things profane that are divine.
Andelocia. Are you content to wear the jewels by turns? I'll have the purse for a year, you the hat and as much gold 410 as you'll ask; and when my pursership ends, I'll resign and cap you.
Ampedo. I am content to bear all discontents.   *Exit.*
Andelocia. I should serve this bearing ass rarely now, if I should load him; but I will not. Though conscience be, 415 like physic, seldom used (for so it does least hurt), yet I'll take a dram of it. This for him and some gold; this for me, for having this mint about me, I shall want no wishing-cap. Gold is an eagle that can fly to any place; and like Death, that dares enter all places. Shadow, wilt 420 thou travel with me?
Shadow. I shall never fadge with the humour because I cannot lie.

420–1. Shadow... me?] *new line in Q.*

401–6. *Indeed ... gone with both.*] cut for the Tufts performance.
405. *gulleries*] deceptions, trickeries.
411. *pursership*] the position of purser (an office of responsibility) (*OED* 'purser, *n.* derivatives', citing this as its first example).
412. *cap you*] punning on 'take the cap from you' (despite the fact that he would be *giving* the cap *to* him) and 'to arrest' (*OED* † v.2, *Obs.* 1), e.g. the Host in Beaumont's *Knight of the Burning Pestle,* 'Twelve shillings you must pay, or I must cap you' (3.174).
416. *physic*] medicinal substance.
418. *mint*] money, coinage (*OED*, citing this example).
419. *wishing-cap*] *OED* first example.
422–3. *I shall never fadge ... I cannot lie*] Shadow will never be suitable (*fadge*) for travel, because lying is what travellers proverbially do (Dent T476*; see 5.139–40n above).

SC. 5]   THE COMEDY OF OLD FORTUNATUS   165

Andelocia. Thou dolt, we'll visit all the kings' courts in the
    world.   425
Shadow. So we may and return dolts home. But what shall
    we learn by travel?
Andelocia. Fashions.
Shadow. That's a beastly disease. Methinks it's better staying
    in your own country.   430
Andelocia. How? In mine own country? Like a cage-bird and
    see nothing?
Shadow. Nothing? Yes, you may see things enough, for what
    can you see abroad that is not at home? The same sun
    calls you up in the morning and the same man in the   435
    moon lights you to bed at night. Our fields are as green

---

427. travel] *Dilke;* trauaile *Q.*

426–7. *return dolts home ... learn by travel?*] Shadow gives voice to standard anti-travel sentiments from the period, questioning the utility of travelling and asserting that fools return just as foolish as they were when they left. The *ars apodemica* treatises are at pains to educate the would-be traveller in the art of travelling well, to avoid precisely this kind of unprofitable voyage. Justus Lipsius, for example, begins the 'pleasure and profit' section of his advice to the young Earl of Bedford with a desire to avoid the fate of the man 'that was carried faire and softly abroad in a cloake-bagge, and returned home as wise as he went out' (*A Direction for Travailers* (London, 1592), sig. A4r).

428. *Fashions*] Andelocia anticipates learning about fashionable trends in exotic countries; Shadow's reply ('That's a beastly disease', 431) wilfully misconstrues 'fashion' as 'farcin' (or 'farcy'), a disease afflicting horses (e.g. Gervaise Markham, *Markhams maister-peece* (1610), 'The farcy (of our ignorant Smiths called the Fashions)', 392).

431. *cage-bird*] As a compound noun, this example antedates the *OED* by some 26 years.

433–9. *Nothing? ... fair*] As Tiffany Stern notes, Richard Brome reworks this passage in *A Jovial Crew* (c.1640), when Oldrents tries to dissuade Springlove from wandering the countryside with a crew of beggars, asking: 'Does not the sun as comfortably shine / Upon my gardens as the opener fields? / Or on my fields as others far remote? / Are not my walks and greens as delectable / As the highways and the commons? / ... / Do not the birds sing here as sweet and lively / As any other where?' (1.1.192–203). In both plays, the metaphor of a 'cage-bird' (*Fortunatus* 5.431) or 'swallow in a cage' (*Jovial Crew* 1.1.183) triggers the favourable comparison of the home culture to the limitations of the foreign.

as theirs in summer and their frosts will nip us more in winter. Our birds sing as sweetly and our women are as fair. In other countries you shall have one drink to you whilst you kiss your hand and duck, he'll poison you. I confess you shall meet more fools, and asses, and knaves abroad than at home (yet God be thanked we have pretty store of all). But for punks, we put them down. 440

Andelocia. Prepare thy spirits, for thou shalt go with me.
To England shall our stars direct our course; 445
Thither the Prince of Cyprus, our king's son,
Is gone to see the lovely Agrippine.
Shadow, we'll gaze upon that English dame
And try what virtue gold has to inflame.
First to my brother, then away let's fly. 450
Shadow must be a courtier ere he die. *Exit.*

Shadow. If I must, the Fates shall be served. I have seen many clowns courtiers, then why not Shadow? Fortune, I am for thee. *Exit.*

[Scene 6]

Enter ORLEANS *melancholic,* GALLOWAY *with him, a* BOY *after them with a lute.*

---

437. *nip us more*] Daniel suggested 'not more' (a parallel construction to the other examples of domestic qualities equalling or exceeding their foreign counterparts), but the logic of the argument requires foreign winters to exceed domestic ones in their harshness, so the emendation is inappropriate.

440. *kiss your hand ... poison you*] Shadow moves from praising home culture to denigrating foreign cultures for their treachery; Hoy compares with Dekker's *A strange horse-race* (1613): 'After this hee travelled into Italy, and there learned to embrace with one arme, and stabbe with another' (sig. E3r). The meaning of 'duck' here is 'to bow humbly' (a sign of respect, a formality), cf. *Jew of Malta* 2.3.23–5: 'I learned in Florence how to kiss my hand, / Heave up my shoulders when they call me dog, / And duck as low as any bare-foot friar'.

443. *But for punks*] Shadow's sentiments might be paraphrased as: 'except for (their abundance of) prostitutes, we outshine them in every count'. This sentence was cut for the Tufts performance (perhaps it was too bawdy?).

0.1. SD] There is a general analogy between the opening of this scene, with the love-sick melancholic accompanied by music, and the opening of Shakespeare's *Twelfth Night* (1601), where Orsino similarly enjoys and then

SC. 6]   THE COMEDY OF OLD FORTUNATUS   167

Orleans. [*To* BOY] Be gone. Leave that with me and leave me
  to myself. If the king ask for me, swear to him I am sick
  and thou shalt not lie. Pray thee, leave me.
Boy. I am gone, sir.   *Exit.*
Orleans. This music makes me but more out of tune.   5
  Oh, Agrippina.
Galloway.   Gentle friend, no more.
  Thou sayst love is a madness; hate it then,

---

dismisses the 'sweet sound' (1.1.5). Rhys adds the setting: 'London. The
Court of Athelstane'. As Conover notes, if there is no intermission between
the previous scene (where Andelocia embarks on his adventures) and this
one, the Orleans action provides some 250 lines for the actor playing
Andelocia to change into 'a more sumptuous costume for the English court'
(Conover, *Thomas Dekker*, 71).
  0.1. Enter ORLEANS melancholic] Greg (*Henslowe Papers*, 144) attempted
to argue that the plot of the lost '2 Fortune's Tennis' play was somehow
related to Dekker's play, by noting the similarities between the plays' titles
('Fortune's Tennis' / *Fortunatus*) and quoting the present SD in comparison
with the plot's 'Enter Orleaunce musing'. Although Dekker had been paid
for 'his boocke called the fortewn te*n*es' on 6 September 1600 (Foakes, 137),
there does not appear to be any connection whatsoever between that first
part or its ostensible sequel ('2 Fortune's Tennis') and *Old Fortunatus*. See
McInnis, '"2 Fortune's Tennis" and the Admiral's Men', in *Lost Plays in
Shakespeare's England*, ed. David McInnis and Matthew Steggle (Basingstoke:
Palgrave Macmillan, 2014), 105–26.
  1–4. *Be gone ... sir.*] Orleans's command may reflect the boy's lack of skill
(his performance cannot cure Orleans's melancholy); the music efficiently
signifies Orleans's 'preoccupation with his own melancholy' (Ketterer, 229–
30). Alternatively, if the boy is skilled at playing, his role here may simply be
to serve as a marker of the courtly setting. These lines were cut for the Tufts
performance.
  5 79. *This music ... grave.*] Charles Lamb reproduced this passage in his
Specimens of English Dramatic Poets (pp. 60–2), noting: 'The humour of a
frantic Lover is here done to the life. Orleans is as passionate an Inamorato
as any which Shakspeare ever Drew. He is just such another adept in Love's
reasons. ... He talks "pure Biron and Romeo", he is almost as poetical as
they, quite as philosophical, only a little madder' (62–3n). Swinburne took
Lamb to task on this point, replacing 'almost' with 'fully', adding: 'Sidney
himself might have applauded the verses which clothe with living music a
passion as fervent and as fiery a fancy as his own. Not even in the rapturous
melodies of that matchless series of songs and sonnets which glorify the
inseparable names of Astrophel and Stella will the fascinated student find a
passage more enchanting than this' (*The Age of Shakespeare*, 64–5).
  7. *love is a madness*] proverbial (Dent L505.2).

Even for the name's sake.
Orleans.   Oh, I love that madness,
Even for the name's sake.
Galloway.   Let me tame this frenzy
By telling thee thou art a prisoner here;   10
By telling thee she's daughter to a king;
By telling thee the King of Cyprus' son
Shines like a sun between her looks and thine,
Whilst thou seemst but a star to Agrippine.
He loves her.
Orleans.   If he do? Why, so do I.   15
Galloway. Love is ambitious and loves majesty.
Orleans. Dear friend, thou art deceived; love's voice doth sing
As sweetly in a beggar as a king.
Galloway. Dear friend, thou art deceived. Oh, bid thy soul
Lift up her intellectual eyes to heaven   20
And in this ample book of wonders read
Of what celestial mould, what sacred essence,
Her self is formed; the search whereof will drive
Sounds musical among the jarring spirits
And in sweet tune set that which none inherits.   25
Orleans. I'll gaze on heaven if Agrippine be there.
If not: *fa, la, la, sol, la, &c.*

---

11. *she's daughter to a king*] Rhys, referring to l. 388 ('the queen (my mother)'), notes that the historical Athelstan had neither wife nor daughter. Hoy notes that '[t]he love interest between Agripyne and her suitors, Orleans and the Prince of Cyprus, is the chief addition to this second part', noting of the present scene in particular: 'it is tempting to see in the scene, which is an interpolation in the Fortunatus story, a distinctly Dekkerean touch' (84).

17–18. *love's voice ... king*] Hoy compares with the proverb 'Love lives in cottages as well as in courts' (Tilley L519; not in Dent).

27. fa, la, la, sol, la] Ketterer (230) notes that, although Orleans retains the boy's lute in l. 1, there is no explicit direction for him to use it when he sings here at l. 27, and indeed his use of solmization (a mnemonic device indicating sound intervals) suggests that he does not use the lute.

Galloway. Oh, call this madness in! See from the windows
    Of every eye derision thrusts out cheeks
    Wrinkled with idiot laughter; every finger   30
    Is like a dart shot from the hand of scorn,
    By which thy name is hurt, thine honour torn.
Orleans. Laugh they at me, sweet Galloway?
Galloway.   Even at thee.
Orleans. Ha, ha, I laugh at them. Are not they mad,
    That let my true, true sorrow make them glad?   35
    I dance and sing only to anger grief,
    That in that anger, he might smite life down
    With his iron fist. Good heart, it seemeth then
    They laugh to see grief kill me. Oh, fond men,
    You laugh at others' tears; when others smile,   40
    You tear yourselves in pieces. Vile, vile, vile.
    Ha, ha! When I behold a swarm of fools
    Crowding together to be counted wise,
    I laugh because sweet Agrippine's not there,
    But weep because she is not anywhere,   45
    And weep because whether she be or not,
    My love was ever, and is still, forgot. Forgot, forgot,
        forgot.
Galloway. Draw back this stream. Why should my Orleans
    mourn?
Orleans. Look yonder, Galloway. Dost thou see that sun?
    Nay good friend, stare upon it, mark it well.   50

28–9. *the windows / Of every eye*] The association of eyes with windows is a familiar Petrarchan conceit, cf. Sidney's *Astrophil and Stella* (1591), sonnet 9: 'The Windowes now, through which this heavenly guest / Lookes ore the world' (4).

30. *idiot laughter*] First example in the *OED* of 'idiot' as 'Of, relating to, or characteristic of an idiot or idiocy, idiotic' (n. and adj., B. adj. (attrib.) 2).

36–41. *I dance ... vile.*] cut for the Tufts performance.

38. *iron fist*] denoting firmness/ruthlessness in behaviour or authority; *OED* first instance.

39. *fond*] infatuated, foolish.

47. *forgot ... forgot*] Cf. Anne's repetition of 'farewell' five times at the end of Anon. (Dekker?), *A Warning for Fair Women* (1599), sig. K3r.

Ere he be two hours older, all that glory
Is banished heaven and then (for grief) this sky
That's now so jocund will mourn all in black.
And shall not Orleans mourn? Alack, alack.
Oh, what a savage tyranny it were   55
T'enforce care, laugh and woe. Not shed a tear?
Dead is my love, I am buried in her scorn;
That is my sunset, and shall I not mourn?
Yes by my troth I will.
Galloway.   Dear friend, forbear.
Beauty, like sorrow, dwelleth everywhere.   60
Raze out this strong idea of her face;
As fair as hers shineth in any place.
Orleans. Thou art a traitor to that white and red
Which, sitting on her cheeks (being Cupid's throne),
Is my heart's sovereign. Oh, when she is dead,   65
This wonder (beauty) shall be found in none.
Now Agrippine's not mine, I vow to be
In love with nothing but deformity.
O fair Deformity, I muse all eyes
Are not enamoured of thee. Thou didst never   70
Murder men's hearts or let them pine like wax,
Melting against the sun of destiny.
Thou art a faithful nurse to chastity.
Thy beauty is not like to Agrippine's,
For cares, and age, and sickness hers deface,   75

---

51. older] *Dilke;* elder *Q.*   61. Raze] *this ed.;* Rase *Dilke;* Race *Q.*   72. of destiny] *Dilke;* of thy deformitie *Daniel;* of thy disdain *Swinburne* (65n); of thy destinie *Q.*

---

53. *jocund ... black*] Cf. *R&J* 17.9–10: 'Night's candles are burnt out, and jocund day / stands tiptoe on the misty mountain tops'.
  63–4. *white and red ... cheeks*] The comparison between damask roses (or roses and lilies) and the cheeks is a standard Petrarchan conceit; cf. 1.249 above, or Shakespeare's sonnet 130, ll. 5–6.
  68. *In love ... deformity*] Ironically, Orleans's vow is fulfilled when Agrippine is punished with the deformity of horns when she eats Vice's apples (scenes 8–9) (Conover, *Thomas Dekker,* 69 and 78).
  69–79. *O fair ... grave.*] cut for the Tufts performance.
  72. *Melting ... sun of destiny*] Cf. the potentially offensive lines at 5.221 above.

But thine's eternal. O Deformity,
Thy fairness is not like to Agrippine's,
For (dead) her beauty will no beauty have,
But thy face looks most lovely in the grave.

Enter Prince of CYPRUS *and* AGRIPPINE.

Galloway. See where they come together hand in hand. 80
Orleans. Oh, watch, sweet Galloway, when their hands do part.
Between them shalt thou find my murdered heart.
Cyprus. [*To* AGRIPPINE] By this then it seems a thing impossible, to know when an English lady loves truly.
Agrippine. Not so, for when her soul steals into her heart, and 85
her heart leaps up to her eyes, and her eyes drop into her hands, then if she say, 'Here's my hand', she's your own; else never.
Cyprus. Here's a pair of your prisoners; let's try their opinion.
Agrippine. My kind prisoners, well encountered! The Prince 90
of Cyprus here and myself have been wrangling about a question of love. My Lord of Orleans, you look lean and likest a lover: Whether is it more torment to love a lady and never enjoy her, or always to enjoy a lady, whom you cannot choose but hate? 95
Orleans. To hold her ever in mine arms whom I loathe in my heart were some plague, yet the punishment were no more than to be enjoined to keep poison in my hand, yet never to taste it.

---

78. dead] *Dilke;* dread *Q.*

84. *an English lady loves*] Wiggins suggests that this line and ll. 181–2 in this scene 'seem to echo' the title of a lost play from the Admiral's Men's repertory in 1594, 'The Love of an English Lady', and further conjectures that, if the present scene were derived from the (hypothetical) lost '2 Fortunatus' play, that play and 'Love of an English Lady' might be identical, 'though that play's dislocation from any performances of 1 *Fortunatus* keeps the possibility very remote' (Wiggins, #851).

93–5. *Whether is it ... hate?*] Prior to writing *Murphy*, Samuel Beckett read these lines and transcribed Agrippine's dilemma into his notebook, where it 'would become the pattern of Neary's yearnings for Miss Counihan and Miss Dwyer' (C. J. Ackerley, *Demented Particulars: The Annotated Murphy* (Edinburgh University Press, 2004, rpt 2010), 7).

Agrippine. But say you should be compelled to swallow the poison? 100
Orleans. Then a speedy death would end a speeding misery. But to love a lady and never enjoy her? Oh, it is not death, but worse than damnation; 'tis hell, 'tis –
Agrippine. No more, no more, good Orleans. Nay then, I see 105
my prisoner is in love too.
Cyprus. Methinks soldiers cannot fall into the fashion of love.
Agrippine. Methinks a soldier is the most faithful lover of all men else, for his affection stands not upon compliment. His wooing is plain home-spun stuff: there's no outland- 110
ish thread in it, no rhetoric. A soldier casts no figures to get his mistress' heart; his love is like his valour in the field, when he pays downright blows.
Galloway. True, madam, but would you receive such payment? 115
Agrippine. No, but I mean I love a soldier best for his plain dealing.
Cyprus. That's as good as the first.
Agrippine. Be it so, that goodness I like. For what lady can abide to love a spruce, silken-face courtier that stands 120
every morning two or three hours learning how to look by his glass, how to speak by his glass, how to sigh by his glass, how to court his mistress by his glass? I would wish

---

108–11. *soldier ... no rhetoric*] Perhaps recalling the courtship of Henry V and Catherine in 5.2 of Shakespeare's play, as Lisa Hopkins suggests (*From the Romans to the Normans*, 180).

110. *home-spun stuff*] simple, plain, unsophisticated (*OED*, citing this as its second example).

111–19. *A soldier ... I like.*] cut for the Tufts performance.

111. *casts no figures*] i.e. rhetorical figures.

119–23. *what lady ... glass?*] another discussion about the relative merits of knowledge acquired through experience and knowledge acquired through reading; cf. the debate above (5.426–7n) about travelling well.

120. *spruce, silken-face*] 'spruce' here means 'dapper', as in Jonson's description of Fastidious Brisk as a 'neat, spruce, affecting courtier; one that wears clothes well and in fashion, practiseth by his glass how to salute' (*Every Man Out*, *CWBJ*, Characters 28). For 'silken-face' as elegant, cf. Marston, *The metamorphosis of Pigmalions image And certaine satyres* (1598), 'yonder sober man ... with his silken face / Smiles on the holy crue' (sig. D2v).

SC. 6]   THE COMEDY OF OLD FORTUNATUS   173

 him no other plague but to have a mistress as brittle as
 glass. 125
Galloway. And that were as bad as the horn plague.
Cyprus. Are any lovers possessed with this madness?
Agrippine. What madmen are not possessed with this love?
 Yet by my troth, we poor women do but smile in our
 sleeves to see all this foppery. Yet we all desire to see our 130
 lovers attired gallantly, to hear them sing sweetly, to
 behold them dance comely and such like. But this apish
 monkey fashion of effeminate niceness, out upon it! Oh,
 I hate it worse than to be counted a scold.
Cyprus. Indeed men are most regarded when they least regard 135
 themselves.
Galloway. And women most honoured when they show most
 mercy to their lovers.
Orleans. But is't not a miserable tyranny to see a lady triumph
 in the passions of a soul languishing through her cruelty? 140
Cyprus. Methinks it is.
Galloway. Methinks 'tis more than tyranny.
Agrippine. So think not I; for as there is no reason to hate any
 that love us, so it were madness to love all that do not
 hate us. Women are created beautiful only because men 145
 should woo them; for 'twere miserable tyranny to enjoin
 poor women to woo men. I would not hear of a woman
 in love, for my father's kingdom.
Cyprus. I never heard of any woman that hated love.
Agrippine. Nor I. But we had all rather die than confess we 150
 love. Our glory is to hear men sigh whilst we smile, to

---

127. with] *Q;* of *Dilke.*

126–38. *And that ... lovers.*] cut for the Tufts performance.
126. *horn plague*] i.e. being cursed (plagued) with the sign of a cuckold: horns (not in *OED*); an ominous foreshadowing of the fates of Andelocia (7.102-3), Agrippine (9.5-0), Montrose (9.64-71), and Longueville (9.72).
 129–30. *smile in our sleeves*] To laugh or smile in one's sleeve is proverbial (Dent S535), meaning 'to laugh to oneself; to nurse inward feelings of amusement or derision' (*OED* v. P1. Phrases d, noting the origin of the phrase in post-classical Latin *ridere in sinum*).
 151–4. *Our glory ... night-cap*] Agrippine's admission lends credibility to the sartorial instructions Malvolio reads in the forged letter in *Twelfth Night.*

kill them with a frown, to strike them dead with a sharp
eye; to make you this day wear a feather and tomorrow
a sick night-cap. Oh! Why, this is rare. There's a certain
deity in this, when a lady by the magic of her looks can   155
turn a man into twenty shapes.
Orleans. [*Aside to* GALLOWAY] Sweet friend, she speaks this
but to torture me.
Galloway. [*Aside to* ORLEANS] I'll teach thee how to plague
her: love her not.
Agrippine. [*Aside*] Poor Orleans, how lamentably he looks; if
he stay, he'll make me surely love him for pure pity. I   160
must send him hence, for of all sorts of love I hate the
French. [*To* ORLEANS] I pray thee, sweet prisoner,
entreat Lord Longueville to come to me presently.
Orleans. I will, and esteem myself more than happy that you
will employ me.   *Exit.*   165
Agrippine. Watch him, watch him for God's sake, if he sigh
not or look not back.
Cyprus. He does both: but what mystery lies in this?
Agrippine. Nay, no mystery, 'tis as plain as Cupid's forehead.
Why, this is as it should be: 'and esteem myself more   170
than happy that you will employ me'. My French pris-
oner is in love over head and ears.
Cyprus. It's wonder how he 'scapes drowning.
Galloway. With whom, think you?
Agrippine. With his keeper, for a good wager. Ah, how glad is   175
he to obey? And how proud am I to command in this
empire of affection? Over him and such spongy-livered

---

156. *shapes*] disguises (*OED*) or otherwise altered appearances.

172. *in love over head and ears*] indicating complete immersion in love; the modern phrase 'head over heels in love' (which makes little sense) is a corruption originating in the eighteenth century (*OED*).

175. *keeper*] Agrippine is his gaoler ('keeper') and Andelocia is a (political?) prisoner (cf. 'My French prisoner', 171–2, and earlier references to his imprisonment).

177–9. *Over him ... sword.*] cut for the Tufts performance.

177. *spongy-livered*] The use of 'spongy' (having porous texture resembling that of a sponge) antedates the *OED*'s earliest example (1628) of the adjective being used in a figurative context.

youths that lie soaking in love I triumph more with mine
eye than ever he did over a soldier with his sword. Is't
not a gallant victory for me to subdue my father's enemy   180
with a look? Prince of Cyprus, you were best take heed
how you encounter an English lady.
Cyprus. God bless me from loving any of you, if all be so
cruel.
Agrippine. God bless me from suffering you to love me, if you   185
be not so formable.
Cyprus. Will you command me any service, as you have done
Orleans?
Agrippine. No other service but this: that (as Orleans) you
love me, for no other reason but that I may torment you.   190
Cyprus. I will, conditionally; that in all company I may call
you my tormenter.
Agrippine. You shall, conditionally; that you never beg for
mercy. Come, my Lord of Galloway.
Galloway. Come, sweet Madam.   *Exeunt.* CYPRUS *remains.*   195
Cyprus. The ruby-coloured portals of her speech
Were closed by mercy but upon her eye,
Attired in frowns, sat murd'ring cruelty.

Enter AGRIPPINE *and listens.*

She's angry that I durst so high aspire.
Oh, she disdains that any stranger's breast   200
Should be a temple for her deity.
She's full of beauty, full of bitterness.
Till now, I did not dally with love's fire,
And when I thought to try his flames indeed,
I burnt me even to cinders. O my stars,   205

---

195. SD] *this ed.; Manet* CYPRUS *Q (and placed on the following line).*   203. not dally] *Q;* but dally *Dilke.*

181–2. *Prince ... English lady*] See 84n above.
186. *formable*] That may be formed (*OED*, citing this example). Dilke suggests 'if you cannot be formed or moulded in the manner I describe'.
196. *ruby-coloured ... speech*] i.e. her lips; Hoy compares Shakespeare's *Venus and Adonis* 451–2: 'Once more the ruby-coloured portal opened, / Which to his speech did honey passage yield'.

176   THE COMEDY OF OLD FORTUNATUS   [SC. 6

Why from my native shore did your beams guide me
To make me dote on her that doth deride me?
                    She kneels. He walks, musing.
Agrippine. [Aside] Hold him in this mind, sweet Cupid, I
conjure thee. Oh, what music these hey-hoes make! I was
about to cast my little, little self into a great love-trance   210
for him, fearing his heart had been flint. But since I see
'tis pure virgin wax, he shall melt his belly full, for now
I know how to temper him.   *Exit.*
Cyprus. Never beg mercy? Yet be my tormenter.
                                            He spies her.
I hope she heard me not. Doubtless she did,   215
And now will she insult upon my passions
And vex my constant love with mockeries.
Nay, then I'll be mine own physician
And outface love, and make her think that I
Mourned thus because I saw her standing by.   220

                    Enter CORNWALL.

What news, my Lord of Cornwall?
Cornwall.   This, fair prince:
One of your countrymen is come to court.
A lusty gallant, brave in Cyprus isle,

---

207. SD] *this ed.; centred and placed in the following line in* Q.   220.1. SD] *placed after* 221 *in* Q.   221. This, fair prince:] *Bowers;* This fair prince, Q.   223. brave] Q; born *Daniel.*

---

209. *hey-hoes*] alternative (probably onomatopoeic) local name for the 'hickwall' or Green Woodpecker (*OED*).

221. SD] Marking Cornwall's entrance seems somewhat redundant after Cyprus's salutation (which is where the SD occurs in *Q*). Hoy attributed such redundancies in the German *Von Fortunato* play to it being a reported text (the faulty memory of the reporter leading to an attempt to 'reconstruct the stage action' using the *Volksbuch*, 90), but Schlueter, who convincingly argues against its status as a reported text, suggests such redundancies are the product of the German editor of the 1620 volume, Frederick Menius (see Schlueter, 'New Light', 129).

223. *brave*] Daniel's conjectural emendation 'born' is plausible but introduces redundancy, since the King of Cyprus's 'countrymen' are necessarily 'born' in Cyprus, whereas *Q*'s 'brave' adds a detail that isn't tautological.

With fifty bar'd horses prancing at his heels,
Backed by as many strong-limbed Cypriots, 225
All whom he keeps in pay; whose offered service
Our king with arms of gladness hath embraced.
Cyprus. Born in the isle of Cyprus? What's his name?
Cornwall. His servants call him Fortunatus' son.
Cyprus. Rich Fortunatus' son? Is he arrived? 230

Enter LONGUEVILLE, GALLOWAY, *and*
CHESTER *with jewels.*

Longueville. This he bestowed on me.
Chester. And this on me.
Galloway. And this bounteous hand enforced me take.
Longueville. I prize this jewel at a hundred marks,
Yet would he needs bestow this gift on me.
Cyprus. My lords, whose hand hath been thus prodigal? 235
Galloway. Your countryman, my lord; a Cypriot.
Longueville. The gallant sure is all compact of gold.
To every lady hath he given rich jewels,
And sent to every servant in the court
Twenty fair English angels.
Cyprus. This is rare. 240

Enter LINCOLN.

Lincoln. My lords, prepare yourselves for revelling.
'Tis the king's pleasure that this day be spent
In royal pastimes, that this golden lord
(For so all that behold him christen him)
May taste the pleasures of our English court. 245
Here comes the gallant, shining like the sun.

---

224. *bar'd*] barded/barbed (armed or covered with bards, 'the protective covering for the breast and flanks of a war-horse, made of metal plates, or of leather set with metal spikes or bosses', *OED* n2). Dilke compares with Heywood, *The Four Prentices of London*: 'Shall our bar'd horses clime yond Mountaine tops' (1615, sig. G3v).

240. *English angels*] angels (cf. 2.37n) because the purse supplies local currency (1.307) and the current location is England.

178   THE COMEDY OF OLD FORTUNATUS   [SC. 6

  Trumpets sound. Enter ATHELSTAN, ANDELOCIA,
  AGRIPPINE, ORLEANS, *ladies, and other attendants,*
  [*and*] INSULTADO *a Spanish lord. Music sounds within.*

Andelocia. For these your royal favours done to me
 (Being a poor stranger), my best powers shall prove
 By acts of worth the soundness of my love.
Athelstan. Herein your love shall best set out itself: 250
 By staying with us. If our English isle
 Hold any object welcome to your eyes,
 Do but make choice and claim it as your prize.
Andelocia. I thank your grace.
      The KING *and* CYPRUS *confer aside.*
 [*Aside*] Would he durst keep his word,
 I know what I would claim. Tush, man, be bold!   255
 Were she a saint, she may be won with gold.
Cyprus. [*To* ATHELSTAN] 'Tis strange, I must confess, but
 in this pride
 His father Fortunatus (if he live)
 Consumes his life in Cyprus. Still he spends,
 And still his coffers with abundance swell.   260
 But how he gets these riches, none can tell.

---

254. SD] *this ed.; placed at line* 253 *in* Q.

246.1. SD] Smeaton starts a new scene here, specifying the setting: '*The Palace of Athelstane*'.

246.3. SD INSULTADO a Spanish lord] The inclusion of this cameo appears to be unique to the court performance (it is not in the 1620 German play, which is apparently based on the pre-court version of *Old Fortunatus*). It follows the inclusion (probably a late insertion) of the Spanish soldier Signor Bragadino in the second scene of Chapman's *The Blind Beggar of Alexandria* (1596), presumably in response to the success of Don Armado in Shakespeare's *Love's Labour's Lost* (1596).

246.3. SD Music sounds within] As Ketterer notes, what follows appears to be 'the longest continuous musical performance evidenced in the extant repertory of the company' (231). The music sounds for nine continuous quarto pages of the play. Duffin notes that, in addition to music appropriate to the Spanish *pavane* danced by Insultado at l. 315 below, allusions in the dialogue suggest two possible pieces that may have been played in this sequence (see 324n, below). The Tufts performance called for 'a trumpet flourish of the period, and, immediately following, "The King's Pavan", date unknown'.

258. *if he live*] News of Fortunatus's death has apparently not spread.

SC. 6]   THE COMEDY OF OLD FORTUNATUS   179

Athelstan. [*To* CYPRUS] Hold him in talk. [*To* AGRIPPINE]
   Come hither, Agrippine.
                    The KING *and* AGRIPPINE *confer aside.*
Cyprus. [*To* ANDELOCIA] But what enticed young
   Andelocia's soul
   To wander hither?
Andelocia. [*To* CYPRUS] That which did allure
   My sovereign's son: the wonder of the place.   265
Agrippine. [*To* ATHELSTAN] This curious heap of wonders,
   which an empress
   Gave him, he gave me; and by Venus' hand
   The warlike *amorato* needs would swear
   He left his country Cyprus for my love.
Athelstan. [*To* AGRIPPINE] If by the sovereign magic of
   thine eye   270
   Thou canst enchant his looks to keep the circles
   Of thy fair cheeks, be bold to try thy charms.
   Feed him with hopes and find the royal vein
   That leads this Cypriot to his golden mine.
   [*To all*] Here's music spent in vain! Lords, fall to
   dancing!   275
Cyprus. [*To* AGRIPPINE] My fair tormentor, will you lend a
   hand?
Agrippine. [*Indicating* ANDELOCIA] I'll try this stranger's
   cunning in a dance.

262.1. SD] *this ed.; placed before line 262 in Q.*

---

268. amorato] One who is enamoured; a lover (usually with a connotation of extravagance); more frequently in the form *'innamorato'*.

270-4. *If ... golden mine*] In the German play, the King and Agrippine conceive this plan to uncover the secret of Andelocia's wealth only after they impose the ban on firewood sales (6.348-50 in Dekker) and Andelocia has solved this dilemma by purchasing expensive spices to burn for fuel (cf. Dekker 6.452-7). The German Andelocia succeeds in his banquet preparations, and *then* Agrippine discovers and removes the source of his fabulous wealth. Dekker's Andelocia has to furnish a banquet without firewood *or* the means to purchase spices to burn; possibly this conflation and acceleration of events was the product of Dekker's need to condense his play sufficiently to include the additional material for court.

277. *cunning*] literally 'knowledge' or 'craft' but with a less positive sense of 'craftiness' and possibly even 'occult craft' (*OED* n.1. †4) in reference to Andelocia's supernaturally enabled riches (cf. 6.365-7 below).

277. *dance*] The Tufts performance specified '[f]or the Court Dance; "King Harry the Eighth's Pavan", date unknown'.

Andelocia. My cunning is but small, yet who'll not prove
   To shame himself for such a lady's love?
            [AGRIPPINE *and* ANDELOCIA *dance.*]
Orleans. [*Aside*] These Cypriots are the devils that torture
   me.   280
   He courts her and she smiles, but I am born
   To be her beauty's slave and her love's scorn.
Andelocia. I shall never have the face to ask the question
   twice.
Agrippine. What's the reason: cowardliness or pride?
Andelocia. Neither: but 'tis the fashion of us Cypriots, both   285
   men and women, to yield at first assault, and we expect
   others should do the like.
Agrippine. It's a sign, that either your women are very black
   and are glad to be sped, or your men very fond and will
   take no denial.   290
Andelocia. Indeed, our ladies are not so fair as you.
Agrippine. But your men more vent'rous at a breach than you,
   or else they are all dastardly soldiers.
Andelocia. He that fights under these sweet colours and yet
   turns coward, let him be shot to death with the terrible   295
   arrows of fair ladies' eyes.
Athelstan. Nay Insultado, you must not deny us.

---

288. *very black*] Agrippine appears to use 'black' figuratively, in a negative sense, in judgement of the apparently lax morals of Cypriot women; Andelocia deflects the insult and comments on the difference in skin colour between his countrywomen and the 'fair' (291) English Agrippine.

289. *glad to be sped*] an ambiguous phrase; 'to be sped' may possibly mean 'to be provided or furnished with' (in this case, a partner) (*OED* v. I. 6. †d) or 'to be brought to a desired condition' (i.e. satisfied by a partner) (*OED* v. I. 7. a) – or more simply 'sped' may be being used in the sense of 'hastily' courted (cf. 'to yield at first assault', l. 286).

292–6. *But your ... eyes*] cut for the Tufts performance.

292. *vent'rous*] cf. Cho.1, 29n.

294–6. *He that fights ... eyes*] Andelocia plays with the Petrarchan conceit of love as war, wooing as besieging, and with the idea that the eyes are vulnerable to love's advances. Cf. Romeo's account of Rosaline: 'She will not stay the siege of loving terms, / Nor bide th'encounter of assailing eyes', *R&J*, 2.199–200).

SC. 6]   THE COMEDY OF OLD FORTUNATUS   181

Insultado. Mi corazón es muy pesado, mi ánima muy atormen-
  tado. No, por los cielos! El pie de español, no hace música en
  tierra inglesa.   300
Cyprus. Sweet Insultado let us see you dance.
  I have heard the Spanish dance is full of state.
Insultado. Verdad, Signor. La danza española, es muy alta,
  Majestuosa, y para monarcas: vuestra inglesa, baja, fantás-
  tica, y muy humilde.   305

298–300. Mi corazón ... inglesa] *this ed.;* My Corocon es muy pesada, my Anima muy atormentada, No per los Cielos: La piede de Espagnoll, no haze musica in Tierra Inglesa. *Q.*   298–9. atormentado. No] *Smeaton;* atormentada, – No *Dilke; mid-line space in Q due to composition error.*   303–5. Verdad ... humilde] *this ed.;* Verdad Signor: la danza spagnola, es muy alta, Maiestica, y para Monarcas: vuestra Inglesa, Baxa, Fantastica, y muy humilde. *Q.*

298–315. *Mi ... alta!*] Dekker's lines appear to be a genuine attempt at plausible Spanish, rather than comical send-up; accordingly, this edition presents the lines in a modernized Spanish in keeping with the modernized English presented throughout the rest of the edition. (I am grateful to Kathryn Vomero Santos for providing the modernized Spanish and its translation here and below; Dekker's attempts at Spanish are included in the collation notes.) Marianne Montgomery notes that the context renders the Spaniard's words intelligible to an audience, and likens this episode to 'the Welshwoman's speech and song in 1 *Henry IV*', noting that Insultado's 'Spanish language and Spanish dance are complementary: two forms of theatrical entertainment that package the foreign for public consumption and public comprehension'. Montgomery looks past the cultural stereotyping to note Dekker's censure of the English princess Agrippine: 'By showing an imperious English queen, Dekker sets up a contrast that highlights his compliment of Elizabeth I later in the play and also problematizes an easy reading of the English as virtuous and the Spanish as cruel. ... Dekker suggests that [Insultado] deserves better treatment than to be made a show' (*Europe's Languages on England's Stages*, 1590–1620 (Farnham: Ashgate, 2012), 92).

298–300. Mi corazón ... inglesa] 'My heart is very heavy, my soul greatly tormented. No, by heaven! The Spanish foot does not make music on English land'. In Hoy's translation, the Spanish foot 'has no music in England', but this is not quite accurate; the verb '*hacer*' means 'to do' or 'make', which suggests that the Spanish foot 'does not make music' (i.e. cannot dance) in England.

303–5. Verdad ... humilde] 'True, Sir. The Spanish dance is very lofty, majestic, and for monarchs: your English [dance] is low, fantastic, and very humble'. 'Signor' is retained here in preference to the Spanish 'Señor' on account of the overwhelming popularity of the Italian 'Signor' in the drama of the period. (Montgomery, for example, finds a comparable case of Italian and Spanish standing in for one another where 'both are clearly supposed to be heard as Spanish against the normative English of the play' in Heywood's *If You Know Not Me, You Know Nobody, Part* 1 (93).)

182   THE COMEDY OF OLD FORTUNATUS   [SC. 6

Agrippine. Doth my Spanish prisoner deny to dance? He has sworn to me by the cross of his pure Toledo to be my servant. By that oath, my Castilian prisoner, I conjure you to show your cunning: though all your body be not free, I am sure your heels are at liberty.   310
Insultado. No lo quiero contradecir: vuestra ojo hace conquista á su prisionero. Oyes, la pavana española sea vuestra música y [*con*] *gravedad, y majestad. Paje, dadme tabaco. Toma mi capa, y mi espada. Más alta, más alta! Desviaos, desviaos, compañeros, más alta, más alta!*   *He dances.* 315
Athelstan. Thanks, Insultado.
Cyprus. 'Tis most excellent.
Agrippine. The Spaniard's dance is as his deeds be: full of pride.
Athelstan. The day grows old and what remains unspent   320
Shall be consumed in banquets. Agrippine,
Leave us a while. If Andelocia please,

311-15. No lo ... alta.] *this ed.*; Nolo quire contra dezir: vuestra oio haze conquesto a su prisionero: Oyes, la pauyne Hispanola, sea vuestra musica y grauidad, y maiestad: Paie, dadime Tabacca, Tonia my capa, e my espada. Mas alta, Mas alta: Desuiaios, Desuiaios, Companieros, Mas alta, Mas alta. *Q.* 315. SD] *this ed.; centred on the next line in Q.*

307. *pure Toledo*] a sword (or its blade) made at Toledo, Spain.
311-15. No lo ... alta!] 'I do not want to contradict: your eye conquers its prisoner. Listen, let the Spanish *pavane* be your music and [with] gravity, and majesty. Page, give me tobacco. Take my cape and my sword. Louder, louder! Stand aside, stand aside, friends, louder, louder!' (following Hoy, 'with'/'*con*' is supplied as the missing word).
312. Oyes] As Hoy notes, 'Oyez!' is a public crier's call for attention or silence prior to issuing a proclamation – e.g. Mistress Quickly in *Merry Wives*: 'Crier Hobgoblin, make the fairy oyes' (5.5.33) – and it was also used to mark the commencement of a song or dance in drama.
315. SD] Ketterer notes that, although 'the music here serves to mark out Insultado as a foreigner within Athelstan's court', the Spanish *pavane* was actually familiar to English courtiers, and 'the Spanish dance the musicians provide functions well to accompany his dance and allows the English monarch a triumph of both will and culture over the Spanish prisoner' (231). Hoy cites other examples of the *pavane* on the English stage, including Lazarillo (a Spaniard) dancing it in *Blurt, Master Constable* 4.2.30-3. Sir Toby Belch refers to 'a passy-measures pavan' in *Twelfth Night* (5.1.188). The Tufts performance specified '[f]or the Dance of Insultado, Gaillard and Pavan, by Dr. John Bull, Published in 1611'.

SC. 6] THE COMEDY OF OLD FORTUNATUS 183

    Go bear our beauteous daughter company.
Andelocia. Fortune, I thank thee: now thou smil'st on me.
    Exeunt AGRIPPINE *and* ANDELOCIA, *and Ladies.*
Athelstan. This Cypriot bears a gallant princely mind.   325
    [*To* CYPRUS] My lord, of what birth is your
    countryman?
    Think not, sweet prince, that I propound this question
    To wrong you in your love to Agrippine:
    Our favours grace him to another end.
    Nor let the wings of your affection droop   330
    Because she seems to shun love's gentle lure.
    Believe it on our word: her beauty's prize
    Only shall yield a conquest to your eyes.
    But tell me what's this Fortunatus' son?
Cyprus. Of honourable blood and more renowned   335
    In foreign kingdoms (whither his proud spirit,
    Plumed with ambitious feathers, carries him)
    Than in his native country. But last day,
    The father and the sons were, through their riots,
    Poor and disdained of all. But now they glister   340
    More bright than Midas. If some damnèd fiend
    Fed not his bags, this golden pride would end.
Athelstan. His pride we'll somewhat tame and curb the
    head

---

    323. *Go bear ... company*] Clearly Athelstan is complicit in the plan to ensnare Andelocia and discover the source of his wealth here, but it is Agrippine (386–401) who devises the plan to drug Andelocia and substitute a false purse for the genuine artefact. In the German play (Act 3, p. 159, ll. 2–12), it is the king who suggests having a bag maker ('*Seckler*') counterfeit the purse (ll. 4–6) and having their physician create a soporific potion for Agrippine to pour into Andelocia's wine (ll. 6–11), so that Agrippine can confiscate the purse from him when unconscious (ll. 11–12).

    324. *Fortune ... smil'st on me*] Reading this as 'a parody of the famous ballad *Fortune my foe*, which begins "Fortune my foe, why dost thou frown on me"', Duffin suggests that the tune of that ballad might play in the background of the present scene (*Some Other Note*, 304).

    327–9. *Think not ... end*] Athelstan explains that his interest in Andelocia's background is not motivated by a desire to set him up with Agrippine, and that Cyprus remains the favoured suitor.

    341. *Midas*] Here the Midas allusion refers to the Phrygian king's ability to turn everything he touched to gold (cf. the allusion to Midas's ears at 1.293 above).

   Of his rebellious prodigality.
   He hath invited us and all our peers   345
   To feast with him tomorrow; his provision,
   I understand, may entertain three kings.
   But Lincoln, let our subjects secretly
   Be charged on pain of life that not a man
   Sell any kind of fuel to his servants. [*Exit* LINCOLN.] 350
Cyprus. This policy shall clip his golden wings,
   And teach his pride what 'tis to strive with kings.
Athelstan. Withdraw a while. *Exeunt.* ATHELSTAN *remains.*
   None filled his hands with gold, for we set spies
   To watch who fed his prodigality.   355
   He hung the marble bosom of our court
   As thick with glist'ring spangles of pure gold
   As e'er the spring hath stuck the earth with flowers.
   Unless he melt himself to liquid gold
   Or be some god, some devil, or can transport   360
   A mint about him by enchanted power,
   He cannot rain such showers. With his own hands
   He threw more wealth abroad in every street
   Than could be thrust into a chariot.
   He's a magician sure, and to some fiend   365
   His soul (by infernal covenants) has he sold,
   Always to swim up to the chin in gold.
   Be what he can be, if those doting fires
   Wherein he burns for Agrippina's love
   Want power to melt from him this endless mine, 370

---

353. SD] *Manet* ATHELSTAN *Q.*

 348–50. *let ... fuel to his servants*] See 270–4n above. It is curious that Athelstan explicitly instructs Lincoln 'let our subjects secretly / Be charged', yet, in ll. 442–6 below, Shadow is clearly acquainted with the king's secret injunction.
 353. SD Exeunt] Cyprus, Insultado, and the French and English lords exit here, leaving Athelstan alone on stage.
 365–6. *to some fiend ... sold*] Athelstan's insinuation of a Faustian pact is the closest Dekker's play comes to explicitly engaging with Marlowe's famous tragedy, but it is only Athelstan's conjecture; Fortunatus's compact with Lady Fortune differs importantly from Faustus's diabolical contract (see Introduction, 49–50).
 367. *swim ... chin in gold*] A common image of Ovid's Golden Age in corruption, cf. Jonson, *Volpone* 1.3.69–72 (*CWBJ*).

SC. 6]   THE COMEDY OF OLD FORTUNATUS   185

    Then (like a slave) we'll chain him in our tower,
    Where tortures shall compel his sweating hands
    To cast rich heaps into our treasury.
        Music sounding still. A curtain being drawn, where
        ANDELOCIA *lies sleeping in* AGRIPPINE'S *lap; she has*
        his purse, and herself and another Lady *tie another (like it)*
        in the place and then rise from him.
Agrippine. I have found the sacred spring that never ebbs.
    [*To* Lady] Leave us.   *Exit* Lady.
                But I'll not show't your majesty,   375
    Till you have sworn by England's royal crown
    To let me keep it.
Athelstan.   By my crown I swear,
    None but fair Agrippine the gem shall wear.
Agrippine. Then is this mine. See, father, here's the fire
    Whose gilded beams still burn. This is the sun   380
    That ever shines, the tree that never dies.
    Here grows the Garden of Hesperides.
    The outside mocks you, makes you think 'tis poor,
    But entering it, you find eternal store.

373.1. SD] Rhys begins a new scene here, introducing stage directions for Athelstan to first exit then re-enter immediately.

---

373. SD] As Dilke notes (see 385n below), this tableau resembles Delilah's outwitting of Samson (Judges 16: 19). The Tufts performance specified the playing of a '[s]ong by Robert Jones, "Farewell, Dear Love," published in 1601' for this scene (see Jones, *The first booke of songes & ayres* (London, 1600), song 12).

377. *crown I swear*] According to Drayton in his *Polyolbion*, Athelstan was the first English king to wear a crown – see Hopkins, *From the Romans to the Normans*, 168.

382. *Garden of Hesperides*] One of Hercules' final labours was to pick golden apples from a dragon-guarded tree at the world's end, in the garden tended by the Hesperides nymphs (see H. J. Rose, *A Handbook of Greek Mythology* (London: Methuen, rpt 1950), 216). The apples were said to provide eternal life, hence Agrippine's 'eternal store' (6.384). This episode may have been dramatized in the lost 'Hercules' plays in the Admiral's Men's repertory in 1595. Although Agrippine evokes the apples for their golden quality here (she is alluding to Fortunatus's purse), it may also recall (for the audience) Vice's tree which reappears later in the play with 'apples like gold' (7.74).

186   THE COMEDY OF OLD FORTUNATUS   [SC. 6

Athelstan. Art sure of this? How didst thou drive it out?   385
Agrippine. Fear not his waking yet. I made him drink
That soporiferous juice which was composed
To make the queen (my mother) relish sleep
When her last sickness summoned her to heaven.
He sleeps profoundly. When his amorous eyes   390
Had singed their wings in Cupid's wanton flames,
I set him all on fire and promised love.
In pride whereof, he drew me forth this purse
And swore by this he multiplied his gold.
I tried and found it true, and secretly   395
Commanded music with her silver tongue
To chime soft lullabies into his soul.
And whilst my fingers wantoned with his hair
T'entice the sleepy juice to charm his eyes,
In all points was there made a purse, like his,   400
Which counterfeit is hung in place of this.
Athelstan. More than a second kingdom hast thou won.
Leave him, that when he wakes he may suspect
Some else has robbed him. Come, dear Agrippine.
If this strange purse his sacred virtues hold,   405
We'll circle England with a waist of gold.
                Exeunt. [ANDELOCIA *remains, asleep.*]

Music still. Enter SHADOW *very gallant, reading a bill,
with empty bags in his hand, singing.*

---

406. waist] *Dilke;* wast *Q;* wall *Rhys.*   406.1. SD] *Dilke;* Saddow *Q.*

385. *drive it out?*] Dilke proposes a debt to the Book of Judges, 'where Samson is described as made to sleep on Delilah's knees till his locks were shaven and his strength taken from him'.
396. *music with her silver tongue*] See 1.338n above.
406. *circle England with a waist of gold*] a common fantasy of wealth-enabled security/power, cf. Greene's *Friar Bacon and Friar Bungay* where Burden accuses Bacon of plans to 'compass England with a wall of brasse' (*Queen's Men Editions* Quarto TLN 204), or the desire of Marlowe's Faustus to 'wall all Germany with brass' (B-text, 1.1.87).
406. SD] The Tufts performance specified: 'Shadow sings a little from an old song of the time, "Canst thou not hit it?" The immediately following music consists of two Slow Dances, author unknown. Then No. XI [see 373 SD above] is repeated.'

SC. 6]   THE COMEDY OF OLD FORTUNATUS   187

Shadow. These English occupiers are mad Trojans: let a man
pay them never so much, they'll give him nothing but the
bag. Since my master created me steward over his fifty
men and his one-and-fifty horse, I have rid over much   410
business, yet never was galled, I thank the Destinies.
Music? Oh, delicate warble! Oh, these courtiers are most
sweet triumphant creatures. Signor, sir, monsieur, sweet
signor – this is the language of their accomplishment. Oh,
delicious strings! These heavenly wire-drawers have   415
stretched my master even out at length. Yet at length he
must wake. Master?

413–14. Signor ... signor] Seignior ... seignior *Q*.

---

407. *occupiers*] Dilke notes that 'occupant' was a term for 'a woman of the town' and 'occupier' was 'a wencher'. Hoy suggests 'tradesmen', but notes that '[t]he word has bawdy implications'.
408–9. *give him ... the bag*] to slip away, leave without warning (*OED* 19. †); e.g. Greene's account of a swindler cheating a maid in *The Defence of Conny Catching* (1592): 'if he meane to give her the bagge, he selleth whatsoever he can, and so leaues hir spoild' (sig. D2r). Cf. Andelocia's own 'Have you given me the slip?' at ll. 430–1 below.
409–11. *Since my ... Destinies.*] cut for the Tufts performance.
411. *galled*] made sore by chafing or rubbing (*OED*).
412–16. *Music? ... out at length*] Duffin detects an 'obscure' reference here to 'the "consort of six" mixed instruments that was developing a repertoire and had associations with the theater through this period'; the *Fortune my foe* tune alluded to in l. 324 above was 'part of the special ensemble repertoire'; a further piece from that repertoire, *Mounsieur Almaine*, may be alluded to by Shadow in ll. 413–14's 'Signor, sir, monsieur' (*Some Other Note*, 304–5). The 'consort of six' ensemble (that Duffin is confident provided the music throughout this scene) consisted of 'one bass and one treble bowed string instrument, a woodwind instrument, a flexible gut-strung plucked instrument with a wide range, and two wire-strung plucked instruments for texture and percussive effect' (Duffin, 'Music and the Stage in the Time of Shakespeare', in R. Malcolm Smuts, ed. *The Oxford Handbook of the Age of Shakespeare* (Oxford University Press, 2016), 749).
412. *delicate warble*] referring (probably) to the flute or recorder (Duffin, *Some Other Note*, 305).
415. *wire-drawers*] persons who play stringed instruments such as the cittern or bandora (antedating *OED* n. †3 by over 25 years). Duffin suggests there may have been a theatrical joke here, since 'Wyerdrawers' (people who draw metal into wire) were listed by Tilney in the 1607–8 Revels accounts as having attended the Officers of the Revels periodically (*Malone Society Collections XIII*, ed. W. R. Streitberger (Oxford: Clarendon Press, 1986), p. 29, item 12b; Duffin, *Some Other Note*, 304).

188   THE COMEDY OF OLD FORTUNATUS   [SC. 6

Andelocia. Wake me not yet, my gentle Agrippine.
Shadow. One word, sir, for the billets and I vanish.
Andelocia. There's heaven in these times. Throw the
   musicians   420
   A bounteous largesse of three hundred angels.
Shadow. Why sir, I have but ten pound left.
                     ANDELOCIA *starts up.*
Andelocia. Ha, Shadow? Where's the Princess Agrippine?
Shadow. I am not Apollo, I cannot reveal.
Andelocia. Was not the princess here when thou cam'st in?   425
Shadow. Here was no princess but my princely self.
Andelocia. In faith?
Shadow. No, in faith, sir.
Andelocia. [*To* AGRIPPINE] Where are you hid? Where stand
   you wantoning? Not here? Gone i'faith? Have you given   430
   me the slip? Well, 'tis but an amorous trick and so I
   embrace it. [*To* SHADOW] My horse, Shadow, how fare
   my horse?
Shadow. Upon the best oats my under-steward can buy.
Andelocia. I mean are they lusty, sprightly, gallant, wanton,   435
   fiery?

---

420. times] *Q;* tunes *Dilke.*   426. my princely] *Q;* thy princely *Deighton.*

---

419. *billets*] wood cut for fuel (required for preparing the banquet for the king; cf. 440–6 below).

420. *times*] Dilke's emendation to 'tunes' is attractive but unnecessary; as Bowers explains via analogy with *Sun's Darling* 2.1.39–40, Dekker is known to distinguish between 'tunes' and 'times' in the context of sounds, and Andelocia might just as easily 'find heaven in the polyphonic rhythms of the music as well as in its melodies'.

424. *Apollo*] the sun-god, famed for his prophecies; a reference to the Delphic oracle, cf. Fortune's offer of wisdom at 1.233 ('thou (like Phoebus) shalt speak oracle').

426. *my princely self*] Deighton's emendation is unnecessary; Shadow is as likely to refer to himself humorously as to esteem Andelocia as princely.

433. *horse*] plural, though the same as the singular (common into the seventeenth century; *OED*). Cf. ll. 435–7 below: 'are they lusty', 'They are as all horses are'.

432–8. *My horse ... munching.*] cut for the Tufts performance. In the German play, the servant offers to sell his horse to help his master: '*mein Pferd und Harnisch wil ich verkauffen / und euch das Geldt geben / und zu Fuss nachlauffen / wohin ihr kommet*' (Act 3, p. 162, ll. 8–10; 'I will sell my horse and armour / and give you the money / and I will follow you on foot / wherever you will go').

SC. 6]   THE COMEDY OF OLD FORTUNATUS   189

Shadow. They are as all horses are, caterpillars to the commonwealth; they are ever munching. But sir, for these billets, and these faggots and bavins?
Andelocia. S'heart, what billets, what faggots? Dost make me a woodmonger? 440
Shadow. No, sweet seignior, but you have bid the king and his peers to dinner and he has commanded that no woodmonger sell you a stick of wood and that no collier shall cozen you of your measure but must tie up the mouth of 445 their sacks, lest their coals kindle your choler.
Andelocia. Is't possible? Is't true, or hast thou learnt of the English gallants to gull?
Shadow. He's a gull that would be taught by such gulls.
Andelocia. Not a stick of wood? Some child of envy has 450 buzzed this stratagem into the king's ear, of purpose to disgrace me. I have invited his majesty and though it cost me a million, I'll feast him. Shadow, thou shalt hire a hundred or two of carts. With them post to all the grocers in London, buy up all the cinnamon, cloves, nutmegs, 455 liquorice and all other spices that have any strong heart and with them make fires to prepare our cookery.
Ere Fortunatus' son look red with shame,
He'll dress a king's feast in a spicèd flame.

---

437. *caterpillars*] parasites to the commonwealth; cf. Ithamore's 'two religious caterpillars' in *Jew of Malta* (4.1.21) and Bushy and Bagot's accomplices, the 'caterpillars of the commonwealth', in *Richard II* 2.3.165.

439. *bavins*] 'A bundle of brushwood or light underwood ... differing from a fagot in being bound with only one band instead of two' (*OED*).

441. *woodmonger*] a dealer in wood/timber (*OED*).

446. *coals kindle your choler*] to carry (or in this case, be offered) coals is to be insulted (Dent C464*), which in turn leads to anger (choler); cf. Samson and Gregory's exchange in *R&J* 2.1-4.

447-9. *Is't possible ... gulls.*] cut for the Tufts performance.

452-7. *I have invited ... cookery*] Cf. Sir Vaughan's extravagant banquet of plums, caraway, comfits, apples and wine in *Satiromastix* 4.1.

454-5. *grocers in London*] In the German play, the servant (called '*Jung*', i.e. 'young' or 'boy') is mentioned for the first time here, and is sent specifically to the Venetian grocers ('*den Venediger Krämern*', Act 3, p. 153, l. 25), which is consistent with the *Volksbuch* of 1509, fol. 73. (Hoy, 'Introduction', 78, quotes the 1670 English translation of the Fortunatus legend, which specifies 'all the Grocers in London' rather than a Venetian grocer as here.)

Shadow. This device, sir, will be somewhat akin to Lady 460
Pride. 'Twill ask cost.
Andelocia. Fetch twenty porters, I'll lade all with gold.
Shadow. First, master, fill these bags.
Andelocia. [*Tries the purse.*] Come then, hold up, how now?
Tricks, new crotchets, Madam Fortune? Dry as an eel- 465
skin? Shadow, take thou my gold out.
Shadow. Why sir, here's none in.
Andelocia. Ha, let me see. Oh, here's a bastard cheek.
I see now 'tis not mine. 'Tis counterfeit,
'Tis so. Slave, thou hast robbed thy master. 470
Shadow. Not of a penny. I have been as true a steward –
Andelocia. Vengeance on thee and on thy stewardship.
Yet wherefore curse I thee? Thy leaden soul
Had never power to mount up to the knowledge
Of the rich mystery closed in my purse. 475
Oh no, I'll curse myself. Mine eyes I'll curse,
They have betrayed me. I will curse my tongue,
That hath betrayed me. I'll curse Agrippine,
She hath betrayed me. Sirens, cease to sing;

---

462. lade] *Dilke;* laid *Q.*

465. *new crotchets*] Andelocia suspects a new ruse; 'crotchet' = 'a whimsical fancy, a perverse conceit' (*OED* 9a).

Dry as an eel-skin] Eels are usually slippery or wet (Dent 59*, 60, 61); either 'dry' here is meant in terms of 'yielding no fruit, result, or satisfaction' (*OED* †15.a), with the eel-skin itself being evoked for its sense of narrowness or tightness; or 'dry' refers to 'lacking adornment or embellishment' (*OED* 16), which in this case would be the gold lacking from the otherwise plain ('eel-skin') purse.

468. *bastard cheek*] 'cheek' in the sense of insolence is a nineteenth-century meaning; Andelocia more likely refers metaphorically to the counterfeit ('bastard') purse than to the cheekiness of attenuating the purse's power.

473–4. *Thy leaden soul ... mount up*] Cf. the parallel construction of 5.175–7, where Fortunatus makes the same allegation against Ampedo for his failure to appreciate 'the incomprehensible glory' of travel.

479. *Sirens, cease to sing*] In Book 12 of Homer's *Odyssey*, the sirens (hybrid creatures that are part women, part feathered and clawed birds) use their enchanting song to lure sailors to their death; Andelocia here recognizes the seductive, soporific role played by music in cheating him of his purse. Music has featured prominently throughout this episode in Dekker's play; the German play contains extensive stage directions for a dumbshow enacting the siren-like seduction of Andelocia through the use of a violin or fiddle,

SC. 6]   THE COMEDY OF OLD FORTUNATUS   191

  Your charms have ta'en effect, for now I see 480
  All your enchantments were to cozen me.
             Music ceaseth.
Shadow. What shall I do with this ten pound, sir?
Andelocia. Go buy with it a chain and hang thyself.
  Now think I on my father's prophecy:
  'Tell none', quoth he, 'the virtue. If you do, 485
  Much shame, much grief, much danger follows you'.
  With tears I credit his divinity.
  O fingers, were you upright Justices,
  You would tear out mine eyes: had not they gazed
  On the frail colour of a painted cheek, 490
  None had betrayed me. Henceforth I'll defy
  All beauty and will call a lovely eye
  A sun whose scorching beams burn up our joys,
  Or turn them black like Ethiopians.
  O women, wherefore are you born men's woe; 495

488. Justices] *Q;* Justicers *Daniel.*

---

specifically. See Act 3, p. 160, ll. 5–12: '*Jetzt fangen sie an zu geigen* / ANDOLOSIA *nimbt den Tranck zu sich* / *setzet darnach das Glaesslein bey seit* / *hat die* AGRIPPIN *bey den Armen* / *und kuesset sie* / *nicht lange darnach fallen ihm die Augen zu* / *wird entschlaffen* / *da holet* AGRIPPINA *den Gluckseckel auss den Hosen* / *stecket ihm den andern an dessen statt wieder ein* / *gehet damit in frewden davon* / *unter dessen wird submissè musiciret* / *harret ein wenig* / *darnach erwacht er* / *siehet umb sich*' ('Now they begin to play the violin / Andolosia drinks the potion / puts down the glass / takes Agrippina into his arms / and kisses her / not long after that his eyes fall shut / and he falls asleep / Agrippina retrieves the moneybag out of his pants / replaces it with the fake moneybag / leaves happily with the real moneybag / during all this, the musicians keep playing music / he starts moving / wakes up / looks around him'). This action corresponds to unseen events that take place chronologically in Dekker's play between 6.325 and the present passage.
  483. *chain ... hang thyself*] Hanging in chains was deemed worse than mere hanging; cf. Anon. (Dekker?), *A Warning for Fair Women* (1599), sig. H4v, where the law '[c]ondemnes a murtherer to be hangd in chaines'.
  487. *divinity*] presumably in the sense of having 'divined' or 'disclosed', rather than being 'god-like', but no record in the *OED* of this sense.
  488–94. *O fingers ... Ethiopians.*] cut for the Tufts performance.
  494. *black like Ethiopians*] another reference (cf. 1.86n) to Phaeton's disastrous attempt to drive the sun chariot, which, according to Ovid (*Met.* 3), resulted in the people of Ethiopia being exposed to such extreme heat that their skin darkened.
  495. *men's woe*] a relatively common misogynistic pun and false etymology ('woe-man') referring to Woman as cause of the fallen world.

Why are your faces framed angelical?
Your hearts of sponges, soft and smooth in show,
But touched, with poison they do overflow.
Had sacred wisdom been my father's fate,
He had died happy, I lived fortunate.   500
[*Indicating the purse*] Shadow, bear this to beauteous Agrippine,
With it this message: tell her I'll reprove
Her covetous sin the less, because for gold
I see that most men's souls too cheap are sold.
Shadow. Shall I buy these spices today or tomorrow?   505
Andelocia. Tomorrow? Ay, tomorrow thou shalt buy them.
Tomorrow tell the princess I will love her,
Tomorrow tell the king I'll banquet him.
Tomorrow, Shadow, will I give thee gold,
Tomorrow pride goes bare and lust a-cold.   510
Tomorrow will the rich man feed the poor,
And vice tomorrow virtue will adore.
Tomorrow beggars shall be crownèd kings;
This no-time, morrow's-time, no sweetness sings.
I pray thee hence. Bear that to Agrippine.   515
Shadow. I'll go hence, because you send me; but I'll go weeping hence, for grief that I must turn villain as many do and leave you when you are up to the ears in adversity.
Exit.
Andelocia. She hath robbed me and now I'll play the thief.
I'll steal from hence to Cyprus, for black shame   520
Here (through my riots) brands my lofty name.
I'll sell this pride for help to bear me thither,
So pride and beggary shall walk together.
This world is but a school of villainy,
Therefore I'll rob my brother, not of gold   525

---

520. shame] *Dilke;* shame. *Q.*

514. *no-time*] chiefly poetical, 'a time which does not exist' (*OED*, first instance).
515. *Bear that*] i.e. the message.
522. *this pride*] his 'gaudy and costly dress' (Dilke).
523. *walk together*] *OED* cites this as its second example of the sense 'To be associated, work or get along *together*, act harmoniously *with*'.

(Nor of his virtues; virtue none will steal)
But, if I can, I'll steal his wishing-hat.
And with that, wand'ring round about the world,
I'll search all corners to find Misery,
And where she dwells, I'll dwell, languish, and die.   530
                                                                    Exit.

[Chorus 2]

                    [*Enter* CHORUS.]

Chorus. Gentles, if ere you have beheld the passions,
    The combats of his soul, who being a king,
    By some usurping hand hath been deposed
    From all his royalties: even such a soul,
    Such eyes, such heart swoll'n big with sighs and tears,   5
    The star-crossed son of Fortunatus wears.
    Though thoughts crowned him a monarch in the morn,
    Yet now he's bandied by the seas in scorn
    From wave to wave. His golden treasure's spoil
    Makes him in desperate language to entreat   10
    The winds to spend their fury on his life.
    But they, being mild in tyranny, or scorning

---

7. Though] *this ed.;* Tho *Bowers;* His *Dilke;* The *Q.*

527. *wishing-hat*] *OED* first example (though see 5.419 above).

6. *star-crossed*] The Chorus (like *R&J*, 1.6) implies that fate, rather than free will, determines the tragic outcome of the protagonist here – even though Andelocia has been seen to exercise little self-restraint or discipline since acquiring the purse. The present example is the *OED*'s second instance of the adjective, following Shakespeare.

7–8. *the morn / Yet now*] The morning/day imagery reinforces natural cycles, and, by extension, Fortune's wheel (see also the metaphor of Fortunatus's life and death offered at 5.335: 'The flower that's fresh at noon, at sunset fades').

8. *bandied by the seas*] Tossed from one to another (*OED*, first instance); a continuation of the fatalistic rhetoric of l. 6. The image is a medieval commonplace exploring the tension between steering (free will) versus being buffeted by the winds (determinism). Jill L. Levenson explains that 'the boat at sea without a sense of direction represents the lover who feels confusion and dislocation' ('The Definition of Love', *Shakespeare Studies* 15 (1982), 25).

9. *golden treasure's spoil*] the purse has become a 'spoil' in the sense of goods seized by the conqueror from the defeated enemy (*OED*).

To triumph in a wretch's funeral,
Toss him to Cyprus. Oh, what treachery
Cannot this serpent gold entice us to?   15
He robs his brother of the Sultan's prize,
And having got his wish (the wishing-hat)
He does not, as he vowed, seek misery
But hopes by that to win his purse again,
And in that hope from Cyprus is he fled.   20
If your swift thoughts clap on their wonted wings,
In Genoa may you take this fugitive,
Where having cozened many jewellers,
To England back he comes. Step but to court
And there (disguised) you find him bargaining   25
For jewels with the beauteous Agrippine,
Who wearing at her side the virtuous purse,

---

18. vowed] *Q;* would *Dilke.*

---

15. *serpent gold*] a further instance of Edenic imagery; gold is here associated with the temptation offered by Satan in the guise of a serpent, rather than with the forbidden fruit which has tempted characters in the form of the golden apples throughout the play.

16–20. *He robs ... fled*] This episode is dramatized in the German play (Act 3, p. 164, l. 11 – p. 166, l. 12). There, Andelocia tells his brother about the loss of the purse, and, after an initial moment of shock, Ampedo proposes raising funds by selling the magic hat back to the Sultan. Andelocia rejects the suggestion and tricks his brother out of the hat, which he ultimately plans to use to return to England and retrieve the stolen purse from Agrippine.

22–6. *In Genoa ... Agrippine*] In the German play, this scene (corresponding to this Choric summary) is also still extant. See Act 4, p. 168, l. 10 – p. 170, l. 4, where Andelocia recounts his trip to Venice and the theft of three valuable pieces of jewellery. Explaining his plan to use the jewels to kidnap Agrippine, he disguises himself with a mask and cloak and positions himself along Agrippine's route to the church. When she passes, he flatters her for being the richest woman in the world and she lets him follow her to show her his wares. They haggle over the price and Agrippine reluctantly pays 4,000 gold coins for the jewels. See Introduction, 17.

27–31. *Who wearing ... wilderness*] The German play's Agrippine produces the purse in order to pay the disguised Andelocia for the jewels he is selling (see 22–6n above); it is at that point that he grabs her and transports them both to the woods in Ireland (see *Von Fortunato*, Act 4, p. 170, ll. 1-4). The *Volksbuch* also specifies that the 'wilderness' is Irish, and Dekker may have had this in mind when Andelocia and Shadow subsequently adopt the disguise of Irish costermongers (8.28.1-2 SD).

27. *virtuous purse*] 'virtuous' in the sense of having magical power (*OED* 8c; cf. 1.304), but also perhaps with a latent sense of irony, in that the purse has demonstrably corrupted its bearers rather than inspiring virtue.

He clasps her in his arms and as a raven
Gripping the tender-hearted nightingale,
So flies he with her, wishing in the air   30
To be transported to some wilderness.
Imagine this the place.

Enter ANDELOCIA *and* AGRIPPINE.

See here they come.
Since they themselves have tongues, mine shall be
dumb.   *Exit.*

[Scene 7]

Enter ANDELOCIA *with the wishing-hat on,* AGRIPPINE
in his hand.

Agrippine. What devil art thou that affrightst me thus,
Haling a princess from her father's court
To spoil her in this savage wilderness?

28–9. *raven / Gripping*] Cf. 'as a dove gripped in a falcon's claw' (2.47) and 'a rascal kite having swept up / A chicken in his claws' (9.172–3).

32. SD] a prompter's note; cf. the authorial direction at 7.0.1 SD below.

0.1. SD] The earlier entrance marked in *Q* at Cho.2, 32 is probably a prompter's note, as the entrance is necessary for the Chorus's injunction, 'see here they come', to make sense. The repetition of Andelocia and Agrippine's entrance here (with greater detail) is more likely authorial. Rhys specifies 'A Wilderness' as the setting; Smeaton locates the action in 'A Desert Place', but clearly it takes place in the forest where Virtue and Vice previously planted their trees (first mentioned in l. 69 below, though Andelocia also refers to the presence of 'nut trees' earlier in l. 42). The forest is specified as an Irish one in the German play when, at the end of Act 4, after Agrippine accidentally vanishes with the wishing-hat and Fortune returns, Andelocia says: '*denn jetzt bin ich noch in Hibernia*' (Act 4, p. 174, ll. 20–1, 'because now I am still in Hibernia [i.e. the Classical Latin term for Ireland]').

2. *Haling*] hauling or dragging; see 0.2 SD's '*in his hand*' above.

3. *spoil*] Agrippine fears assault from a stranger (not having yet recognized Andelocia), as Andelocia himself threatens to do at ll. 30–4 below, but the dramatic irony here is that 'spoil' more appropriately means to strip of goods (in this case the purse) by violence or force (*OED* v.1, 2a).

Andelocia. Indeed the devil and the pick-purse should always
    fly together, for they are sworn brothers. But, Madam
    Covetousness, I am neither a devil as you call me, nor a
    jeweller as I call myself. No, nor a juggler, yet ere you
    and I part, we'll have some legerdemain together. Do you
    know me?
Agrippine. [*Aside*] I am betrayed: this is the Cypriot.
    [*To* ANDELOCIA] Forgive me, 'twas not I that changed
      thy purse,
    But Athelstan my father. Send me home
    And here's thy purse again. Here are thy jewels,
    And I in satisfaction of all wrongs—
Andelocia. Talk not you of satisfaction; this is some recompense that I have you. 'Tis not the purse I regard. Put it off and I'll mince it as small as pie meat. The purse? Hang the purse! Were that gone, I can make another, and another, and another, ay and another. 'Tis not the purse I care for, but the purser: you. Ay, you. Is't not a shame that a king's daughter, a fair lady, a lady not for lords but for monarchs, should for gold sell her love? And when she has her own asking and that there stands nothing

---

    4. *devil and the pick-purse*] Agrippine accused Andelocia of being a 'devil' (l. 1), so he responds by labelling her a 'pick-purse' (she having stolen his magical purse), overstating the magnitude of her crime by suggesting the fittingness of the devil and pick-purse flying together.
    5–6. *Madam Covetousness*] because Agrippine has desired the purse which rightfully belongs to Andelocia.
    7. *juggler*] one who uses magic to work wonders or who uses sleight of hand to perform tricks (*OED* 2).
    7–8. *yet ere ... together*] cut for the Tufts performance.
    8. *legerdemain*] trickery, juggling, deception (from the French for 'light of hand') (*OED*).
    10. *this is the Cypriot*] Agrippine had not recognized Andelocia until now because he was 'disguised' (Cho.2, 25) as 'a jeweller' (7.6–7).
    11–12. *'twas not I ... father*] Although the German play's Athelstan was more actively involved in the plot (see 6.323n), Agrippine's absolute denial here of any involvement is false in either version of the play.
    20. *purser*] Andelocia clearly means the person who stole the purse, the pickpocket; not one who makes purses (*OED* n. †1) nor a 'bursar' (n. 2b) who administers funds. The present example antedates the *OED* (n. †3.) by 40 years.

SC. 7]   THE COMEDY OF OLD FORTUNATUS   197

    between, then to cheat your sweetheart? Oh, fie, fie, a
    she cony-catcher? You must be dealt soundly with.   25
Agrippine. Enjoin what pains thou wilt and I'll endure them,
    So thou wilt send me to my father's court.
Andelocia. Nay, God's lid, y'are not gone so. Set your heart
    at rest, for I have set up my rest, that except you can run
    swifter than a hart, home you go not. What pains shall I 30
    lay upon you? Let me see. I could serve you now but a
    slippery touch. I could get a young king or two, or three,
    of you and then send you home and bid their grandsire
    king nurse them. I could pepper you, but I will not.
Agrippine. Oh, do not violate my chastity!   35
Andelocia. No, why I tell you I am not given to the flesh,
    though I savour in your nose a little of the devil. I could
    run away else and starve you here.

---

24. your sweetheart] *Q;* her sweetheart *Dilke.*   25. soundly] *Q;* fondly *Rhys.*   26–7. Enjoin ... court] *Rhys; set as prose in Q.*

---

    24. *your sweetheart*] Dilke emends to 'her sweetheart' (in agreement with 'her love' and 'her own asking' in the previous line), but as Andelocia is clearly referring to Agrippine's behaviour (e.g. l. 25, 'You must be'), it is only natural that he slips from the third person to the second person pronoun in the course of his denunciation.
    24–5. *Oh, fie ... with.*] cut for the Tufts performance.
    25. *she cony-catcher?*] a female swindler, cheater.
    28. *God's lid*] a mild oath ('by God's eyelid'); cf. Sir Andrew's "Slid, I'll after him again, and beat him' in *Twelfth Night* 3.4.334. The present example from Dekker is the *OED*'s earliest (P3. In oaths. b. † (by) God's lid int. Obs.).
    29. *set up my rest*] As Hoy notes, this is a gambling term meaning 'to stake one's all'. Andelocia's fate depends on holding on to Agrippine.
    30. *hart*] a male deer.
    30–1. *What pains ... you?*] cut for the Tufts performance.
    31–7. *I could ... devil,*] cut for the Tufts performance (perhaps on account of the subject matter?).
    32. *slippery touch*] 'slippery' here means '[c]haracterized by shiftiness, deceitfulness, or want of sincerity' (*OED* 4b), and 'touch' is 'sexual contact or activity' (*OED* 6c); cf. the hostess who cannot kiss a mystical saint's relic lest it reveal her infidelity and she 'be suspected to have playd her husband a slippery touch' in Richard Carew, trans., *A World of Wonders* (London, 1607), 350.
    34. *pepper*] have sex with (*OED* II. †5. trans. slang. A. Obs., citing this as its first example).
    37. *though I savour ... devil*] There is some analogy with a passage in Jonson's *The Devil Is an Ass* (1616), where the Newgate Keepers suspect

Agrippine. If I must die, doom me some easier death.
Andelocia. Or transform you (because you love picking) into   40
a squirrel and make you pick out a poor living here
among the nut trees; but I will not neither.
Agrippine. What will my gentle Andelocia do?
Andelocia. Oh, now you come to your old bias of cogging.
Agrippine. I pray thee, Andelocia, let me go.   45
Send me to England and by heaven I swear,
Thou from all kings on earth my love shalt bear.
Andelocia. Shall I in faith?
Agrippine.   In faith, in faith thou shalt.
Andelocia. Here, God-a-mercy. Now thou shalt not go.
Agrippine. Oh, God!   50
Andelocia. Nay, do you hear lady? Cry not, y'are best. No,
nor curse me not. If you think but a crabbed thought of
me, the spirit that carried you in mine arms through the
air will tell me all. Therefore set your Sunday face upon't.
Since you'll love me, I'll love you. I'll marry you, and lie   55

---

diabolical meddling in similar terms; the Third Keeper suggests the dead body 'savours of the devil strongly' and the Second Keeper responds 'I ha' the sulphur of hell-coal i'my nose' (*CWBJ* 5.7.9–10). The analogy is imperfect, though, since the present example is pointedly about *Agrippine's* nose, not Andelocia smelling something sulphurous about her. It may be that there was something distinctively diabolical about Agrippine's nose (its steepness?). The general sense seems to be that Andelocia would simply leave Agrippine to starve except ('though') that he suspects she would be saved by infernal assistance.

41–2. *squirrel ... nut trees*] Agrippine's potential fate resembles that of Fortunatus at the start of the play, lost in the wood, at Fortune's mercy; ironically, it anticipates Andelocia's actual fate later in this same scene (ll. 98–101).

43–4. *What will ... cogging.*] cut for the Tufts performance.

44. *old bias*] another bowls metaphor (cf. 2.26n); here, as Hoy notes, the bias is 'the construction or form of the bowl which causes it to swerve when rolled'.

44. *cogging*] 'Deceitful flattery; fawning' (*OED*).

49. *God-a-mercy*] expression of surprise or thanks, here used ironically.

53. *spirit that carried you*] This is the first reference to the wishing-hat-enabled transportations involving any kind of spirit aid, and may not be a clue to staging so much as an attempt by Andelocia to mystify the voyaging process and keep Agrippine confused.

54. *Sunday face*] The *OED*'s first instance of this term, meaning 'a solemn, somewhat sanctimonious expression'.

55–7. *Since you'll ... not.*] cut for the Tufts performance.

with you, and beget little jugglers. Marry, home you get
not. England you'll say is yours; but Agrippine, love me
and I will make the whole world thine.
Agrippine. I care not for the world; thou murd'rest me.
Between my sorrow and the scalding sun   60
I faint and quickly will my life be done.
My mouth is like a furnace and dry heat
Drinks up my blood. Oh, God, my heart will burst.
I die, unless some moisture quench my thirst.
Andelocia. [*Aside*] S'heart, now I am worse than ere I was
    before: 65
For half the world I would not have her die.
Here's neither spring nor ditch, nor rain, nor dew,
Nor bread, nor drink. [*To* AGRIPPINE] My lovely
    Agrippine,
Be comforted, see here are apple trees.
Agrippine. Climb up for God's sake, reach me some of
    them.   70
Andelocia. Look up, which of these apples likes thee best?
Agrippine. This hath a withered face, 'tis some sweet fruit.
Not that, my sorrows are too sour already.
Andelocia. Come hither, here are apples like gold.

57–8. England ... thine] *Q; Bowers sets as verse.*

56. *little jugglers*] little tricksters or conjurors; see l. 7 above. The modern sense of a person who practises juggling is not supported prior to the nineteenth century.

65. *S'heart*] God's heart; another mild oath (cf. l. 28 above).

71. *which of these apples*] Andelocia refers to Virtue's tree first, but Agrippine prefers the golden apples of Vice's tree (referred to in ll. 74–5). Neither, of course, knows the trees' true identities. Of the superficial discrepancies between the apples on offer, Hillary M. Nunn notes that '[p]erhaps to the benefit of the playhouse vendors, *Old Fortunatus* shows that if the fruit available cannot be judged beautiful, it just might be better for you' ('Playing with Appetite in Early Modern Comedy', in *Shakespearean Sensations: Experiencing Literature in Early Modern England*, ed. Katharine A. Craik and Tanya Pollard (Cambridge University Press, 2013), 116).

72. *This ... fruit*] Bowers queries whether this line should rather be assigned to Andelocia and only l. 73 to Agrippine; he concedes, though, that Agrippine may be pointing to one apple and then another.

Agrippine. Oh, ay, for God's sake, gather some of these. 75
   Ay me, would God I were at home again.
                                                    [*He*] *climbs up.*
Andelocia. Stand farther, lest I chance to fall on thee.
   Oh, here be rare apples, rare red-cheeked apples, that cry
   'come kiss me'. Apples, hold your peace; I'll teach you
   to cry.   [*He*] *eats one.* 80
Agrippine. O England, shall I ne'er behold thee more?
Andelocia. Agrippina, 'tis a most sugared delicious taste in
   one's mouth; but when 'tis down, 'tis as bitter as gall.
Agrippine. Yet gather some of them. Oh, that a princess
   Should pine for food! Were I at home again, 85
   I should disdain to stand thus and complain.
Andelocia. Here's one apple that grows highest, Agrippina;
   and I could reach that, I'll come down.
                    He stands fishing with his girdle for it.
Agrippine. Make haste, for the hot sun doth scald my cheeks.
Andelocia. The sun kiss thee? Hold, catch, put on my hat. I 90
   will have yonder highest apple, though I die for't.
Agrippine. [*Puts on hat.*] I had not wont be sunburnt, wretched
   me.
   O England, would I were again in thee.   *Exit.*

82–3. *sugared ... gall*] Cf. the apples of Sodom (the legendary apples growing on the site of the destroyed city of Sodom), e.g. Webster, *The White Devil* (1612): 'You see my Lords what goodly fruict she seemes, / Yet like those apples travellers report / To grow where *Sodom* and *Gomora* stood, / I will but touch her and you straight shall see / Sheele fall to soote and ashes' (*The Works of John Webster*, vol. 1, ed. David Gunby, David Carnegie, and Antony Hammond and Doreen DelVecchio (Cambridge University Press, 1995), 3.2.63–7).

88. *and*] in the conditional sense ('if').

90. *put on my hat*] The German Andelocia makes the same foolish mistake; see Act 4, p. 170, ll. 18-24. The stage directions read: '*Andolosia setzt auss unbedacht ihr den Wuenschhut auff / und gehet nach den Bawm*' (ll. 18/19; 'Andolosia thoughtlessly puts the magic hat on to her head / and walks over to the tree').

93. *O England ... thee*] In the *Gesta Romanorum* and in Hoccleve's redaction, Jonathas (the Andelocia character) uses his magic cloth to transport Fellicula (the Agrippine character) to the end of the world; there, he promptly falls asleep on her lap, and she extricates herself, using the cloth to return home and leave him in the wilderness. See Introduction, 19–20.

Andelocia. 'Swounds Agrippina, stay! Oh, I am undone.
                                              He leaps down.
Sweet Agrippina, if thou hearst my voice,   95
Take pity of me and return again.
She flies like lightning. Oh, she hears me not.
I wished myself into a wilderness
And now I shall turn wild. Here I shall famish,
Here die, here cursing die, here raving die,   100
And thus will wound my breast and rent mine hair.
What hills of flint are grown upon my brows?
Oh, me! Two forkèd horns. I am turned beast.
I have abused two blessings, wealth and knowledge;
Wealth in my purse and knowledge in my hat,   105
By which being borne into the courts of kings
I might have seen the wondrous works of Jove,
Acquired experience, learning, wisdom, truth.
But I in wildness tottered out my youth,
And therefore must turn wild, must be a beast,   110
An ugly beast. My body horns must bear,
Because my soul deformity doth wear.
Lives none within this wood? If none but I
Live here, thanks heaven – for here none else shall die.

98. wished] *Dilke;* will'd *Daniel;* wish *Q.*   98. wilderness] *Q;* wildness *Dilke.*   109. wildness] *Dilke;* wildernesse *Q.*

---

94. *'Swounds*] a further mild oath ('God's wounds'), cf. ll. 65 and 28 above.

100–1. *Here die ... hair*] Andelocia's predicament parallels that of his father in the play's opening scenes, offering a neat symmetry to the plot (see Conover, *Thomas Dekker*, 75, on other examples of such unifying devices of repetition that 'give the work the appearance of an artistic whole by referring to earlier parts of the play').

102. *hills of flint*] 'Flint' here means a flint-like substance, and indicates the newly sprouting horns on Andelocia's head; the *OED*'s first example of this transferred sense is dated 1712 (*n.* II.5.a).

111–12. *My body ... doth wear*] Andelocia refers to the Neoplatonic idea that outward appearance is indicative of moral fibre (cf. Miranda's evaluation of Ferdinand in *The Tempest* 1.2.457: 'There's nothing ill can dwell in such a temple').

114. SD] Smeaton starts a new scene here, again identifying the setting as '*A Desert Place*'. The Tufts performance specified '[f]or the entrance of Fortune, etc., with Satyrs: a tune said to date from the fourteenth century'.

THE COMEDY OF OLD FORTUNATUS   [SC. 7

He lies down and sleeps under the tree. Enter FORTUNE, VICE, VIRTUE [*with crowns and bay-garlands*], *the* PRIEST, [*and*] *satyrs with music, playing as they come in before* FORTUNE. *They play awhile.*

Fortune. See where my new-turned devil has built his hell.   115
Vice. Virtue, who conquers now? The fool is ta'en.
Virtue. Oh, sleepy sin!
Vice.   Sweet tunes wake him again.
                                    Music awhile, and then cease.
Fortune. Vice sits too heavy on his drowsy soul,
   Music's sweet concord cannot pierce his ear.
   Sing, and amongst your songs mix bitter scorn.   120
Virtue. Those that tear Virtue must by Vice be torn.

                        The Song.

1. Verse. Virtue stand aside: the fool is caught.
   Laugh to see him, laugh aloud to wake him.

---

118. sits] *Dilke;* sets *Q.*

Ketterer draws attention to the use of music as an 'aural barrier between the fictional world in which Agrypine and Andelocia have been picking apples, and the imaginative realm in which the occult figures exist', creating a distinction between worlds occupying the same physical space of the stage (232).

   116. *The fool is ta'en*] Vice most probably refers to the sleeping Andelocia whose horns mark him as Vice's foolish victim, and who is described again as a fool throughout the song; but see ll. 191–2n below.

   117. SD] Wilfred T. Jewkes suggests this is an example of a prompter's 'warning note' which duplicates the stage direction at 114.3 above, but the satyrs could enter playing music, cease whilst the supernatural characters converse, then resume (with the specific purpose of attempting to wake Andelocia, as instructed by Vice) (*Act Division in Elizabethan and Jacobean Plays, 1591–1616* (Hamden, CT: The Shoestring Press, 1958), 138).

   121.1 *The Song*] Duffin, noting the 'constant citing of fools' in these lyrics, suggests that the song 'might have had some association with the tune *Walking in a country town ...* which later became identified with English clowns on the Continent under the title *Pots hondert tausetn slapferment*, or *Pekelharing*' (*Some Other Note*, 302). He reproduces a musical setting from Thomas Robinson's *Schoole of Musicke* (1603). The Tufts performance used a '[s]ong-tune of about 1600, author unknown'. Presumably it is the Priest (cf. 3.20–35 above) and possibly the satyrs who do the singing here, not Virtue and Vice, whom the lyrics address.

SC. 7]   THE COMEDY OF OLD FORTUNATUS   203

  Folly's nets are wide and neatly wrought.
  Mock his horns and laugh to see Vice take him.   125
Choir. Ha, ha, ha, ha, ha, laugh, laugh in scorn,
      ANDELOCIA *wakens and stands up.*
  Who's the fool? The fool, he wears a horn.
2. Verse. Virtue stand aside: mock him, mock him, mock
  him.
  Laugh aloud to see him, call him fool.
  Error gave him suck, now sorrows rock him.   130
  Send the riotous beast to madness' school.
Choir. Ha, ha, ha, ha, ha, laugh, laugh in scorn,
  Who's the fool? The fool, he wears a horn.
3. Verse. Virtue stand aside: your school he hates.
  Laugh aloud to see him, mock, mock, mock him.   135
  Vanity and hell keep open gates.
  He's in, and a new nurse (Despair) must rock him.
Choir. Ha, ha, ha, ha, ha, laugh, laugh in scorn,
  Fool, fool, fool, fool, fool, wear still the horn.
    When they have done singing, VICE *and* VIRTUE *hold*
    apples out to him, VICE *laughing,* VIRTUE *grieving.*
Andelocia. Oh, me! What hell is this? Fiends, tempt me not.   140
  [*To* VICE] Thou glorious devil, hence. Oh, now I see
  This fruit is thine; thou hath deformèd me.
  Idiot, avoid! Thy gifts I loathe to taste.
  Away! Since I am entered madness' school,
  As good to be a beast as be a fool.   145

---

126. Choir] *this ed.;* Quire *Q;* Chorus *Dilke, Rhys.*   132. Choir] *this ed.;* Quire *Q;* Chorus *Dilke, Rhys.*   138. Choir] *this ed.;* Quire *Q;* Chorus *Dilke, Rhys.*

---

126. SP] *Q*'s 'Quire' is an early modern variant of 'choir' (a gathering), signifying that these lines are sung by multiple voices rather than only being a refrain (as Dilke and Rhys's emendation might suggest).
126. SD] *Q* spreads this SD across ll. 126–7, but editors place invariably place it in l. 127. It would make more sense that Andelocia is woken by the choir of voices commencing in l. 126 than that he conveniently remains sleeping until they finish their chorus.
141. *Thou glorious devil*] i.e. Vice.

Away! Why tempt you me? Some powerful grace
Come and redeem me from this hideous place.
Fortune. To her hath Andelocia all his life
Sworn fealty; wouldst thou forsake her now?
Andelocia. Whose blessèd tongue names Andelocia? 150
Fortune. Hers who, attended on by Destinies,
Shortened thy father's life and lengthens thine.
Andelocia. O sacred queen of chance, now shorten mine,
                                                                Kneels.
Else let thy deity take off this shame.
Fortune. [*Indicating* VICE] Woo her. 'Twas she that set it on
thy head. 155
Andelocia. She laughs to see me metamorphosèd.
Virtue. Woo me and I'll take off this ugly scorn.   *Rises.*
Vice. Woo me and I'll clap on another horn.
Andelocia. I am beset with anguish, shame, and death.
[*To* FORTUNE] Oh, bid the Fates work fast and stop
my breath. 160
Fortune. No, Andelocia, thou must live to see
Worse torments (for thy follies) light on thee.
This golden tree, which did thine eyes entice,
Was planted here by Vice. Lo, here stands Vice.
How often hast thou sued to win her grace? 165
Andelocia. Till now, I never did behold her face.
Fortune. Thou didst behold her at thy father's death,
When thou in scorn didst violate his will.
Thou didst behold her when thy stretched-out arm
Catched at the highest bough, the loftiest vice; 170
The fairest apple, but the foulest price.
Thou didst behold her when thy lickerish eye
Fed on the beauty of fair Agrippine;

---

153. SD] *line 152 in Q.*   171. price] *Q;* prize *Daniel.*

146. *Some*] Dilke insists that he emended *Q*'s 'sour' to 'some', but all copies of *Q* collated for this edition read 'some'. Curiously, in l. 149 below, Dilke prints 'desert her now' for *Q*'s 'forsake her now', but does not mark it as an emendation (i.e. it is presented as if it were the reading found in the copy of *Q* used by Dilke).
167–77. *Thou didst ... eye.*] cut for the Tufts performance.
172. *lickerish*] See 5.95n above.

Because th'hadst gold, thou thoughtst all women thine.
When lookst thou off from her? For they whose souls 175
Still revel in the nights of vanity,
On the fair cheeks of Vice still fix their eye.
Because her face doth shine and all her bosom
Bears silver moons, thou wast enamoured of her.
But hadst thou upward looked and seen these shames, 180
Or viewed her round about and in this glass
Seen idiots' faces, heads of devils and hell,
And read this 'Ha, ha, he', this merry story,
Thou wouldst have loathed her where, by loving her,
Thou bearst this face and wearst this ugly head. 185
And if she once can bring thee to this place,
Loud sounds, these 'ha, ha, he', she'll laugh apace.
Andelocia. Oh, re-transform me to a glorious shape
And I will learn how I may love to hate her.
Fortune. I cannot re-transform thee; woo this woman. 190
          [*She indicates* VIRTUE.]
Andelocia. This woman? Wretched is my state when I,
To find out wisdom, to a fool must fly.
Fortune. Fool, clear thine eyes, this is bright Aretë.
This is poor Virtue. Care not how the world
Doth crown her head. The world laughs her to scorn, 195
Yet *sibi sapit*, Virtue knows her worth.
Run after her, she'll give thee these and these,
Crowns and bay-garlands (Honour's victories).

---

174. th'hadst] *Rhys;* thou'dst *Dilke;* th'adst *Q*. 187. she'll] *Dilke;* sheele *Q;* He'll *Smeaton.* 189. love to hate] *Q;* live to hate *Daniel.*

---

179. *silver moons*] Cf. the description of 'silver half-moons' on Vice's clothing in 3.0.3 SD above.

191–2. *This woman? ... a fool*] From Virtue's first appearance in scene 3 she has worn 'a coxcomb on her head' (3.0.10 SD), which she continues to wear as a badge of honour ('I am proud to wear the scorn of fools', 3.77). The German play's stage directions explicitly call for Virtue to again enter wearing a fool's cap at this point (Act 4, p. 167, ll. 2-3: '*Jetzt koempt die Goettin der Laster und die Goettin der Tugendt / hat ein Narrenhuetlein auf*'; 'Enter the Goddess of Vice and the Goddess of Virtue / wearing a fool's cap').

193. *Aretë*] Greek for excellence or virtue (as in Aristotle's *Nicomachean Ethics*, Book 2).

196. *sibi sapit*] See 3.0.10 SDn above.

Serve her and she will fetch thee pay from heaven,
Or give thee some bright office in the stars. 200
Andelocia. Immortal Aretë, Virtue divine; *Kneels.*
Oh, smile on me and I will still be thine.
Virtue. Smile thou on me and I will still be thine.
Though I am jealous of thy apostasy,
I'll entertain thee. Here, come taste this tree; 205
Here's physic for thy sick deformity.
Andelocia. 'Tis bitter. This fruit I shall ne'er digest.
Virtue. Try once again, the bitterness soon dies.
Vice. Mine's sweet, taste mine.
Virtue. But being down, 'tis sour,
And mine being down has a delicious taste. 210
The path that leads to Virtue's court is narrow,
Thorny and up a hill; a bitter journey,
But being gone through, you find all heav'nly sweets.
The entrance is all flinty, but at th'end
To towers of pearl and crystal you ascend. 215
Andelocia. Oh, delicate! Oh, sweet Ambrosian relish!
And see, my ugliness drops from my brows.
Thanks, beauteous Aretë. Oh, had I now
My hat and purse again, how I would shine
And gild my soul with none but thoughts divine. 220
Fortune. That shall be tried. Take fruit from both these trees;
By help of them win both thy purse and hat.

---

199. *pay from heaven*] 'pay' in the obsolete sense of satisfaction, pleasure (*OED* n. I. †1).

204. *jealous of thy apostasy*] Virtue is upset that Andelocia abandoned her for Vice's principles.

206. *Here's physic ... deformity*] In the *Volksbuch* a hermit points Andelocia in the direction of the apples that treat his deformity.

211–15. *The path ... ascend*] noted by Allott in *Englands Parnassus* under 'Virtue' (p. 290). Allott's excerpt contains minor variants to punctuation but also substitutes 'Two towers of pearles' for 'To towers of pearl' in l. 18. This emendation implies one tower being pearl and another crystal, but offers no clear advantage over *Q*'s 'towers of pearl and crystal' *to* which the subject journeys.

221–3. *Take fruit ... how*] In the German play, Andelocia asks Fortune if he can take apples from each tree (Act 4, p. 173, l. 28 – p. 174, l. 2), and she consents to his wish (p. 174, ll. 4–5). The plan is not explicitly stated and Fortune does not offer instructions.

I will instruct thee how, for on my wings
To England shalt thou ride. Thy virtuous brother
Is (with that Shadow who attends on thee)   225
In London. There I'll set thee presently.
But if thou lose our favours once again,
To taste her sweets, those sweets must prove thy bane.
Virtue. Vice, who shall now be crowned with victory?
Vice. She that triumphs at last, and that must I.   230
                                                    Exeunt.

[Scene 8]

Enter ATHELSTAN, LINCOLN *with* AGRIPPINE, CYPRUS,
GALLOWAY, CORNWALL, CHESTER, LONGUEVILLE,
and MONTROSE.

Athelstan. Lincoln, how setst thou her at liberty?
Lincoln. No other prison held her but your court.
There, in her chamber hath she hid herself
These two days, only to shake off that fear
Which her late violent rapture cast upon her.   5
Cyprus. Where hath the beauteous Agrippina been?
Agrippine. In heaven or hell, in or without the world,
I know not which. For as I oft have seen

---

227. *lose our favours*] to spend unprofitably or in vain, to waste (*OED v.*1 6a). Fortune refers to the possibility that Andelocia will actively squander her gifts (by pursuing Agrippine again) rather than merely fall out of favour.

228. *bane*] that which causes death or ruin; especially poison (*OED*).

0.1.] Rhys adds the setting: 'London, The Court of Athelstane'. Conover notes that the opening lines devoted to the Cyprus–Agrippine betrothal here afford the actor playing Andelocia time to change into his new costume and pick up the required props before entering as an Irish costermonger after l. 28 (Conover, *Thomas Dekker*, 71).

4. *two days*] A period of two days has lapsed since the previous scene.

5. *her late violent rapture*] her abduction; 'rapture' here means the 'action or an act of carrying off a woman by force' (*OED* †2.a, citing this line as its second example).

7–8. *In heaven ... not which*] Dilke suspects an allusion to 2 Corinthians 12 here, in which case Agrippine avails herself of an alternative meaning of 'rapture' (conveyance to heaven; *OED* 4. †a., though this would antedate the *OED* by 9 years).

When angry Thamesis hath curled her locks,
A whirlwind come and from her frizzled brows   10
Snatch up a handful of those sweaty pearls
That stood upon her forehead, which awhile,
Being by the boist'rous wind hung in the air,
At length hath flung them down and raised a storm.
Even with such fury was I wherried up,   15
And by such force held prisoner in the clouds
And thrown by such a tempest down again.
Cornwall. Some soul is damned in hell for this black deed.
Agrippine. I have the purse safe and anon your grace
  Shall hear this wondrous history at full.   20
Cyprus. Tell me, tormenter, shall fair Agrippine
  Without more difference be now christened mine?
Agrippine. My choice must be my father's fair consent.
Athelstan. Then shall thy choice end in this Cyprus prince.
  Before the sun shall six times more arise,   25
  His royal marriage will we solemnize.
  Proclaim this honoured match. Come Agrippine,
  I am glad th'art here, more glad the purse is mine.

---

9. *angry Thamesis*] 'Thamesis' is Latin for 'Thames', however this may not quite capture the full richness of the allusion; Agrippine's use here probably also invokes the mythological Greek sea-goddess Thamesis who (usually with Amphitrite) typically appears accompanied by Tritons, as in the *Gesta Grayorum* (c.1594, printed 1688), 57. The pun on the river and the goddess is common, and is also made (for example) in Neptune's speeches in Dekker's own *Troia Nova Triumphans* (1612), sig. Br.

10. *frizzled*] See 2.22–3n above.

11. *pearls*] small drops (especially dewdrops or tears) resembling pearls (*OED* III.4); e.g. Shakespeare, *Luc.*, l. 1213: 'And wiped the brinish pearl from her bright eyes'.

15. *wherried*] to be carried in or as in a light rowing boat used on rivers to carry passengers ('wherry'; perhaps with the suggestion of rapid movement) (as a transitive verb, antedating *OED*).

19. *I have the purse safe*] Agrippine neglects to mention the wishing-hat, which is also in her possession, because it was the purse alone that she and her father had set their sights on acquiring (also, given her description here of her transportation, she may as yet still be uncertain of the hat's full significance). That she has the purse safely with her is attributable to Andelocia still having been infatuated with her to the point of distraction in the previous scene, and his failure to anticipate that she might suddenly and unexpectedly escape his captivity through the aid of the hat before he could retrieve the purse from her.

As they are all going in, enter ANDELOCIA *and* SHADOW, *like Irish costermongers.* AGRIPPINE, LONGUEVILLE, *and* MONTROSE *stay listening to them, the rest exeunt.*

Both. Buy any apples, feene apples of Tamasco, feene Tamasco peepins. Peeps feene, buy Tamasco peepins. 30
Agrippine. Damasco apples? Good my lord Montrose, Call yonder fellows.
Montrose.   Sirrah costermonger.
Shadow. Who calls? Peeps of Tamasco, feene peeps. I'fat, 'tis de sweetest apple in de world, 'tis better den de pomewater, or apple-john. 35

---

29. any] *Q;* my *Dilke.* 29. Tamasco] *Dilke;* Tamasio *Q.* 33. I'fat,] *this ed.;* I fat *Q;* and fat *Dilke;* Ay, fat *Rhys.*

---

29. SP] 'Both' refers to Andelocia and Shadow as costermongers (applesellers); cf. l. 77 below.
30. *peepins. Peeps*] Pippins were any of the various late-ripening, sweet apple varieties available at the time (*OED* n. 3a); the *OED* lists 'pip' separately as referring to the same kind of apples specifically in 'Elizabethan and Jacobean satirical writings' where it is 'attributed as a cry to Irish costermongers', citing the present example. Nunn suggests that, in addition to the thematic importance of the forbidden fruit in Dekker's play, product placement is occurring in the costermonger episode, where the 'onstage selling ... serves as more than an active reminder of the merchandise for sale in the theater; it makes the exchange familiar and desirable by acting out the interplay between vendor and customer'. By encouraging the circulation of apples amongst playgoers, the play invites 'a new awareness of the moral significance' underlying the desire to satisfy bodily cravings ('Playing with Appetite', 116).
30. *Peeps feene*] A typical London street cry, cf. the costermonger in Jonson's *Bartholomew Fair* (1614), 'Buy any pears, pears, fine, very fine pears!' (*CWBJ,* 2.2.26) or the broadside 'A new Ballad intituled, I haue fresh Cheese and Creame' (c.1610; *English Broadside Ballad Archive* ID 20013): 'Will you buy pippins fine'.
31. *Damasco apples?*] Noting that Dekker's characters sell fine apples of Damascus, rather than the English apples available to Dekker's audiences, Chew explains that '[t]he associations of the words damask and damascene with ideas of beauty and luxury and exquisite craftsmanship and with a sense of refreshment are due in part to the city's reputation for wealth and ease and voluptuousness as well as to the quality of the commodities that came thence' (*Crescent and the Rose,* 82).
33-7. *I'fat ... else.*] cut for the Tufts performance.
33. *I'fat*] In faith.
34-5. *pomewater, or apple-john*] both were types of apple; the pomewater was a 'large, juicy, sharp-tasting variety', whilst the apple-john would supposedly 'keep for two years' and have 'a shrivelled, withered appearance' thereafter (*OED*).

210   THE COMEDY OF OLD FORTUNATUS   [SC. 8

Andelocia. By my trat Madam, 'tis reet Tamasco peepins, look here else.
Shadow. I dare not say, as de Irishman my countryman say, taste de goodness of de fruit. No say't, 'tis farie teere, mistriss, by Saint Patrick's hand 'tis teere Tamasco apple.   40
Agrippine. The fairest fruit that ever I beheld. Damasco apples? Wherefore are they good?
Longueville. What is your price of half a score of these?
Both. Half a score, half a score? Dat is doos many, mester.
Longueville. Ay, ay, ten; half a score, that's five and five.   45
Andelocia. Feeve and feeve? By my trat and as Creeze save me la, I cannot tell, wat be de price of feeve and feeve, but 'tis tree crown for one peepin, dat is the preez if you take 'em.
Shadow. I'fat, 'tis no less for Tamasco.   50
Agrippine. Three crowns for one? What wondrous virtues have they?
Shadow. Oh, 'tis feene Tamasco apple and shall make you a great teal wise, and make you no fool, and make feene memory.   55

---

39. No say't,] *this ed.;* No fayt *Q;* no fait *Dilke;* no, sayt *Rhys.*   50. I'fat] *this ed.;* I fat *Q;* Ay fat *Dilke.*

---

36. *By my trat*] By my troth.
36. *reet*] right.
39. *farie teere*] very dear.
44. *doos many, mester*] too many, master.
46. *Creeze*] Christ.
46–7. *By my ... la,*] cut for the Tufts performance, perhaps on account of the profanity? (see 64–5n below).
47. *la*] 'An exclamation formerly used to introduce or accompany a conventional phrase or an address, or to call attention to an emphatic statement' (*OED*). Cf. *Merry Wives* 1.1.61: 'And I thank you always with my heart, la'.
48. *tree crown*] three crowns; a crown was a gold English coin (the Crown of the Double Rose) worth 5s when first issued in 1526 but which dipped in value to 3s 4d during Elizabeth's reign, and was discontinued in 1601 (Fischer, *Econolingua*, 63).
dat] *OED* first instance (though it appears above in l. 44) in the sense of 'that' (pronoun) and the context of representing speech of non-native English speakers (esp. Irish).
preez] price.
54. *teal*] deal.

Andelocia. And make dis fash be more fair and amiable, and make dis eyes look always lovely, and make all de court and country burn in desire to kiss di none sweet countenance.
Montrose. Apples to make a lady beautiful? 60
Madam, that's excellent.
Agrippine. These Irishmen,
Some say, are great dissemblers and I fear
These two the badge of their own country wear.
Andelocia. By my trat, and by Saint Patrick's hand, and as Creez save me la, 'tis no dissembler. De Irish man now 65
and den cut di countryman's throat, but yet in fayt he love di countryman, 'tis no dissembler. Dis feene Tamasco apple can make di sweet countenance, but I can take no less but three crowns for one. I wear out my naked legs

---

58. di none sweet] *Q;* di honeysweet *Dilke.*

56. *dis fash*] this face.
58–9. *di none sweet countenance*] i.e. 'thine own sweet countenance'; the false Irish accent has metanalysed 'thine own' into 'di none' (cf. the etymology of 'nickname' from 'an eke name'). Dilke's emendation to 'di honeysweet' is just plausible in the context of 'countenance' but is exposed as unnecessary by the parallel construction in l. 85 below ('di none sweet self', i.e. 'thine own sweet self').
61–3. *These Irishmen ... wear*] The Master of the Revels, Edmund Tilney, must have allowed these 'Irish' costermonger episodes, but their topicality in late 1599 would not have been wasted on the audience. Essex left London for Dublin on 27 March 1599 as part of England's military campaign in Ireland, but returned to London, against express orders, on 28 September and by the time of the play was in disgrace and under house arrest at York House. Meanwhile the Irish rebels controlled virtually the whole of Ireland outside the Pale, making it accessible to the Spanish as a base for attacking England. Dekker here characterizes the Irish in general as illiterate peasants (cf. 'kern' at 9.66); untrustworthy, but not ultimately a serious threat (Richard Dutton, personal correspondence).
64–5. *and as Creez ... la*] cut for the Tufts performance (cf. 46–7n above).
69–72. *I wear out ... la*] cut for the Tufts performance.
69. *naked legs*] Citing this example, Robert I. Lublin notes that '[u]nlike all other nationalities depicted on the English stage, Irish characters often appeared with bare lower legs and sometimes without shoes'. Originally a pragmatic fashion related to the need to 'walk among the bogs', the distinctiveness of the attire came to represent the stage-Irishman: 'the incivility of appearing with bare legs marked the nation that embraced the fashion' (*Costuming the Shakespearean Stage* (Farnham: Ashgate, 2011), 113).

and my foots and my toes, and run hidder and didder to 70
Tamasco for dem.
Shadow. As Creez save me la, he speaks true. Peeps feene.
Agrippine. I'll try what power lies in Damasco fruit.
Here are ten crowns for three, so fare you well.
Montrose. Lord Longueville, buy some.
Longueville. I buy? Not I. 75
Hang them, they are toys. Come madam, let us go.
Exeunt. [ANDELOCIA *and* SHADOW *remain.*]
Both. Saint Patrick and Saint Peter, and all de holy angels look upon dat fash and make it fair.

Enter MONTROSE *softly.*

Shadow. Ha, ha, ha, she's sped, I warrant.
Andelocia. Peace, Shadow. [*To* MONTROSE] Buy any peepins, 80
buy?
Both. Peeps feene, feene Tamasco apples.
Montrose. Came not Lord Longueville to buy some fruit?
Andelocia. No fat, master, here came no lords nor ladies, but di none sweet self. 85
Montrose. 'Tis well. Say nothing, here's six crowns for two.
You say the virtues are to make one strong?
Both. Yes fat, and make sweet countenance and strong too.
Montrose. 'Tis excellent. Here. [*Offers crowns.*] Farewell. If these prove,
I'll conquer men by strength, women by love. *Exit.* 90

Enter LONGUEVILLE.

---

70. toes] *Daniel;* tods *Q.*   74. three] *Q;* thee *Dilke.*

---

70. *toes*] Rhys follows *Q* in printing 'tods', which he explains as 'Stockings probably, from the use of the term for bales of wool', and Smeaton qualifies Rhys's suggestion by offering 'clothes' rather than 'stockings' as the meaning. But these glosses ignore the specific mention of 'naked legs' earlier in the line, and 'legs ... foots ... toes' is a cogent alternative.

70. *didder*] thither.

74. *three*] Dilke's emendation to 'thee' is unnecessary; the price of one apple is three crowns, and Agrippine is generously offering ten crowns (instead of nine) for three apples. Montrose offers 'six crowns for two' (86). Consequently, *Q*'s printing of Longueville's 'nine crowns for thee' (97) should be emended to 'for three', following Rhys.

76. *toys*] trifles; things of no importance (*OED* n.5).

SC. 8]   THE COMEDY OF OLD FORTUNATUS   213

Andelocia. Ha, ha, ha! Why, this is rare.
Shadow. Peace, master, here comes another fool.
Both. Peeps feene, buy any peeps of Tamasco?
Longueville. Did not the Lord Montrose return to you?
Both. No fat, sweet master, no lord did turn to us. Peeps   95
    feene.
Longueville. I am glad of it. Here are nine crowns for three.
    What are the virtues besides making fair?
Andelocia. Oh, 'twill make thee wondrous wise.
Shadow. And dow shall be no more a fool, but sweet face and   100
    wise.
Longueville. 'Tis rare. Farewell, I never yet durst woo.
    None loves me. Now I'll try what these can do.   *Exit.*
Andelocia. Ha, ha, ha. So, this is admirable, Shadow. Here
    end my torments in Saint Patrick's Purgatory, but thine   105
    shall continue longer.
Shadow. Did I not clap on a good false Irish face?
Andelocia. It became thee rarely.
Shadow. Yet that's lamentable, that a false face should become
    any man.   110
Andelocia. Thou art a gull. 'Tis all the fashion now, which
    fashion because we'll keep, step thou abroad; let not the
    world want fools. Whilst thou art commencing thy

---

91. SP] *this ed.;* Both Q.   97. three] *Rhys;* thee Q.

---

91. SP] Q assigns this line to both Andelocia and Shadow, but Shadow pointedly advises Andelocia to be silent upon sighting Longueville. Q is surely correct, *pace* Dilke (who places Longueville's entrance after l. 91), that Longueville must enter before Andelocia speaks, otherwise Shadow need not silence him.
    100. *dow*] thou.
    105. *Saint Patrick's Purgatory*] a cavern in Lough Derg (a lake in County Donegal, Ireland), where Christ is said to have appeared to St Patrick and showed him a cave or deep pit; according to legend, it was a portal to purgatory. Dekker may be recalling here a detail from the German *Volksbuch* in which Fortunatus and the nobleman Lüpoldus visit Ireland and St Patrick's Purgatory as part of their adventures; see Introduction, 21–22.
    113–16. *Whilst thou ... fly.*] cut for the Tufts performance.

214   THE COMEDY OF OLD FORTUNATUS   [SC. 8

  knavery there, I'll proceed Doctor Dodypoll here. That
  done, thou, Shadow and I will fat ourselves to behold the   115
  transformation of these fools. Go, fly.
Shadow. I fear nothing, but that whilst we strive to make
  others fools, we shall wear the coxcombs ourselves. Pips
  fine &c.   *Exit* SHADOW.

        Enter AMPEDO.

Andelocia. [*Aside*] S'heart, here's my brother, whom I have
  abused.   120
  His presence makes me blush. It strikes me dead
  To think how I am metamorphosèd.
  [*To* AMPEDO] Feene peepins of Tamasco &c.
Ampedo. For shame cast off this mask.
Andelocia. Wilt thou buy any pips?
Ampedo.   Mock me no longer   125
  With idle apparitions. Many a land
  Have I with weary feet and a sick soul
  Measured, to find thee; and when thou art found,
  My greatest grief is that thou art not lost.
  Yet lost thou art: thy fame, thy wealth are lost,   130

---

121. strikes] *Dilke;* stcikes *Q.*   128. found] *Dilke;* fonnd *Q.*

  114. *proceed*] graduate, to the title of (academic) doctor.
  114. *Doctor Dodypoll*] conventional character type but also the subject of a Children of Paul's play, *The Wisdom of Doctor Dodypoll*, entered in the Stationers' Register 7 October 1600 and printed that year (i.e. well after Dekker's play was published), but with the claim 'As it hath bene sundrie times Acted', which implies it may have been performed early enough to be the subject of this allusion. In that play, Dodypoll is a French doctor, which is probably the point of relevance here: when Andelocia next enters, it is explicitly '*like a French doctor*' (9.85 SD). Dodypoll is initially an unsuccessful suitor for the love of Cornelia, who unwittingly supplies her father (Flores) with a love potion that Flores will attempt to use to ensnare his preferred candidate for his daughter's hand. Dodypoll subsequently turns against Flores and rejects Cornelia.
  115. *fat ourselves*] Rhys suggests to '[g]row jolly, at the spectacle'.
  122. *metamorphosèd*] Andelocia refers to his Irish costermonger disguise, but cf. his earlier metamorphosis at 7.156 and his angst over the deformity of his soul that it occasions (7.111–12). Ampedo's lamentation in l. 142 below reinforces the concern about Andelocia's degeneration.

SC. 9]   THE COMEDY OF OLD FORTUNATUS   215

   Thy wits are lost and thou hast, in their stead,
   With shame and cares and misery crowned thy head.
   That Shadow that pursues thee filled mine ears
   With sad relation of thy wretchedness.
   Where is the purse and where my wishing-hat?   135
Andelocia. Where? And where? Are you created constable,
   you stand so much upon interrogatories? The purse is
   gone, let that fret you; and the hat is gone, let that mad
   you. I run thus through all trades to overtake them. If
   you'll be quiet, follow me and help; if not, fly from me   140
   and hang yourself. Wilt thou buy any pippins?   *Exit.*
Ampedo. Oh, how I grieve, to see him thus transformed.
   Yet from the circles of my jealous eyes
   He shall not start till he have repossessed
   Those virtuous jewels, which found once again,   145
   More cause they ne'er shall give me to complain.
   Their worth shall be consumed in murd'ring flames,
   And end my grief, his riot, and our shames.   *Exit.*

[Scene 9]

Enter ATHELSTAN; AGRIPPINE, MONTROSE, *and* LONGUEVILLE
       with horns; LINCOLN *and* CORNWALL.

---

142. transformed.] *this ed.;* transformd? *Q.*

   131. *Thy wits are lost*] The *OED*'s earliest instance of losing one's wits (from emotion or excitement) is from 1604, and postdates *Old Fortunatus* (*v.*1 10.c).
   139. *run thus through all trades*] 'to run trade' is an obsolete phrase usually pertaining to ships and the regularity or constant course of trade-winds, but here being applied to Andelocia's persistent travels in search of the purse and hat. The present example is not mentioned by the *OED* but is as early as its first instance (*n.* I. †3. †d). There is possibly a secondary sense of 'trades' (i.e. Irish costermongers).
   0. SD] Rhys adds the location, 'London. The Court of Athelstane'. As Schlueter notes, it is only in Dekker's play (and the German play derived from Dekker) that the lords grow horns after eating the apples (122); this is not a feature of the *Volksbuch* or Hans Sachs's earlier German play of 1553. The incident may recall the Knight's sprouting of horns in the A-text of *Faustus* (4.1.76.2 SD).

Athelstan. In spite of sorcery try once again.
   Try once more in contempt of all damned spells.
Agrippine. Your majesty fights with no mortal power.
   Shame and not conquest hangs upon his strife.
   [*To* LINCOLN] Oh, touch me not, you add but pain to
      pain.   5
   The more you cut, the more they grow again.
Lincoln. Is there no art to conjure down this scorn?
   I ne'er knew physic yet against the horn.

               Enter CYPRUS.

Athelstan. See, Prince of Cyprus, thy fair Agrippine
   Hath turned her beauty to deformity.   10
Cyprus. Then I defy thee, Love. Vain hopes, adieu.
   You have mocked me long, in scorn I'll now mock you.
   I came to see how the Lord Longueville
   Was turned into a monster and I find
   An object which both strikes me dumb and blind.   15

---

4. his] *Q;* this *Dilke.*

---

   4. *his*] Bowers defends *Q*'s reading ('his') over Dilke's emendation ('this') on the grounds that 'there is no reason to suppose that the reference is not to Lincoln's efforts, off-stage, to remove the horns'.
   7–8. *Is there ... horn.*] cut for the Tufts performance.
   8. *physic ... against the horn*] i.e. no safeguard against being cuckolded (conventionally signified by the sprouting of horns: a sign of betrayal visible to all but the bearer).
   9–10. *fair ... deformity*] Cf. 7.111–12n.
   9–55. *See ... sight*] In the trope of the 'rejected girl ... saved from disgrace by the quick response of a faithful suitor', Arthur M. Sampley finds a 'striking' analogue between Agrippine's rejection by Cyprus and acceptance by Orleans, and Cordelia's rejection by Burgundy and acceptance by France in the opening scene of Shakespeare's *King Lear*: 'In each play the King of England has an attractive daughter who is sought by two foreign suitors. When the daughter falls into disgrace, the suitor apparently favored is informed by the father of the daughter's plight and in each play rejects her. The less favored suitor accepts the girl, praising her highly in spite of her misfortune. The King in each play commands the successful suitor to carry the daughter from his sight' ('Two Analogues to Shakespeare's Treatment of the Wooing of Cordelia', *Shakespeare Quarterly* 12.4 (1961), 469).

Tomorrow should have been our marriage-morn,
But now my bride is Shame, thy bridegroom Scorn.
Oh, tell me yet, is there no art, no charms,
No desperate physic for this desperate wound?
Athelstan. All means are tried, but no means can be found. 20
Cyprus. Then England, farewell. Hapless maid, thy stars
Through spiteful influence set our hearts at wars.
I am enforced to leave thee and resign
My love to grief.

Enter ORLEANS *and* GALLOWAY.

Agrippine.   All grief to Agrippine.
Cyprus. Adieu, I would say more, had I a tongue 25
Able to help his master. Mighty king,
I humbly take my leave. To Cyprus I,
My father's son, must all such shame defy.   *Exit.*
Orleans. So doth not Orleans. I defy all those
That love not Agrippine and him defy 30
That dares but love her half so well as I.
Oh, pardon me, I have in sorrow's jail
Been long tormented; long this mangled bosom
Hath bled and never durst expose her wounds
Till now, till now, when at thy beauteous feet, 35

---

25. Adieu,] *comma clear only in Bodleian and Harvard (B).*

16. *marriage-morn*] *OED* first example. In the previous scene, Athelstan decreed that Cyprus would marry Agrippine '[b]efore the sun shall six times more arise' (8.25), so five days appear to have lapsed between then and the present scene if '[t]omorrow' is the scheduled wedding ceremony. At l. 67 below, though, Montrose claims to have bought apples only 'Some two hours since', which seems impossible to reconcile with Cyprus's comment.

19. *wound*] wounds are typically abrasions or incisions of the flesh (as in l. 34 below), rather than external projections like these horns (though the *OED* does include 'an external injury' in its primary definition); it seems, though, that Dekker uses the term in the uncommon, obsolete sense (†6.) of an imperfection or flaw (antedating the *OED*'s only example of 1646).

24. SD Orleans] Conover suggests that '[t]he regularity with which the scenes of the Orleans plot provide for the necessities of the stage creates the suspicion that that is their prime function' (*Thomas Dekker*, 71); in the present instance, the actor playing Andelocia is preparing to enter disguised after l. 85, having last appeared on stage at the end of the previous scene.

I offer love and life. Oh, cast an eye
Of mercy on me; this deformèd face
Cannot affright my soul from loving thee.
Agrippine. Talk not of love, good Orleans, but of hate.
Orleans. What sentence will my love pronounce on me? 40
Galloway. Will Orleans then be mad? O gentle friend –
Orleans. O gentle, gentle friend I am not mad.
He's mad, whose eyes on painted cheeks do dote.
O Galloway, such read beauty's book by rote.
He's mad that pines for want of a gay flower 45
Which fades when grief doth blast, or sickness lower,
Which heat doth wither and white age's frost
Nips dead. Such fairness, when 'tis found, 'tis lost.
I am not mad for loving Agrippine.
My love looks on her eyes with eyes divine, 50
I dote on the rich brightness of her mind;
That sacred beauty strikes all other blind.
Oh, make me happy then, since my desires
Are set a burning by love's purest fires.
Athelstan. So thou wilt bear her far from England's sight, 55
Enjoy thy wishes.
Agrippine.   Lock me in some cave
Where staring Wonder's eye shall not be guilty
To my abhorred looks and I will die
To thee, as full of love as misery.

46. lower] *Q;* lour *Dilke.* 55. England's sight] *Dilke;* England sight *Q.*
58. die] *Q;* die, *Bowers.*

36–8. *Oh ... loving thee*] Agrippine has hardly conducted herself with sufficient virtue to warrant such devotion, but, as Conover observes, '[t]he emphasis here is on Orleans rather than Agripyne. He is to be rewarded for constancy and for his refusal to be deceived by appearances. If she benefits too, that is her good fortune' (*Thomas Dekker,* 79).

46. *lower*] i.e. the flower may droop and thus 'lower' (cf. being blasted with grief). Dilke emends to 'lour', implying that sickness might lour (scowl) at the flower. *Q's* 'lowre' could be modernized either way (cf. 1.74 or 10.359 but 'lower' makes sufficient sense here.

47–8. *Which heat ... lost.*] cut for the Tufts performance.

47. *white age's*] Cf. 'silver-handed age' (Prologue at Court 42) and 'grey-wingèd age' (Epilogue at Court 15).

58–9. *die / To thee*] Bowers's comma implies Agrippine's actual death, rather than merely her symbolic death 'To thee'.

SC. 9]   THE COMEDY OF OLD FORTUNATUS   219

Athelstan. I am amazed and mad. Some speckled soul   60
  Lies pawned for this in hell, without redemption.
  Some fiend deludes us all.
Cornwall.   O unjust Fates,
  Why do you hide from us this mystery?
Lincoln. My Lord Montrose, how long have your brows worn
  This fashion, these two feather-springs of horn?   65
Montrose. An Irish kern sold me Damasco apples
  Some two hours since and (like a credulous fool)
  He swearing to me that they had this power,
  To make me strong in body, rich in mind,
  I did believe his words, tasted his fruit,   70
  And since have been attired in this disguise.
Longueville. I fear that villain hath beguiled me too.
Cornwall. Nay, before God he has not cozened you;
  You have it soundly.
Longueville.   Me he made believe
  One apple of Damasco would inspire   75
  My thoughts with wisdom and upon my cheeks
  Would cast such beauty that each lady's eye
  Which looked on me should love me presently.
Agrippine. Desire to look more fair makes me more foul.

---

60. *speckled*] spotted, maculated; tainted.

65. *feather-springs of horn*] It is unlikely that Dekker has anticipated, by more than two hundred years, the use of 'feather-spring' to connote part of a gun-lock; it is more likely this is an original coinage derived from the use of 'feather' as a 'tuft or ridge of hair' (*OED* III.11.a, citing Baret's *Alvearie* (1574), 'Feather ... the curled bush of frizzled hair'); horns typically consist of keratin – hair – often over bone.

66. *Irish kern*] a lightly armed Irish foot-soldier drawn from the poorer classes (cf. *Macbeth* 5.8.4-5: 'I cannot strike at wretched kerns whose arms / Are hired to bear their staves'); *transf.* (contemptuously) a vagabond.

66-81. *An Irish ... deformity*] Here the confessions of Montrose, Longueville, Cornwall, and Agrippine reveal a strong analogy between their responses to temptation and Fortunatus's response to Fortune's offers in 1.221-304.

72-4. *I fear...soundly*] Longueville echoes Montrose's dismay at having been fooled, but Cornwall jokes that, far from being cozened, Longueville has received horns every bit as good as Montrose's.

79. *foul*] Dilke thought the reading in *Q* was 'fool' (it is actually 'fowle'); Rhys emended to 'fool', noting a pun on the two terms.

220   THE COMEDY OF OLD FORTUNATUS   [SC. 9

 Those apples did entice my wand'ring eye 80
 To be enamoured of deformity.
Athelstan. This proves that true which oft I have heard in
 schools:
 Those that would seem most wise do turn most fools.
Lincoln. Here's your best hope: none needs to hide his face,
 For hornèd foreheads swarm in every place. 85

 Enter CHESTER *bringing* ANDELOCIA *like a French doctor.*

---

85. *hornèd foreheads*] a comment on the ubiquity of cuckoldry; see 8n above.
85. SD French doctor] Portrayals of the French accent were often the source of mirth on the early modern stage (e.g. Barabas as French music teacher in Marlowe's *Jew of Malta*, c.1589), but the specific figure of the French doctor appears to have been a staple in its own right, with examples including Doctor Caius in Shakespeare's *Merry Wives of Windsor* and the eponymous role in *The Wisdom of Doctor Dodypoll* (1600; see 8.115n above). Characters disguised as French doctors include Lorrique in Henry Chettle's *The Tragedy of Hoffman* (acted 1602) and Master Philomusus in *The Return from Parnassus, Part 2* (St John's College, Cambridge 1602), as well as Medina in Dekker's *The Noble Spanish Soldier*, Angelo in his *The Wonder of a Kingdom* (acted before 1631), and Picentio in his *The Tell-Tale*. Henslowe records a play called 'The French Doctor' in his entries for October 1594 – November 1596 at the Rose, and Star Chamber proceedings reveal there was also a French doctor in the lost play by George Chapman, 'The Old Joiner of Aldgate' (acted in 1603 by the Children of Paul's); see C. J. Sisson, *Lost Plays of Shakespeare's Age* (Cambridge: Cambridge University Press, 1936), 12–79, and the *Lost Plays Database* entry for Chapman's play. It is clear from Thomas Nashe that the figure was an inherently untrustworthy one: 'The hungry druggier, ambitious after preferment, agrees to anything, and to Court he goes; where being come to interview, he speaks nothing but broken English like a French Doctor pretending to have forgotten his natural tongue by travel, when he hath never been farther than either the Low Countries or Ireland, enforced thither to fly either for getting a maid with child, or marrying two wives' (*The terrors of the night* (1594), sig. Eiir). What a French doctor disguise looked like on stage remains unknown. The German play differs slightly on this detail of Andelocia's disguise: he introduces himself as '*Doctor der Medicin / komme jetzt aus Barbarien / habe den König in Spanien 6 Jahr mit meiner Kunst gedient*' (Act V, p. 183, ll. 3–4, 'Doctor of medicine / I have come from Barbarien [i.e. a barbarous/foreign country] / and have served the King of Spain for 6 years'). In the Covent Garden adaptation, Fortunatus (not Andelocia) arrives 'disguised as an Armenian, with long beard &c.' (55).

SC. 9]   THE COMEDY OF OLD FORTUNATUS   221

Athelstan. Now Chester, what physicians hast thou found?
Chester. Many, my liege, but none that have true skill
   To tame such wild diseases. Yet here's one,
   A doctor and a Frenchman, whom report
   Of Agrippina's grief hath drawn to court.   90
Athelstan. Cure her and England's treasury shall stand
   As free for thee to use as rain from heaven.
Montrose. Cure me and to thy coffers I will send
   More gold from Scotland than thy life can spend.
Longueville. Cure Longueville and all his wealth is thine.   95
Andelocia. He, Monsieur Long-villain, gra tanck you; gra
   tanck your mashesty a great teal artely, by my trat. Where
   be dis Madam Princeza dat be so mush tormenta? O
   Jeshu! One, two, an tree, four an five, seez horn? Ha, ha,
   ha! *Pardona moy,* pray wid all mine art, for by my trat, 100

---

90. Agrippina's] *Bowers;* Agripynes *Q.* 96–104.] *this ed.;* He Monsieur Long-villaine gra tanck you: Gra tanck your mashestie a great teale artely by my trat: where be dis Madam Princeza dat be so mush tormenta? O Jeshu: one, 2: an tree, 4 & 5, seez horn? Ha, ha, ha, pardona moy prea wid al mine art, for by my trat, me can no point shose but laugh, Ha, ha, ha, to marke how like tree bul-beggera, dey stand. Oh, by my trat and fat, di diuela be whoreson, scurvie, paltry, ill fauore knaue to mocke de Madam, and gentill-home so: Ha, ha, ha, ha. *Q.*

86–95. *Now Chester ... thine*] In the *Gesta Romanorum* and in Hoccleve, Jonathas (the Andelocia character) serendipitously learns that Fellicula (the Agrippine character) is in need of a cure for leprosy (which takes the form of both fruit and water, not just fruit); here, Andelocia has orchestrated the need for a physician by selling the apples to Agrippine, knowing full well the effect that they will produce when she eats them.
   90. *Agrippina's*] Bowers presumably emends for metrical purposes.
   96–104] None of the earlier editors attempted to explicate this passage and Andelocia's subsequent speeches as a French doctor; Rhys politely suggested that '[e]lucidation of his jargon must be left to the discretion of the reader'. Unlike Dekker's apparently genuine attempt at Spanish in 6.298–315, the 'French' of the present passage is clearly meant in jest, like the Irish accents of scene 8. Andelocia alternates between attempts at genuinely French words ('*pardona moy*' for '*pardonnez moi*' / 'excuse me'; '*gentill-home*' for '*gentilhomme*' / 'gentleman'), and English words uttered with an exaggerated French accent ('mashesty' for 'majesty'). (Spelling has been modernized except where it possibly conveys a sense of the French Doctor's affected pronunciations.) 'Long-villain' is evidently meant as a deliberate mistake for 'Longueville'. Presumably 'gra tanck' means 'great (*grand*) thanks'; 'teal artely' = 'deal heartily'; 'an tree' = 'and three'; 'pray wid all mine art' = 'pray with all my heart'; 'shose' = 'choose'; and 'trat and fat' = 'troth and faith'.

me can no point shose but laugh, ha, ha, ha, to mark how
like tree bul-beggera, dey stand. Oh, by my trat and fat,
di divela be whoreson, scurvy, paltry, ill favour knave to
mock de Madam and *gentill-home* so. Ha, ha, ha, ha.
Lincoln. This doctor comes to mock your majesty. 105
Andelocia. No, by my trat, la; but me lova musha musha mer-
rymant. Come Madam, pray artely stand still and letta
me feel you. Dis horn, oh, dis pretty horn, dis be *facile*,
easy for pull de vey. But Madam dis, oh, be grand, grand
horn, *difficill* and very deep; 'tis perilous, a grand laroon. 110
But Madam, pray be patient, we shall take it off vell.
Athelstan. Thrice have we pared them off, but with fresh
pain
In compass of a thought they rise again.
Andelocia. It's true, 'tis no easy mattra, to pull horn off; 'tis
easy for pull on, but hard for pull off. Some horn be so 115
good fellow, he will still inhabit in de man's pate, but 'tis
all one for dat; I shall snap away all dis. [*Offers medicine.*]
Madam trust dis down into your little belly.
Agrippine. Father, I am in fear to taste his physic.
First let him work experiments on those. [*Indicating*
LONGUEVILLE and MONTROSE] 120

106–11.] *this ed.;* No by my trat la, but me loua musha musha merymant:
Come Madam, prea-artely stand still, and letta mee feele you: dis horne, O
tis prettie horne, dis be facile, easie for pull de vey but Madame dis O be
grand, grand horne, difficill, and very deepe, tis perilous, a grand Laroone.
But Madam, prea be patient, we shall take it off vell. Q.   108. dis] *this ed.;*
'tis *Dilke*; tis Q.   114–18.] *this ed.;* Its true, tis no easie mattra, to pull horne
off, tis easie for pull on, but hard for pull off, some horne bee so good fellow,
hee will still inhabit in de mans pate, but tis all one for tat, I shall snap away
all dis: Madam trust dis downe into your little belly. Q.

---

102. *bul-beggera*] As Dilke notes, 'bull-beggar' is an alternative to 'bug-
bear' (a spectre, bogy, object of groundless terror; *OED*).
102–4. *Oh … so.*] cut for the Tufts performance.
106–11] Presumably '*facile*' is meant as genuine French, glossed the very
next word, whereas '*difficill*' ('*difficile*') later that same line is its opposite,
'difficult'; 'pull de vey' = 'pull away' (or 'this way'?); 'oh, be grand' may be
a mistake for 'oh, de grand' ('oh, the grand'): Andelocia suggests that the
pretty little horn is relatively easy to remove, but the bigger horn ('grand')
will be more challenging to remove.
110. *laroon*] *Larron* (French) or 'Laron' (English); a robber or thief.
114–18.] See 96–104n above. 'mattra' = 'matter'; 'trust' = 'thrust'.
116. *pate*] head.

SC. 9]   THE COMEDY OF OLD FORTUNATUS   223

Andelocia. [*Aside*] I'll sauce you for your infidelity.
   In no place can I spy my wishing-hat.
Longueville. Thou learnèd Frenchman, try thy skill on me;
   More ugly than I am, I cannot be.
Montrose. Cure me and Montrose' wealth shall all be thine.   125
Andelocia. 'Tis all one for dat. Shall do presently. Madam,
   pray mark me. Monsieur, shamp dis in your two shaps,
   so; now Monsieur Long-villain, dis so. Now dis, fear
   noting, 'tis eshelent medicyne. So, now cram dis into
   your guts and belly. So, now snap away dis whoreson four   130
   divela. Ha, ha. Is no point good?
   [*Pulls* MONTROSE *and* LONGUEVILLE'S *horns off.*]
Athelstan. This is most strange.
                         Was't painful, Longueville?
Longueville. Ease took them off and there remains no pain.
Agrippine. Oh, try thy sacred physic now on me.

126–31.] *this ed.;* Tis all one for dat: shall doe presently; Madam, prea marke me: Monseiur, shamp dis in your two shaps, so, now Monsieur Long-villaine, dis so: nowe dis, feare noting, tis eshelent medicyne: so, now cram dis into your guts, and belly: So, now snap away dis whoreson fowre diuela; Ha, ha, Is no point good? *Q.* 131.1. SD] *Dilke; Puts Gallowayes hornes off., Q.* 132. strange. / Was't] *line break in Q.* 134. physic now on] *Bowers;* physic upon *Dilke;* Physicke on *Q.*

---

123. *Thou learnèd Frenchman*] It must be with a heavy irony that the Frenchman, Longueville, is duped by Andelocia's disguise as a French doctor.

125. *Montrose' wealth*] Clearly 'Montrose's wealth' is meant here, but introducing the *s* would cause metrical irregularity ('Montrose' should be treated as a personal name ending with an *s*, whose possessive form would entail an apostrophe rather than an apostrophe *and* an additional *s* in modern grammatical usage).

126–31.] Presumably 'shamp dis in your two shaps' = 'champ (chew vigorously) this in your two chaps (jawbones)'; 'fear noting, 'tis eshelent medicyne' = 'fear nothing, 'tis excellent medicine'.

130–1. *four divela*] The 'four devils' Andelocia refers to are presumably 'four horns', two on Montrose's head and two on Longueville's. See 137 below.

132. strange. / Was't] The line break in *Q*, preserved here, presumably indicates a pause occasioned by Athelstan's wonder.

134. *physic now on*] The line requires an extra syllable; Bowers's emendation is better suited to the metre than Dilke's, and is followed here.

Andelocia. No by my trat, 'tis no possibla, 'tis no possibla; all 135
de mattra, all de ting, all de substance, all de medicyne,
be among his and his belly. [*Indicating* MONTROSE
and LONGUEVILLE] 'Tis no possibla, till me prepare
more.
Athelstan. Prepare it then and thou shalt have more gold 140
From England's coffers than thy life can waste.
Andelocia. I mush buy many costily tings dat grow in Arabia,
in Asia, and America. By my trat, 'tis no possibla till
anoder time, no point.
Agrippine. There's nothing in the world but may for gold 145
Be bought in England. Hold your lap, I'll rain
A shower of angels.

135–9.] *this ed.;* No by my trat, tis no possibla, tis no possibla, al de mattra, all de ting, all de substance, all de medicyne, be among his and his belly: tis no possibla, till me prepare more. *Q.* 142–4.] *this ed.;* I mush buy many costily tings dat grow in Arabia, in Asia, and America, by my trat tis no possibla, till anoder time, no point. *Q.* 146. lap, I'll] *Dilke;* lap ile *Q.*

135–9.] In claiming he has used up all his medicine curing Longueville (and Montrose? See 137n below), and that he cannot presently cure Agrippine, Andelocia feigns a need for money in the hope of catching a glimpse of the hat and purse's whereabouts.

137. *his and his belly*] Who has Andelocia cured here? In his previous speech, Andelocia addressed only Longueville, and Athelstan similarly asks only Longueville whether the procedure was painful. In the German play, when Longueville and Montrose later encounter Shadow and Andelocia, one of the lords (presumably Montrose) retains his horns, by which Shadow recognizes him (Act V, p. 201, ll. 18–21 and p. 203, ll. 20–3). Andelocia's reference to the four horns (if that is what's meant by 'four divela', ll. 130–1) and to 'his *and* his belly' reads as though he has administered his cure to both Longueville *and* Montrose though, and, in l. 183 below, Montrose refers to the taste of 'the medicine which he gave us', which unambiguously demonstrates that he received the cure too. The matter is complicated by the fact that the SD at l. 131 in *Q* appears faulty; it reads '*Puts Gallowayes hornes off*'. Editors since Dilke have emended 'Galloway' to 'Montrose and Longueville' but *Q* may be correct in applying the action to a single lord, which should have been Longueville, rather than Galloway. At some point between the draft of the playtext corresponding to the German play, and the draft corresponding to the performance at court (printed as *Q*), Dekker may have altered the plot so that Montrose as well as Longueville is cured by Andelocia.

SC. 9]   THE COMEDY OF OLD FORTUNATUS   225

Andelocia. Fie, fie, fie, fie, you no credit le dockature? Ha,
   but vell, 'tis all one for tat. 'Tis no mattera for gold. Vell,
   vell, vell, vell, vell, me have some more. Pray, say noting,   150
   shall be presently prepara for your horns.
   [*Aside*] She has my purse and yonder lies my hat.
   Work brains and once more make me fortunate.
   [*To* AGRIPPINE] Vell, vell, vell, vell, be patient Madam,
   presently, presently, be patient. Me have two, tree, four   155
   and five medicines for de horn. Presently Madam, stand
   you der, pray wid all mine art, stand you all der and say
   noting, so. Nor look noting dis vey. So, presently, presently Madam, snip dis horn off wid de rushes and anoder
   ting by and by, by and by, by and by. Pray, look none dis   160
   vey and say noting.   *Gets his hat up.*
Athelstan. Let no man speak or look, upon his life.
   [*To* ANDELOCIA] Doctor, none here shall rob thee of
   thy skill.
Andelocia. So, taka dis hand. Wink now, pray artely, wid your
   two nyes. Why, so.   165
   [*Aside*] Would I were with my brother Ampedo.
                                                  Exit with her.
Agrippine. Help, father, help! I am hurried hence perforce!

148–51.] *this ed.;* Fie, fie, fie, fie, you no credit le dockature? Ha, but vel, tis all one for tat: tis no mattera for gold: Uel, vel, vel, vel, vel, me haue some more, prea say noting, shall bee presently prepara for your hornes. Q.   154–61.] *this ed.;* Uel, vel, vel, vel, be patient Madam, presently, presently, be patient, mee haue two, tree, fowre and fiue medicines for de horne: presently Madam, stand you der, prea wid all mine art, stand you all der: and say noting, so: nor looke noting dis vey: so, presently, presently Madam, snip dis horne off wid de rushes & anoder ting by and by, by and by, by and by, prea looke none dis vey, and say noting. Q.   164–5.] *this ed.;* So, taka dis hand: winck now prea artely wid your two nyes: why so. Q.

148. *you no credit le dockature?*] 'you don't credit the doctor?'
164. *Wink ... wid your two nyes*] The instruction is to close both eyes, not to close a single eye in the more recent sense of conveying intimate or humorous information.
167. *Help ... perforce*] A further clue to the stage business associated with transportation by wishing-hat: Agrippine's exit must be slow enough for her to register what's happening and speak about it for at least one full line.

Athelstan. Draw weapons! Where's the princess? Follow
him!
Stay the French doctor, stay the doctor there!

CORNWALL *and some other[s] run out and enter presently.*

Cornwall. Stay him? S'heart, who dare stay him? 'Tis the
devil   170
In likeness of a Frenchman, of a doctor.
Look: how a rascal kite having swept up
A chicken in his claws, so flies this hell-hound
In th'air with Agrippina in his arms.
Orleans. Mount every man upon his swiftest horse.   175
Fly several ways, he cannot bear her far.
Galloway. These paths we'll beat.
       Exeunt GALLOWAY *and* ORLEANS.
Lincoln.   And this way shall be mine.
Cornwall. This way, my liege, I'll ride.
Athelstan.   And this way I:
No matter which way, to seek misery.
       Exit ATHELSTAN.
Longueville. I can ride no way to outrun my shame.   180
Montrose. Yes, Longueville, let's gallop after too.
Doubtless this doctor was that Irish devil
That cozened us. The medicine which he gave us
Tasted like his Damasco villainy.
To horse, to horse! If we can catch this fiend,   185
Our forkèd shame shall in his heart-blood end.

---

168. SP *Athelstan*] Dilke; Andel. Q.   169.1. SD] *Dilke*; Q *prints in black-letter as a continuation of Athelstan's speech.*   174. *Agrippina*] *Bowers;* Agripyne Q.

---

168. *Draw weapons!*] Under normal circumstances it was forbidden to draw a weapon in the presence of a monarch (cf. the confrontation between Essex and Elizabeth in the summer of 1598, when she struck his head and he reached for his sword, causing the Lord Admiral to restrain him).
 172–4. *rascal kite ... arms*] Another instance of violent bird of prey imagery, cf. 2.47 and Cho.2, 28–9.
 186. *heart-blood*] vital blood, blood shed in death (cf. lifeblood) (*OED*); cf. 'life's little river in my breast', 10.159 below.

SC. 10]   THE COMEDY OF OLD FORTUNATUS   227

Longueville. Oh, how this mads me, that all tongues in scorn,
   Which way so e'er I ride, cry, '''Ware the horn'. *Exeunt.*

[Scene 10]

   Enter ANDELOCIA, *with* AGRIPPINE, AMPEDO
   and SHADOW.

Agrippine. O gentle Andelocia, pity me.
   Take off this infamy, or take my life.
Andelocia. Your life? You think then that I am a true doctor indeed, that tie up my living in the knots of winding-sheets? Your life? No, keep your life, but deliver your   5
   purse. You know the thief's salutation: 'Stand and deliver'. So, this is mine and these yours. I'll teach you to live by the sweat of other men's brows.
Shadow. And to strive to be fairer than God made her.
Andelocia. Right, Shadow. [*To* AGRIPPINE] Therefore vanish;   10
   you have made me turn juggler and cry 'hey-pass', but your horns shall not repass.
Agrippine. O gentle Andelocia.
Andelocia. Andelocia is a nettle: if you touch him gently, he'll sting you.   15
Shadow. Or a rose; if you pull his sweet stalk, he'll prick you.
Andelocia. Therefore not a word. Go, trudge to your father.

   187–8. *Oh ... horn.*] cut for the Tufts performance.
   188. *'Ware*] Beware; possibly also a pun on 'wear'.

   0. SD] Rhys adds the setting: 'An open Space near London: A Prison and a Pair of Stocks in the background'.
   3–5. *You think ... sheet?*] cut for the Tufts performance.
   7. *this ... these*] 'this' is Andelocia's purse, 'these' are Agrippine's deserved horns.
   11–12. *you have ... repass*] cut for the Tufts performance.
   11. *hey-pass*] A conjuror's exclamation, ordering something to move or change position (the *OED*'s second example, after *Faustus*: 'pass, v. †36. Conjuring. b. intr.').
   12. *repass*] heal; the present example antedates the *OED* (†, v.2, citing Donne) by 31 years. Andelocia is punning on 'pass and repass' as a sleight of hand action performed by conjurors (*OED*, v.1, †3. trans. Conjuring).
   14–17. *Andelocia ... Therefore*] cut for the Tufts performance.

Sigh not for your purse: money may be got by you as well as by the little Welshwoman in Cyprus, that had but one horn in her head; you have two, and perhaps you shall cast both, as you use me. Mark those words well: as you use me. Nay, y'are best fly, I'll not endure one word more. Yet stay too, because you entreat me so gently and that I'll make some amends to your father, although I care not for any king in Christendom. Yet hold you, take this apple; eat it as you go to court and your horns shall play the cowards and fall from you.

Agrippine. O gentle Andelocia.

Andelocia. Nay, away, not a word.

Shadow. Ha, ha, ha, *&c.* 'Ware horns!

Exit AGRIPPINE *weeping.*

Andelocia. Why dost thou laugh, Shadow?

Shadow. To see what a horn plague follows covetousness and pride.

Ampedo. Brother, what mysteries lie in all this?

Andelocia. Tricks, Ampedo. Tricks, devices, and mad hieroglyphics. Mirth, mirth and melody. Oh, there's more

---

21. both, as] *Dilke;* both: as *Q.*

18–21. *Sigh not ... cast both*] cut for the Tufts performance.

19–20. *Welshwoman ... her head*] Unexplained (and possibly the reason these lines were cut in the Tufts production), though clearly intended as a sideshow attraction of the kind Caliban is imagined to be by Trinculo in *The Tempest,* 2.2.23–32. Dilke alludes to two instances of this phenomenon recorded in the *Encyclopedia Britannica* (untraced) and relates that 'the horns and picture of one woman are at present at the British Museum'. Welsh characters and language feature in much of Dekker's writings, including *Patient Grissil* (Admiral's Men, 1600) and *Satiromastix* (Chamberlain's Men and Children of Paul's, 1601) around the time of *Fortunatus.*

21. *cast both ... use me*] Andelocia's meaning is unclear. Previous editors differ in their punctuation of these lines and fail to offer an explanatory gloss. His sense seems to be that Agrippine might succeed in casting off her horns just as she has previously cast Andelocia aside.

30. *'Ware horns*] See 9.188n above.

35–6. *Tricks ... hieroglyphics*] Loewenstein suggests that Amorphus in Jonson's *Cynthia's Revels* may draw inspiration from Andelocia's lines when he makes Asotus 'the horribly paltry gift of his own hat' (Loewenstein, 81 and 171 n55; *Cynthia's Revels* (Q), *CWBJ*, 1.4.142–3: "tis a relic I could not so easily have departed with, but as the hieroglyphic of my affection. You shall alter it to what form you please, it will take any block').

36–42. *Oh, there's ... seek us.*] cut for the Tufts performance.

music in this than all the gamut airs and *sol fa res* in the world. Here's the purse and here's the hat. Because you shall be sure I'll not start, wear you this [*Indicates the wishing-hat*]; you know its virtue. If danger beset you, fly 40 and away. A sort of broken-shinned limping-legged jades run hobbling to seek us. Shadow, we'll for all this have one fit of mirth more, to make us laugh and be fat.

Shadow. And when we are fat, master, we'll do as all gluttons do: laugh and lie down. 45

Andelocia. Hie thee to my chamber, make ready my richest attire. I'll to court presently.

Shadow. I'll go to court in this attire, for apparel is but the shadow of a man. But Shadow is the substance of his apparel. *Exit* SHADOW. 50

Andelocia. Away, away and meet me presently.

Ampedo. I had more need to cry away to thee.
Away, away with this wild lunacy,
Away with riots.

Andelocia. Away with your purity, brother, y'are an ass. Why 55 doth this purse spit out gold but to be spent? Why lives a man in this world? To dwell in the suburbs of it, as you do? Away, foreign simplicity, away. Are not eyes made to see fair ladies? Hearts to love them? Tongues to court them and hands to feel them? Out you stock, you stone, 60

---

37. gamut airs] Gammoth ares *Q*. 40. its virtue] *Rhys;* his vertue *Q*. 40–1. fly and away] *Rhys;* fly & away *Q*; fly away *Dilke*. 49. Shadow] *Dilke;* shaddow *Q*. 59. ladies?] *Q catchword;* ~: *Q text*

---

37. *gamut airs*] The scale of notes formed by the overlapping hexachords in Guido d'Arezzo's system of music (*OED*, gamut 2a); i.e. all the notes of the musical scale.

sol fa res] The *OED*'s only example of this particular compound (n., C2 † sol-fa-re n. Obs.). Sol, fa and res are notes in d'Arezzo's hexachords.

40–1. *fly and away*] i.e. fly and away you go.

43. *laugh and be fat*] proverbial, to enjoy life rather than worry; Dent L91, cf. Jonson, *Every Man Out*, 'When shall we sup together, and laugh and be fat with those good wenches?' (3.1.30–2).

45. *laugh and lie down*] a card game predicated on making pairs (the player unable to do so laying down their cards and being laughed at by the other players), but also proverbial (Dent L92★, cf. *Shoemaker's Holiday*, 'Lie down sirs, and laugh', 18.130), and frequently with sexual connotation.

60. *you stock, you stone* ...] senseless things, cf. Shakespeare, *Julius Caesar* 1.1.34: 'You blocks, you stones, you worse than senseless things'.

you log's end. Are not legs made to dance and shall mine
limp up and down the world after your cloth-stocking
heels? You have the hat; keep it. Anon I'll visit your virtu-
ous countenance again. Adieu. Pleasure is my sweet mis-
tress; I wear her love in my hat and her soul in my heart. 65
I have sworn to be merry and in spite of Fortune and the
black-browed Destinies, I'll never be sad.   *Exit.*
Ampedo. Go, fool. In spite of mirth, thou shalt be sad.
                                          [*Lights a fire.*]
I'll bury half thy pleasures in a grave
Of hungry flames. This fire I did ordain 70
To burn both purse and hat: as this doth perish,
So shall the other. Count what good and bad
They both have wrought; the good is to the ill
As a small pebble to a mighty hill.
Thy glory and thy mischiefs here shall burn. 75
Good gifts abused to man's confusion turn.

   Enter LONGUEVILLE, *and* MONTROSE *with soldiers.*

Longueville. This is his brother. Soldiers, bind his arms.
Montrose. Bind arms and legs and hale the fiend away.
Ampedo. Uncivil! Wherefore must I taste your spite?
Longueville. Art thou not one of Fortunatus' sons? 80
Ampedo. I am, but he did never do you wrong.
Longueville. The devil thy brother has, villain. Look here.
Montrose. Where is the beauteous purse and wishing-hat?
Ampedo. My brother Andelocia has the purse.
This way he'll come anon to pass to court. 85
Alas, that sin should make men's hearts so bold
To kill their souls for the base thirst of gold.
The wishing-hat is burnt.
Montrose.   Burnt? Soldiers bind him.

---

83. beauteous] *Q;* bountious *Bowers (suggested).*

61–3. *Are not legs ... heels?*] cut for the Tufts performance.
76. *Good gifts ... turn*] noted by Allott in *Englands Parnassus* under 'Gifts' (p. 108).
78. *hale*] haul (see 7.2n).
88. *Burnt ... bind him*] As Blamires notes, there is an irony in the fact that Ampedo burns the hat that could have facilitated his escape from this confinement (*Fortunatus in His Many English Guises*, 51).

SC. 10]   THE COMEDY OF OLD FORTUNATUS   231

  Tortures shall wring both hat and purse from you.
  Villain, I'll be revenged for that base scorn   90
  Thy hell-hound brother clapped upon my head.
Longueville. And so will Longueville.
Montrose.   Away with him.
  Drag him to yonder tower. There shackle him,
  And in a pair of stocks lock up his heels
  And bid your wishing-cap deliver you.   95
  Give us the purse and hat, we'll set thee free;
  Else rot to death and starve.
      [*The soldiers drag Ampedo away.*]
Ampedo.   Oh, tyranny!
  You need not scorn the badge which you did bear:
  Beasts would you be, though horns you did not wear.
Montrose. Drag hence the cur. Come noble Longueville,   100
  One's sure and were the other fiend as fast,
  Their pride should cost their lives. Their purse and hat
  Shall be both ours, we'll share them equally.
Longueville. That will be some amends for arming me.

   Enter ANDELOCIA *and* SHADOW *after him.*

Montrose. Peace, Longueville, yonder the gallant comes.   105
Longueville. Y'are well encountered.
Andelocia.   Thanks, Lord Longueville.
Longueville. The king expects your presence at the court.
Andelocia. And thither am I going.

---

92. Away with him] *Bowers; assigned to Longaville in* Q.   97–8. Oh ... bear] *Dilke; one line in* Q.   104. arming] Q; harming *Dilke.*

---

 93. *yonder tower*] perhaps upstage (i.e. the discovery space, appropriately altered) or above the stage.
 98. *scorn the badge ... wear*] Ampedo's meaning depends on identifying 'badge' with 'horn' (= ornamental helmet, made of horn, as badge of honour); he's telling Montrose not to despise his horns. Cf. the song in *As You Like It*: 'Take thou no scorn to wear the horn' (4.2.11).
 104. *arming*] Providing with spurs (cock-fighting; *OED* 3b) or other addition; Longueville refers to the addition of horns. Most editors emend to 'harming', following Dilke, but, as Bowers notes, '[t]he ordinary sense of *arm* is sufficient to give specific pertinence to the Q reading, even if special senses as in falconry and cock-fighting were not also peculiarly applicable'.

232   THE COMEDY OF OLD FORTUNATUS   [SC. 10

Shadow. Pips fine, fine apples of Tamasco, ha, ha, ha.
Montrose. Wert thou that Irishman that cozened us?   110
Shadow. Pips fine, ha, ha, ha! No, not I, not Shadow.
Andelocia. Were not your apples delicate and rare?
Longueville. The worst that e'er you sold. Sirs, bind him
   fast.
Andelocia. What, will you murder me? Help, help, some
   help!
Shadow. Help, help, help!   *Exit* SHADOW [, *running*].   115
Montrose. Follow that dog and stop his bawling throat.
Andelocia. Villains, what means this barbarous treachery?
Longueville. We mean to be revenged for our disgrace.
Montrose. And stop the golden current of thy waste.
Andelocia. Murder! They murder me! Oh, call for help!   120
Longueville. Thy voice is spent in vain. Come, come, this
   purse,
This wellspring of your prodigality.
Andelocia. Are you appointed by the king to this?

---

116. bawling] Dilke; balling *Q*.

---

109. *Pips fine ... ha*] As Dilke notes, '[t]his unseasonable jesting of Shadow's, was not only dangerous but unnatural, as he could not be ignorant of the consequence of a discovery both to his master and himself'. Dilke attributes the imprudent outburst to the fact that Shadow plays a clown role and that 'the propriety or impropriety of the speeches of these characters was seldom sufficiently attended to'. In the German play, Shadow notices the dukes before they see him and Andelocia. Recognizing them (by the horns still worn by one) as the gulls who purchased the apples previously, Shadow carelessly slips into the old costermonger routine, apparently forgetting that he and Andelocia are not assuming the disguise this time: '*Gnädiger Herr wen sehen wir da? Es seynd die beyden Herrn / den wir am nechsten zu Lundun Epffel verkaufften / und zwar der eine hat noch Hörner / Epffelchen von* DAMASCO, *Epffelchen*' (Act V, p. 203, ll. 20–3, 'Milord who are we seeing here? It is the two gentlemen / whom we initially sold apples to in London / and one of them still has horns / Apples from Damasco, apples').
115. SD] *Q* notes the exit for Shadow here, after he cries for help, but the German play's stage directions explicitly call for Shadow to be stabbed: '*Die* GRAFEN *kommen / und lauffen sie mit blossen Gewehr an / erstechen den* DIENER' (Act V, p. 203, ll. 27–8, translated by Elena Benthaus as: 'The dukes come / and start running with bayonets / stab the servant'). The brothers subsequently lament their servant's death in German. His reappearance below at l. 200 means that, if he is stabbed in the English version, he does not die of his wounds.
119. *waste*] the consumption of material or resources (*OED* 8a).

Montrose. No, no. Rise. Spurn him up. Know you who's
    this?   [AMPEDO *is discovered.*]
Andelocia. My brother Ampedo? Alas, what fate   125
    Hath made thy virtues so unfortunate?
Ampedo. Thy riot and the wrong of these two lords,
    Who (causeless) thus do starve me in this prison.
Longueville. Strive not, y'are best. Villains, lift in his legs.
                    [*They place Andelocia in stocks.*]
Andelocia. Traitors to honour, what do you intend?   130
Longueville. That riot shall in wretchedness have end.
    Question thy brother with what cost he's fed,
    And so assure thou shalt be banqueted.
          Exeunt they two [LONGUEVILLE *and* MONTROSE].
Ampedo. In want, in misery, in woe and care,
    Poor Ampedo his fill hath surfeited.   135
    My want is famine, bolts my misery.
    My care and woe should be thy portion.
Andelocia. Give me that portion, for I have a heart
    Shall spend it freely and make bankrupt
    The proudest woe that ever wet man's eye.   140
    Care with a mischief? Wherefore should I care?
    Have I rid side by side by mighty kings,
    Yet be thus bridled now? I'll tear these fetters.

---

139. bankrupt] *Dilke;* bankerowte *Bowers (suggested);* bankrowt, *Q.*

124. *Spurn*] to strike, trample or kick (*OED* 5b); cf. 214 below.
124. *Know you who's this?*] *Q* does not supply a stage direction, but clearly Ampedo must be discovered here. Dilke's suggestion – '(*Draws a curtain and discovers Ampedo in fetters and in prison*)' – is conjectural, but some kind of revelation must take place. See 93n above for the possible setting of the 'tower' in which Ampedo is discovered.
129. *best. Villains, lift*] *Q*'s punctuation is ambiguous (cf. collation); Longueville might either be advising the villainous brothers not to struggle, then subsequently instructing soldiers to lift Andelocia's legs into stocks or shackles (hence Bowers's inclusion of an editorial stage direction, '[Andelocia *in stocks.*]' at the end of l. 129), or he might be using 'villains' in the older sense of being low-born, and thus referring to the soldiers shackling Andelocia.
136. *bolts*] irons or fetters for fastening the leg (*OED* n1 6).
142–3. *Have I rid ... bridled now?*] Another image of Fortune's wheel turning a full revolution, recalling the debasement of once mighty kings and emperors in Fortune's entourage at 1.68–318, and perhaps more specifically the 'pampered jades of Asia', Trebizon and Soria, who drag Tamburlaine's chariot in Marlowe's *2 Tamburlaine* 4.3.1.

Murder! Cry murder, Ampedo, aloud.
To bear this scorn our fortunes are too proud. 145
Ampedo. O folly, thou hast power to make flesh glad,
When the rich soul in wretchedness is clad.
Andelocia. Peace, fool, am not I Fortune's minion?
These bands are but one wrinkle of her frown.
This is her evening mask, her next morn's eye 150
Shall overshine the sun in majesty.
Ampedo. But this sad night will make an end of me.
Brother, farewell; grief, famine, sorrow, want,
Have made an end of wretched Ampedo.
Andelocia. Where is the wishing-hat?
Ampedo.   Consumed in fire.   155
Andelocia. Accursed be those hands that did destroy it;
That would redeem us, did we now enjoy it.
Ampedo. Wanton, farewell, I faint. Death's frozen hand
Congeals life's little river in my breast.
No man before his end is truly blessed.   *Dies.*   160
Andelocia. Oh, miserable, miserable soul.
Thus a foul life makes death to look more foul.

Enter LONGUEVILLE *and* MONTROSE *with a halter.*

Longueville. Thus shall this golden purse divided be,
One day for you, another day for me.
Montrose. Of days anon. Say, what determine you: 165
Shall they have liberty, or shall they die?
Longueville. Die sure. And see, I think the elder's dead.
Andelocia. Ay, murderers, he is dead. O sacred wisdom,
Had Fortunatus been enamourèd

---

160. *No man ... blessed*] noted by Allott in *Englands Parnassus* under 'Man' (p. 198).
160. SD] The chronology of events and the clarity of their detail differs in the German play; there, Andelocia is captured by the lords and Shadow is killed, *then* Ampedo enters, laments Shadow's death and Andelocia's abduction (which he has clearly heard about), and decides to destroy the hat, which he promptly burns by throwing into a fire on stage, before dying of grief (Act V, p. 205, ll. 6-25). In Q, Shadow clearly does not die at l. 115 since he speaks again at l. 197.
162. SD halter] A rope or cord with a noose, for fastening horses or cattle.

> Of thy celestial beauty, his two sons   170
> Had shined like two bright suns.
Longueville.   Pull hard, Montrose.
Andelocia. Come you to strangle me? Are you the hangman?
> Hellhounds, y'are damned for this impiety!
> Fortune, forgive me, I deserve thy hate;
> Myself have made myself a reprobate.   175
> Virtue, forgive me, for I have transgressed
> Against thy laws. My vows are quite forgot,
> And therefore shame is fallen to my sins' lot.
> Riches and knowledge are two gifts divine;
> They that abuse them both as I have done,   180
> To shame, to beggary, to hell must run.
> O conscience hold thy sting, cease to afflict me.
> Be quick, tormentors, I desire to die.
> No death is equal to my misery.
> Cyprus, vain world and vanity farewell.   185
> Who builds his heaven on earth, is sure of hell.
>   [ANDELOCIA *dies.*]
Longueville. He's dead. In some deep vault let's throw their
> bodies.
Montrose. First let us see the purse, Lord Longueville.
Longueville. Here 'tis. By this we'll fill this tower with gold.

---

171. *shined ... bright suns*] Cf. Fortunatus's earlier, misguided belief that gold would enable his sons to '[s]hine in the streets of Cyprus like two stars' (2.206).

172. *hangman*] The Tufts promptbook here specifies: 'Two brothers in stocks, front right'.

179–81. *Riches ... must run*] Andelocia's remorse here was cut for the Tufts performance.

182–6. *O conscience ... hell*] Conover notes that the strength of Andelocia's dying words 'are completely dissipated by what follows', with Virtue's triumph clumsily overshadowing what ought to be the principal climax of the action: the denouement of the Andelocia–Ampedo plot (*Thomas Dekker*, 74).

186. SD] The SD 'with a halter' at l. 162, and the references to 'pulling hard' and 'strangling' in ll. 171-2 make clear that strangling is the means of Andelocia's death; in the German play, the strangulation is specified even more explicitly: '*Er thut ihn einen Strick umb den Halß und erwürgen ihn / der Todte wird hinein getragen*' (Act V, p. 206, ll. 11-12, '*He puts a rope around his neck and they strangle him / the deceased is carried inside*').

Montrose. Frenchman, this purse is counterfeit.
Longueville.   Thou liest.   190
  Scot, thou hast cozened me; give me the right,
  Else shall thy bosom be my weapon's grave.
Montrose. Villain, thou shalt not rob me of my due.
                                                                They fight.

Enter ATHELSTAN, AGRIPPINE, ORLEANS, GALLOWAY, CORNWALL, CHESTER, LINCOLN, *and* SHADOW *with weapons at one door;* FORTUNE, VICE, *and their attendants at another door.*

All. Lay hands upon the murderers, strike them down.
Fortune. Surrender up this purse, for this is mine.   195
All. Are these two devils, or some powers divine?
Shadow. Oh, see, see! Oh, my two masters, poor Shadow's substances! What shall I do? Whose body shall Shadow now follow?

---

190. *purse is counterfeit*] Actually, the purse is genuine, but its magical properties have ceased with the death of Fortunatus's sons, in line with Fortune's warning, 'The virtue ends when thou and thy sons end' (1.311). This is more obvious in the German version, where the lords test the purse before killing Andelocia, and each succeeds in withdrawing ten gold pieces from it (Act V, p. 206, ll. 3 and 6: '*er greifft hat 10. stueck goldes*' and '*Er holet auch zeben Stueck Goldes herauss*'), but immediately after they strangle Andelocia, the purse is suddenly empty (Act V, p. 207, l. 1: '*er wil ihn gehen / der Seckel ist leer*').

193.2 SD] The Tufts promptbook here specifies: 'Ampedo & Andel. are in front, bound & dead'.

193.2-5. SD] Another moment in which events depicted in full in German are elided in English. In the German play (Act 5, p. 207, l. 25 – p. 208, l. 25), the sword fight between Longueville and Montrose is interrupted by the King, Agrippine, and a servant who, following the King's instructions, removes one of the lords from the stage. The remaining lord confesses that they killed Andelocia and were fighting over the purse, which they believed to be counterfeit. The King and Agrippine, however, authenticate the purse as genuine. Agrippine asks the King for justice for Andelocia's murder; the King sentences both killers to death, and the lord who had remained onstage is escorted away. Only then does Fortune enter to reclaim the purse (Vice and Virtue never enter the stage again; they last appeared in Act IV when they planted the trees). The King and Agrippine kneel before Fortune and thank her for her generosity towards them, asking her to be generous to their kingdom in the future. Fortune grants them their wish.

194. SP] The reference to 'two devils' (meaning Fortune and Vice) in l. 196 suggests that 'All' here refers to the non-supernatural characters.

SC. 10]   THE COMEDY OF OLD FORTUNATUS   237

Fortune. [*To* SHADOW] Peace, idiot, thou shalt find rich
   heaps of fools   200
  That will be proud to entertain a shadow.
  I charm thy babbling lips from troubling me.
  [*To the others*] You need not hold them; see, I smite
   them down
  Lower than hell. Base souls, sink to your heaven.
Vice. I do arrest you both my prisoners.   205
Fortune. Stand not amazed, you gods of earth, at this:
  She that arresteth these two fools is Vice.
  They have broke Virtue's laws; Vice is her sergeant,
  Her jailer and her executioner.
  Look on those Cypriots, Fortunatus' sons;   210
  They and their father were my minions.
  My name is Fortune.
All.   O dread deity.   [*They kneel.*]
Fortune. Kneel not to me. If Fortune list to frown,
  You need not fall down, for she'll spurn you down.
  Arise. But fools, on you I'll triumph thus.   215
  What have you gained by being covetous?
  This prodigal purse did Fortune's bounteous hand
  Bestow on them; their riots made them poor
  And set those marks of miserable death
  On all their pride. The famine of base gold   220
  Hath made your souls to Murder's hands be sold,
  Only to be called rich. But, idiots, see:
  The virtue's to be fled. Fortune hath caused it so.
  Those that will all devour, must all forgo.
Athelstan. Most sacred goddess –
Fortune.   Peace, you flatterer.   225
  Thy tongue but heaps more vengeance on thy head.
  Fortune is angry with thee. In thee burns

---

    203. *them*] i.e. Longueville and Montrose.
    208-9. *Virtue's laws ... executioner*] This is the first suggestion of such a relationship between Virtue and Vice.
    220. *famine of base gold*] This is only the second example in the *OED* of 'famine' in the chiefly figurative sense of '[v]iolent appetite, as of a famished person'. It recalls Fortune's Virgilian warning against 'gold's sacred hunger' in 1.253.
    224. *Those ... all forgo*] noted by Allott in *Englands Parnassus* under 'Avarice' (p. 12).

238   THE COMEDY OF OLD FORTUNATUS   [SC. 10

  A greedy covetous fire, in Agrippine
  Pride like a monarch revels; and those sins
  Have led you blindfold to your former shames. 230
  But Virtue pardoned you and so doth Fortune.
Athelstan and Agrippine. All thanks to both your sacred
  deities.
Fortune. As for these metal-eaters, these base thieves
  Who rather than they would be counted poor
  Will dig through hell for gold: you were forgiven 235
  By Virtue's general pardon, her broad seal
  Gave you your lives when she took off your horns.
  Yet having scarce one foot out of the jail,
  You tempt damnation by more desperate means.
  You both are mortal and your pains shall ring 240
  Through both your ears to terrify your souls,
  As please the judgement of this mortal king.
Athelstan. Fair empress of the world, since you resign
  Your power to me, this sentence shall be mine:
  [*To* LONGUEVILLE *and* MONTROSE] Thou shalt be
   tortured on a wheel to death, 245
  Thou with wild horses shalt be quarterèd.
Vice. Ha, ha! Weak judge, weak judgement. I reverse

228–31. *in Agrippine ... Fortune*] Fortune pardons Agrippine for her sinful pride but as Conover notes, it is not clear whether Orleans (who was rewarded for loving Agrippine despite her temporary deformity) will still marry her now that she is once again attractive to all. The Orleans–Cyprus–Agrippine subplot lacks resolution: Conover suggests that the only viable solution is 'some pantomime or dumb show' in which a 'pairing off of Orleans with Agripyne might satisfy part of this lack, but no indication of such a conclusion remains in the published play' (*Thomas Dekker*, 69).

233. *metal-eaters*] a pejorative term alluding to their subsistence on gold rather than food (cf. 2.251-2n). Fortune is referring here to Longueville and Montrose.

245–6. *Thou shalt be tortured... quarterèd*] Both are specifically French methods of execution; it is impossible to say which punishment is being assigned to Longueville and which to Montrose.

247–54. *Weak judge ... you free*] Vice's reprieve does not exist in the German play, where the King's sentence of capital punishment is final; it may have been added by Dekker as part of his revisions for performance at court. Dilke had similar suspicions: 'I fear no better reason can be assigned for this strange deliverance than that the general conclusion of the play was to be more cheerful than it could have been if Montrose and Longavile had been led to execution'.

SC. 10]   THE COMEDY OF OLD FORTUNATUS   239

  That sentence, for they are my prisoners.
  Embalm the bodies of those Cypriots
  And honour them with princely burial.   250
  For those do as you please. But for these two:
  I kiss you both, I love you, y'are my minions.
  Untie their hands. Vice doth reprieve you both.
  I set you free.
[*Longueville and Montrose*]. Thanks, gracious deity.
Vice. Be gone, but you in liberty shall find   255
  More bondage than in chains. Fools, get you hence.
  Both wander with tormented conscience.
Longueville. Oh, horrid judgement! That's the hell indeed.
Montrose. Come, come, our death ne'er ends if conscience
  bleed.
[*Longueville and Montrose*]. Oh, miserable, miserable men. 260
    Exeunt [LONGUEVILLE *and* MONTROSE].
Fortune. Fortune triumphs at this, yet to appear
  All like myself, that which from those I took,
      [*She points to the purse.*]
  King Athelstan I will bestow on thee,
  And in it the old virtue I infuse.
  But, king, take heed how thou my gifts dost use. 265
  England shall ne'er be poor if England strive
  Rather by virtue than by wealth to thrive.

---

254. SP] Both *Q*.   260. SP] Both *Q*.   260.1. SD] *Exeunt they two. Q.*

 253. *reprieve*] OED cites this amongst its earliest examples of 'reprieve' in the sense '[t]o grant a respite to (a person) from impending punishment'.
 263. *bestow on thee*] As Dilke points out, Fortune has only just censured Athelstan for the 'greedy covetous fire' that burns in him (l. 228); her subsequent bestowal of the revitalised purse on him 'seems indeed to *be like herself*, and not calculated to promote the moral purposes of the drama' but rather to serve Dekker 'as a proper introduction to denote the national prosperity in the reign of his royal mistress'.
 266-7. *England ... thrive*] Wiggins (#851) tentatively offers the 'impressionistic judgement' that these lines' apparent echo of the final couplet of *James IV* ('Thus warres have end, and after dreadfull hate, / Men learne at last to know their good estate', sig. K4r) may be evidence of Greene's authorship of a lost 'Fortunatus, part 2' play from c.1590.
 267. SD] The Tufts performance specified '[f]or the entrance of Virtue, crowned, an Italian Moresca, by Claudio Monteverde [*sic*], published in 1608'. This final part of the scene, in which the supernatural characters

240   THE COMEDY OF OLD FORTUNATUS   [SC. 10

 Enter VIRTUE, *crowned; nymphs and kings attending on her,*
 crowned with olive branches and laurels; music sounding.
Vice. Virtue? Alas good soul, she hides her head.
Virtue. What envious tongue said, 'Virtue hides her head'?
Vice. She that will drive thee into banishment.   270
Fortune. She that hath conquered thee. How dar'st thou
 come
 Thus tricked in gaudy feathers and thus guarded
 With crowned kings and muses, when thy foe
 Hath trod thus on thee and now triumphs so?
 Where's virtuous Ampedo? See, he's her slave.   275
 For following thee, this recompense they have.
Virtue. Is Ampedo her slave? Why, that's my glory.
 The idiot's cap I once wore on my head

267.1. SD attending] *Eton copy of Q;* attendin *in all other copies.*   273.
With]   *Dilke;* Which *Q.*

---

directly address Queen Elizabeth, was criticized by Herford as corresponding 'not only to nothing in the *Volksbuch*, but to nothing in the rest of the play' (except for the other Virtue/Vice/Fortune scenes, which he considers 'an after-thought') (*Studies in the Literary Relations*, 211–12). Schlueter, however, whilst noting that the final scene of the German play 'brings closure to a leaner Virtue/Vice subplot' than the one present in the version Dekker prepared for court (and ultimately printed), views the English ending as 'complicated' more than 'muddled', and part of Dekker's attempt to please Elizabeth – an attempt in which 'his embellished subplot succeeded in honoring the true Virtue that sat on England's throne' ('New Light', 123, 126).

 277–86. *Is Ampedo … poor*] Critics have been troubled by the apparent injustice of the virtuous Ampedo's death in l. 186 above and by Virtue's uncharitable appraisal of him here; as the author of the Tufts production programme quips, '[u]nfortunately for poetic justice, the innocent Ampedo suffers with his guilty brother' (5). Ellis reads Ampedo's demise as the visitation of the sins of the father on the son; Fortunatus's indulgences are the direct cause of Ampedo's abstemiousness, which is here punished by death (*Old Age*, 150). Schlueter observes that Virtue here sounds like 'the contemptuous Fortune' and bases her judgement of Ampedo 'on nothing that is dramatized in the play'. She suggests that Dekker (perhaps in haste) failed to make earlier adjustments to Ampedo's character but needed here to rationalize Ampedo's death as part of the moralized ending of the play ('New Light', 127). However, George R. Price points out that, 'possessed of the means to do good to the needy (the magic purse and hat), Ampedo did nothing. In short, his sin was sloth' (*Thomas Dekker* (New York: Twayne Publishers, 1969), 48). An allusion to the Parable of the Talents (Matt. 25: 14–30; Luke 19:12–19) seems probable: Ampedo fails to actively promote virtue, preferring merely to criticise his brother's failings.

　　　　Did figure him. Those that (like him) do muffle
　　　　Virtue in clouds and care not how she shine,　　　　　280
　　　　I'll make their glory like to his decline.
　　　　He made no use of me, but like a miser
　　　　Locked up his wealth in rusty bars of sloth.
　　　　His face was beautiful but wore a mask,
　　　　And in the world's eyes seemed a blackamoor.　　　　285
　　　　So perish they that so keep Virtue poor.
Vice. Thou art a fool to strive, I am more strong
　　　　And greater than thyself. Then Virtue fly,
　　　　And hide thy face, yield me the victory.
Virtue. Is Vice higher than Virtue? That's my glory,　　　290
　　　　The higher that thou art, thou art more horrid.
　　　　The world will love me for my comeliness.
Fortune. Thine own self loves thyself: why on the heads
　　　　Of Agrippine, Montrose, and Longueville
　　　　(English, Scot, French) did Vice clap ugly horns,　　295
　　　　But to approve that English, French, and Scot,
　　　　And all the world else, kneel and honour Vice,
　　　　But in no country Virtue is of price?
Virtue. Yes, in all countries Virtue is of price.
　　　　In every kingdom some diviner breast　　　　　　　300
　　　　Is more enamoured of me than the rest.
　　　　Have English, Scot, and French bowed knees to thee?
　　　　Why, that's my glory too, for by their shame
　　　　Men will abhor thee and adore my name.
　　　　Fortune, thou art too weak, Vice th'art a fool　　　　305
　　　　To fight with me. I suffered you awhile
　　　　T'eclipse my brightness, but I now will shine
　　　　And make you swear your beauty's base to mine.
Fortune. Thou art too insolent. [*Gesturing to Elizabeth's
　　　　court*] See here's a court
　　　　Of mortal judges; let's by them be tried　　　　　　310
　　　　Which of us three shall most be deified.

---

296. *to approve*] to show to be true (*OED*).
298. *of price*] of great reputation; worthy, excellent (*OED*).

242   THE COMEDY OF OLD FORTUNATUS   [SC. 10

Vice. I am content.
Fortune.   And I.
Virtue.   So am not I.
   [*Gesturing to Elizabeth*] My judge shall be your sacred
      deity.
Vice. Oh, miserable me! I am undone.
                              Exit VICE *and her train.*
All. Oh, stop the horrid monster!
Virtue.   Let her run.   315
   Fortune, who conquers now?
Fortune.   Virtue, I see
   Thou wilt triumph both over her and me.
All. Empress of heaven and earth!
                          [*They kneel before* FORTUNE.]
Fortune.   Why do you mock me?
   Kneel not to me, to her transfer your eyes.
                              [*She gestures to Elizabeth.*]
   There sits the Queen of Chance. I bend my knees   320
   Lower than yours. [*To Elizabeth*] Dread goddess, 'tis
      most meet
   That Fortune fall down at thy conqu'ring feet,
   Thou sacred Empress that commandst the Fates.
   Forgive what I have to thy handmaid done,
   And at thy chariot wheels Fortune shall run,   325
   And be thy captive and to thee resign
   All powers which heaven's large patent have made
      mine.
Virtue. Fortune, th'art vanquished. [*To Elizabeth*] Sacred
      deity,
   Oh, now pronounce who wins the victory.
   And yet that sentence needs not, since alone   330
   Your virtuous presence Vice hath overthrown.

---

   313. *your sacred deity*] i.e. Queen Elizabeth; the remainder of the dialogue centres on the Queen.
   327. *All powers ... mine.*] The metre requires 'powers' and 'heaven's' to be monosyllabic.
   330–1. *since alone...overthrown*] i.e. the Queen's virtuous presence has overthrown Vice.

SC. 10]   THE COMEDY OF OLD FORTUNATUS   243

    Yet to confirm the conquest on your side,
    Look but on Fortunatus and his sons.
    Of all the wealth those gallants did possess,
    Only poor Shadow is left, comfortless.   335
    Their glory's faded and their golden pride.
Shadow. Only poor Shadow tells how poor they died.
Virtue. All that they had, or mortal men can have,
    Seems only but a shadow from the grave.
    Virtue alone lives still, and lives in you;   340
    I am a counterfeit, you are the true.
    I am a shadow, at your feet I fall,
    Begging for these and these, myself and all.
    All these that thus do kneel before your eyes
    Are shadows like myself, dread nymph; it lies   345
    In you to make us substances. Oh, do it!
    Virtue I am sure you love, she woos you to it.
    I read a verdict in your sun-like eyes,
    And this it is: Virtue the victory.
All. All loudly cry, Virtue the victory!   350
Virtue. Virtue the victory: for joy of this,
    Those self-same hymns which you to Fortune sung,
    Let them be now in Virtue's honour rung.

---

333. sons.] *sonnes: (colon not inked in most copies of Q)*.   339. Seems] *Daniel;*
Sends *Q*.   347. woos] *Dilke;* woes *Q*.

338–40. *All ... lives still*] noted by Allott in *Englands Parnassus* under
'Virtue' (p. 292).

339. *Seems*] Daniel prefers the variant reading 'seems', found in Allott's
quotation (instead of *Q*'s 'sends') and emends accordingly.

341–2. *counterfeit ... shadow*] As Shirley notes, this is a memorable
example of how Shadow's name is used in the play 'to initiate statements
concerning the difference between *shadow* and *substance*' (*Serious and Tragic
Elements*, 44).

345. *Are shadows*] As Hoy suggests, with a Puck-like pun on 'shadows' =
'players' (cf. *Dream*, 8.53ff: 'If we shadows have offended').

350. *All loudly cry*] Dilke thought this should have been a stage direction,
but did not emend the text to reflect his supposition. The line is metrical as
it stands, but would be incomplete if Dilke's theory of stage directions were
accepted.

The Song.

Virtue smiles, cry holiday,
Dimples on her cheeks do dwell.   355
Virtue frowns, cry welladay,
Her love is heaven, her hate is hell.
Since heaven and hell obey her power,
Tremble when her eyes do lour.
Since heaven and hell her power obey,   360
Where she smiles, cry holiday.
Holiday with joy we cry,
And bend, and bend, and merrily
Sing hymns to Virtue's deity:
Sing hymns to Virtue's deity.   365

As they all offer to go in, enter the TWO OLD MEN.

---

359. lour] *Dilke;* lowre *Q.*

353.1. The Song] The song is, of course, a mirror of that sung in 1.69–84, with Virtue's name now substituted for Fortune's. The tune identified by Duffin is thus again *Dulcina* (*Some Other Note*, 303). The Tufts performance specified a 'Repetition of II' ('Song by Coprario, published in 1614'; see 1.69–84n).

365.1. offer to go in] i.e. express readiness to exit; this seems to imply that they all remain on stage during the Epilogue that follows (confirmed by 1 Old Man's first line, 'Nay, stay, poor pilgrims').

The Epilogue at Court

1 Nay, stay, poor pilgrims; when I entered first
 The circle of this bright celestial sphere,
 I wept for joy; now I could weep for fear.
2 I fear we all, like mortal men, shall prove
 Weak, not in love but in expressing love.   5
1 Let every one beg once more on his knee,
 One pardon for himself and one for me;
 For I enticed you hither. O dear goddess,
 Breathe life in our numbed spirits with one smile
 And from this cold earth we with lively souls   10
 Shall rise like men newborn and make heav'n sound
 With hymns sung to thy name and prayers that we
 May once a year so oft enjoy this sight,
 Till these young boys change their curled locks to white.
 And when grey-wingèd age sits on their heads,   15
 That so their children may supply their steads,
 And that heaven's great arithmetician,
 Who in the scales of number weighs the world,
 May still to forty-two add one year more,

19. add] *Dilke;* and *Q.*

 1. *pilgrims*] The two old men from the Prologue at Court were making a pilgrimage to visit the Queen.
 3. *I wept*] Bowers notes that since it is the second old man, not the first, who weeps for joy in the Prologue at Court (l. 34 SD), Dekker 'has confused the precise circumstances of the Prologue' here (Bowers, Prol. at Court 38n).
 15. *grey-wingèd age*] See Prologue at Court 40-2n. *OED*'s second example of parasynthetic use of 'grey'.
 17. *heaven's great arithmetician*] Probably a reference to God's omniscience, possibly derived from Psalm 147: 4 (God counting the number of stars). The notion was relatively commonplace in the period, e.g. Thomas Walkington's *Rabboni Mary Magdalens teares, of sorrow, solace* ... (London, 1620): 'the very bristles of Hogs, are numbred to God, that heavenly Arithmetician' (53). It may alternatively be derived from the work of the German astronomer Johannes Kepler (1571–1630), whose *Mysterium Cosmographicum* (1596) proposed a divine geometrical design for the universe.
 19. *forty-two*] Elizabeth acceded to the throne on 17 November 1558 and the court performance of *Old Fortunatus* took place on 27 December 1599;

246   THE EPILOGUE AT COURT

  And still add one to one, that went before, 20
  And multiply four tens by many a ten:
  To this I cry Amen.
All.   Amen, Amen.
1 Good night, dear mistress. Those that wish thee harm,
  Thus let them stoop under destruction's arm.
All. Amen, Amen, Amen.   *Exeunt.* 25
      FINIS.

              Tho. Dekker.

1558–59 was the first regnal year, and there had thus been 41 regnal years by the time of the performance at court. The first old man declares his desire to see not just a forty-second but a number of additional regnal years.

23. *wish thee harm*] perhaps a specific reference to the numerous assassination attempts on Elizabeth (most famously by the Catholics in 1584–85), or even Essex's recent (September 1599) and bold behaviour in returning unscheduled from Ireland and bursting into the Queen's chamber whilst she was incompletely dressed; an intrusion that resulted in his confinement and, in November 1599, the public justification in Star Chamber of Essex's imprisonment. At Christmas, the time of the *Fortunatus* performance, Essex appeared to be on his deathbed, and churches rang their bells for him, infuriating the Queen (*ODNB*).

25. *Amen*] Michael Hattaway compares this prayer-as-epilogue to the possibly Shakespearean 'As the Dial Hand Tells O'er' poem (Cambridge University Library, MS Dd.5.75, fol. 46r), whose conceits – including 'the wish for a life so long for the queen that she might see the locks of boys turn white, followed by the mathematical imagery'– it closely resembles, suggesting that Dekker either wrote the poem or borrowed from it for this epilogue ('Dating *As You Like It*, Epilogues and Prayers, and the Problems of "As the Dial Hand Tells O'er"', *Shakespeare Quarterly* 60.2 (2009), 164). Helen Hackett argues more forcefully for Dekker's authorship of the Dial Hand poem on the strength of the parallel with the *Fortunatus* epilogue – in particular 'the conceits of Elizabeth's reign extending into an infinite perpetuity, and of her subjects' children becoming old in her service while she remains the same' – assigning it to *Shoemaker's Holiday* ('"As the Diall Hand Tells Ore": The Case for Dekker, Not Shakespeare, as Author', *Review of English Studies* 63 (2012), 38).

27. *Tho. Dekker*] The explicit announcement of authorship at the foot of the play-text rather than on the title-page is unusual, occurring in only two other plays in the late Elizabethan to early Jacobean period (*Promos and Cassandra*, 1578; and *Edward I*, Q1 1593 and Q2 1599); see Lukas Erne, *Shakespeare and the Book Trade* (Cambridge University Press, 2013), 95, who notes that there are 'no further examples up to 1660'.

Index

A Delectable Little History (1698), pp. 27-9
Admiral's Men, pp. 1, 3, 27, 29-33, 48, 51, 85, 89, 96, 105, 125, 127, 167, 171, 185, 228
Age is like love, it cannot be hid, 5.129-30
agree with, 5.395
Agrippine, Chars.45
alabaster, 5.389
A Looking Glass for London, p. 32
all hail, 5.22
Allot, Robert, pp. 10, 68, 106, 108, 109, 128, 131, 133, 153, 162, 206, 230, 234, 237, 243
alvarado, 4.94
amain, 5.250
amorato, 6.268
Ampedo, Chars.23
Andelocia, Chars.25
an you will come off, so, 5.25
apish, childish, and Italianate, 5.230
Apollo, 6.429
apple-john, 8.35
Apply, 3.18
approve, 10.296
Arabian phoenix, 5.171
Aragon, Cho.1.17
Aretë, 7.193
arming, 10.104
Astraea, Pro. at Court.4, p. 128
Athelstan, Chars.51

Babylon, Cho.1.35
Bajazeth, 1.192
bald fashion, 5.319
bandied, Cho.2.8
bane, 7.228
Barbarossa, 1.186-7
bar'd, 6.224
bastard cheek, 6.468
bavins, 6.439

Beckett, Samuel, p. 171
Belgia, 4.16
Belphoebe, Pro. at Court.3-4
* benumbing Pro.4
bewray, Cho.1.40
bias, 7.44
billets, 6.419
Bishop, Henry R., pp. 39-40, 41, 45
black, 6.288
Blamires, David, pp. 23, 24, 26, 53, 230
block, 5.321
bolts, 10.136
bosom stick, 3.3
Bowers, Fredson, pp. 5, 7, 8-10, 59, 62-64, 188, 199, 216, 218, 221, 223, 231, 233, 245
brave, 2.149
break out, 1.55
broad-brim fashions, 2.38
Browne, Robert, pp. 34-5
busied, 5.220

* cage-bird 5.431
cage of cuckoos' nests, 1.58
candlesticks, Pro. at Court.25-6
cap you, 5.412
casts no figures, 6.111
caterpillars, 6.437
cattle, 1.46
cedar, 3.23, 5.247
Chambers, E. K., pp. 2, 3, 5, 121
chameleon, 2.143
Chapman, George
 Blind Beggar of Alexandria, pp. 30, 178
 'Old Joiner of Aldgate', pp. 94, 220, *The Widow's Tears*, p. 160
characters of black, 1.172
Chester, Chars.49
cheverel consciences, 2.84
chinks, 1.15-16

circle England with a waist of gold, 6.406
circumference, Pro.15
coals kindle your choler, 6.446
cogging, 7.44
Coleridge, Samuel Taylor, pp. 40–1
Collier, John Payne, pp. 25, 48
complement, 5.227
confounds, Pro.7
conjuring circle, 1.20
Conover, James H., pp. 21, 52, 78, 126, 161, 167, 170, 201, 207, 217, 218, 235, 238
cook's shop, 5.94
Cornwall, Chars.47
corslets, 4.38
covetous earl, Cho.1.19
coxcomb, 3.0.10
crab-tree-faced, 2.64
crack me this nut, 1.57
Crescit Eundo, 3.0.5
crochets, 6.465
crusado, 5.63
* cudgels 5.285–6
cunning, 6.277
Current in any realm, 1.307
Cypriots, Pro. at Court.53

Dagger in Cyprus, 5.107
daggers drawing, 5.111
Damasco apples, 8.31
dance after her pipe, 5.103–4
* dat 8.48
deformity, 3.85
Dekker, Thomas
 The Dead Term, p. 130
 '1 Fortune's Tennis', p. 167
 1 Honest Whore, pp. 41, 45, 59
 in debt, pp. 56, 117, 119
 London's Tempe, p. 155
 Lust's Dominion, p. 117
 News from Grave's End, p. 125
 News from Hell, p. 112
 Noble Spanish Soldier, p. 155, 220
 Old Fortunatus (see separate entry)
 Patient Grissel, p. 228
 payments to, p. 1–6, 97, 119
 'Phaeton', p. 97
 Satiromastix, pp. 143, 228

The Seven Deadly Sins of London, pp. 55, 119, 126, 143
 'The Seven Wise Masters', pp. 31, 144
 The Shoemaker's Holiday, pp. 24, 29, 59, 82, 112, 129, 145
 A Strange Horse-Race, p. 166
 Sun's Darling, p. 188
 The Tell-Tale, p. 220
 Troia Nova Triumphans, p. 208
 The Wonder of a Kingdom, p. 220
delicate warble, 6.412
Dilke, Charles Wentworth, pp. 45, 62, 102, 108, 114, 120, 149, 175, 177, 185, 186, 187, 192, 204, 207, 219, 222, 228, 232, 233, 238, 239, 243
* divinity 6.487
Doctor Dodypoll, 8.114
dog has his day, 5.212
Dominabitur astris, 3.0.13–14
Don Dego, 5.285
Doric, Lydian, and Phrygian, 5.166–7
dormouse, 5.353
dram, 5.19
Dread Queen of Fairies, Pro. at Court.55
dribble out the sea by drops, 1.308
drop my soul out at mine eyes, 5.342
Dry as an eel-skin, 6.465
ducats, 2.194
Duckert, Lowell, pp. 54–5
Dutch botcher, 1.211–13
Dutton, Richard, pp. 29, 90, 152, 211
Dyce, Rev. Alexander, p. 9

eagle, Cho.1.28
eaten metals, 5.252
eatst bull beef, 2.11
Echo, Chars.6
Elizium, Pro. at Court.10, 5.334, 5.395
Ellis, Anthony, pp. 53–4, 85, 93, 95, 117, 118, 119, 131, 148
empery, 1.213
English angels, 6.240

Essex, Earl of (Robert Devereux),
    pp. 9–11, 153, 211, 226, 246
execution, 2.87

fadge, 5.422
fairies, 5.380
falcon, 5.142
falling sickness, 2.118
false brows, 1.112
Famagusta, 2.119
famine of base gold, 10.220
fan of Proserpine, 4.54
* fantasticoes 5.165
Fashions, 5.428
Fasting day, 2.13
fatal choice, 1.266
fat ourselves, 8.115
* feather-springs 9.65
fegaries, 5.126
field argent, 2.91
fig for a famine, 2.184–5
Fleay, F. G., pp. 2, 4, 5
* flint 7.102
flip-flap, 2.173
flourish, 2.70–1
fond, 6.39
Fonteyn, Bernard, p. 5
foot-cloths, 2.164
formable, 6.186
Fortunatus, Chars.4
Fortunatus, and His Sons (1819) the
    Covent Garden production,
    pp. 36–41, 123, 135, 140, 220
Fortune playhouse, pp. 29–30, 60,
    89
French crown, 5.320
French doctor, 9.85 SD
frizzled groatsworth of hair, 2.22–3
frosty hand of age, 5.153

gallant, 2.140.1
galled, 6.416
galleries, 5.405
Galloway, Chars.42
gammer, 1.36
gamut airs, 10.37
Ganymede, 1.247
Garden of Hesperides, 6.382
German emperor, / Henry the
    Fifth, 1.180–1

Gesta Romanorum, pp. 19–20, 29,
    200, 221
gilded wantons, 1.254–8
give him...the bag, 6.408–9
glad to be sped, 6.289
Gloriana, Pro. at Court.3–4
Glückssäckel und Wünschhut (puppet
    play), pp. 35–6, 48, 62
God-a-mercy, 7.49
God's lid, 7.28
go dwell with cares, 1.317
golden circle, 1.204
* golden hooks 2.53
gold's sweet music, 2.169
good angel, 2.37
goodfellow, 1.5
gossip, 1.333
great bell ... in Cyprus, 1.47–8
great Cham of Tartary, 2.212
Great landlady, Pro. at Court.37
Green, John, pp. 33, 48
Greene, Robert, pp. 3, 66, 98, 123,
    127, 186, 187, 239
Greg, W. W., pp. 4, 5, 65, 167
Greville, Fulke, pp. 10–11
grey-wingèd age, Epi.15

hale, 10.78
Haling, 7.2
halter, 10.162 SD
hart, 7.30
hasped, 5.368
heart-blood, 9.186
heaven's great arithmetician, Epi.17
Henslowe, Philip, pp. 1–6, 16, 26,
    27, 29, 30, 48, 65, 119, 121,
    125, 127, 144, 220
Herford, Charles H., pp. 15–16, 19,
    20, 23, 24, 47–50, 51, 52, 60–1,
    75, 240
hey-hoes, 6.209
hey-pass, 10.11
hoary wand'ring knight, 1.27–8
Hoccleve, Thomas, pp. 19–20, 29,
    200, 221
Homan, Sidney R., Jr., pp. 49–50
home-spun stuff, 6.110
horn-mad, 2.127
* horn-plague 6.126
horse, 6.433

hotshot, 5.30
Hoy, Cyrus, pp. 25, 48, 49, 69, 87, 92, 95, 102, 103, 104, 105, 108, 116, 120, 121, 123, 126, 130, 140, 143, 144, 148, 153, 155, 159, 160, 166, 168, 175, 176, 181, 182, 187, 189, 197, 198, 243
huffing, 5.361
hungry dog eats dirty puddings, 5.77–8

I am so full of chinks, 1.16
I cashier you, 1.332
idiot laughter, 6.30
idiot's cap, 1.125
idiot's hood, 3.75
India, 5.313
Indian, 1.343
inky thread, 5.259
in riots, 5.253
Insultado, Chars.53
in love over head and ears, 6.172
in their minority, 5.109
Irish kern, 9.66
iron fist, 6.38

jeopardy, 2.194
Jove, 4.22
Jove's daughters, 5.270
juggler, 7.7
jugglers, 7.56
juggling, 1.90

keeper, 6.175
Knave in Grain New Vamped, p. 66
knights of the post, 2.1
Knutson, Roslyn L., pp. 2, 4, 30, 72, 144

Lamb, Charles, pp. 40–1, 45, 106, 148, 167
* lamb's skin 1.343
lapped all in damask, 2.89–90
latten, 5.368
laugh and be fat, 10.43
laugh and be lean, 1.23
laugh and lie down, 10.45
laws of poesy, Pro.22
leaden slumber, 5.367
lead the world in a string, 5.29

lean diet makes fat wit, 2.18–19
lean fellow, 1.275
lean, tawny-faced tobacconist Death, 1.345
leap at a crust, 5.102
legerdemain, 7.8
Leyden, John, 1.211–13
lickerish, 5.95, 7.172
light, 2.76
lights, Cho.1.30
* limbs 1.93
lime-twigs to catch wealth, 2.78–9
logger-headed jade, 2.31–2
Longueville, Chars.48
lose our favours, 7.227
lost plays
  'Antony and Cleopatra', pp. 10–11
  'Chinon of England', p. 30
  'Fair Constance of Rome', p. 31
  '1 Fortunatus', pp. 1–6, 26–7, 30, 48, 66
  '2 Fortunatus', pp. 4–5, 65
  '1 Fortune's Tennis', p. 167
  '2 Fortune's Tennis', p. 167
  'The French Doctor', p. 220
  'Harry the 5', p. 30
  'King of England's Son and King of Scotland's Daughter', p. 32
  'Long Meg of Westminster', p. 65
  'Longshanks', p. 30
  'Lord and His Three Sons', p. 27
  'Love of an English Lady', p. 171
  'Merchant of Emden', p. 2
  'New World's Tragedy', p. 30
  'Old Joiner of Aldgate', pp. 94, 220
  'Paradox', p. 2
  'Phaeton', p. 97
  'Play of a Maiden's Suitors', p. 31
  '2 Seven Deadly Sins', p. 32
  'Seven Wise Masters', p. 31, 144
  'A Stately Tragedy ... of the Great Cham', p. 77
  '1 Tamar Cham', p. 4
  'Tristram of Lyons', p. 31
  'Valentine and Orson' (1598), p. 31, 77
  'The Whore New Vamped', p. 66
  'Wise Man of West Chester', p. 30

Louis the Meek, 1.189
love's sweet war, Pro.1
lower, 9.46

* maggot 1.12
maintain, 5.60
Malone, Edmond, p. 9
* man...of wax 2.110–11
* marked me well 5.114
Marlowe, Christopher, alleged influence on Dekker, pp. 3, 47–51
  Doctor Faustus, pp. 11, 30, 32, 33, 47–51, 56, 75, 80, 92, 94, 108, 152, 153, 184, 186, 215, 227
  Jew of Malta, pp. 30, 32, 158, 166, 189, 220
marriage-morn, 9.16
Marston, John: *Antonio's Revenge*, pp. 31, 141, 146
Marx, Karl, p. 53
massy gold, 5.386
meanly attired, 1.0.1
Menius, Frederick, pp. 11, 17, 176
men's woe, 6.495
mere, 3.66
metal-eaters, 10.233
Midas, 6.341
Midas' ears, 1.293
mind-travelling, pp. 56–7, 90, 125, 133, 159
mint, 5.418
monarchize, 3.25
monk Gregory, 1.207–8
moon, Pro. at Court.26
motley, 5.21
motley-scorn, 3.51
mourn the less, 5.339
moving of the spheres, 1.100
Mulready, Cyrus, pp. 32, 58, 90
Murad, Orlene, pp. 16, 33
music with her silver tongue, 6.396
musk, 1.327–8

naked legs, 8.69
Nashe, Thomas, pp. 32, 105, 113, 143, 150, 220
negro, 1.163
nice, Pro.5
noddy, 1.67
No does?, 4.101

no time, 6.514
not corporal, 2.4
Nunn, Hillary M., pp. 57–8, 199, 209
nutcrackers, 1.54
nymphs, Pro. at Court.32

occupiers, 6.407
of price, 10.298
Old Fortunatus
  adapted for Covent Garden see *Fortunatus, and His Sons* (1819)
  copy-text of, pp. 6–7, 59–64
  depiction of gold in, pp. 53–6
  depiction of old age in, pp. 53–4
  depiction of travel in, pp. 53–7
  form of, pp. 45–6, 48–51, 52–3, 58, 59–63
  German redaction (see entry for '*Von Fortunato*')
  perceived quality of, pp. 45–6, 49–53, 58
  performed at court, pp. 1, 29, 60, 61
  performed at Tufts College, pp. 41–3
  performed at University of Ottawa, pp. 43–4, 60
  post-publication offence, pp. 8–11
  reading of at Shakespeare Institute, p. 45
  reading of at Shakespeare Association of America, p. 45
  repertorial context of, pp. 29–33
  staged reading of at the Globe, p. 45
ordained by destiny, 1.223
ordinary, 5.55
ostrich, 5.251
out-valuing, 4.66
owl, 5.172
Oyes, 6.312

Pandora, Pro. at Court.3
pantheon, Pro. at Court.30
paradoxes, 5.52
Parcae, 1.227–8
pay from heaven, 7.199
pearls, 8.11

peepins, 8.30
Peeps, 8.30
peise, 4.106
pepper, 7.34
Phaetons, 1.86
Phoebus, 1.233
physic, 5.416
pinions, Pro.7
planet-stricken, 5.124
pomewater, 8.34–5
pour golden showers into their laps, 2.155
Prester John, 2.211
Price, George R., pp. 51–2, 240
priceless wonders, 4.63
Primislaus, 1.206–7
proceed, 8.114
progress, 5.238
proves, 5.7
* purse net 2.80–1
* purser 7.20
pursership, 5.411
purse strings, 2.172

quick imaginations, Cho.1.5

rank multitude, 5.191
rapt to a third heaven, 5.207
* rapture 8.7–8
rare, 2.190, 3.94
rear, Pro.12
relish, 1.144
* repass 10.12
reprieve, 10.253
Rhys, Ernest, pp. 62–3
riding post, 2.31
Rose playhouse, pp. 1, 29, 31, 48, 60
roundure, 1.99
rub out and shift, 2.26
rumbling, 1.49
* run thus through all trades 8.139
running woodbine, 3.13

Sachs, Hans, pp. 24, 34, 44, 215
sacred, 1.253
sacred inspiration, 4.32
Saint Patrick's Purgatory, 8.105
Satyrs, Chars.39
saucy brows, 3.93

scenes, Pro.20
Schelling, Felix E., p. 45
Scherer, Hans, p. 62
Schlueter, June, pp. 16–17, 24, 25, 33, 34, 96, 176, 215, 240
Scythian, 1.196
semi-gods, 1.114
Sempsters, 5.275
serpent gold, Cho.2.15
set up my rest, 7.29
seven liberal sciences, 5.95
seven wise masters, 5.48
Shadow, Chars.24
shadows, 10.345
Shakespeare, William: *2H4* pp. 31, 86, *AYLI* p. 32, *H5* pp. 31, 90, 172, *JC* p. 229, *KJ* p. 140, *KL* p. 216, *LLL* p. 178, *Luc.* pp. 139, 208, *MM* p. 120, *MND* p. 46, *MW* p. 220, *R2* p. 31, *R&J* pp. 31, 126, 193, *T&C* p. 95, *TN* pp. 32, 166, *V&A* p. 175, *WT* p. 110
shapes, 6.156
S'heart, 2.1, 7.65
she cony-catcher, 7.25
Sherman, William H., p. 53
shift for myself, 5.338
Sibi sapit, 3.0.11, 7.196
Sidney, Sir Philip, pp. 31–2, 58, 90, 91, 167, 169
silver-handed age, Pro. at Court.40–2
silver moons, 7.179
Sirens, 6.479
Sirrah, 2.23
sit with folded arms, Cho.1.21
slippery touch, 7.32
small compass, 5.300
Smeaton, Oliphant, pp. 6, 62–3, 212
smile in our sleeves, 6.129–30
* Snip-snap 1.52
Snudges, 2.85
Soho, 5.354
sol fa res, 10.37
sovereigness, 1.97
speckled, 9.60
spoil, Cho.2.9, 7.3
* spongy 6.177
spruce, silken-face, 6.120

Spurn, 10.124
square, 5.26
squint-eyed, 2.56
squint-eyed soul, Cho.1.24
stalks, 5.227
star-crossed, Cho.2.6
Stationers' Register, pp. 1, 5, 25, 29
still one, Pro. at Court.47
strews, 5.154
strive, 3.95
such red and white, 1.246
Suleiman, 4.10
Sunday face, 7.54
sun-like radiance, 1.95
* swag-bellies 5.59
swear like Puritans, 2.24
sweet music...silver sound, 1.338
Swinburne, Algernon Charles, pp. 46–7, 167
'Swounds, 7.94
Syme, Holger, pp. 3–4, 30

tapers of the night, Pro. at Court.24
Tartarian slaves, 1.177
Taurus, 2.10
* temple 2.189
terrible eaters, 5.82
Tilney, Edmund, pp. 10, 187, 211
Thamesis, 8.9
The Three Destinies, Chars.38
This travel now expires, 1.164
three blue beans, 2.176–7
throw squibs, 1.59–60
* Thy wits are lost 8.131
tobacco, 1.327–8
Toledo, 6.307
toys, 8.76
travel, 5.158
travel can transform, 1.53–4
travellers must lie, 5.139–40
tree of gold with apples, 3.0.9
Tricked in, 5.228
Trollope, Anthony, pp. 45–6
True grief is dumb, 5.345

unconstancy, Cho.1.26

vagaries, 5.126
vent'rous, Cho.1.29, 6.292
Viriat, 1.205
virtuous, Cho.2.27
Vitkus, Daniel, pp. 54, 56
vizards, 3.0.8
Volksbuch, pp. 16, 20–7, 48, 51, 60–1
Von Fortunato
  performance of, pp. 33–4, 48
  relationship to Dekker's play, pp. 15–18, 24, 33, 49, 51, 57, 62, 82, 96, 133, 163, 176, 178, 179, 183, 188, 189, 190, 194, 195, 196, 205, 206, 215, 220, 224, 232, 234, 235, 236, 238, 240
  relationship to Kassel MS play, p. 34
  relationship to puppet play, p. 35
  summary of, pp. 11–15

wags, 2.187
walking your stations, 5.162
walk together, 6.523
'Ware, 9.188
waste, 5.271, 10.119
waxing kernels, 1.56
welladay, 1.71
* wherried 8.15
white age's, 9.47
White-headed, 5.201
Whittemore, Thomas, p. 41
Who's the fool now?, 2.121–2
Wiggins, Martin, pp. 3, 4, 45, 65, 66, 102, 104, 171, 239
wild beast Multitude, 1.110
Wink, 9.164
* wire-drawers 6.415
wish, 4.87
wishing cap, 5.419
* wishing-hat 6.527
with a full mouth, 5.69
Woe worth, 5.277
wooden, 2.3
woodmonger, 6.441
* wound 9.19
wrack, 5.42
wretch, 1.298–300

you stock, you stone, 10.60
youth's glory, Pro. at Court.43

EU authorised representative for GPSR:
Easy Access System Europe, Mustamäe tee 50,
10621 Tallinn, Estonia
gpsr.requests@easproject.com